MODERN CURRICULUM PRESS

PHONICS

A complete phonics and word study program in 7 levels: K, A-F

This program has helped 50 million children learn to read. It can help your students, too.

MCP "Plaid" Phonics
A Complete Program Newly Revised

A+ FOR MCP PHONICS

"Every year I have a range of students in my class. I need a flexible program that gives me a way to provide each child what he or she needs to become a reader. MCP Phonics teacher edition has enough variety to reach children of all levels in each lesson."

Carol Sibila
Third Grade Teacher
St. Joseph School
Cuyahoga Falls, Ohio

— **has an unparalleled track record of student success.**

— **is the standard** by which every other program is measured.

— **has lots of practice with kid-appeal!** In phonics, practice really does make perfect. **MCP Phonics** packs practice into lots of fun riddles, rhymes, games, puzzles, and activities that challenge students to read aloud, write, review, and check their work.

— **is flexible. MCP Phonics** is tailor-made for classes that represent a wide range of ability levels. It helps all students become successful readers through multiple approaches that reach visual, auditory, and kinesthetic learners.

Call MCP "Plaid" Phonics at
800-321-3106

MCP Phonics has helped more than 50 million kids learn to read in the past 40 years.

It can help your students, too.

— is research-based.
MCP Phonics has been continuously revised to reflect the latest classroom research and to maintain a relevance for each generation of students and teachers.

— is systematic and explicit.
Studies show that most students benefit from explicit phonics instruction. Like training wheels on a bike, **MCP Phonics** provides the systematic, intensive support children need to become independent readers.

— earns a teacher's trust, year after year.
The method is sound; the materials are first-rate. Reading trends may come and go — **MCP Phonics** steers students on a steady course to success.

TEACHERS!
DO YOU HAVE A GREAT *"PLAID" PHONICS* IDEA TO SHARE WITH OTHER TEACHERS?

ANNOUNCING
"PLAID" PHONICS PARTNERS GRANTS!
MCP is awarding grants to teachers who want to create a phonics workshop using *MCP Phonics*. Grants include a $400 stipend in money and materials. For an application, write to:

Modern Curriculum Press
attn. Marketing Dept.
299 Jefferson Road
Parsippany, NJ 07054

or call
800-321-3106
Share your teaching strategies with others!

Ten key features in MCP Phonics

1 **Easy-to-use Teaching Plan with all you need at point of use**

This teaching plan is the easiest ever! **Quick-scan lesson plans** put everything you need at your fingertips. No confusion, no page flipping, no losing your place.

MCP Phonics' Teaching Plan includes...

- simple step-by-step lesson plans
- strategies to help every learner
- lesson objectives that serve as a guide to informal assessment
- spelling practice that flows from phonics
- quick and easy curriculum connections

Lesson 40
Pages 85–86

Short

a

INFORMAL ASSESSMENT OBJECTIVES

Can children

- identify picture names and words that contain the short sound of *a*?
- write words that contain the short sound of *a* to complete sentences?

Lesson Focus

PHONEMIC AWARENESS

Say a word that begins with the short *a* sound. Have children say the word, repeating /a/ twice before the word. For example, children would respond *a-a-apple*. Use these words: *alligator, accident, ant, animal, ax, apple*.

SOUND TO LETTER

- Write these words on the board and read each one: *cat, cab, fan, map, dad, ham, bag, sad, can*. Call on volunteers to use colored chalk to underline the letter *a*. Have children name the sound in each word.
- Give children an opportunity to name other words that contain the short *a* sound. Write the words on the board as they are suggested.

USING THE PAGES

- Help children identify the pictures on pages 85 and 86.
- **Critical Thinking** Read aloud the Think! question at the bottom of page 85 and discuss answers with the children.

85

Look at the picture. Circle the word that will finish the sentence. Print it on the line.

1. Max is my ___cat___. **(cat)** sat can
2. He licks my ___hand___. land **(hand)** ham
3. Max sits on my ___lap___. pad rap **(lap)**
4. He likes my ___dad___. sad **(dad)** bad
5. He plays with a ___bag___. bat rag **(bag)**
6. Max takes a ___nap___. **(nap)** cap cab

 Why does the girl like Max?

Lesson 40
Short vowel a: Words in context **85**

FOCUS ON ALL LEARNERS

ENGLISH LANGUAGE LEARNERS/ESL

Before beginning page 85, have children talk about pets they have or would like to have.

VISUAL LEARNERS

SMALL GROUP Materials: paper bag, index cards or slips of paper

Have each child in the group write three short *a* words on separate cards or slips of paper and place the words in the bag. Ask children to take turns picking a card, reading the word aloud and using it in a sentence.

KINESTHETIC LEARNERS

SMALL GROUP Have children say a sentence leaving out a short *a* word which they can pantomime for others to guess. They might suggest *cat, sat, nap, lap, pan,* or *man*.

Teacher Resource Guide, page 85, Level A

Lessons begin with phonemic awareness activities (Levels K, A, B).

Find approaches for auditory, visual, kinesthetic, ESL, gifted, and those who need extra support in every lesson.

2 **Approaches you need to reach every learner**

The Focus On All Learners supports students' **preferred learning styles** while also helping them develop other ways to learn.

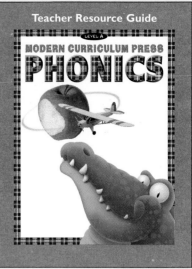

Teacher Resource Guide, Level A

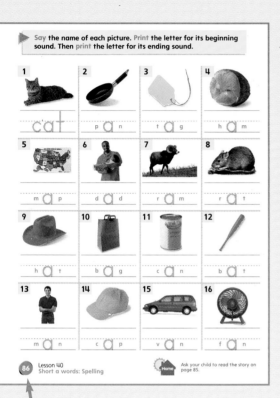

Say the name of each picture. Print the letter for its beginning sound. Then print the letter for its ending sound.

1. c _a_ t
2. p _a_ n
3. t _a_ g
4. h _a_ m
5. m _a_ p
6. d _a_ d
7. r _a_ m
8. r _a_ t
9. h _a_ t
10. b _a_ g
11. c _a_ n
12. b _a_ t
13. m _a_ n
14. c _a_ p
15. v _a_ n
16. f _a_ n

86 Lesson 40
Short a words: Spelling

Home Ask your child to read the story on page 85.

CURRICULUM CONNECTIONS ✳ ⦁ ▪ ◆

SPELLING
Write the List Words *bag, can, cat, fan, ham,* and *map* on the chalkboard and read them with children. Give clues for each word such as *It is food*. Have volunteers touch and spell the word that goes with the clue.

WRITING
Portfolio
Have the children reread the story about Max on page 85. Then suggest that they write and draw their own stories that tell more about Max. Brainstorm a list of short *a* words and write them on the board for children to use in their stories. Invite volunteers to share their stories with the class.

MATH
Invite children to name pets they have or would like to have. List the kinds of pets, such as gerbils, fish, cats, and dogs. Record the names of children who have or would like to have each kind of pet on a chart under the pet name. Have children count the names to determine which pets are the most popular and which are the most unusual.

Technology

AstroWord Short Vowels: *a, i.*
©1998 Silver Burdett Ginn Inc.
Division of Simon & Schuster.

AUDITORY/KINESTHETIC LEARNERS
LARGE GROUP
Materials: fingerpaints; paper

Have children listen to words and paint a picture for each one with a name that contains a short *a*. They can write *a*'s under the pictures. Use: *apple, ant, dog, cat, dad*.

GIFTED LEARNERS
Challenge children by having them write a song that contains short *a* words, using a familiar tune. Encourage them to perform their songs.

LEARNERS WHO NEED EXTRA SUPPORT
Materials: Letter Cards

Use Letter Cards to make groups of words with the same phonogram. For example, use cards to spell *bat*. Ask children to change the *b* to *c* to make *cat*, the *c* to *f* to form *fat*, the *f* to *h* to make *hat*, and so on. See Daily Phonics Practice, page 312.

Book Corner
PHONICS CONNECTION
Riley, Kana. *That Fly*. Ready Readers. (Modern Curriculum Press, 1996). A girl unwittingly gets a fly to stop bothering her.

THEME CONNECTION
Michelson, Richard. *Animals Ought to Be: Poems About Imaginary Pets*. (Simon & Schuster, 1996). This collection of short poems tells about such animals as the Roombroom and the Channel Changer.

86

Teacher Resource Guide, page 86, Level A

Curriculum Connections include suggestions for integrating phonics with a range of content areas. The writing activities make great additions to student portfolios.

New! References appear for technology phonics practice.

Book Corner suggests favorite titles to reinforce the lesson's phonics / thematic connection (Levels K, A, B, C).

A+ FOR MCP PHONICS

"I look for ease of use in a teaching plan with quick tips and ideas for reaching all learners. I find that in MCP Phonics. If I were a beginning teacher, I'd really appreciate the step-by-step approach MCP Phonics presents."

Karen Gordon
First Grade Teacher
Alimacani Elementary
Jacksonville, Florida

No more confusion! Page numbers align! The page number you see in the student edition is the one you'll find in the teaching plan.

③ The only program with all photographic picture clues

In MCP Phonics you'll find page after page of **powerful photography** — all easy for students to identify.

In MCP Phonics, picture clues are...
- easy and fun to identify
- representative of our nation's diversity
- kid-tested

Take-Home Books with powerful photography engage young readers in nonfiction.

Say **the name of each picture.** Circle **its name.**

1. bat bad ban
2. ant wax ax
3. nap can cat
4. cab cap nap
5. man bag band
6. tag rag tap
7. fat fan tan
8. had hand land
9. tap lap lamp
10. van had ran
11. bad cab dad
12. pat pan ran

Short vowel a: Picture-text match 81
Lesson 38

page 81, Level A

Think about fish. Fish are amazing!

Can you tell what this fish is called?

148 Lesson 71
Review short vowels a, i, u, o, e: Take-Home Book

page 148, Level A

Say **and spell the words in the tic-tac-toe grids.** Follow the directions for each grid. Draw **straight lines through three words across, up and down, or on a diagonal to win.**

1. Match **ly** words.

blasting	sunless	lovely
stars	biggest	slowly
hopeful	roared	nicely

2. Match **ness** words.

darkness	cheerful	sweetly
longest		
fearful		

3. Match **ful** words.

warmly	swiftness	joyful
smarter	joined	trying
careful	helpful	wishful

4. kindr
   nea
   lig

166 Lesson 77
Review Suffixes -ly, -ful, -less, -ness

page 166, Level B

Read **the words in the blue box.** Print a word **in the puzzle to name each picture.**

Across →
2.
5.
6.

Down ↓
1.
3.
4.

| bag | cat | hand |
| hat | map | pan |

Use **some of the words from the box to write a sentence.**

82 Lesson 38
Short vowel a

Make up riddles using some of the words from the box. Ask your child to guess the word.

page 82, Level A

④ A variety of fun formats provide practice galore!

Now you'll find an even **greater variety** of exercise formats.

MCP Phonics practice pages...
- feature photographs and realistic up-to-date illustrations
- motivate students with kid-friendly puzzles, games, and quizzes
- provide for a range of levels and learning styles
- make phonics learning FUN!

5 Skills presented in kid-friendly, thematic contexts

> MCP Phonics introduces **every skill in context** to help students apply their phonics learning to their reading.

MCP Phonics features...

- popular unit themes kids love (and teachers love to teach!)
- interest-grabbing openers with lots of ways for kids to apply phonics skills
- engaging rhyme, rhythm, and repetition so essential in building phonics skills

A variety of unit openers include poems, songs, and activities that provide context and foster discussion.

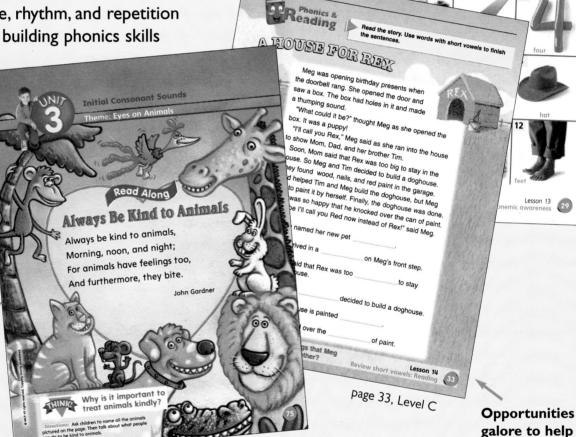

You'll find lots of "let's recite" and "read-again rhymes" throughout MCP Phonics.

page 29, Level A

Five furry foxes
Fanning in the heat.
They all run away
On furry fox feet.

Five begins with the sound of f. Circle each picture whose name begins with the sound of f.

four

hat

feet

Lesson 13
Phonemic awareness 29

A HOUSE FOR REX

Read the story. Use words with short vowels to finish the sentences.

Meg was opening birthday presents when the doorbell rang. She opened the door and saw a box. The box had holes in it and made a thumping sound.

"What could it be?" thought Meg as she opened the box. It was a puppy!

"I'll call you Rex," Meg said as she ran into the house to show Mom, Dad, and her brother Tim. Soon, Mom said that Rex was too big to stay in the house. So Meg and Tim decided to build a doghouse. They found wood, nails, and red paint in the garage. Meg helped Tim and Meg build the doghouse, but Meg got to paint it by herself. Finally, the doghouse was done. Meg was so happy that he knocked over the can of paint. Maybe I'll call you Red now instead of Rex!" said Meg.

___ named her new pet ___.

___ arrived in a ___ on Meg's front step.

___ said that Rex was too ___ to stay ___ house.

___ decided to build a doghouse.

___ house is painted ___.

___ over the ___ of paint.

___ things that Meg ___ together?

Review short vowels: Reading Lesson 14 33

page 33, Level C

Opportunities galore to help kids make the phonics/reading connection.

page 75, Level K

UNIT 3 — Initial Consonant Sounds
Theme: Eyes on Animals

Read Along

Always Be Kind to Animals

Always be kind to animals,
Morning, noon, and night;
For animals have feelings too,
And furthermore, they bite.

John Gardner

THINK! Why is it important to treat animals kindly?

Directions: Ask children to name all the animals pictured on the page. Then talk about what people can do to be kind to animals.
Unit 3 • Introduction 75

6 Clear, concise directions and rules for students

> MCP Phonics pages win loud praise from teachers **for easy-to-follow directions** for students.

In MCP Phonics student pages...

- directions are boxed and easy to find
- key words "pop" in bold, red type
- directions for students are highlighted in yellow

page 89, Level B

Name

Gentle giraffes,
Gaze through the trees.
Bigger than giants,
They nibble the leaves.

Say the name of each picture. If the name has a soft g sound, circle the picture. If it has a hard g sound, draw a line under it.

RULE
When g is followed by e, i, or y, it usually has a soft sound. You can hear the soft g sound in giraffe.

1   2   3

7 Purposeful writing and spelling connections

MCP Phonics helps children see the phonics / reading / spelling / writing connection. Phonics **builds decoding skills** which helps students in their reading. Spelling **develops encoding skills** which helps them in their writing.

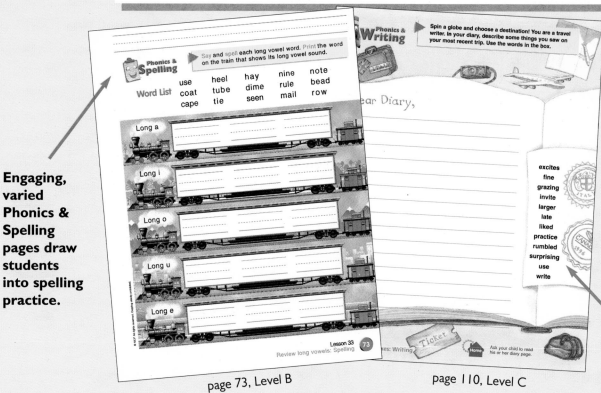

Engaging, varied Phonics & Spelling pages draw students into spelling practice.

page 73, Level B

Students apply newly learned phonics skills to their writing.

page 110, Level C

8 Critical Thinking Questions develop comprehension

Critical Thinking Questions provide a springboard for the necessary discussion that helps students **develop vocabulary, oral language**, and **comprehension**. Critical Thinking Questions appear in unit openers, sentence practice pages, and story pages.

This Critical Thinking Question prompts discussion that checks students' understanding.

page 225, Level B

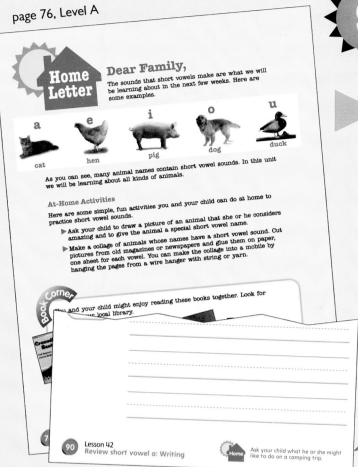

9 Fun, effective ways to foster reinforcement at home

With MCP Phonics, you always have an answer for parents who ask how they can **help their child** develop phonics skills.

Make a stronger Home Connection with...

- Home Letters that include suggested books to read (no need to copy, just send them home!)
- colorful, "just the right level" Take-Home Books

Workbook pages include simple tips for sharing at home to make it easy for parents to follow phonics learning in the classroom. (Levels K, A, B, C).

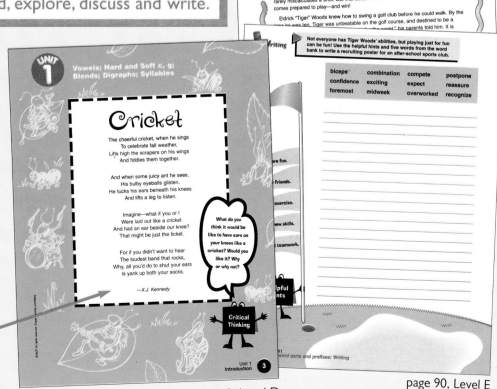

10 Big word strategies for big kids!

MCP Word Study levels D, E, and F provide **word study** and more **challenging structural analysis** for older students. They offer lots of opportunities to read, explore, discuss and write.

MCP Word Study levels D, E, and F provide review and prepare students for...

- multi-syllable words
- base words
- roots
- more difficult prefixes
- suffixes
- dictionary skills

Each unit opener shows words in context, in a playful, appealing way.

MCP Phonics and Stories Libraries
Four levels of books make it easy and fun for students to apply decoding skills to reading for comprehension.

Level K

Consonants

Level A

Consonants
Short Vowels
Long Vowels
Consonant Blends
Consonant Digraphs

Level B

Short Vowels
Long Vowels
Hard, Soft g
Consonant Blends
Consonant Digraphs
r-Controlled Vowels
Contractions
Plurals
Suffixes
Endings
Variant Vowels
Prefixes

Level C

Short Vowel Review
Long Vowel Review
Consonant Blends
r-Controlled Vowels
Contractions
Plurals
Endings
Diphthongs
Vowel Pairs
Suffixes/Prefixes
Syllabication
Synonyms
Multiple-meaning Words

20 different books in each Library!

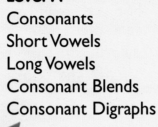

Phonics Power Packs

Available at Levels K, A, B

Complement instruction with posters, audio cassettes, picture cards, word cards and more! Packaged in a pocket-chart storage bag. Each component is also available separately.

AstroWord

The first and only multimedia program that provides comprehensive reading skills and strategies instruction for students of all ages!

17 individual CD-ROMs for Macintosh or Windows. Modules available separately or as Lab Packs.

Call 800-321-3106 for more information

A research-based scope and sequence for student success

MCP PHONICS PROGRAM SCOPE AND SEQUENCE OF SKILLS

LEVELS	K	A	B	C	D	E	F
ALPHABETIC AWARENESS	•	•	•	•			
AUDITORY DISCRIMINATION	•	•					
COMPOUND & TWO-SYLLABLE WORDS			•	•	•	•	•
CONSONANT BLENDS			•	•	•	•	•
CONSONANT DIGRAPHS			•	•	•	•	•
CONSONANT LETTER-SOUND ASSOCIATIONS	•	•	•	•	•		
CONSONANT VARIATIONS					•	•	•
CONSONANT-VOWEL-CONSONANT BLENDING		•					
CONTRACTIONS			•	•	•	•	•
CRITICAL THINKING	•	•	•	•	•	•	•
DICTIONARY SKILLS				•	•	•	•
INFLECTIONAL ENDINGS		•	•				
LETTER IDENTIFICATION	•	•					
LISTENING & SPEAKING SKILLS	•	•	•	•	•	•	•
LISTENING COMPREHENSION STRATEGIES	•	•	•	•	•	•	•
LONG VOWEL LETTER-SOUND ASSOCIATIONS		•	•	•	•		
MOTOR SKILLS	•						
MULTIPLE-MEANING WORDS						•	•
ORTHOGRAPHIC AWARENESS	•	•	•	•	•	•	•
PHONEMIC/PHONOLOGICAL AWARENESS	•	•	•				
PLURALS			•	•	•	•	•
POSSESSIVES, APOSTROPHE					•	•	•
PREFIXES			•	•	•	•	•
PRINT AWARENESS	•	•	•				
R-CONTROLLED VOWELS			•	•	•		
READING COMPREHENSION STRATEGIES	•	•	•	•	•	•	•
ROOTS					•	•	•
SHORT VOWEL LETTER-SOUND ASSOCIATIONS	•	•	•				
SILENT LETTERS					•	•	•
SOUNDS OF HARD & SOFT c, g			•	•	•		
SUFFIXES			•	•	•	•	•
SYLLABICATION			•	•	•	•	•
SYNONYMS, ANTONYMS, HOMONYMS			•	•	•		
VISUAL DISCRIMINATION	•	•					
VOWEL DIPHTHONGS			•	•	•	•	•
VOWEL PAIRS, VOWEL DIGRAPHS			•	•	•	•	
Y AS A VOWEL		•	•	•			

MCP PHONICS PROGRAM FEATURES

LEVELS	K	A	B	C	D	E	F
HOME LETTERS	•	•	•	•	•	•	•
LITERATURE SELECTIONS, SONGS, ACTIVITY PAGES	•	•	•	•	•	•	•
PHONICS & READING; READING & WRITING PAGES		•	•	•	•	•	•
PHONICS & SPELLING PAGES		•	•	•			
PHONICS & WRITING PAGES		•	•	•			
TAKE-HOME BOOKS		•	•	•			

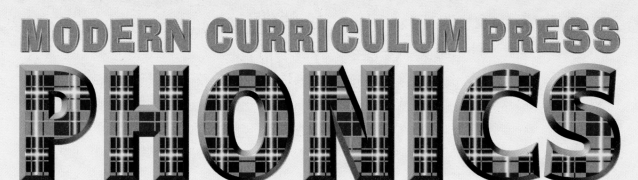

LEVEL E

MODERN CURRICULUM PRESS
WORD STUDY

ELWELL • MURRAY • KUCIA

TEACHER ADVISORY BOARD

Robert Figueroa
Cheektowaga, NY

Jackie Fonte
Gretna, LA

Karen Gordon
Jacksonville, FL

Tim Hamilton
Hermitage, TN

Sr. Denise Lyon, I. H. M.
Philadelphia, PA

Rachel Musser
Jackson, NJ

Sr. Mary Jean Raymond, O. S. U.
Cleveland, OH

Gloria Tuchman
Santa Ana, CA

ACKNOWLEDGEMENTS

EXECUTIVE EDITOR
Ronne Kaufman

EDITORIAL DEVELOPMENT
Brown Publishing Network

COVER DESIGN
Bill Smith Studios

PRODUCT MANAGER
Christine A. McArtor

PRODUCTION
Julie Ryan, Helen Wetherill

CREATIVE DIRECTOR
Doug Bates

ART DIRECTORS
Rosanne Guararra, Elaine Sandersen

ELECTRONIC PUBLISHING DIRECTOR
Sandy Kerr

IMAGE SERVICES MANAGER
Sandy Gregg

PROJECT EDITORS
Leslie Feierstone-Barna, Nancy Ellis,
Beth Fernald, Donna Garzinsky, Betsy Niles

MANUFACTURING & INVENTORY PLANNING
Karen Sota, Danielle Duchamp

COMPOSITION
Desktop Media, Devost Design, Hester Hull Associates, Caragraphics

LAYOUT AND PRODUCTION
Deena Uglione, Terri Shema
Larry Berkowitz, Peter Herrmann, Rachel Avenia-Prol, Pat Carlone, Diane Fristachi, Mary Jean Jones,
Chris Otazo, Andrea Schultz, Nancy Simmons, Dave Simoskevitz, Melinda Judson, Diana Rudio,
Murray Levine, Johanna Moroch, Sarah Balogh, Ruth Leine, Jennifer Peal

DESIGN
Judi DeSouter, Michele Episcopo, Denise Ingrassia, Aggie Jaspon, Diedre Mitchel,
Karolyn Necco, Ruth Otey, Siok-Tin Sodbinow, Terry Taylor, Deborah Walkoczy

ILLUSTRATION CREDITS
Sharon Vargo: p. 4; Chris Reed: p. 34, 114, 161o, 162; Bill Bossert: p. 63o, 113o;
Mary Keefe: p. 64; Jim Connolly: p. 113o; Terry Taylor: p. 135o; Peter Fasolino: bulletin board frames

PHOTO CREDITS
All photographs by Silver Burdett Ginn & Parker/Boon Productions for Silver Burdett Ginn.

IMAGE SERVICES
Barbara Haugh
Photographers: John Paul Endress; Michael Gaffney, Michael Provost;
Image Research: Leslie Laguna, Betsy Levin
Digital Photographers: John Serafin, Bob Grieza, Douglas Carney; Stylists: Judy Mahoney, Debbie Gaffney

REDUCED STUDENT PAGES
Modern Curriculum Press gratefully acknowledges the following for the use of copyrighted materials:
"Fiddle-Faddle" by Eve Merriam. From A WORLD OR TWO WITH YOU by Eve Merriam. Copyright ©1981 Eve Merriam.
Used by permission of Marian Reiner.

CONTENTS

Variants, Combinations, Syllables

UNIT 1

Vowel Pairs, Digraphs, Diphthongs, Syllables

UNIT 2

Prefixes

UNIT 3

Roots, Compound Words, Possessives, Contractions

UNIT 4

Suffixes

Suffixes, Plurals

Dictionary Skills

Assessment Strategy Overview

Throughout Unit 1, assess students' ability to read and write words with consonant variants, consonant combinations, and vowel combinations. There are various ways to assess students' progress. You may also want to encourage students to evaluate their own work and participate in setting goals for their own learning.

FORMAL ASSESSMENT

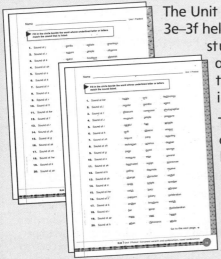

The Unit 1 Pretest on pages 3e–3f helps to assess a student's knowledge at the beginning of the unit and to plan instruction.

The Unit 1 Posttest on pages 3g–3h helps to assess mastery of unit objectives and to plan for reteaching, if necessary.

INFORMAL ASSESSMENT

The Reading & Writing pages and Unit Checkup in the student book are an effective means of evaluating students' performance.

Skill	Reading & Writing Pages	Unit Checkup
k Sound	17–18	31–32
qu and kn Words	17–18	31–32
Sounds of ch	17–18	31–32
Sounds of c	17–18	31–32
Sounds of g	17–18	31–32
f Sound	17–18	31–32
Sounds of s	17–18	31–32
Sounds of sh, th, wh	17–18	31–32
Sounds of sc	29–30	31–32
gn Words	29–30	31–32
Sounds of rh, wr	29–30	31–32
/air/	29–30	31–32
Sounds of ear	29–30	31–32
ild, ind, ost, old Sounds	29–30	31–32
Syllables	29–30	31–32

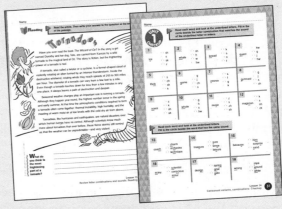

PORTFOLIO ASSESSMENT

This logo appears throughout the teaching plans. It signals opportunities for collecting students' work for individual portfolios. You may also want to collect the following pages.

❖ Unit 1 Pretest and Posttest, pages 3e–3h

❖ Unit 1 Checkup, pages 31–32

❖ Unit 1 Reading & Writing, pages 17–18, 29–30

STUDENT PROGRESS CHECKLIST

Use the checklist on page 3i to record students' progress. You may want to cut the sections apart to place each student's checklist in his or her portfolio.

Administering and Evaluating the
Pretest and Posttest

DIRECTIONS

To help you assess students' progress in learning Unit 1 skills, tests are available on pages 3e–3h. Administer the Pretest before students begin the unit. The results of the Pretest will help you identify each student's strengths and needs in advance, allowing you to structure lesson plans to meet individual needs. Administer the Posttest to assess students' overall mastery of skills taught in the unit and to identify specific areas that will require reteaching.

PERFORMANCE ASSESSMENT PROFILE

The following chart will help you identify specific skills as they appear on the tests and enable you to identify and record specific information about an individual's or the class's performance on the tests.

Depending on the results of the tests, refer to the Reteaching column for lesson-plan pages where you can find activities that will be useful for meeting individual needs or for daily word study practice.

ANSWER KEYS

Unit 1 Pretest, page 3e (BLM 1)

1. quiz	11. scarecrow
2. agent	12. decorate
3. photographer	13. change
4. museum	14. knight
5. wriggle	15. whisper
6. unique	16. celebration
7. leisure	17. anchor
8. technician	18. rhododendron
9. guest	19. mare
10. several	20. whole

Unit 1 Pretest, page 3f (BLM 2)

21. same	26. same	31. same
22. different	27. different	32. different
23. same	28. different	33. same
24. different	29. same	34. different
25. different	30. same	35. different

36. 1	38. 2	40. 1	42. 3	44. 3
37. 3	39. 3	41. 2	43. 2	45. 2

Unit 1 Posttest, page 3g (BLM 3)

1. agitate	8. excellent	15. garden
2. observe	9. rhythm	16. scalp
3. boutique	10. wholesale	17. champion
4. edition	11. quicksand	18. whimper
5. sandwich	12. phantom	19. orchestra
6. compose	13. wrinkle	20. aware
7. kneel	14. measure	

Unit 1 Posttest, page 3h (BLM 4)

21. same	26. different	31. same
22. different	27. different	32. different
23. same	28. different	33. same
24. same	29. same	34. different
25. different	30. same	35. different

36. 3	38. 3	40. 2	42. 2	44. 1
37. 1	39. 2	41. 1	43. 3	45. 2

PERFORMANCE ASSESSMENT PROFILE

Skill	Pretest Questions	Posttest Questions	Reteaching Focus on All Learners	Reteaching Daily Word Study Practice
k, ck, que: /k/	6, 28	3, 28	5–6, 17–18	180
qu: /kw/; kn, gn: /n/	1, 14, 28, 31	7, 11, 28, 31	5–6, 17–20, 29–30	180
ch: /k/, /ch/, /sh/	13, 17	17, 19	7–8, 17–18	180
c: /k/, /s/	12, 16	6, 8	7–8, 17–18	180–181
g: /g/, /j/	2, 9	1, 15	9–10, 17–18	180–181
f, ff, ph: /f/	3	12	11–12, 17–18	180–181
s: /z/, /s/, /sh/, /zh/	4, 7, 10	2, 5, 14	11–12, 17–18	180–181
wh: /h/, /hw/	15, 20, 29, 30	10, 18, 29, 30	13–18	181–182
sh, ci, ce, ti: /sh/	8	4	13–18	181–182
thin; then	25, 26	25, 26	15–18, 29–30	181–182
sc: /sk/, /s/, /sh/	11, 24	16, 24	19–20, 29–30	182
rh, wr: /r/	5, 18, 23	9, 13, 23	21–22, 29–30	182
are, air: /air/	19, 21, 22	20, 21, 22	21–22, 29–30	182
ear: /ear/, /air/, /ur/	21, 22, 27	21, 22, 27	23–24, 29–30	182–183
ild: /ild/; ind: /ind/;	34, 35	34, 35	25–26, 29–30	182–183
ost: /ost/; old: /old/	32, 33	32, 33	25–26, 29–30	182–183
Syllable Recognition	36–45	36–45	27–28	193

> Fill in the circle beside the word whose underlined letter or letters match the sound listed.

1. Sound of *kw*   ○ ta**ck**le   ○ **qu**iz   ○ te**ch**nology
2. Sound of *j*   ○ re**g**ular   ○ **g**azebo   ○ a**g**ent
3. Sound of *f*   ○ **p**leasure   ○ com**p**oser   ○ **ph**otographer
4. Sound of *z*   ○ mu**s**eum   ○ **s**imple   ○ pre**ss**ure
5. Sound of *r*   ○ ca**r**eful   ○ ha**ir**   ○ **wr**iggle
6. Sound of *k*   ○ **qu**ilt   ○ **ch**eese   ○ uni**que**
7. Sound of *zh*   ○ lei**s**ure   ○ **s**ong   ○ a**ss**uring
8. Sound of *sh*   ○ techni**ci**an   ○ **sci**ence   ○ de**s**pair
9. Sound of *g*   ○ pa**g**e   ○ **g**uest   ○ spon**g**e
10. Sound of *s*   ○ mea**s**ure   ○ wi**s**e   ○ **s**everal
11. Sound of *sk*   ○ fa**sc**inated   ○ re**s**ign   ○ **sc**arecrow
12. Sound of *k*   ○ **c**eiling   ○ de**c**orate   ○ re**c**eive
13. Sound of *ch*   ○ **ch**ange   ○ **ch**aracter   ○ or**ch**id
14. Sound of *n*   ○ qui**ck**   ○ **kn**ight   ○ spea**k**er
15. Sound of *hw*   ○ cat**ch**   ○ **h**arp   ○ **wh**isper
16. Sound of *s*   ○ pop**c**orn   ○ **c**olony   ○ **c**elebration
17. Sound of *k*   ○ an**ch**or   ○ bro**ch**ure   ○ wat**ch**
18. Sound of *r*   ○ **f**air   ○ **w**asp   ○ **rh**ododendron
19. Sound of *air*   ○ m**are**   ○ **y**ear   ○ h**ear**d
20. Sound of *h*   ○ **wh**en   ○ **rh**inoceros   ○ **wh**ole

Go to the next page. →

BLM 1 Unit 1 Pretest: Consonant variants and combinations, vowel combinations

3e

> **Read both words and decide if the underlined letters stand for sounds that are the same or different. Fill in the circle with the correct response.**

21. h<u>air</u>, p<u>ear</u>   ○ same   ○ different

22. f<u>ear</u>, m<u>are</u>   ○ same   ○ different

23. <u>wr</u>eath, <u>r</u>amp   ○ same   ○ different

24. <u>sc</u>ience, <u>sc</u>andal   ○ same   ○ different

25. <u>th</u>in, <u>th</u>an   ○ same   ○ different

26. mara<u>th</u>on, <u>th</u>under   ○ same   ○ different

27. cl<u>ear</u>, s<u>ear</u>ch   ○ same   ○ different

28. <u>qu</u>estion, anti<u>que</u>   ○ same   ○ different

29. <u>wh</u>istle, <u>wh</u>eat   ○ same   ○ different

30. <u>wh</u>o, <u>h</u>istory   ○ same   ○ different

31. forei<u>gn</u>, campai<u>gn</u>   ○ same   ○ different

32. lo<u>st</u>, gho<u>st</u>   ○ same   ○ different

33. <u>g</u>old, f<u>o</u>lder   ○ same   ○ different

34. rem<u>ind</u>, h<u>ind</u>er   ○ same   ○ different

35. w<u>ild</u>, w<u>ild</u>erness   ○ same   ○ different

> **Read each word in the list. On the line in front of the word, write how many syllables (1, 2, or 3) the word has.**

36. ____ whose   41. ____ freedom

37. ____ difficult   42. ____ disappear

38. ____ cartoon   43. ____ cabin

39. ____ elephant   44. ____ telephone

40. ____ risk   45. ____ transfer

Possible score on Unit 1 Pretest is 45. Number correct _____

Fill in the circle beside the word whose underlined letter or letters match the sound that is listed.

1. Sound of *j* ○ <u>g</u>orilla ○ a<u>g</u>itate ○ <u>g</u>reetings

2. Sound of *z* ○ a<u>ss</u>ure ○ <u>s</u>imple ○ ob<u>s</u>erve

3. Sound of *k* ○ <u>qu</u>est ○ bouti<u>que</u> ○ <u>ch</u>eetah

4. Sound of *sh* ○ edi<u>ti</u>on ○ <u>ch</u>orus ○ <u>sc</u>enic

5. Sound of *s* ○ mi<u>ss</u>ion ○ ri<u>s</u>e ○ <u>s</u>andwich

6. Sound of *k* ○ <u>c</u>ompose ○ <u>c</u>ease ○ di<u>c</u>e

7. Sound of *n* ○ tri<u>ck</u>y ○ <u>kn</u>eel ○ pi<u>ck</u>le

8. Sound of *s* ○ ex<u>c</u>ellent ○ confec<u>ti</u>on ○ <u>c</u>urtain

9. Sound of *r* ○ <u>d</u>are ○ <u>w</u>alk ○ <u>r</u>hythm

10. Sound of *h* ○ <u>wh</u>isker ○ <u>r</u>hombus ○ <u>wh</u>olesale

11. Sound of *kw* ○ <u>qu</u>icksand ○ <u>kn</u>ow ○ bu<u>ck</u>le

12. Sound of *f* ○ <u>p</u>ierce ○ <u>ph</u>antom ○ re<u>p</u>air

13. Sound of *r* ○ <u>wr</u>inkle ○ <u>s</u>pare ○ <u>t</u>ear

14. Sound of *zh* ○ <u>sh</u>uttle ○ pla<u>s</u>tic ○ mea<u>s</u>ure

15. Sound of *g* ○ enra<u>g</u>e ○ <u>g</u>arden ○ en<u>g</u>ine

16. Sound of *sk* ○ <u>sc</u>alp ○ <u>sc</u>issors ○ <u>sc</u>ene

17. Sound of *ch* ○ <u>ch</u>oir ○ <u>ch</u>ampion ○ ar<u>ch</u>itect

18. Sound of *hw* ○ <u>wh</u>imper ○ <u>h</u>eart ○ <u>ch</u>apter

19. Sound of *k* ○ or<u>ch</u>estra ○ <u>ch</u>ocolate ○ <u>ch</u>amber

20. Sound of *air* ○ b<u>ear</u>d ○ y<u>ear</u>n ○ aw<u>are</u>

Go to the next page. →

> ▶ **Read both words and decide if the underlined letters stand for sounds that are the same or different. Fill in the circle with the correct response.**

21. f<u>air</u>, w<u>ear</u> ○ same ○ different

22. sh<u>ear</u>, sh<u>are</u> ○ same ○ different

23. <u>wr</u>ist, <u>r</u>ope ○ same ○ different

24. con<u>sc</u>ience, lu<u>sc</u>ious ○ same ○ different

25. <u>th</u>ink, <u>th</u>ose ○ same ○ different

26. fa<u>th</u>er, <u>thr</u>oat ○ same ○ different

27. <u>ear</u>th, <u>gear</u> ○ same ○ different

28. <u>qu</u>arrel, mysti<u>qu</u>e ○ same ○ different

29. <u>wh</u>eel, <u>wh</u>ich ○ same ○ different

30. <u>wh</u>olesome, <u>h</u>andsome ○ same ○ different

31. rei<u>gn</u>, resi<u>gn</u> ○ same ○ different

32. c<u>o</u>stly, m<u>o</u>stly ○ same ○ different

33. sc<u>old</u>, beh<u>old</u> ○ same ○ different

34. beh<u>ind</u>, w<u>ind</u>y ○ same ○ different

35. ch<u>ild</u>, ch<u>ild</u>ren ○ same ○ different

> ▶ **Read each word in the list. On the line in front of the word, write how many syllables (1, 2, or 3) the word has.**

36. ____ honeycomb

37. ____ threat

38. ____ magazine

39. ____ meanwhile

40. ____ recent

41. ____ sold

42. ____ renew

43. ____ imagine

44. ____ file

45. ____ teapot

Possible score on Unit 1 Posttest is 45. Number correct _____

BLM 4 Unit 1 Posttest: Consonant variants and combinations, vowel combinations, syllables

Student Progress Checklist

Make as many copies as needed to use for a class list. For individual portfolio use, cut apart each student's section. As indicated by the code, color in boxes next to skills satisfactorily assessed and mark an X by those requiring reteaching. Marked boxes can later be colored in to indicate mastery.

STUDENT PROGRESS CHECKLIST

Code: ■ Satisfactory   ☒ Needs Reteaching

Student: _____ _____ Pretest Score: _____ Posttest Score: _____	Skills ❑ /k/ ❑ *qu, kn* Words ❑ Sounds of *ch* ❑ Sounds of *c* ❑ Sounds of *g* ❑ /f/ ❑ Sounds of *s* ❑ Sounds of *sh, th, wh* ❑ Sounds of *sc* ❑ *gn* Words ❑ /r/ ❑ /air/ ❑ Sounds of *ear* ❑ *ild, ind, ost, old* Sounds ❑ Syllables	Comments / Learning Goals
Student: _____ _____ Pretest Score: _____ Posttest Score: _____	Skills ❑ /k/ ❑ *qu, kn* Words ❑ Sounds of *ch* ❑ Sounds of *c* ❑ Sounds of *g* ❑ /f/ ❑ Sounds of *s* ❑ Sounds of *sh, th, wh* ❑ Sounds of *sc* ❑ *gn* Words ❑ /r/ ❑ /air/ ❑ Sounds of *ear* ❑ *ild, ind, ost, old* Sounds ❑ Syllables	Comments / Learning Goals

Spelling Connections

INTRODUCTION

The Unit Word List is a comprehensive list of spelling words drawn from this unit. The words are grouped according to the skills developed in this unit. To incorporate spelling into your word study program, use the activity in the Curriculum Connections section of each teaching plan.

The spelling lessons utilize the following approach for each set of words.

1. Administer a pretest of the words that have not yet been introduced. Dictation sentences are provided.

2. Provide practice.

3. Reassess. Dictation sentences are provided.

A final test is provided at the end of the unit on page 32.

DIRECTIONS

Make a copy of Blackline Master 6 for each student. After administering the pretest for each set of words, give students a copy of the appropriate word list.

Students can work with a partner to practice spelling the words orally and identifying the appropriate sound in each word. They can also create letter cards to use to form the words on the list. You may want to challenge students to identify other words that have the same sound variant or combination. Students can write words of their own on *My Own Word List* (see Blackline Master 6).

Have students store their list words in envelopes or plastic zipper bags in the back of their books or notebooks. You may want to suggest that students keep a spelling notebook, listing words with similar patterns. You could also invite students to build word-wall displays in the classroom. Each section of the wall could focus on words with a single word study element. The walls will become a good spelling resource when students are writing.

UNIT WORD LIST

k* Sound; *qu/kn, ch, c, g; f* Sound; *s

queen
knee
cheap
character
race
game
page
different
dolphin
measure

wh, sh, th, sc, gn

whole
whale
ship
special
partial
science
conscience
scare
gnat
sign

r* and *air* Sounds; *ear, ild, ind, ost, old

rhyme
wrist
hair
aware
year
pearl
wild
reminded
ghost
behold

Name _____

 **Spelling** # UNIT 1 WORD LIST

k Sound; qu/kn, ch, c, g; f Sound; s

queen
knee
cheap
character
race
game
page
different
dolphin
measure

wh, sh, th, sc, gn

whole
whale
ship
special
partial
science
conscience
scare
gnat
sign

r and air Sounds; ear, ild, ind, ost, old

rhyme
wrist
hair
aware
year
pearl
wild
reminded
ghost
behold

My Own Word List

Word Study Games, Activities, and Technology

The following collection of ideas offers a variety of opportunities to reinforce word study skills while actively engaging students. The games, activities, and technology suggestions can easily be adapted to meet the needs of your group of learners. They vary in approach so as to consider students' different learning styles.

● CREATE A MAP

Provide students with blank paper on which they can create a map showing accurate directions to the school from their home or from a common reference point (such as city hall or a ball field). Tell them to complete the map by inserting as many street or road names as possible whose names contain the phonemes discussed in this unit. If the school is in a rural area, you might vary the activity by asking students to include landmarks, physical features, or other identifiers along the route.

▲ I SPY

Have students list on the chalkboard some of the vowel and consonant combinations discussed in this unit. Then have them look around the room and think of words containing the listed sounds. Ask volunteers to say *I spy* . . . followed by a simple definition of an object visible to most class members. Other students can try to identify the object being described. Encourage those who guess correctly to write the word on the chalkboard, underlining the appropriate letter combinations. You might model the first by saying *I spy an outer covering for my foot* (*sh*oe). Other examples might include *chalkboard, desk, pencil, shirt, child, hair*.

◆ TONGUE TWISTERS

Encourage students to repeat a tongue twister such as *She sells seashells by the seashore* or *How much wood would a woodchuck chuck if a woodchuck could chuck wood?* Invite students to make up silly sentences or phrases of their own that use alliteration or other repetition to create tongue twisters.

■ SILLYSAURUS

Tell students that the word *dinosaur* comes from two Greek words: *dino*, meaning "terrible," and *sauros*, meaning "lizard." Ask volunteers to share with the class what they know about dinosaurs, including names, physical traits, and behaviors. Tell students to draw a picture of a dinosaur engaged in a humorous or silly activity. Then invite students to name their creations by using a word that contains one of the sounds covered in the unit. You might provide examples such as these.

✳ GNOMES NEED FRIENDS, TOO

Display a picture of a gnome. Explain that in folklore, gnomes are tiny people who live alone in caves and guard a treasure. Invite students to write and illustrate a story about a gnome. Tell them to include words that contain one or more of at least six different consonant or vowel combinations discussed in this unit. Challenge them to include as many of the following words as possible: *gnarled, gnash, gnat, gnaw,* and *gnu.* Students may consult classroom dictionaries as needed.

● WHAT'S MY SOUND?

List the following combinations on the board: *c, ck, que, ch, ff, ph, gn, kn, wh, th, sh, sc, gn, air, ear.* Provide groups of four students with fifteen index cards per group from which to make a deck. Tell each group to write one of the consonant or vowel combinations listed on the board on one side of each card. Suggest that students draw a colorful design on the opposite side. Have them shuffle the cards and place the deck in the center of the circle. Taking turns, each student draws the top card from the deck and suggests a word that contains that letter combination.

▲ ROUND TABLE

Have small groups of students sit around a table or arrange their desks in a circle. Provide each group with a sheet of paper on which a sound from the unit is printed at the top. Taking turns, each group passes the paper around the circle, writing words containing that sound until no group member can add any more. Tally the total. The group with the most words wins that round.

◆ LYRICAL PHONEMES

Distribute a printed copy of the lyrics from a traditional, patriotic, popular, or folk song. Tell students to read along as you play a recording of the song for the class. Play the song a second time and invite students to underline words on the printout that contain sounds discussed in this unit. Call on students to identify and correctly pronounce words they have underlined. Encourage volunteers to sing a stanza. Tell them to substitute humming for two words containing sounds studied in this unit. Afterward, call on others to identify and pronounce the words that were hummed.

■ PLANTING A PHONETIC GARDEN

Ask a volunteer to write the words *Vegetables* and *Flowers* on the chalkboard. With the class, brainstorm and list appropriate words containing the consonant and vowel combinations discussed in this unit. If possible, show the class pictures of garden layouts from magazines or seed catalogs. Have students design and draw a picture of a garden plot. Tell them to indicate where different plants will be placed. They should include labels with phonemes from the unit.

✳ JUST A BOWL OF PHONEMES

Arrange students in small groups. Provide each group with up to 28 gift tags or paper labels and a bowl. Tell each group to write one of the consonant or vowel combinations discussed in this unit on one side of each tag. One member can drop the tags in the bowl and swirl the bowl to mix the tags. Tell group members to take turns closing their eyes and picking a tag from the bowl. You might suggest students use two unsharpened pencils as "chopsticks" to draw a tag from the bowl; if this method is used, students should not close their eyes. After picking a tag, each student should say the sound associated with the letter combination and use the sound in a word identifying a kind of food. Encourage students to use the word in a sentence describing the food.

● SOUND HUNT

Have students look through books to find words that have these sounds: /k/, /kw/, /kn/, /ch/, /c/, /s/, /sh/, /th/, /wh/, /sc/. Tell them to make a list and count the words containing each sound. Then demonstrate how to make a horizontal or vertical bar graph. Invite students to create their own graphs illustrating how often each sound appears in the words on their list.

▲ FURNISHING A CASTLE

Students might work individually, with a partner, or in small groups to complete the following activity. Display a master copy of Blackline Master 7 for students to view. Tell them to imagine that this is a floor plan of an ancient castle. Ask them to suggest people who might have visited this site. Write these words on the chalkboard, underlining phonemes discussed in this unit (such as _king_, _queen_, _prince_, _knight_). Explain that students should decide what types of furniture and other objects they would place in each room and then write the name of each item in the appropriate location on the floor plan. When their project is completed, students are to circle words that include consonant and vowel combinations studied in this unit.

Technology

The following software products are designed to reinforce students' logical-thinking and language skills.

Smart Games Word Puzzles 1   Four types of word puzzles—such as "Word Melt," which involves changing one word into another, and "Word Hunter," which involves finding hidden words—provide students with practice in word play. Each puzzle addresses a broad range of ability levels (from older children to adults).
** Random Soft
   201 East 50th Street
   New York, NY 10022
   (800) 788-8815

Mind Castle: The Spell of the Word Wizard   By solving word puzzles and decoding passwords, students (Grade 3 and up) can escape from the dungeon tower the Word Wizard has locked them in.
** Lawrence Productions
   1800 South 35th Street
   Galesburg, MI 49053
   (616) 665-7075

Reading Blaster   Through hundreds of word-skill games, students in third grade through sixth grade can hone their skills.
** Davidson & Associates, Inc.
   19840 Pioneer Avenue
   Torrance, CA 90503
   (800) 545-7677

Name _____

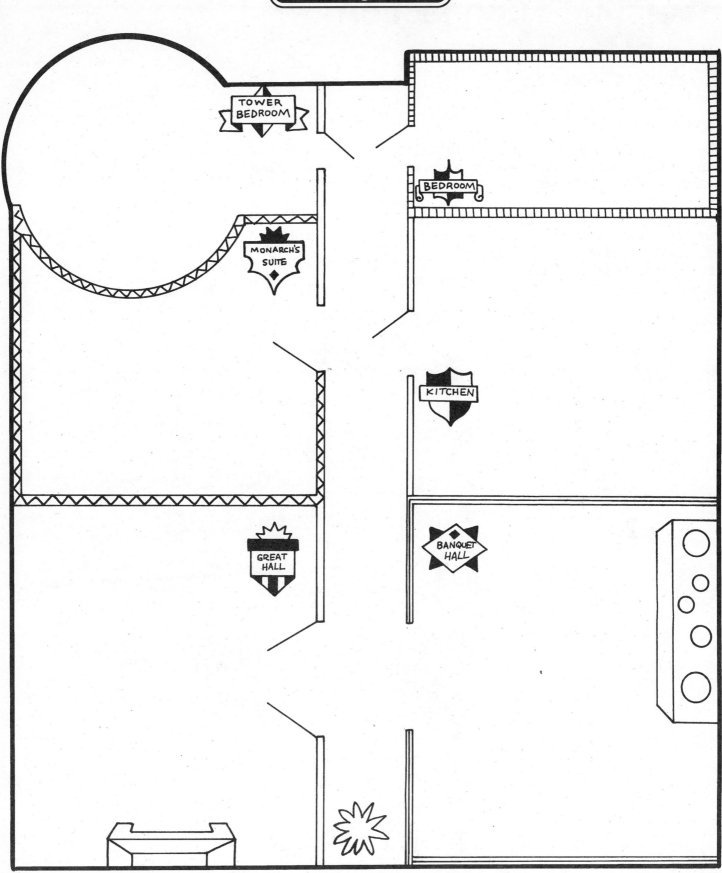

TOWER BEDROOM

BEDROOM

MONARCH'S SUITE

KITCHEN

GREAT HALL

BANQUET HALL

Home Connection

HOME LETTER

A letter is available to be sent home at the beginning of Unit 1. This letter informs family members that children will be learning to read and write words containing consonant variants, consonant combinations, and vowel combinations. The suggested home activity focuses on the poem "Fiddle Faddle." This activity promotes interaction between child and family members while supporting the student's learning of reading, identifying, and writing words with the targeted word study skills. A letter is also available in Spanish on page 3q.

Dear Family,

In the next few weeks, your child will be learning the different sounds associated with vowels and consonants. Following are some activities that you might enjoy sharing.

At-Home Activities

▶ Read the poem "Fiddle Faddle" on the other side of this letter with your child to feel the rhyme and rhythm of the language used in the poem.

▶ Ask your child to find the words with the sounds of s, k, qu, sh, wh, th, g, and r in the poem. Then ask your child to complete another verse of the poem. Post the child's additional verse in a prominent place.

▶ With your child, discuss what success means in your family. Then, brainstorm ways that success can be achieved. Have your child create a poster to illustrate these paths to success. Hang the poster as a reminder to everyone in your family.

Book Corner

Another way to extend the learning experience is to read aloud with your child. Here are two poetry collections that you can probably find in the library.

Poetry from A to Z
by Paul B. Janeczko

Poets comment candidly on their work in this useful and encouraging resource for beginining poets.

Remembering and Other Poems
by Myra C. Livingston

Enjoy these forty-five imaginative poems that explore how ordinary sights can provoke playful journeys through the imagination.

Sincerely,

_____

4 Unit 1
Introduction

Carta para la casa

Estimada familia,

En las semanas próximas, su hijo/a va a estudiar los diferentes sonidos asociados con las vocales y las consonantes en palabras en inglés. Las siguientes son actividades que quizás quieran compartir juntos.

Actividades para hacer en casa

He aquí algunas actividades que su hijo/a y ustedes pueden realizar juntos.

▶ Lean con su hijo/a el poema **"Fiddle Faddle"** al dorso de esta carta para sentir la rima y el ritmo del lenguaje usado en el poema.

▶ Pídanle a su hijo/a que busque las palabras con los sonidos de la **s**, **k**, **qu**, **sh**, **wh**, **th**, **g** y **r** en el poema. Luego pídanle que complete otro verso del poema. Exhiban el verso adicional hecho por su hijo/a en un lugar destacado.

▶ Con su hijo/a, hablen sobre lo que quiere decir el éxito en su familia. Juntos, generen ideas sobre cómo se puede lograr el éxito. Luego, pídanle a su hijo que cree un cartel para ilustrar estos caminos al éxito. Cuelguen el cartel en casa para que le sirva de recordatorio a toda la familia.

Otra manera de ampliar la experiencia de aprendizaje es leer en voz alta con su hijo/a. He aquí dos colecciones de poesía que probablemente puedan hallar en la biblioteca.

Poetry from A to Z
por Paul B. Janeczko

Los poetas hablan con franqueza acerca de su obra en este recurso útil y estimulante para poetas principiantes.

Remembering and Other Poems
por Myra C. Livingston

Disfruten estos originales cuarenta y cinco poemas que exploran cómo las vistas ordinarias pueden provocar travesías juguetonas por medio de la imaginación.

Atentamente, _____

Unit 1

Pages 3–4

Consonant Variants, Letter Combinations, Vowel Combinations, and Syllables

ASSESSING PRIOR KNOWLEDGE

To assess students' prior knowledge of consonant variants, combinations, vowel combinations, and syllables, use the pretest on pages 3e–3f.

Unit Focus

USING THE PAGE

- Read "Fiddle Faddle" aloud.
- Invite students to read along as you read the poem again. Emphasize the rhythm and rhyme in the poem.
- Discuss the meaning of the poem. Help students identify the word play in each character's statement. Point out that *M.D.* signifies a medical doctor.
- Ask students what they enjoy about the poem. In what ways do they think the poem is humorous?
- **Critical Thinking** Read aloud the question the character asks at the bottom of page 3. Encourage students to share their choice for helpful advice.

BUILDING A CONTEXT

As you read the poem again, have children identify words that start with *s, k, qu, sh, wh, th, g,* and *r.* Make lists of their words on the board.

Fiddle Faddle

Riddle me no,
riddle me yes,
what is the secret
of sweet success?

Said the razor, "Be keen."
"String along," said the bean.
"Push" said the door.
"Be polished" said the floor.
Said the piano, "Stand upright and grand."
"Be on the watch," said the second hand.

"Be cool," said the ice cube.
"Be bright," said the TV tube.
"Bounce back," said the yo-yo.
"Be well bred," said the dough.
"Plug," said the stopper.
"Shine," said copper.

"Be game," said the quail.
"Make your point," said the nail.
"Have patience," said the M.D.
"Look spruce," said the tree.
"Press on," said the stamp.
"Shed some light," said the lamp.
"Oh, just have a good head,"
the cabbage said.

—Eve Merriam

What's your favorite piece of advice in this poem?

Critical Thinking

Unit 1 Introduction **3**

UNIT OPENER ACTIVITIES

SPEAK UP

Read the poem again, asking students to pay special attention to the quotations. Ask students to develop different voices for each character as they take turns reading the poem aloud.

PUN AGAIN

Challenge students to choose one of the images from the poem and elaborate on it. For example, to continue the time subject from *"Be on the watch," said the second hand,* students might suggest *"Time out," said the stop watch; "That's alarming," said the clock radio; "Give me a hand," said the broken watch.*

DEAR ADDIE OR DEAR ABNER

Invite students to take turns being the class advice columnist. Have students make a "Help Box," where they can put in their anonymous questions about school or friends.

Home Letter

Dear Family,

In the next few weeks, your child will be learning the different sounds associated with vowels and consonants. Following are some activities that you might enjoy sharing.

At-Home Activities

▶ Read the poem "Fiddle Faddle" on the other side of this letter with your child to feel the rhyme and rhythm of the language used in the poem.

▶ Ask your child to find the words with the sounds of s, k, qu, sh, wh, th, g, and r in the poem. Then ask your child to complete another verse of the poem. Post the child's additional verse in a prominent place.

▶ With your child, discuss what success means in your family. Then, brainstorm ways that success can be achieved. Have your child create a poster to illustrate these paths to success. Hang the poster as a reminder to everyone in your family.

Book Corner

Another way to extend the learning experience is to read aloud with your child. Here are two poetry collections that you can probably find in the library.

Poetry from A to Z
by Paul B. Janeczko

Poets comment candidly on their work in this useful and encouraging resource for beginining poets.

Remembering and Other Poems
by Myra C. Livingston

Enjoy these forty-five imaginative poems that explore how ordinary sights can provoke playful journeys through the imagination.

Sincerely,

- The Home Letter on page 4 is intended to acquaint family members with the word study skills for the unit. Students can tear out page 4 and complete it with a family member. Encourage students to look for the books pictured on page 4 in the library and to read them with family members.

- The Home Letter can also be found on page 3q in Spanish.

CURRICULUM CONNECTIONS ✳

WRITING

Have students write a paragraph about an expertise they have that they could share with others. Then pair them with students who would like advice on that particular subject.

SCIENCE

Students can choose one of the subjects of the poem to research, such as clocks and time or the way light bulbs or TV tubes work.

DRAMATIC ARTS

Students might enjoy working in groups to perform the poem as Readers' Theatre or to dramatize it. One student can act as narrator as others say the characters' words.

BULLETIN BOARD

Challenge students to create a "Fun With Puns" bulletin-board display with illustrations of the puns in the poem and any other puns they have learned or invented. Have them use art materials to make the characters into cartoon figures and then write captions on speech balloons to attach near the "mouth" of each speaker.

Lesson 1

Pages 5–6

Words with the k Sound and qu and kn Words

INFORMAL ASSESSMENT OBJECTIVES

Can students

✔ identify words with /k/?

✔ use *qu* and *kn* words?

Lesson Focus

INTRODUCING THE SKILLS

- Read the following words aloud: *king, back , fickle, unique, mark, take.* Ask students what sound is heard in each of the words. *(/k/)*

- Write the words on the board and tell students that the letters *k, ck,* or *que* stand for /k/.

- Invite volunteers to underline the letter or letters that stand for /k/ in each word.

- Repeat the activity above, helping students identify the letters that stand for /kw/ in *queen, quilt,* and *quarter* and then /n/ in *knee, knock,* and *knight*.

USING THE PAGES

- Give students help as necessary to complete pages 5 and 6. After they have completed the pages, encourage them to discuss what they have learned about the sounds of *k* and about *qu* and *kn* words.

- **Critical Thinking** Read aloud the question at the bottom of page 5 and discuss answers with students.

5

Name _____

▶ Circle the letter or letters that stand for the **k** sound in each word in the box. Then use the words to complete the sentences.

> **RULE**
> When you hear the **k** sound in a syllable or word, the letters **k, ck,** or **que** will usually stand for that sound.
> **k**angaroo   pi**ck**le
> techni**que**

back	black	blacksmith	jackets	
kept	kettles	kinds	knack	look
pockets	quick	techniques	thick	unique

1. The early English settlers in America wore simple clothing that was often tan, gray, or _____black_____ .

2. Native Americans showed them which _____kinds_____ of plants could be used for dying cloth.

3. Bark, roots, seeds, and berries were sometimes boiled in large _____kettles_____ to create shades of yellow, red, and brown.

4. The plain clothing of these settlers often had no decoration on the front or _____back_____

5. Children were dressed to _____look_____ like small adults.

6. Women sewed clothes from cloth made with different _____techniques_____ , such as spinning and weaving.

7. Clothing was also made from animal skins and fur, which _____kept_____ people warm in winter.

8. Because materials were scarce, the settlers had a _____knack_____ for using every scrap.

9. Their _____thick_____ , heavy clothes were mended many times.

10. A _____quick_____ glance at a person's clothing could tell you about the work they did.

11. A _____blacksmith_____ wore a leather apron for protection from flying sparks.

12. A peddler often wore a coat with many _____pockets_____ for carrying small items.

13. Farmers would wear leather _____jackets_____ that looked like vests.

14. Since all of the colonists' clothing was homemade, each piece was _____unique_____ .

> **How do you think the children of early settlers felt when they got new clothing?**

Critical Thinking

Lesson 1
Words with the k sound
5

FOCUS ON ALL LEARNERS ✳ ● ◆ ■ ◆

ENGLISH LANGUAGE LEARNERS/ESL

Before beginning page 5, guide a discussion about the colonial era in America and the life of early English settlers.

VISUAL LEARNERS

LARGE GROUP

Have the class play "name that word" by giving clues whose answers begin with *qu,* such as *another word for argue (quarrel).* Ask a volunteer to write the answers on the board and underline the letters that make /kw/. Then give clues whose answers begin with *kn.*

KINESTHETIC LEARNERS

LARGE GROUP

Ask students to look in a pocket each time they hear a word with /k/, to tap one knee each time they hear a word that begins with *kn,* and to point to an imaginary queen's crown on their heads each time they hear a word that begins with *qu.*

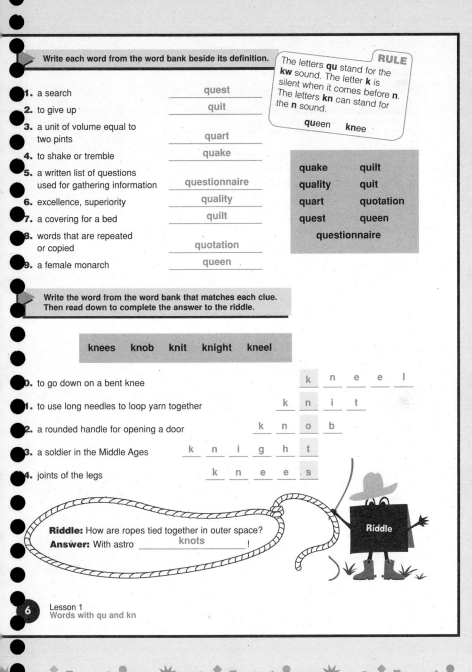

1 Write each word from the word bank beside its definition.

1. a search — quest
2. to give up — quit
3. a unit of volume equal to two pints — quart
4. to shake or tremble — quake
5. a written list of questions used for gathering information — questionnaire
6. excellence, superiority — quality
7. a covering for a bed — quilt
8. words that are repeated or copied — quotation
9. a female monarch — queen

> **RULE**
> The letters **qu** stand for the **kw** sound. The letter **k** is silent when it comes before **n**. The letters **kn** can stand for the **n** sound.
>
> **qu**een   **kn**ee

quake	quilt
quality	quit
quart	quotation
quest	queen
questionnaire	

2 Write the word from the word bank that matches each clue. Then read down to complete the answer to the riddle.

knees	knob	knit	knight	kneel

10. to go down on a bent knee — k n e e l
11. to use long needles to loop yarn together — k n i t
12. a rounded handle for opening a door — k n o b
13. a soldier in the Middle Ages — k n i g h t
14. joints of the legs — k n e e s

Riddle: How are ropes tied together in outer space?
Answer: With astro ___knots___ !

Riddle

Lesson 1
Words with qu and kn

6

SPELLING

The following sentences can be used as a pretest for this set of spelling words.

1. **queen** — The **queen** had tea in the afternoon.
2. **knee** — He hurt his **knee** playing basketball.
3. **cheap** — The play tickets were **cheap**.
4. **character** — My favorite **character** is the pig.
5. **race** — I came in first in the **race**.
6. **game** — Ping pong is a good **game**.
7. **page** — She read the first **page**.
8. **different** — He knew five **different** bird calls.
9. **dolphin** — The **dolphin** swam in front of us.
10. **measure** — **Measure** my height.

WRITING

Portfolio Invite students to write a story about what they imagine it would be like to be a child their age in colonial America.

PHYSICAL EDUCATION

Students can compile a number of sports articles about professional football quarterbacks. They might also like to research famous quarterbacks such as Joe Namath, Joe Montana, and Dan Marino.

SCIENCE

Ask students to research earthquakes and their causes. Have them report on the earthquake information and how it compares to earthquakes they have seen in movies.

AUDITORY/KINESTHETIC LEARNERS

PARTNER

Tell pairs of students to head three columns with *k*, *ck*, and *que*. Have one partner dictate to the other as many words as possible that contain *k*, *ck*, and *que*. After the listener has written each word in the appropriate column, have students switch roles and repeat the activity.

GIFTED LEARNERS

Challenge students to write about a technique they have learned in sports or the arts. Ask them to describe the technique and to explain how they acquired this specialized knowledge.

LEARNERS WHO NEED EXTRA SUPPORT

To help students having difficulty with the silent *k*, have them use a dictionary to look up words that begin with *kn*. Make sure they read the words before and after the *kn* words so that they see and hear the difference between /k/ and /n/ spelled *kn*. **See Daily Word Study Practice, page 180.**

Lesson 2

Pages 7–8

The Sounds of ch and the Sounds of c

INFORMAL ASSESSMENT OBJECTIVES

Can students

✓ identify the sounds of *ch*?

✓ distinguish the hard and soft sounds of *c*?

Lesson Focus

INTRODUCING THE SKILLS

● Ask a volunteer to come to the board and write the words *checkers*, *character*, and *chandelier*.

● Encourage students to tell you how the words are alike and how they are different.

● Help students conclude that the *ch* in *checkers* sounds like /ch/, the *ch* in *character* sounds like /k/, and the *ch* in *chandelier* sounds like /sh/.

● Challenge students to name additional words with the three *ch* sounds and to write them on the board.

● Repeat the activity with *column, cubic, cane, ceramic, cinder,* and *cymbal* to illustrate the hard and soft sounds of *c*.

● Help students conclude that *c* is usually hard when it is followed by *a, o,* or *u* and soft when it is followed by *e, i,* or *y*.

USING THE PAGES

● Have students review their work on pages 7 and 8 with a partner.

● **Critical Thinking** Read aloud the question at the bottom of page 7 and discuss answers with students.

7

Name _____

▶ **Read the sentences. Underline the words in which ch stands for the sound you hear in child. Circle the words in which ch stands for the k sound. Mark an X on the words in which ch stands for the sh sound.**

> **RULE**
> Usually **ch** stands for the sound you hear at the beginning of **child**. Sometimes the letters **ch** can stand for the **k** or **sh** sounds.
>
> **ch**eap   **ch**aracter   **ch**ef

1. You can <u>watch</u> a professional baseball game in many American cities.

2. Some large cities like New York and Chicago have more than one major league baseball team.

3. The fans are a (chorus,) cheering the teams to victory.

4. At a professional baseball game, you can <u>purchase</u> a brochure with the players' names.

5. In it you can <u>check</u> each player's records of hits and runs.

6. In the game of baseball, <u>pitching</u> is a skill that takes great strength and (character.)

7. <u>Champion</u> teams have good <u>pitchers</u> to (anchor) their infield.

8. During a game, the <u>coaches</u> may <u>change</u> <u>pitchers</u> several times.

9. They might, for instance, <u>choose</u> to play a left-handed <u>pitcher</u> against a left-handed batter.

▶ **Complete each sentence with a word from the word bank.**

check	reach	chest	coaches
character	catchers	change	attached

10. The _____character_____ of each baseball position is different.

11. The manager and _____coaches_____ decide who will play in the game.

12. The _____catchers_____ spend most of their time at home plate.

13. They carefully _____check_____ their equipment before each inning.

14. They use a mask and padding to protect their face, _____chest_____, and legs.

15. The cage-like mask is _____attached_____ by straps to the back of the catcher's head.

16. Fielders sometimes _____change_____ their position during a game.

17. They want to be in the best position to _____reach_____ a ball.

Why is baseball a popular sport?

Critical Thinking

Lesson 2
The sounds of ch   **7**

© MCP All rights reserved. Copying strictly prohibited.

FOCUS ON ALL LEARNERS

ENGLISH LANGUAGE LEARNERS/ESL

Before beginning page 7, ask students to talk about their own favorite sport. How do the rules and action compare to baseball? Students might want to demonstrate their prowess in a particular skill of their chosen sport.

VISUAL LEARNERS

SMALL GROUP

Materials: magazines, newspapers

Instruct pairs of students to search in newspapers or magazines for words that contain the letters *ch*. Have students write the words on a sheet of paper, say them aloud, and circle *ch*. Encourage them to discuss which *ch* sound each word contains—/ch/, /sh/, or /k/.

KINESTHETIC LEARNERS

PARTNER

Materials: index cards

Distribute two index cards to each student. Have students draw a picture clue for a word that begins with /ch/, /sh/, or /k/ on each card. Then have them play a guessing game with their partners to guess the words.

Read the article, and circle each word with the letter **c** that is followed by a vowel. Then write each word you circled in the correct column. Use each word only once.

A NATIONAL FAVORITE

People in America love to eat ice cream. We produce and consume more ice cream than any other country in the world. Americans from the past loved ice cream as much as we do today. George Washington and Thomas Jefferson were no exceptions. Ice cream was served as a dessert course when each man was president. At that time, ice cream was considered a treat reserved for special celebrations because it was so hard to make. Ice needed to be cut from frozen ponds to keep the confection cold.

After the ice cream freezer was invented, ice cream vendors could sell all kinds of new treats. The ice cream cone was invented at the 1904 World's Fair, when a vendor ran out of dishes and placed the ice cream in a rolled up waffle instead. His customers thought that this was an excellent idea, and it remains a popular combination today!

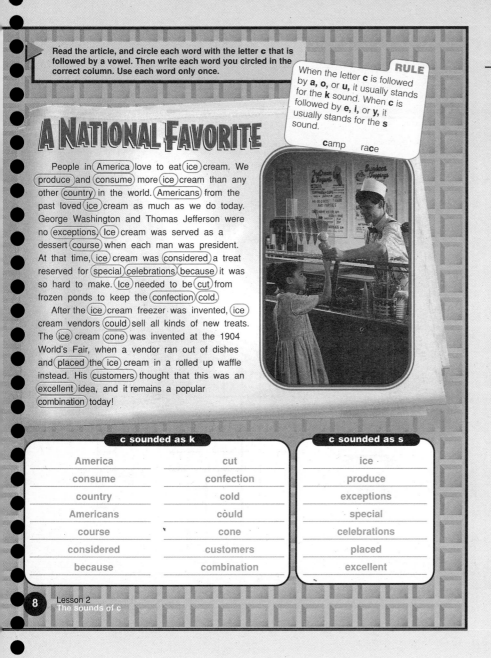

c sounded as k		c sounded as s
America	cut	ice
consume	confection	produce
country	cold	exceptions
Americans	could	special
course	cone	celebrations
considered	customers	placed
because	combination	excellent

SPELLING

Write these words on the chalkboard and ask students to use each one in a sentence: *queen, knee, cheap, character, race, game, page, different, dolphin, measure.*

WRITING

Portfolio Invite students to write a thank-you letter to the inventor of the ice-cream cone. Encourage them to mention their favorite flavors and to suggest some new flavors they would like to taste.

SOCIAL STUDIES

Challenge students to use a map of the United States to mark every city that has a major league baseball team. They may want to use the newspaper sports pages or a sports magazine for research.

FINE ARTS

Invite an artist who works with ceramic pottery to visit the classroom. Ask the artist to display some ceramic pieces and demonstrate his or her techniques for forming, glazing, and firing. Provide each student with a small amount of self-hardening potter's clay. Encourage students to make their own creations, incorporating some of the techniques the artist described.

LARGE GROUP

AUDITORY/KINESTHETIC LEARNERS

Instruct students to put their thumbs in the air when you say a word that contains hard *c*, and to put their thumbs down when you say a word that contains soft *c*. Use the words *castle, cylinder, clerk, centennial, uncover, cypress, fancy,* and *particular.* Then have students suggest words.

GIFTED LEARNERS

Challenge students to write sentences using more than one meaning of words such as *watch*. An example is: *Do you ever watch your watch to see if it is keeping correct time?*

LEARNERS WHO NEED EXTRA SUPPORT

Materials: word cards, lunch bags, markers

Have students decorate three bags—one with a chair, one with a parachute, and one with corn. Distribute word cards representing words with /ch/, /sh/, or /k/. Have students work together to divide the cards into groups according to the three sounds. Have students place the cards in the appropriate bag. **See Daily Word Study Practice, pages 180–181.**

Lesson 3

Pages 9–10

Sounds of g

Lesson Focus

INTRODUCING THE SKILL

- Write the following sentences on the board, omitting the underlines: *Gina is an excellent gymnast. Go open the gate immediately!* Ask volunteers to read each sentence and to underline the words that contain *g*.

- Ask the class whether the *g*'s in *Gina* and *gymnast* stand for the same sound as the *g*'s in *go* and *gate*. *(no)*

- Help students understand that when *g* is followed by *e, i,* or *y*, it usually stands for the soft sound, or /j/. If *g* is followed by *a, o,* or *u*, it usually stands for the hard sound, or /g/.

USING THE PAGES

- Give students help as necessary to complete pages 9 and 10.

- **Critical Thinking** Read aloud the question on page 10 and discuss answers with students.

Name _____

▶ Read each word. Write **g** on the line if the word has the hard sound of **g**. Write **j** on the line if the word has the soft sound of **g**.

RULE
When the letter **g** is followed by **a, o,** or **u**, it has the hard sound of **g**. When **g** is followed by **e, i,** or **y**, it usually has a soft sound. Soft **g** has a **j** sound.

game   pa**g**e

1. gymnast — j
2. guest — g
3. gazebo — g
4. galloping — g
5. arrangement — j
6. gym — j
7. rage — j
8. sponge — j
9. region — j
10. guess — g
11. age — j
12. tragedy — j

▶ Use the words from above to solve the crossword puzzle.

Across

4. a disaster or serious event
5. a summerhouse from which a person can gaze at the scenery
6. extreme anger
7. moving very fast
9. an expert in gymnastics
11. number of years a person has lived

Down

1. the way in which something is put together or shown
2. a part of the earth's surface
3. someone who is visiting
8. give an estimate
10. something full of holes, used for cleaning

Crossword answers:
Across: 4. TRAGEDY, 5. GAZEBO, 6. RAGE, 7. GALLOPING, 9. GYMNAST, 11. AGE
Down: 1. ARRANGEMENT, 2. REGION, 3. GUEST, 8. SPONGE, 10. GUESS

Lesson 3
The sounds of g   **9**

FOCUS ON ALL LEARNERS

ENGLISH LANGUAGE LEARNERS/ESL

Before beginning page 10, ask students to read the sentences on the board to be sure they are pronouncing the sounds of *g* correctly. Be sure they understand how to work a crossword puzzle.

VISUAL LEARNERS

PARTNER   Invite pairs of students to play tic-tac-toe, with one partner writing words with the soft *g* sound, the other partner words with the hard *g* sound. If a player writes a word with the wrong sound of *g*, he or she loses a turn.

KINESTHETIC/VISUAL LEARNERS

LARGE GROUP   Students choose words that contain *g* and pantomime the definitions of each word. The rest of the class guesses what word is being acted out and uses that word in a sentence.

9

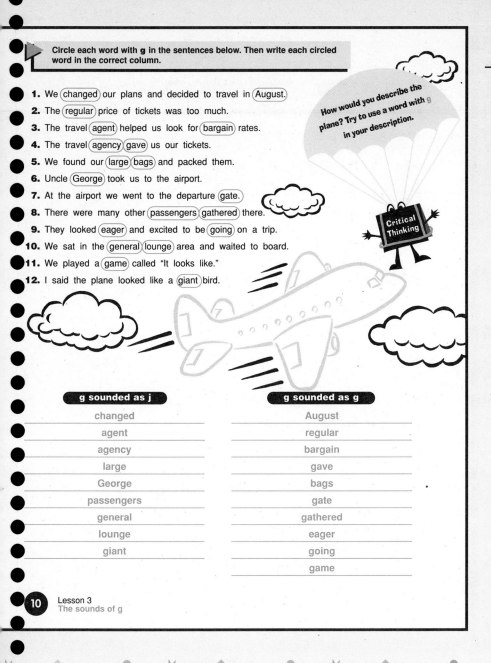

Circle each word with g in the sentences below. Then write each circled word in the correct column.

1. We (changed) our plans and decided to travel in (August).
2. The (regular) price of tickets was too much.
3. The travel (agent) helped us look for (bargain) rates.
4. The travel (agency) (gave) us our tickets.
5. We found our (large) (bags) and packed them.
6. Uncle (George) took us to the airport.
7. At the airport we went to the departure (gate).
8. There were many other (passengers) (gathered) there.
9. They looked (eager) and excited to be (going) on a trip.
10. We sat in the (general) (lounge) area and waited to board.
11. We played a (game) called "It looks like."
12. I said the plane looked like a (giant) bird.

How would you describe the plane? Try to use a word with g in your description.

Critical Thinking

g sounded as j	g sounded as g
changed	August
agent	regular
agency	bargain
large	gave
George	bags
passengers	gate
general	gathered
lounge	eager
giant	going
	game

AUDITORY/KINESTHETIC LEARNERS

LARGE GROUP

Make two columns on the board, *Hard g* and *Soft g*. Say a word with *g* such as *goat*. Ask a student to write the word in the correct column. Then that student says another word with *g* for a classmate to write.

GIFTED LEARNERS

Challenge students by having them create advertisements for nonsense products with names that contain the letter *g*, such as *Raging Gifts* or *Gurgling Gadgets*. Each must contain both sounds of *g*.

LEARNERS WHO NEED EXTRA SUPPORT

Work with students as they begin page 9, having each child, in turn, read a word aloud and identify the sound of *g*. Have them read the clues for the crossword puzzle to be sure they understand what each means. **See Daily Word Study Practice, pages 180–181.**

CURRICULUM CONNECTIONS

SPELLING

Prepare slips of paper for a box with the spelling words *queen, knee, cheap, character, race, game, page, different, dolphin,* and *measure.* Invite students to draw a word from the box to act out as classmates try to guess the word. The student who guesses correctly, spells the word aloud and writes it on the board.

WRITING

Portfolio Invite students to write a story about a realistic or a fantasy trip using a form of transportation other than an airplane. Encourage them to use some of the *g* words listed on page 10.

SOCIAL STUDIES

Portfolio Make a chart with the following headings for three columns: *Name, /g/, /j/.* Have students use maps, an atlas, and a globe to find geographical names that begin with *G* then write them on the chart, putting an X in the correct column to indicate whether the *g* in each name has /g/ or /j/.

PHYSICAL EDUCATION

Suggest students read about national and international gymnastic competitions, then choose one gymnast to learn more about. They could give an oral report to the class or make a poster celebrating that gymnast's life, with information about where he or she was born, where he or she trains, and what medals he or she has won.

Lesson 4

Pages 11–12

Words with the **f** Sound and the Sounds of **s**

INFORMAL ASSESSMENT OBJECTIVES

Can students

✔ identify the letters that stand for /f/?

✔ distinguish among variations of the sound of *s*?

Lesson Focus

INTRODUCING THE SKILLS

- Have students listen as you say the words *follow*, *photograph*, and *afflict*. Ask what sound is heard in all three words. *(/f/)*

- On the board, write *follow*, *photograph*, and *afflict*. Ask a volunteer to underline the letter(s) in the words that stand for /f/. (*f, ph, ff*) Challenge students to name additional words that contain these letters.

- Write *sing*, *posy*, *treasure*, and *sure* as students say the words aloud.

- Guide students to understand that the *s* in *sing* stands for /s/, the *s* in *wise* stands for /z/, the *s* in *treasure* stands for /zh/, and the *s* in *sure* stands for /sh/.

USING THE PAGES

If students need help to complete pages 11 and 12, have them first read the page aloud. After they have completed the pages, encourage them to discuss what they have learned about the sounds of *f* and *s*.

11

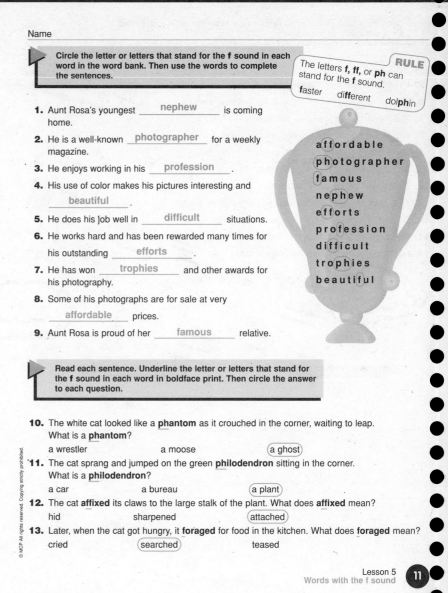

Name _____

▶ Circle the letter or letters that stand for the **f** sound in each word in the word bank. Then use the words to complete the sentences.

> **RULE**
> The letters **f**, **ff**, or **ph** can stand for the **f** sound.
> faster   di**ff**erent   dol**ph**in

1. Aunt Rosa's youngest ____nephew____ is coming home.

2. He is a well-known ____photographer____ for a weekly magazine.

3. He enjoys working in his ____profession____.

4. His use of color makes his pictures interesting and ____beautiful____.

5. He does his job well in ____difficult____ situations.

6. He works hard and has been rewarded many times for his outstanding ____efforts____.

7. He has won ____trophies____ and other awards for his photography.

8. Some of his photographs are for sale at very ____affordable____ prices.

9. Aunt Rosa is proud of her ____famous____ relative.

Word Bank:
a**ff**ordable
photogra**ph**er
famous
ne**ph**ew
e**ff**orts
pro**f**ession
di**ff**icult
tro**ph**ies
beauti**f**ul

▶ Read each sentence. Underline the letter or letters that stand for the **f** sound in each word in boldface print. Then circle the answer to each question.

10. The white cat looked like a **phantom** as it crouched in the corner, waiting to leap. What is a **phantom**?
    a wrestler   a moose   (a ghost)

11. The cat sprang and jumped on the green **philodendron** sitting in the corner. What is a **philodendron**?
    a car   a bureau   (a plant)

12. The cat **affixed** its claws to the large stalk of the plant. What does **affixed** mean?
    hid   sharpened   (attached)

13. Later, when the cat got hungry, it **foraged** for food in the kitchen. What does **foraged** mean?
    cried   (searched)   teased

FOCUS ON ALL LEARNERS

ENGLISH LANGUAGE LEARNERS/ESL

Before beginning page 11, invite those who wish to do so to bring in photographs that they or their family members have taken. Encourage a discussion of the technique of taking good photographs.

VISUAL LEARNERS

SMALL GROUP

Students may enjoy working in pairs to design a word-search puzzle using words that contain /f/ and the sounds of *s*. Suggest that students begin by brainstorming a list of words they can use. Encourage partners to exchange their puzzle with another pair of students.

KINESTHETIC LEARNERS

LARGE GROUP

Divide the group in half. Ask the members of one group to stand every time they hear a word with /f/ at the beginning of a word, and the members of the other group to stand when they hear /f/ in the middle of a word. Use words such as *nephew*, *phantom*, *philodendron*, *professor*, and *fantasy*.

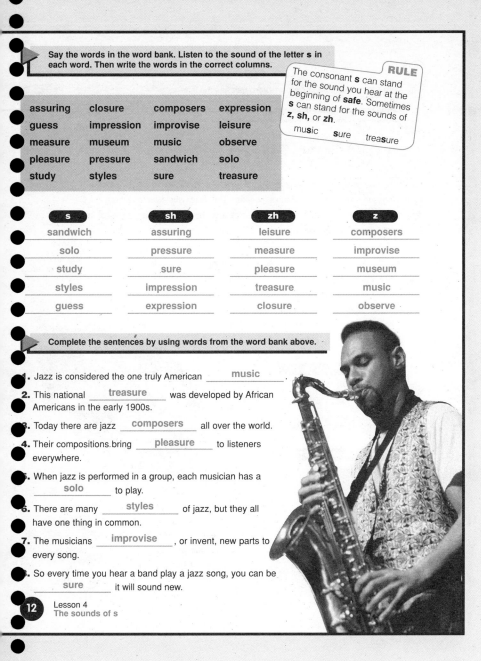

Say the words in the word bank. Listen to the sound of the letter **s** in each word. Then write the words in the correct columns.

assuring	closure	composers	expression
guess	impression	improvise	leisure
measure	museum	music	observe
pleasure	pressure	sandwich	solo
study	styles	sure	treasure

RULE

The consonant **s** can stand for the sound you hear at the beginning of **safe**. Sometimes **s** can stand for the sounds of **z, sh,** or **zh**.

mu**s**ic   **s**ure   trea**s**ure

s	**sh**	**zh**	**z**
sandwich	assuring	leisure	composers
solo	pressure	measure	improvise
study	sure	pleasure	museum
styles	impression	treasure	music
guess	expression	closure	observe

Complete the sentences by using words from the word bank above.

1. Jazz is considered the one truly American ____music____

2. This national ____treasure____ was developed by African Americans in the early 1900s.

3. Today there are jazz ____composers____ all over the world.

4. Their compositions bring ____pleasure____ to listeners everywhere.

5. When jazz is performed in a group, each musician has a ____solo____ to play.

6. There are many ____styles____ of jazz, but they all have one thing in common.

7. The musicians ____improvise____, or invent, new parts to every song.

8. So every time you hear a band play a jazz song, you can be ____sure____ it will sound new.

12 Lesson 4
The sounds of s

SPELLING

The following sentences can be used as a spelling posttest.

1. **queen** The **queen** wears a crown.
2. **knee** She scraped her **knee**.
3. **cheap** That is a **cheap** price.
4. **character** Tom Sawyer is a book **character**.
5. **race** We **race** to school every morning.
6. **game** The home team won the **game**.
7. **page** Each **page** had a drawing of a face.
8. **different** My cap is **different** from yours.
9. **dolphin** I saw a **dolphin** at the aquarium.
10. **measure** Use a ruler to **measure**.

WRITING

Portfolio Invite students to write a story about taking a photograph of a family pet that they have or wished they had. Brainstorm a list of descriptive words with /f/ and /s/ that they might use in their work.

FINE ARTS

Gather a collection of music by various traditional and contemporary composers and recording artists with an emphasis on jazz. Then invite children to contribute to the "listening fest" by bringing in recordings by their favorites. Help children make a music chart that categorizes the types of music and their creators and/or performers.

SOCIAL STUDIES

Display a number of books with documentary photographs from around the world. Ask students to pick one photograph to share with the class. Ask them to explain what they learned about the people or place pictured from examining the photograph.

INDIVIDUAL

AUDITORY/KINESTHETIC LEARNERS

Materials: index cards

Distribute four index cards to each student. Have students write *s, z, sh,* or *zh* in large letters on separate cards. As you name words that contain the consonant*s*, have students hold up the card that represents the sound they hear.

GIFTED LEARNERS

Challenge students to write sentences using words with as many of the different *s* sounds as they can. An example is *The wise man sang a song assuring us we would find the treasure.*

LEARNERS WHO NEED EXTRA SUPPORT

Materials: word cards

Distribute word cards representing the different sounds of *s*. Have students work together to divide the cards into groups according to the four sounds of *s*. Have students color-code the cards to help them group the variations of the sound. **See Daily Word Study Practice, pages 180–181.**

Lesson 5

Pages 13–14

The Sounds of *wh* and Words with the *sh* Sound

INFORMAL ASSESSMENT OBJECTIVES

Can students

✔ identify the sounds that the letters *wh* stand for?

✔ identify words that contain /sh/?

Lesson Focus

INTRODUCING THE SKILLS

● Write the words *wheel* and *whose* on the board. Ask the class to read them.

● Have students listen carefully as you say each word, emphasizing /hw/ in *wheel* and /h/ in *whose*. Ask the class to repeat the words.

● Help students conclude that even though both words begin with *wh*, a different sound is heard at the beginning of each word.

● Write *shoulder, invitation,* and *musician* on the board, say the words, and ask what sound is heard in all three words. (/sh/)

● Underline the letters that make /sh/ in the words. (*sh, ti, ci*)

USING THE PAGES

● Give students help as necessary to complete pages 13 and 14.

● **Critical Thinking** Read aloud the question at the bottom of page 13 and discuss answers with students.

13

Name _____

▶ Read the article and circle each word that has the letters **wh.** Then write those words in the correct columns below. Write each word only once.

RULE
The letters **wh** can stand for the **h** sound or the **hw** sound.
whole   **wh**ale

The Amazing Whale

(Where) can you find the largest animal that has ever lived? Some say it's swimming (somewhere) in the earth's oceans. The blue (whale), (whose) body length can reach about 100 feet (30 meters), can be heavier than an elephant and bigger than the largest prehistoric dinosaur.

(When) scientists study these huge animals, they find out (why) they are some of the most fascinating animals found (anywhere) on earth. For example, (while) blue (whales) have excellent hearing, they have small ear openings and no real ears at all on the outside of their bodies. These animals, (who) live in water, must breathe air to survive. Although a blue (whale) usually keeps its (whole) body underwater, it must bring the top of its head to the surface regularly in order to breathe.

wh sounded as h
whose
who
whole

wh sounded as hw
where
somewhere
whale(s)
when
why
anywhere
while

What is the most interesting or surprising fact you learned from this article?

Critical Thinking

Lesson 5
The sounds of wh   **13**

FOCUS ON ALL LEARNERS

ENGLISH LANGUAGE LEARNERS/ESL

Before beginning page 13, have students describe the enormous size of a blue whale and what they know about whales.

VISUAL LEARNERS

PARTNER   **Materials:** posterboard, markers

Have students work in pairs to make sound posters for *wh* and *sh.* On one poster, have them draw a picture of a whale labeled *whale,* with the *wh* circled, and on another poster, have them draw a picture of a magician labeled *magician,* with the *ci* circled. Have partners take turns adding words to each poster.

KINESTHETIC LEARNERS

LARGE GROUP   **Materials:** index cards

Divide the class into three groups. Tell students in the first group to write one word that contains the letters *sh* on an index card. Each student in the second group can write *ti* words; the third group can write *ci* words. Have volunteers pick a card, identify which letters stand for /sh/ and use the word in a sentence.

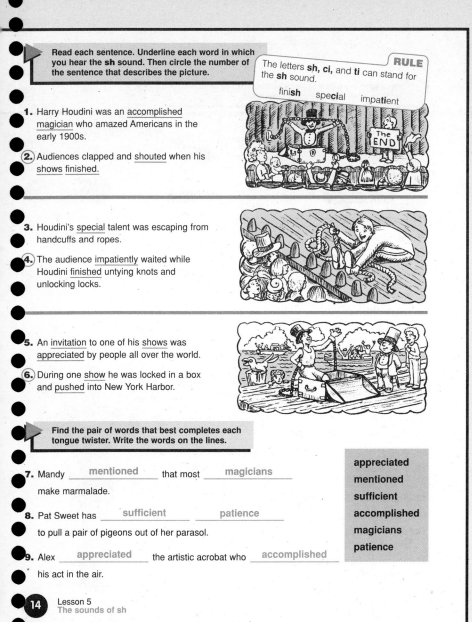

Read each sentence. Underline each word in which you hear the sh sound. Then circle the number of the sentence that describes the picture.

RULE

The letters **sh, ci,** and **ti** can stand for the **sh** sound.

fini**sh**   spe**ci**al   impa**ti**ent

1. Harry Houdini was an <u>accomplished</u> <u>magician</u> who amazed Americans in the early 1900s.

2. Audiences clapped and <u>shouted</u> when his <u>shows</u> <u>finished</u>.

3. Houdini's <u>special</u> talent was escaping from handcuffs and ropes.

4. The audience <u>impatiently</u> waited while Houdini <u>finished</u> untying knots and unlocking locks.

5. An <u>invitation</u> to one of his <u>shows</u> was <u>appreciated</u> by people all over the world.

6. During one <u>show</u> he was locked in a box and <u>pushed</u> into New York Harbor.

Find the pair of words that best completes each tongue twister. Write the words on the lines.

7. Mandy _____mentioned_____ that most _____magicians_____ make marmalade.

8. Pat Sweet has _____sufficient_____ _____patience_____ to pull a pair of pigeons out of her parasol.

9. Alex _____appreciated_____ the artistic acrobat who _____accomplished_____ his act in the air.

| appreciated |
| mentioned |
| sufficient |
| accomplished |
| magicians |
| patience |

14 Lesson 5
The sounds of sh

SPELLING

The following sentences can be used as a pretest for this set of spelling words.

1.	**whole**	She ate the **whole** sandwich.
2.	**whale**	The **whale** is bigger than a horse.
3.	**ship**	When the mast broke, the **ship** sank.
4.	**special**	She is my **special** friend.
5.	**partial**	This is not whole, it is **partial**.
6.	**science**	In **science** we study plants.
7.	**conscience**	My **conscience** says, "don't do it."
8.	**scare**	That movie didn't **scare** me.
9.	**gnat**	A **gnat** is an insect.
10.	**sign**	The stop **sign** is red.

WRITING

Portfolio Invite students to write and illustrate a story about going on a whale watch with their family or classmates. Ask them to consider what kinds of whales they would like to see and what they would learn about how whales live in the sea.

FINE ARTS

Invite students to practice and perform their own magic show, with simple tricks, costumes, and props. Students can create and send invitations to their parents and to students in other classes.

SCIENCE

Challenge students to research the different species of whales to find out which ones are extinct, endangered, or thriving. Have students create a picture graph to show the numbers of whales of each species that scientists estimate are swimming in the ocean today.

AUDITORY/KINESTHETIC LEARNERS

LARGE GROUP

Remind the class that *wh* has two sounds, /h/ as in *whole* and /hw/ as in *whale*. Then tell the class that you are going to say several words that contain *wh*. Invite students to raise their left hands whenever they hear /h/ and their right hands whenever they hear /hw/.

GIFTED LEARNERS

Challenge students to write a newspaper review of a Houdini performance, using as many /sh/ words as they can.

LEARNERS WHO NEED EXTRA SUPPORT

Help students make a /sh/ Word Wall with words representing the three sounds. Have students add to the wall whenever a new word with the sound is introduced. **See Daily Word Study Practice, pages 181–182.**

Lesson 6

Pages 15–16

Sounds of th, sh, wh

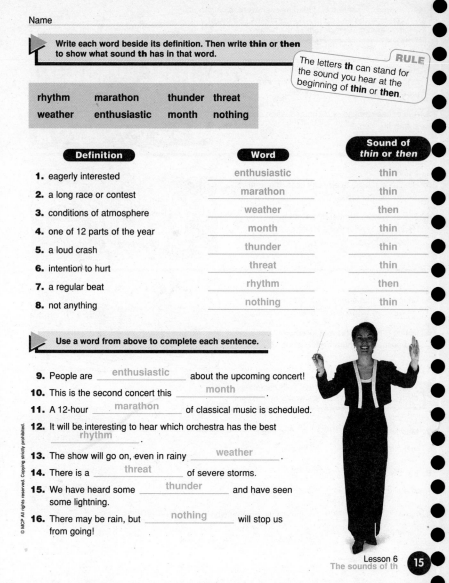

INFORMAL ASSESSMENT OBJECTIVES

Can students

- distinguish the different sounds of *th*?
- identify the sounds that the letters *sh, wh, th* stand for?

Lesson Focus

INTRODUCING THE SKILLS

- Write the words *then* and *thin* on the board and ask students to say them aloud. Ask what sounds they hear that are almost the same in each word. *(th)* Be sure students hear the difference in the two sounds.
- Remind students that a digraph is two consonants together that stand for one sound: the /th/ in *thin*.
- Write these words on the board and underline the digraph *th* in each one: *weather, bothered, farther, throat, forth, thick.*
- Challenge students to name additional words with the sounds of *th*.
- Remind students that *wh* stands for /hw/ and /h/ and that the letters *sh, ti,* and *ci* can stand for /sh/.

USING THE PAGES

- Be sure students understand how to complete pages 15 and 16.
- **Critical Thinking** Read aloud the question on page 16 and discuss answers with students.

Name ____________________

Write each word beside its definition. Then write thin or then to show what sound th has in that word.

RULE The letters **th** can stand for the sound you hear at the beginning of **thin** or **then**.

rhythm	marathon	thunder	threat
weather	enthusiastic	month	nothing

Definition	Word	Sound of *thin* or *then*
1. eagerly interested	enthusiastic	thin
2. a long race or contest	marathon	thin
3. conditions of atmosphere	weather	then
4. one of 12 parts of the year	month	thin
5. a loud crash	thunder	thin
6. intention to hurt	threat	thin
7. a regular beat	rhythm	then
8. not anything	nothing	thin

Use a word from above to complete each sentence.

9. People are ___enthusiastic___ about the upcoming concert!

10. This is the second concert this ___month___.

11. A 12-hour ___marathon___ of classical music is scheduled.

12. It will be interesting to hear which orchestra has the best ___rhythm___.

13. The show will go on, even in rainy ___weather___.

14. There is a ___threat___ of severe storms.

15. We have heard some ___thunder___ and have seen some lightning.

16. There may be rain, but ___nothing___ will stop us from going!

FOCUS ON ALL LEARNERS

ENGLISH LANGUAGE LEARNERS/ESL

Before beginning page 15, briefly discuss weather patterns and weather vocabulary such as *thunder, thunderstorms,* and *lightning.*

VISUAL LEARNERS

INDIVIDUAL Challenge students to write a weather report, using as many words that contain *wh, sh,* and *th* as possible and underlining any words with digraphs that they use. Call on volunteers to read their reports to the class. Then display students' work on a bulletin board.

KINESTHETIC/AUDITORY LEARNERS

SMALL GROUP Ask students to repeat each word you say, then wiggle their thumbs if the word has the sound of /th/ as in *thumb*. Try these words: *thank, tooth, thunder, this, that, thread, there, cloth.*

> Circle the letters that stand for the **sh, wh,** and **th** sounds. Then complete the sentences using words from the word bank.

Word Bank:
- brea**th**ing
- heal**th**y
- **th**en
- **wh**ispered
- **d**i**sh**
- **wh**impering
- **th**ick
- **wh**iskers
- **wh**ose
- fil**th**y
- **sh**ivering
- **s**pecial
- pa**t**ient
- **wh**at

1. Tina thought she heard a _____whimpering_____ sound in the bushes.

2. She wondered _____what_____ it could be.

3. When she looked, she discovered a _____shivering_____ little kitten trying to keep warm.

4. Tina _____whispered_____ softly, and the kitten came over to her.

5. The kitten needed a bath; its fur was _____filthy_____ .

6. Tina wrapped the kitten in her warm, _____thick_____ jacket.

7. She didn't know _____whose_____ kitten this was.

8. Tina gave the kitten a _____dish_____ of food.

9. She _____then_____ gave it some milk.

10. She was very _____patient_____ and gentle as she cleaned the kitten.

11. The kitten seemed to be quite _____healthy_____ but tired.

12. It licked its _____whiskers_____ as it curled up on the floor.

13. Soon all Tina could hear was its gentle _____breathing_____ .

14. Tina got a basket and made a _____special_____ bed for her new friend.

What does this incident tell you about the kind of person Tina is?

Critical Thinking

AUDITORY/KINESTHETIC LEARNERS

LARGE GROUP

Materials: index cards

Have students draw on a card a picture of a word that contains *sh*, /hw/ of *wh*, or a sound of *th*. Call for cards by asking for cards that contain digraphs heard in *whiskers, thistle, father,* and *shampoo*. Students hand in the correct picture as each word is said.

GIFTED LEARNERS

Challenge students to write three tongue-twisters using words with the sounds of *th, sh,* and *wh*.

LEARNERS WHO NEED EXTRA SUPPORT

Help students establish a word wall with headings for the two sounds of *th* and *wh* and the three spellings for /sh/. Students can add words to the wall as they learn them. **See Daily Word Study Practice, pages 181–182.**

CURRICULUM CONNECTIONS

SPELLING

Write the consonant combinations *wh, sh, sc, gn* on separate cards and display them on the chalk ledge. Then say the list words *whole, whale, ship, special, partial, science, conscience, scare, gnat,* and *sign,* one at a time. Call on volunteers to hold up the card with the consonant combination they hear and write the word on the board.

WRITING

Portfolio Invite students to write a story about a special pet they have or would like to have. Brainstorm a list of descriptive words with the *th, wh,* and *sh* sounds that they might use in their work. Let volunteers read their stories to the class.

SOCIAL STUDIES

Have students find out about the organizations or groups in your area that rescue and place abandoned animals. Have students learn from them what kinds of food and treatment a lost or sick cat, dog, bird, or other pet might need if it was found near their home or the school. Have students make a chart to show what pets need to stay healthy.

LANGUAGE ARTS

Explain that hink-pinks are riddles that are answered with two rhyming one-syllable words; hinky-pinkies have answers with two rhyming two-syllable words. Challenge students to answer these riddles then write some of their own. *HINK-PINK: What do you call a fat hen? (thick chick) HINKY-PINKY: What do you call 10 plus 20 people playing in the mud? (dirty thirty)*

Lesson 7

Pages 17–18

Reading ✏ Writing

Reviewing Variants and Combinations

INFORMAL ASSESSMENT OBJECTIVES

Can students

✔ review an article containing words with the sounds of *k*, *qu*, *kn*, *ch*, *c*, *g*, *f*, *ff*, *ph*, *d*, *wh*, *sh*, *ci*, *ti*, and *th*?

✔ write a brochure about joining a scientific expedition, using such words?

Lesson Focus

READING

● Write the following words on the board and review with students what they have learned about them: *pocket, quiz, knife, cheer, chef, choir, juicy, guess, rage, fling, afford, pharmacist, singer, those, sure, pleasure, whose, whale, marsh, suspicion, relation, thought, brother.*

WRITING

Explain that on page 18, students will plan a brochure about a scientific expedition to study penguins. They can use information they learned from reading the article on page 17. Point out that students should use words from the word box when writing their brochures.

Name _____

 Reading ▶ Read the following article. Then write your answer to the question at the end of the story.

Birds With a Sense of Humor

Penguins have always fascinated people. Their formal appearance and unique walk make them look cartoonish. Despite their humorous look, these flightless birds are accomplished hunters and swimmers.

Penguins can swim underwater at speeds of 30 miles per hour. This is five times faster than a human Olympic swimming champion! Using an in-and-out-of-the-water technique, these birds can travel long distances, too. The king penguin, for example, can swim underwater for about 25 feet and then "fly" through the air for about 15 feet.

All 18 species of wild penguins live in the southern hemisphere. Although some penguins live in the steamy tropics near the equator, most penguins live in the very coldest regions of the world under severe weather conditions. Their small feet, wings, and heads help them with heat conservation. They also have a thick layer of fat, or blubber, under their feathers to insulate them.

Scientists and photographers who observe these birds know that penguins take enthusiastic pleasure in each other's company and often live in giant flocks of thousands of birds. One reason there are so many penguins is that their only natural enemies are leopard seals and killer whales.

What characteristic of the penguin's body or behavior would you choose to study. Why? _____
_____
_____
_____

Lesson 7
Review variants, combinations, syllables: Reading **17**

FOCUS ON ALL LEARNERS ✳ ● ◆ ■ ◆

ENGLISH LANGUAGE LEARNERS/ESL

Before they begin page 17, invite students to demonstrate what they know about penguins. Have volunteers mimic the way a penguin walks. Also point out their habitat on a world map or globe.

VISUAL LEARNERS

 SMALL GROUP Invite students to play "sound search" in groups of three or four. Have each group fold a sheet of paper into three columns and label them *Sounds of s, Sounds of wh,* and */sh/*. Challenge the group to use any book to find at least ten words for each category and to write them in the correct column.

KINESTHETIC LEARNERS

LARGE GROUP Invite each student to write, on separate index cards, the 23 words listed on the board for Lesson Focus. Then have students choose a partner, combine their cards, and place all the cards word-side up. Invite students to take turns choosing two words that use the same letters to stand for a certain sound.

Writing

A scientific study of penguins in Antarctica is about to begin. Your job is to locate scientists, photographers, and guides to join the study. Write a brochure about the trip, using the following helpful hints and words from the word bank to help you.

tricks	questions	watch	treasure	anchor	enthusiastic
guest	passengers	photograph	count	appreciate	place

▶ Learn to survive Arctic weather.

▶ Observe Arctic wildlife.

▶ Research penguin habits.

▶ Learn to communicate with penguins.

Helpful Hints

Lesson 7
Review variants, combinations, syllables: Writing

CURRICULUM CONNECTIONS

SPELLING

Write these words on a word wall and ask students to choose one to match each definition you read aloud.

whole whale ship special partial
science conscience scare gnat sign

1. large sea animals that breathe air
2. having all its parts
3. a very big boat
4. knowledge about nature and the universe
5. to make someone feel afraid
6. a board or poster that gives information
7. different from what is usual
8. a biting insect
9. not total, incomplete
10. an inner feeling that tells right from wrong

MATH/SCIENCE

Help students use the measurements in the article to make a demonstration area about penguin mobility. Have students measure out 25 feet and 15 feet on the ground to show how far and high a penguin can swim underwater and leap through the air.

FINE ARTS

Have students research the names of famous artists. Challenge them to find artists whose names have one of the following word-study elements: *ch* /s/ (such as Marc Chagall), *ch* /k/ (such as Michelangelo), *wh* /hw/ (such as James Whistler), *c* /k/ (such as Alexander Calder) and *c* /s/ (such as Paul Cezanne). Have each student share important facts about the artists and pictures of their work with the class.

AUDITORY/KINESTHETIC LEARNERS

SMALL GROUP

Materials: magazines

Divide the class into groups of three or four and assign each group a consonant sound. Invite students to browse through magazines to find pictures whose names contain their consonant sound. Have students cut out the pictures and create collages.

GIFTED LEARNERS

Challenge students to research four more interesting facts about penguins. Have them use the information to write an additional paragraph for the penguin article.

LEARNERS WHO NEED EXTRA SUPPORT

Introduce some of the difficult words in the article before students begin page 17: *fascinated, unique, cartoonish, technique, hemisphere,* and *enthusiastic*. **See Daily Word Study Practice, pages 180–182.**

Sounds of sc and Words with the gn Sound

INFORMAL ASSESSMENT OBJECTIVES

Can students

✔ read words that contain the letters *sc* and *gn*?

✔ recognize words that contain /s/, /sh/, /sk/, and /n/?

Lesson Focus

INTRODUCING THE SKILLS

● Write the following sentences on the board and have volunteers read them aloud: *The painter needed a scaffold. The turkey was luscious. Our science teacher is late.*

● Then ask volunteers to underline the words that contain the letters *sc* and identify the sound *sc* stands for in each word. *(/sk/, /sh/, /s/)* Help students conclude that *sc* can stand for three different sounds.

● Write *gnaw, reign,* and *sign* on the board. Read the words aloud and ask students what sound is heard in all three words. Lead students to notice that the words contain /n/ written with the letters *gn*.

● Ask students to name other words with *gn*. Write their words on the board.

USING THE PAGES

● Be sure students understand how to complete pages 19 and 20.

● **Critical Thinking** Read aloud the question at the bottom of page 19 and discuss answers with students.

Name _____

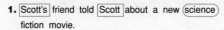

▶ Circle each word in which the letters **sc** stand for the **s** sound. Underline each word in which **sc** stands for the **sh** sound. Draw a box around each word in which **sc** stands for the **sk** sound.

RULE

The letters **sc** can stand for the **s, sh,** or **sk** sounds.

science   conscious
scare

1. Scott's friend told Scott about a new science fiction movie.

2. Now, Scott and his brother were waiting in line to see the scary movie.

3. They could smell the scent of popcorn while they waited.

4. Scott and Stan hurried because they could see all the people scurrying toward seats.

5. In the first scene of the movie, a scientist was working in a lab.

6. He had just discovered a new plant formula.

7. The boys were fascinated as the scary plants got bigger and bigger.

8. The scientist scowled when the huge plants suddenly moved toward him.

9. The plants scattered the formula all over the scientist.

10. He turned into a dreadful monster with big muscles and an ugly scar.

11. There was a terrible scuffle while the monster destroyed the horrid plants and finally collapsed!

12. While the monster was unconscious, the formula wore off.

13. At the end, the main character scooped up the formula and destroyed it.

14. Later, Scott and his brother told their parents that the movie didn't scare them at all.

How do you think the boys really felt during the movie? What makes you think that?

Critical Thinking

Lesson 8
The sounds of sc
19

FOCUS ON ALL LEARNERS

ENGLISH LANGUAGE LEARNERS/ESL

Before students begin page 19, discuss the differences between science and science fiction. Display nonfiction science books and science-fiction novels and have them contrast the titles and illustrations.

VISUAL LEARNERS

SMALL GROUP Divide the class into three groups. Have each group list words in which *sc* stands for a different sound, /s/, /sk/, or /sh/. Ask groups to share their lists with the rest of the class.

KINESTHETIC/AUDITORY LEARNERS

LARGE GROUP **Materials:** letter cards with *g* and *gn*

Distribute cards to students. Ask them hold up the appropriate card with each word you read. Try these words: *giggle, sign, foreign, galvanize, again, cargo, campaign, gnome.*

> Read each sentence and look at the word in boldface print. Then use the sentence to figure out the meaning of the word. Fill in the circle beside the best meaning.

> **RULE**
> The letters **gn** can stand for the **n** sound.
> **gn**at   si**gn**

1. The **sovereign** who governed the country was wise and fair.
   ○ clown   ● ruler   ○ traveler

2. The queen's **reign** would last until she died.
   ○ leather strap   ○ special gown   ● period of rule

3. The queen was a **benign** ruler who was fair and well received.
   ● kindly   ○ cruel   ○ corrupt

4. The queen started a major **campaign** to improve relationships with other countries.
   ● a series of actions   ○ a game   ○ a threat

5. Her new **foreign** relations program with other countries was well liked.
   ○ within one's family   ○ inside one's government   ● outside one's country

6. Her loyal advisors **designed** new laws.
   ○ destroyed   ● thought up   ○ wrote over

7. They presented them for her to **sign**.
   ○ give away   ○ display one's picture   ● write one's name

8. The queen said she would not **resign** unless she could no longer rule.
   ● quit   ○ write again   ○ take over

> Use a word in boldface print from the exercise above to complete each sentence.

9. The former governor had to _____resign_____ from office due to poor health.

10. Journalists covered the new candidate's _____campaign_____ for election.

11. The candidate's staff _____designed_____ her campaign strategy.

12. Newspapers from _____foreign_____ countries carried stories about it.

13. She wanted to be known as a _____benign_____ governor.

14. Her first act would be to _____sign_____ an important and popular bill.

15. Then she would meet with the _____sovereign_____ of a nearby country whose _____reign_____ had just begun.

CURRICULUM CONNECTIONS

SPELLING

The following sentences can be used as a spelling posttest.

1. **whole**   We read the **whole** book.
2. **whale**   Which kind of **whale** did you see?
3. **ship**   The **ship** sailed fifty years ago.
4. **special**   This is a **special** party.
5. **partial**   I have only a **partial** card deck.
6. **science**   Astronomy is **science.**
7. **conscience** She had a good **conscience.**
8. **scare**   Loud noises will **scare** the baby.
9. **gnat**   A **gnat** is a tiny insect.
10. **sign**   There is a **sign** in the window.

WRITING

Portfolio Challenge students to write an essay about a scientific discovery they believe is important. Encourage them to include words with /s/, /sh/, and /sk/.

SOCIAL STUDIES

Suggest students find out about rulers of an ancient culture, such as Egypt or China, and compare them to American presidents. Invite groups of students to collaborate in creating reports telling what they find out.

SCIENCE

Ask students to describe the physical symptoms they feel when they are scared at a horror movie or while reading a ghost story. They might make a chart to show the number of students who have each symptom (heart pounding, shortness of breath, and so on). Then have them use science resources to find out why their bodies react this way to fear. Encourage students to report on what they find out.

AUDITORY LEARNERS

PARTNER Have each student make up three sentences that contain words with *gn* standing for /n/. Then have them read their sentences to each other, leaving out the word with *gn*. The listening partner names the missing word and repeats the sentence with the word.

GIFTED LEARNERS

Challenge students to write silly phrases using words with the letters *g, n,* and *gn*. For example: *The giggling gnu is new.*

LEARNERS WHO NEED EXTRA SUPPORT

Have the student read the rule at the top of each page aloud before beginning to work, so you are sure he or she pronounces the sounds correctly. Work several items together to help the student begin the pages successfully. **See Daily Word Study Practice, page 182.**

Lesson 9
Pages 21–22

Sounds of r and Sound of air

INFORMAL ASSESSMENT OBJECTIVES

Can students

✔ read words that contain the consonant digraphs *rh* and *wr*?

✔ recognize words with /air/ ?

Lesson Focus

INTRODUCING THE SKILLS

- Write *rhubarb,* and *wrap* on the board and call on volunteers to read the words. Ask students what sound they hear at the beginning of each word. (/r/)

- Write the following sentence *Kate dared me to cut my hair short.* Have students underline two words that contain the same sound.

- Write *dare* and *hair* on the board and underline *are* and *air.* Guide students to conclude that the letters *are* and *air* stand for /air/.

- Ask students to suggest other words with /air/ and /r/. Write their suggestions on the board.

USING THE PAGES

- Give students help as necessary to complete pages 21 and 22. After they have completed each page.

- **Critical Thinking** Read aloud the questions on pages 21 and 22 and discuss answers with students.

Name _____

▶ Read the words below. Underline each word in which **rh** is used for the **r** sound. Circle each word in which **wr** is used for the **r** sound.

> **RULE**
> The letters **rh** and **wr** can stand for the **r** sound.
>
> **rh**yme   **wr**ist

1. rhythm
2. (wrote)
3. (wriggle)
4. (wrinkled)
5. rhinestones
6. rhinoceros
7. (wrench)
8. rhododendron
9. rheumatism
10. (wrong)
11. (writing)
12. (wrens)
13. (wrestle)
14. (wrap)
15. rhapsody

▶ Use a word from above to complete each sentence.

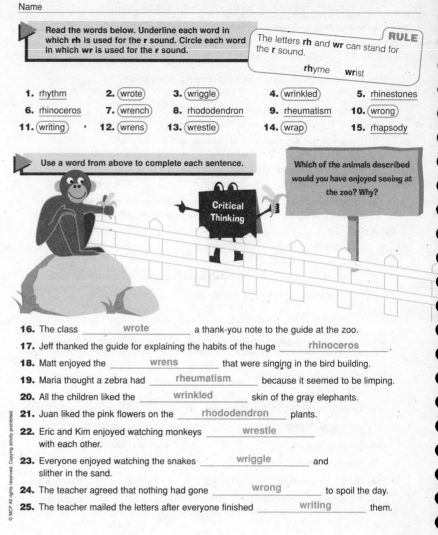

Critical Thinking

Which of the animals described would you have enjoyed seeing at the zoo? Why?

16. The class _____wrote_____ a thank-you note to the guide at the zoo.
17. Jeff thanked the guide for explaining the habits of the huge _____rhinoceros_____ .
18. Matt enjoyed the _____wrens_____ that were singing in the bird building.
19. Maria thought a zebra had _____rheumatism_____ because it seemed to be limping.
20. All the children liked the _____wrinkled_____ skin of the gray elephants.
21. Juan liked the pink flowers on the _____rhododendron_____ plants.
22. Eric and Kim enjoyed watching monkeys _____wrestle_____ with each other.
23. Everyone enjoyed watching the snakes _____wriggle_____ and slither in the sand.
24. The teacher agreed that nothing had gone _____wrong_____ to spoil the day.
25. The teacher mailed the letters after everyone finished _____writing_____ them.

Lesson 9
Words with the r sound   **21**

FOCUS ON ALL LEARNERS

ENGLISH LANGUAGE LEARNERS/ESL

Before beginning page 21, talk about visits to zoos or aviaries students have made, and ask them to name animals or birds they have seen or would like to see. Review the lesson sounds again.

VISUAL/KINESTHETIC LEARNERS

LARGE GROUP

Divide the class into teams lined up in front of *rh, wr, air, are* columns on the board. Students, in turn, write a word in a column until the team has four words in each column. The team that finishes first with the most words spelled correctly wins.

KINESTHETIC/VISUAL LEARNERS

PARTNER

Have students write and illustrate humorous sentences containing words with *ear* and *air*; for example, *The cat didn't care when it fell off the chair.*

▶ **Write a word from the word bank to complete each sentence.**

RULE
The letters **air** and **are** can stand for the **air** sound.
h**air**   c**are**

careful	dare	aware	care	chair
despair	fair	hair	pair	fare
rare	repaired	shared	stared	repair

1. Carlos _____ **stared** _____ at his car for a long time.
2. He was _____ **aware** _____ that the car needed to be fixed.
3. He tugged on his _____ **hair** _____ while he waited for someone to help him.
4. The mechanic asked Carlos to sit on a _____ **chair** _____.
5. The mechanic told Carlos not to _____ **despair** _____.
6. She said the car could be _____ **repaired** _____ at the garage.
7. It would need a new _____ **pair** _____ of tires.
8. She quoted a price to Carlos that seemed to be _____ **fair** _____.
9. But the car _____ **repair** _____ would not be ready until tomorrow.
10. Luckily Carlos had enough money to pay his bus _____ **fare** _____ home.
11. Carlos didn't _____ **care** _____ what it cost as long as the car got fixed.
12. A car like his was unusual and _____ **rare** _____.
13. Carlos _____ **shared** _____ the car with his brother.
14. He didn't _____ **dare** _____ tell his brother about the wreck.
15. Carlos decided to be more _____ **careful** _____ in the future.

Critical Thinking
How do you know that the damage to the car was Carlos's fault?

SPELLING

The following sentences can be used as a pretest for this set of spelling words.

1. **rhyme** — I wrote a **rhyme** about the sea.
2. **wrist** — She wears her watch on her **wrist.**
3. **hair** — The baby has very little **hair.**
4. **aware** — He was **aware** that he was late.
5. **year** — She grew two inches last **year.**
6. **pearl** — The ring had a **pearl** in the middle.
7. **behold** — The snow was a sight to **behold**
8. **reminded** — We **reminded** him to rest.
9. **wild** — The **wild** cats prowled all night.
10. **ghost** — This is my **ghost** costume.

WRITING

Portfolio Invite students to write tongue twisters using words with /r/, especially with digraphs *rh* and *wr*; for example, *The red wrinkled rhino roared the wrong rhyme.*

SCIENCE

Have students choose a zoo animal and research its native habitat and diet. Students can present their findings to the class and pin a picture of their animal in the appropriate place on a world map.

LANGUAGE ARTS

To contrast business and friendly letters, have students write one of each: one from a teacher asking the educational director of a zoo for permission to visit, the second a personal thank-you note to a friend or relative who took them to the zoo.

LARGE GROUP

KINESTHETIC/AUDITORY LEARNERS

Divide the group in half. Ask one group to wrinkle their noses every time you say a word with *wr*, and the other group to tap a rhythm with their feet every time you say a word with *rh*. Try these words: *writer, wriggle, rhinoceros, rhubarb, wrestler, rhyme.*

GIFTED LEARNERS

Challenge students to discover as many *air, are* homonym pairs as they can and to use both words in sentences; for example, *What is the bus fare to the fair?*

LEARNERS WHO NEED EXTRA SUPPORT

Materials: index cards

Have students make cards for *air* and *are* words listed on page 22 and then sort the cards according to the spelling pattern. Then have each student choose a card from each pile and use the words in sentences. **See Daily Word Study Practice, pages 182.**

Lesson 10
Pages 23–24

Sounds of ear

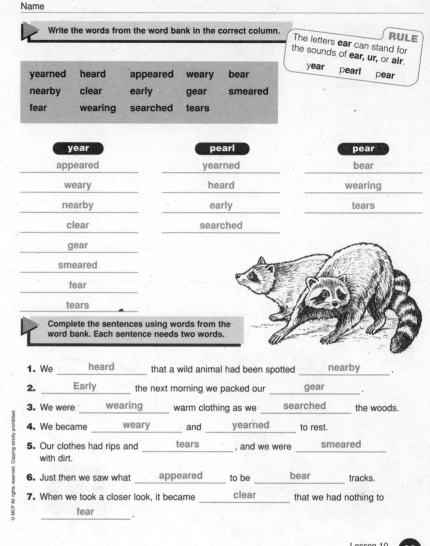

INFORMAL ASSESSMENT OBJECTIVES

Can students

✔ read words that contain the letters *ear*?

✔ recognize words with /ear/, /air/, and /ur/?

Lesson Focus

INTRODUCING THE SKILL

- Have students listen as you say the words *year, pear,* and *pearl* aloud. Ask students if the vowel sounds in the three words are the same. *(no)*

- Then write the words on the board and make three columns labeled /ear/, /air/, and /ur/. Ask students to say the words aloud. Help them understand that *ear* can stand for three different sounds. Ask volunteers to write *year, pear,* and *pearl* in the correct columns.

- Call on volunteers to name other words that contain the letters *ear* and to write them in the correct column. Example words include *fear, near; wear, bear;* and *research, learn.*

USING THE PAGES

Ask students to read the directions for completing pages 23 and 24. Be sure they understand what to do. After they have completed the pages, encourage them to review the lesson by correcting their pages with a partner.

Name _____

▶ Write the words from the word bank in the correct column.

> **RULE**
> The letters **ear** can stand for the sounds of **ear, ur,** or **air.**
> year pearl pear

yearned	heard	appeared	weary	bear
nearby	clear	early	gear	smeared
fear	wearing	searched	tears	

year
appeared
weary
nearby
clear
gear
smeared
fear
tears

pearl
yearned
heard
early
searched

pear
bear
wearing
tears

▶ Complete the sentences using words from the word bank. Each sentence needs two words.

1. We __heard__ that a wild animal had been spotted __nearby__.
2. __Early__ the next morning we packed our __gear__.
3. We were __wearing__ warm clothing as we __searched__ the woods.
4. We became __weary__ and __yearned__ to rest.
5. Our clothes had rips and __tears__, and we were __smeared__ with dirt.
6. Just then we saw what __appeared__ to be __bear__ tracks.
7. When we took a closer look, it became __clear__ that we had nothing to __fear__.

FOCUS ON ALL LEARNERS ✳ ● ◆ ■ ◆ ●

ENGLISH LANGUAGE LEARNERS/ESL

Before beginning page 23, ask students to read the words in the box at the top of the page to be sure they are pronouncing the *ear* words correctly. Help them start sorting the words.

VISUAL LEARNERS

PARTNER Students may enjoy working in pairs to design a word-search puzzle using words that contain /ear/, /air/, and /ur/. Suggest that they begin by brainstorming a list of words they can use. Partner pairs can exchange puzzles for solving.

KINESTHETIC/AUDITORY LEARNERS

LARGE GROUP **Materials:** index cards labeled /ear/, /air/, /ur/

Give each student a card labeled /ear/, /air/, or /ur/. Read *ear* words from the lesson. As you read each word, students with a card with that sound raise their cards in the air.

Complete the crossword puzzle by writing **ear** words that fit the definitions.

Across

2. to gain knowledge
5. hair on the face
6. serious and determined
8. a wheel that has teeth that fit into another wheel
10. listen to
11. ornaments for the ears

Down

1. afraid of nothing
3. close by
4. an animal that is one year old
6. wages or money paid to a person
7. a nickname for someone who is much loved
9. tired

CURRICULUM CONNECTIONS

SPELLING

Materials: small cards or tiles with letters of the alphabet in a paper bag

Draw a square on the board for each letter in one of the list words: *rhyme, wrist, hair, aware, year, pearl, behold, reminded, wild, ghost.* Have a student choose a card from the bag and ask, for example, "Is there an *f*?" If that letter is in the word, write it in place, and ask the player to guess the word. If the letter is not in the word, or the player can not guess the word, let the next player pick another letter. Continue until all the words have been spelled.

WRITING

Portfolio Have students learn more about the history of their families by interviewing family members and writing reports. They might include information about the year their parents or ancestors arrived in this country and where they first lived. Ask them to underline the *ear* words they use. Encourage students to share their reports with the class.

MATH

Invite students to survey their classmates about what they have learned to do in the past year. Did they learn to skate or ski, to identify bears, or to conquer a fear? Anything is possible. Have students complete an "I Learned How To" survey, tally the results, and create a bar graph on the board showing the results.

SCIENCE

Suggest students find out how the human ear allows us to hear sounds. Have them research the process of hearing and make a diagram showing how the ear works. Some students could find out how well humans hear as compared to other mammals.

AstroWord r-Controlled Vowels
©1998 Silver Burdett Ginn, Inc.
Division of Simon & Schuster.

AUDITORY LEARNERS

LARGE GROUP Have students identify the words that contain *ear* from the clues you give and tell what sound *ear* stands for in each word; for example, *What word means "look for"?* (search, /ur/) *What word is 365 days?* (year, /ear/) *What word is a fruit?* (pear, /air/)

GIFTED LEARNERS

Challenge students by having them make their own crossword puzzles of *ear* words.

LEARNERS WHO NEED EXTRA SUPPORT

Materials: index cards

Have students make *ear* word cards. Then shuffle all the cards together and have pairs of students, in turn, choose a card, giving a definition for the word, and using the word in a sentence. **See Daily Word Study Practice, pages 182–183.**

Sounds of ild, ind, ost, old

INFORMAL ASSESSMENT OBJECTIVE

Can students

✓ decode words with the letter combinations *ild*, *ind*, *ost*, and *old*?

Lesson Focus

INTRODUCING THE SKILLS

- Say the following words aloud: *mild, mind, most, mold*. Ask students what is similar about the vowel sound in all the words. *(It is long.)*

- Write the following sentences on the board: *1. Jan had a <u>mild</u> case of the flu. 2. I don't <u>mind</u> cold weather. 3. <u>Most</u> people like apples. 4. The bread had <u>mold</u> on it.*

- Have volunteers read the sentences aloud. Point out that each underlined word has the long *i* or long *o* sound and that each word ends in *-nd*, *-ld*, *-*or *st*. Help students conclude that words ending in *-nd*, *-ld*, or *-st*, and preceded by *i* or *o*, sometimes have the long vowel sound.

- Encourage students to name other words that have a long vowel sound and contain the letters *ild*, *ind*, *ost*, and *old*.

USING THE PAGES

- Give students help as necessary to complete pages 25 and 26.

- **Critical Thinking** Read aloud the question at the bottom of page 25 and discuss the answers with students.

25

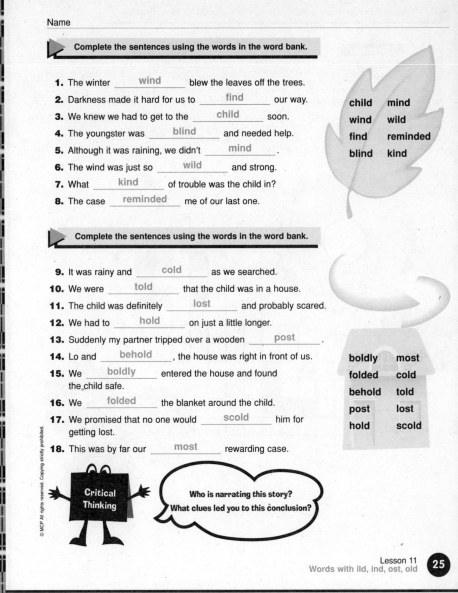

Name _____

► Complete the sentences using the words in the word bank.

1. The winter _____ wind _____ blew the leaves off the trees.
2. Darkness made it hard for us to _____ find _____ our way.
3. We knew we had to get to the _____ child _____ soon.
4. The youngster was _____ blind _____ and needed help.
5. Although it was raining, we didn't _____ mind _____ .
6. The wind was just so _____ wild _____ and strong.
7. What _____ kind _____ of trouble was the child in?
8. The case _____ reminded _____ me of our last one.

child	mind
wind	wild
find	reminded
blind	kind

► Complete the sentences using the words in the word bank.

9. It was rainy and _____ cold _____ as we searched.
10. We were _____ told _____ that the child was in a house.
11. The child was definitely _____ lost _____ and probably scared.
12. We had to _____ hold _____ on just a little longer.
13. Suddenly my partner tripped over a wooden _____ post _____ .
14. Lo and _____ behold _____ , the house was right in front of us.
15. We _____ boldly _____ entered the house and found the child safe.
16. We _____ folded _____ the blanket around the child.
17. We promised that no one would _____ scold _____ him for getting lost.
18. This was by far our _____ most _____ rewarding case.

boldly	most
folded	cold
behold	told
post	lost
hold	scold

Critical Thinking

Who is narrating this story? What clues led you to this conclusion?

FOCUS ON ALL LEARNERS

ENGLISH LANGUAGE LEARNERS/ESL

Before students begin page 25, read the story aloud, then have students briefly summarize the story, using as many of the words with *ild*, *ind*, *ost*, and *old* as possible.

 VISUAL LEARNERS

PARTNER Have partners write a letter to another pair of students, including in their letter words with the letters *ild, ind, ost*, and *old*. Ask pairs to exchange papers and ask partners to work together to identify the *ild, ind, ost*, and *old* words.

KINESTHETIC/AUDITORY LEARNERS

LARGE GROUP **Materials:** colored chalk

Say words from the lesson and let students take turns writing the words on the board, using colored chalk for *ild, ind, ost, old*.

Use a phrase from the word bank to answer each question.

a ghost host	a folder holder	a wild child
a kind mind	sold gold	an old cold

1. What would you call a brain that thinks of ways to help others?
a kind mind

2. What would you call the creature who invites you to a spooky party?
a ghost host

3. What would you call a young person who misbehaves?
a wild child

4. What would you call precious metal that someone has bought?
sold gold

5. What would you call a previous illness?
an old cold

6. What would you call a place to keep papers?
a folder holder

Use words from the word bank to complete the sentences.

find
lost
wind
told
mild
sold
most
cold
gold
blinding

7. Kim wanted to buy a _____ gold _____ pin for her friend Marge before they were _____ sold _____ out.

8. The weather had changed from sunny and _____ mild _____ to snowy and _____ cold _____ .

9. It was the _____ most _____ snow and _____ wind _____ they had all winter.

10. Kim's mother worried that she might get _____ lost _____ in the _____ blinding _____ snowstorm.

11. She _____ told _____ Kim she would have to _____ find _____ another time to go shopping.

CURRICULUM CONNECTIONS

SPELLING

Write the list words *rhyme, wrist, hair, aware, year, pearl, behold, reminded, wild, ghost* on the chalkboard, and ask student to use each one in a sentence.

WRITING

Portfolio Invite students to write a story based on one of the phrases used in items 1–6 on page 26, such as a story about a *ghost host* or a *wild child*. Ask them to circle other words with the same letter combinations they use. Suggest they illustrate their stories and give them a title. Encourage students who based stories on the same phrase to compare what they wrote.

SOCIAL STUDIES

Gold glitters and attracts attention. Students might like to find out why people came from all over the world to search for gold during the California gold rush. Then encourage them to become a "settler" themselves and write a letter home to relatives, describing their life and what they found, or didn't find, in California.

SCIENCE

Encourage students to keep track of the weather for a week. Have them make a weather calendar and fill in each day with a drawing to depict the weather, the high and low temperatures, and a brief written description such as "a mild day with brief mid-afternoon showers."

AUDITORY LEARNERS

PARTNER Have pairs divide a sheet of paper into four sections labeled *ild, ind, ost,* and *old* and write as many words with these combinations as they can in two minutes. Invite pairs to read their lists aloud. Create a class list by combining all the students' words.

GIFTED LEARNERS

Challenge students by having them write as many rhyming phrases, such as *ghost host* or *kind mind,* as they can for words with the endings *-ild, -ind, -ost,* and *-old.* Encourage them to choose two to use as cartoon captions.

LEARNERS WHO NEED EXTRA SUPPORT

Complete page 25 with students, each student, in turn, reading a sentence aloud and deciding which word best completes the sentence before consulting with others on the choice. **See Daily Word Study Practice, pages 182–183.**

Lesson 12

Pages 27–28

Syllabication

Lesson Focus

INTRODUCING THE SKILL

- Write the following words on the board: *numb, magic, powerful, recent, rarity, metal, level, scorn, meter, sign, roundabout, pirate.*

- Help students recall that a word has as many syllables as it has vowel sounds. Then call on volunteers to identify the number of syllables in each word on the board.

- Call on a volunteer to erase the one- and three-syllable words. Ask students whether the first vowel in each remaining two-syllable word is long or short.

- Guide students to understand that when a single consonant comes between two vowels, the word is usually divided after the consonant if the first vowel is short (*met-al*) and before the consonant if the first vowel is long (*pi-rate*).

USING THE PAGES

Help students as necessary to complete pages 27 and 28. When they have completed the pages, review syllabication as you correct the pages together.

Name _____

▶ Read the words in the word bank. Write the words in the correct column.

> **RULE**
> A syllable is a word or part of a word with a single vowel sound. A word has as many syllables as it has vowel sounds.

knight	phantom	arrangement	threat	music
composer	disappear	dare	grind	numb
wheat	bold	climbing	wholesome	whose
find	unique	questionaire	meanwhile	cashier
declare	innermost	honeycomb	refreshment	overwhelm
difficult	foremost			

One Syllable	Two Syllables	Three Syllables
knight	declare	composer
wheat	phantom	difficult
find	unique	disappear
bold	foremost	innermost
dare	climbing	arrangement
threat	wholesome	questionnaire
grind	meanwhile	honeycomb
numb	music	refreshment
whose	cashier	overwhelm

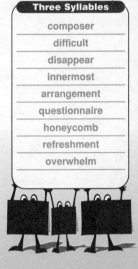

Lesson 12
Recognize syllables **27**

FOCUS ON ALL LEARNERS

ENGLISH LANGUAGE LEARNERS/ESL

Pair fluent English speakers with second-language learners to help them with the pronunciation of words as they work.

VISUAL/KINESTHETIC LEARNERS
PARTNER

Ask pairs of students to walk around the classroom and make a list of objects they see, then divide each word into syllables. Encourage them to use a dictionary to check their work.

KINESTHETIC LEARNERS
LARGE GROUP

Challenge students to play "syllable race." Divide the class into two teams. Have a student from each team write on the board the word that you say aloud and divide it into syllables. The student who finishes correctly first wins a point for the team.

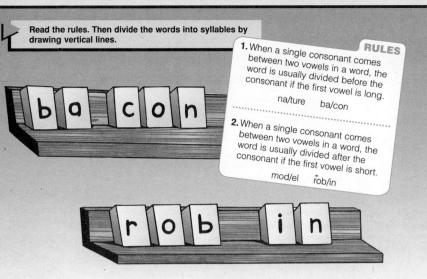

> Read the rules. Then divide the words into syllables by drawing vertical lines.

RULES

1. When a single consonant comes between two vowels in a word, the word is usually divided before the consonant if the first vowel is long.

na/ture   ba/con

2. When a single consonant comes between two vowels in a word, the word is usually divided after the consonant if the first vowel is short.

mod/el   rob/in

1. melon	mel/on		16. final	fi/nal
2. facial	fa/cial		17. recent	re/cent
3. silent	si/lent		18. bison	bi/son
4. lemon	lem/on		19. finish	fin/ish
5. comic	com/ic		20. magic	mag/ic
6. repair	re/pair		21. rotate	ro/tate
7. cabin	cab/in		22. petal	pet/al
8. below	be/low		23. pilot	pi/lot
9. declare	de/clare		24. punish	pun/ish
10. visit	vis/it		25. medal	med/al
11. pities	pit/ies		26. cities	cit/ies
12. modest	mod/est		27. radish	rad/ish
13. design	de/sign		28. famous	fa/mous
14. nasal	na/sal		29. patient	pa/tient
15. music	mu/sic		30. lizard	liz/ard

28 Lesson 12
Recognize syllables

AUDITORY/KINESTHETIC LEARNERS

LARGE GROUP

Materials: index cards

Have students write *1, 2,* and *3* on cards. As you say a word, they raise the card that identifies the number of syllables. Try *product, loose, stand, result, overload, chair, disappoint,* and *sidewalk.*

GIFTED LEARNERS

Challenge students by having them dramatize a magic show in which one-, two-, and three-syllable words are magically cut into the correct number of syllables.

LEARNERS WHO NEED EXTRA SUPPORT

Before students begin the pages, have them read each word in the box on page 27 to themselves as you say it aloud slowly, so they can hear each syllable pronounced distinctly. While they work, remind them to ask for help pronouncing the words if needed. **See Daily Word Study Practice, page 193.**

CURRICULUM CONNECTIONS

SPELLING

Write these words in a column on the board: *rhyme, wrist, hair, aware, year, pearl, behold, reminded, wild, ghost.* Then call students, one at a time, to give a word clue, while others guess the word.

WRITING

Portfolio Invite students to work in pairs to write a five-line poem called a cinquain, such as the following

Puppies

soft and furry

Running, jumping, licking

Always there to snuggle with you

Playful!

Line 1: title of subject—two syllables

Line 2: adjectives—four syllables

Line 3: verbs or actions—six syllables

Line 4: a feeling or a thought—eight syllables

Line 5: one word to sum up—two syllables

MATH

If students did the Visual/Kinesthetic Learners activity, have them make a bar graph showing how many of the classroom words they wrote have one, two, and three syllables.

SOCIAL STUDIES/ART

Invite students to figure out the number of syllables in the first names of members of their families, then make a family portrait or family tree that includes a drawing or photo of each member of the family with his or her name divided into syllables.

Technology

AstroWord Multisyllabic Words ©1998 Silver Burdett Ginn, Inc. Division of Simon & Schuster.

Reading **Writing**

Reviewing Variants and Combinations

INFORMAL ASSESSMENT OBJECTIVES

Can students

✔ read an article containing words with *th, sc, gn, kn, wr, rh, are, air, ear, ind, ild, ost,* and *old*?

✔ write an interview and newspaper article using such words?

Lesson Focus

READING

- Make and display review cards for the words *myth, feather, scalpel, scene, conscious, gnash, wreath, rhythm, repair, rare, spear, pear, search, grind, child, post, gold,* and *know.*
- Tell students you are going to use clues to describe the words.
- Encourage students to come to the board, point to the word or words indicated by a clue, and tell why they selected the word or words.
- **Critical Thinking** Discuss the question.

WRITING

Explain that on page 30, students will plan an interview and a newspaper story about a tornado disaster. They can use information they learned from reading the article on page 29.

Name _____

Reading ▶ Read the article. Then write your answer to the question at the end of the passage.

Tornadoes

Have you ever read the book *The Wizard of Oz*? In the story a girl named Dorothy and her dog, Toto, are carried from Kansas by a wild tornado to the magical land of Oz. The story is fiction, but the frightening power of a tornado is real.

A tornado, also called a twister or a cyclone, is a funnel-shaped cloud of violently rotating air often formed by an intense thunderstorm. Inside the destructive whirlwind, rotating winds may reach speeds of 200 to 300 miles per hour. The diameter of a tornado can vary from a few feet to a mile. Even though a tornado touches down for less than a few minutes in any one place, it always leaves a path of destruction and despair.

Seasonal weather changes play an important role in forming a tornado. Although they happen year-round, the highest number occur in the spring and early summer. At that time the atmospheric conditions required to form a tornado often come together: thermal instability, high humidity, and the meeting of warm moist air at low levels with the cold dry air from above.

Tornadoes, like hurricanes and earthquakes, are natural disasters over which human beings have no control. Although scientists know much more about tornadoes than ever before, these fierce storms still remind us that the weather can be unpredictable—and very violent.

What do you think is the most frightening part of a tornado?

_____

Lesson 13
Review letter combinations and sounds: Reading **29**

FOCUS ON ALL LEARNERS

ENGLISH LANGUAGE LEARNERS/ESL

Before students begin page 29, generate a discussion about weather conditions that turn into natural disasters. Have students share their personal experiences with severe weather. Briefly discuss safety measures to take during severe weather.

VISUAL LEARNERS

LARGE GROUP Write the letters *th, sc, gn, wr, rh, are, air, ear, ind, ild, ost,* and *old* on the board. Then ask one student to begin a story with a sentence that contains a word with one of the letter combinations. Have another student add a sentence with a word containing another combination, and so on, until all the letters have been used.

KINESTHETIC LEARNERS

LARGE GROUP Have students play "categories." One group member announces a letter combination such as *sc* or *ild.* Students stand in a circle and snap their fingers as they take turns saying a word that contains that combination (*scare, science, conscious; wild, child, mild*).

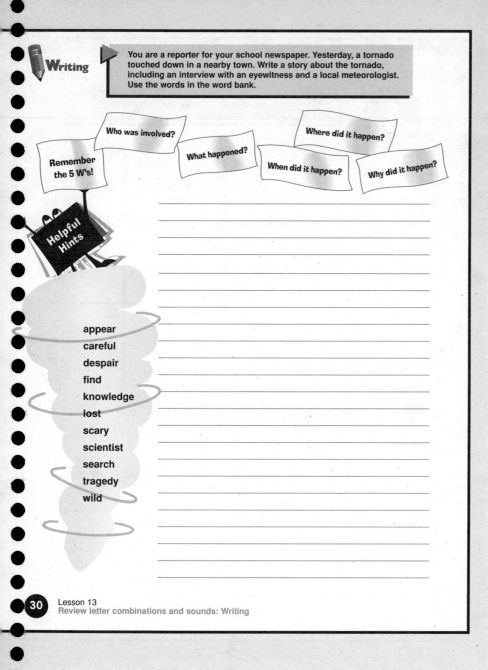

✏️ **Writing**

▶ You are a reporter for your school newspaper. Yesterday, a tornado touched down in a nearby town. Write a story about the tornado, including an interview with an eyewitness and a local meteorologist. Use the words in the word bank.

Remember the 5 W's!

Who was involved?

What happened?

Where did it happen?

When did it happen?

Why did it happen?

Helpful Hints

appear
careful
despair
find
knowledge
lost
scary
scientist
search
tragedy
wild

SPELLING

The following sentences can be used as a spelling posttest.

1. **rhyme** — *Tear* and *pear* **rhyme.**
2. **wrist** — Her **wrist** is sore.
3. **hair** — His **hair** is black and curly.
4. **aware** — Be **aware** of cars and bicycles.
5. **year** — This has been our team's best **year.**
6. **pearl** — I wear a **pearl** on a chain.
7. **behold** — When I **behold** it, it look at it.
8. **reminded** — You **reminded** him to dress up.
9. **wild** — **Wild** animals live in the woods.
10. **ghost** — We painted a **ghost** for Halloween.

SCIENCE/SOCIAL STUDIES

Display a national weather report and weather map from the newspaper and have students find any examples of severe weather across the country. Students might choose to follow a particular storm or weather pattern over the course of a week. They might also enjoy setting up a "weather channel" in the classroom to report on any interesting weather phenomenon.

MATH

Have students look through books and magazines to find words that have these letter combinations: *th, sc, gn, wr, rh, are, air, ear, ind, ild, ost, old*. Have them compile the words they found and count how many words contain each sound. Then demonstrate how to make a horizontal or vertical bar graph and encourage students to show the number of words for each sound on their own graphs.

AUDITORY/KINESTHETIC LEARNERS

SMALL GROUP

Challenge students to make bingo cards by drawing a grid containing five vertical and five horizontal squares. Tell them to write a word containing one of the following letter combinations inside each square: *th, sc, gn, wr, rh, are, air, ear, ind, ild, ost,* and *old*. Divide the class into groups of five to play bingo.

GIFTED LEARNERS

Challenge students to interview someone who has actually lived through a natural disaster such as a tornado or a flood. Students can use the interview as a starting point for researching the actual event that was described by their source in the interview.

LEARNERS WHO NEED EXTRA SUPPORT

Review the words in the word box before students begin writing their story. Help them create a number of model sentences about a tornado that use the words. **See Daily Word Study Practice, pages 180–183.**

Lesson 14

Pages 31–32

Unit Checkup

Reviewing Consonant Variants, Letter Combinations, Syllables

INFORMAL ASSESSMENT OBJECTIVE

Can students

✔ identify consonant variants, combinations, vowel combinations, and the number of syllables in words?

Lesson Focus

PREPARING FOR THE CHECKUP

- On the board, write the heading *Consonant Combinations*. Write these letters to head ten columns: *k, ck, que, qu, kn, ch, c, g, f, s, wh, sh, ci, th, sc,* and *gn,* Have volunteers write these words under the correct heading as you read them aloud: *sure, key, brochure, kneel, cheap, scientist, anchor, race, quiz, game, dolphin, wise, treasure, who, corn, whale, special, technique, thin, age, then, scoop, gnat, trick.*

- Write *rh, wr, air, are, ear, ild, ind, ost, old* on a word wall and ask students to dictate words that contain those sounds as a volunteer writes them in the correct columns.

- Read these words aloud and have students count the number of syllables in each: *climbing, radish, declare, refreshment, disappear,* and *knight.*

USING THE PAGES

Make sure students understand each set of directions on pages 31 and 32. Point out that the directions change after item 12 on page 31.

31

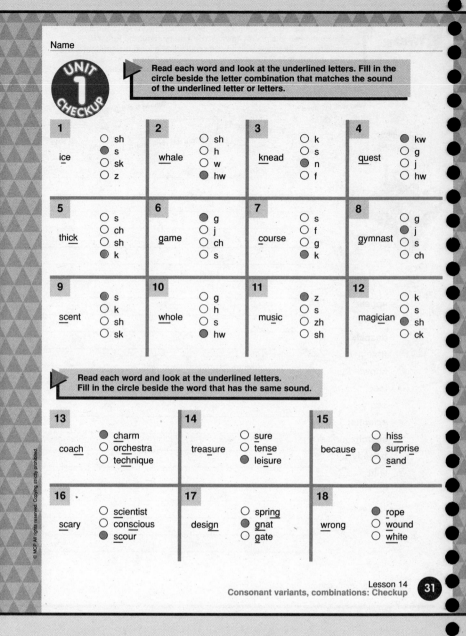

FOCUS ON ALL LEARNERS

ENGLISH LANGUAGE LEARNERS/ESL

Before beginning page 32, generate a discussion about any museums the students have visited as a class or with their families. If possible, display brochures from local museums and compare the information about their collections.

VISUAL LEARNERS

PARTNER Challenge students to work in pairs to design a word-search puzzle using words that contain the sounds of *ch, sh, wh,* and *th.* Suggest that students begin by brainstorming a list of words they can use. Encourage partners to exchange their puzzle with another pair of students.

KINESTHETIC LEARNERS

SMALL GROUP Choose two example words from each consonant variant, consonant combination, and vowel combination lesson in this unit and make two sets of word cards. Then have students work in groups to place a set number of word pair cards face down and play a memory game.

UNIT 1 CHECKUP

Read the words in the word bank. Then read the story. Write the correct word from the word bank on the line to complete each unfinished sentence. Then answer the questions.

collection	rare	country	museums
region	weather	nearby	science
games	quilts	search	

Visiting ___museums___ is educational as well as enjoyable. There are thousands of fascinating museums in every ___region___ of our ___country___. There are famous art museums with ___rare___ paintings and sculptures from cultures all over the world. There are ___science___ museums with exhibits about space, electricity, and unusual ___weather___ conditions. There are electronic museums with computer ___games___ for visitors to play.

Not all museums are giant buildings filled with thousands of items. One tiny museum just shows a ___collection___ of locks and keys. Another shows an arrangement of embroidered ___quilts___ that were sewn by hand. If you ___search___ your own neighborhood or region, you are sure to find an interesting museum ___nearby___.

1. Where can you find museums in the United States?

_____

_____

_____

2. What kinds of exhibits can be shown in science museums?

_____

_____

_____

32 Lesson 14
Consonant variants, combinations: Checkup

ASSESSING UNDERSTANDING OF UNIT SKILLS

Student Progress Assessment Review the observational notes you made as students worked through the activities in the unit. Your notes will help you evaluate the progress students made with consonant variants, combinations, vowel combinations, and syllables.

Portfolio Assessment Review the materials students have collected in their portfolios. You may wish to have interviews with students to discuss their written work and the progress they have made since the beginning of the unit. As you review students' work, evaluate how well they use these phonics skills.

Daily Word Study Practice For students who need additional practice with any of the topics in this unit, quick reviews are provided on pages 180–183, 193 in Daily Word Study Practice.

Word Study Posttest To assess students' mastery of skills covered in this unit, use the posttest on pages 3g–3h.

SPELLING CUMULATIVE POSTTEST

Use the following words and dictation sentences.

1. **queen**   The **queen** is a kind ruler.
2. **character**   Each **character** in the movie was an animal.
3. **race**   After school I **race** home.
4. **game**   Soccer is my favorite **game.**
5. **dolphin**   The boat was decorated with a picture of a **dolphin.**
6. **measure**   Did you **measure** the length of the field?
7. **whale**   The **whale** was enormous.
8. **ship**   The sails on the **ship** billowed in the wind.
9. **partial**   I could only give a **partial** answer to the question.
10. **conscience**   Will your **conscience** bother you if we leave early?
11. **scare**   The clothes stuffed in straw did not **scare** away the birds.
12. **gnat**   The buzzing **gnat** kept her awake.
13. **wrist**   She sprained her **wrist** playing tennis.
14. **pearl**   Each **pearl** was perfectly white and round.
15. **reminded**   I have to be **reminded** to do my chores.
16. **ghost**   We told each other **ghost** stories before we went to sleep.

AUDITORY/KINESTHETIC LEARNERS

INDIVIDUAL

Materials: index cards

Distribute an index card with the name of one of the 50 United States to each student. As each student reads the word on his or her card, have classmates hold up the correct number of fingers to represent the number of syllables in the state name.

GIFTED LEARNERS

Challenge students to choose one word from each possible consonant variant, consonant combination, and vowel combination taught in Unit 1 and look up the phonetic respellings in a dictionary.

LEARNERS WHO NEED EXTRA SUPPORT

Materials: word cards

Make and distribute word cards representing the consonant variants and combinations *k, ck, que, qu, kn, ch,* and *c.* Then ask students to work in pairs to sort the words according to sounds. Have students post their words in the appropriate column on a word wall. **See Daily Word Study Practice, pages 180–183, 193.**

Teacher Notes

Assessment Strategy Overview

Throughout Unit 2, assess students' ability to read and write words with vowel pairs, vowel digraphs, and diphthongs. There are various ways to assess students' progress. You may also want to encourage students to evaluate their own work and participate in setting goals for their own learning.

FORMAL ASSESSMENT

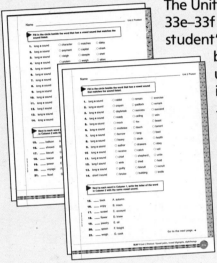

The Unit 2 Pretest on pages 33e–33f helps to assess a student's knowledge at the beginning of the unit and to plan instruction.

The Unit 2 Posttest on pages 33g–33h helps to assess mastery of unit objectives and to plan for reteaching, if necessary.

INFORMAL ASSESSMENT

The Reading & Writing Pages and Unit Checkup in the student book are an effective means of evaluating students' performance.

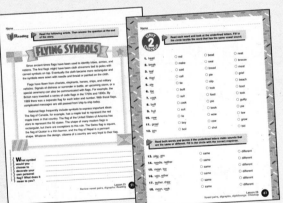

PORTFOLIO ASSESSMENT

Portfolio This logo appears throughout the teaching plans. It signals opportunities for collecting students' work for individual portfolios. You may also want to collect the following pages.

❖ Unit 2 Pretest and Posttest, pages 33e–33h

❖ Unit 2 Reading & Writing, pages 51–52, 59–60

❖ Unit 2 Checkup, pages 61–62

STUDENT PROGRESS CHECKLIST

Use the checklist on page 33i to record students' progress. You may want to cut the sections apart to place each student's checklist in his or her portfolio.

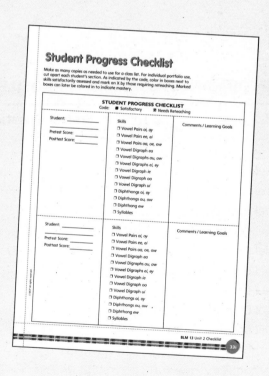

Skill	Reading & Writing Pages	Unit Checkup
Vowel Pairs *ai, ay*	51–52	61–62
Vowel Pairs *ee, ei*	51–52	61–62
Vowel Pairs *oa, oe, ow*	51–52	61–62
Vowel Digraph *ea*	51–52	61–62
Vowel Digraphs *ei, ey*	51–52	61–62
Vowel Digraphs *au, aw*	51–52	61–62
Vowel Digraph *ie*	51–52	61–62
Vowel Digraph *oo*	51–52	61–62
Vowel Digraph *ui*	51–52	61–62
Diphthongs *oi, oy*	59–60	61–62
Diphthongs *ou, ow*	59–60	61–62
Diphthong *ew*	59–60	61–62
Syllables	59–60	61–62

Administering and Evaluating the
Pretest and Posttest

DIRECTIONS

To help you assess students' progress in learning Unit 2 skills, tests are available on pages 33e–33h. Administer the Pretest before students begin the unit. The results of the Pretest will help you identify each student's strengths and needs in advance, allowing you to structure lesson plans to meet individual needs. Administer the Posttest to assess students' overall mastery of skills taught in the unit and to identify specific areas that will require reteaching.

PERFORMANCE ASSESSMENT PROFILE

The following chart will help you identify specific skills as they appear on the tests and enable you to identify and record specific information about an individual's or the class's performance on the tests.

Depending on the results of the tests, refer to the Reteaching column for lesson-plan pages where you can find activities that will be useful for meeting individual needs or for daily word study practice.

ANSWER KEYS

Unit 2 Pretest, page 33e (BLM 9)

1. remain	8. steak	15. G
2. crayon	9. obey	16. E
3. succeed	10. veil	17. A
4. ceiling	11. chief	18. C
5. boast	12. tried	19. D
6. mistletoe	13. recruit	20. B
7. borrow	14. building	21. F

Unit 2 Pretest, page 33f (BLM 10)

22. yes	28. no	34. 1; ea
23. yes	29. no	35. 2; ea
24. no	30. no	36. 2; ie
25. no	31. yes	37. 3; oo
26. yes	32. 1; ui	
27. yes	33. 2; ow	

Unit 2 Posttest, page 33g (BLM 11)

1. daisy	8. break	15. B
2. payment	9. survey	16. D
3. steeple	10. neigh	17. G
4. protein	11. relief	18. A
5. coal	12. cries	19. C
6. tiptoe	13. suit	20. F
7. tomorrow	14. cruise	21. E

Unit 2 Posttest, page 33h (BLM 12)

22. yes	28. no	34. 1; ou
23. no	29. no	35. 2; ay
24. no	30. no	36. 1; oo
25. yes	31. yes	37. 3; ea
26. yes	32. 3; ey	
27. yes	33. 2; oa	

PERFORMANCE ASSESSMENT PROFILE

Skill	Pretest Questions	Posttest Questions	Reteaching Focus on All Learners	Daily Word Study Practice
Vowel Pairs ai, ay /ā/	1, 2, 22, 26	1, 2, 26, 35	35–36, 51–52	183
Vowel Pairs ee, ei /ē/	3, 4, 25	3, 4, 25	37–38, 51–52	183
Vowel Pairs oa, oe, ow /ō/	5, 6, 7, 24	5, 6, 7, 24, 33	39–40, 51–52	183
Vowel Digraph ea /e/, /ā/, /ē/	8, 30, 34, 35	8, 23, 30, 37	41–42, 51–52	184
Vowel Digraphs ei, ey /ā/	9, 10, 22, 25, 27	9, 10, 27, 32	43–44, 51–52	184
Vowel Digraphs au, aw /ô/	17, 23	9, 18, 22	43–44, 51–52	184
Vowel Digraph ie /ē/ /ī/	11, 12, 36	11, 12	45–46, 51–52	184
Vowel Digraph oo /o͞o/ /oo/ /u/	15, 20, 28, 37	15, 21, 28, 36	47–48, 51–52	184
Vowel Digraph ui /i/ /oo/	13, 14, 32	13, 14, 17	49–52	184
Diphthongs oi, oy /oi/	16, 31	20, 31	53–54, 59–60	184–185
Diphthongs ou, ow /ou/	18, 24, 33	19, 24, 34	55–56, 59–60	184–185
Diphthong ew /oo/	19, 29	16, 29	57–60	184–185
Syllables	32–37	32–37	57–60	193

> **Fill in the circle beside the word that has a vowel sound that matches the sound listed.**

1. long **a** sound   ○ rabbit   ○ remain   ○ exercise
2. long **a** sound   ○ crayon   ○ padlock   ○ remark
3. long **e** sound   ○ daybreak   ○ success   ○ succeed
4. long **e** sound   ○ ready   ○ ceiling   ○ vein
5. long **o** sound   ○ mock   ○ fox   ○ boast
6. long **o** sound   ○ mistletoe   ○ touch   ○ torrent
7. long **o** sound   ○ borrow   ○ long   ○ boot
8. long **a** sound   ○ heavy   ○ steak   ○ health
9. long **a** sound   ○ author   ○ drawers   ○ obey
10. long **a** sound   ○ receive   ○ catch   ○ veil
11. long **e** sound   ○ chief   ○ shepherd   ○ untie
12. long **i** sound   ○ wink   ○ tried   ○ field
13. long **u** sound   ○ guilty   ○ biscuit   ○ recruit
14. short **i** sound ○ bruise   ○ building   ○ bridle

> **Next to each word in Column 1, write the letter of the word in Column 2 with the same vowel sound.**

15. ____ book   A. autumn
16. ____ enjoy   B. moon
17. ____ scrawl   C. account
18. ____ flower   D. knew
19. ____ jewelry   E. oil
20. ____ spoon   F. freight
21. ____ weigh   G. cook

Go to the next page. →

> **Read each sentence. Fill in the circle beside yes if the underlined vowels have the same sound or beside no if they do not.**

22. The queen of Sp<u>ai</u>n began her r<u>ei</u>gn last year. ○ yes ○ no

23. A solid gold f<u>au</u>cet is an <u>aw</u>esome sight. ○ yes ○ no

24. I am going tr<u>ou</u>t fishing tomorr<u>ow</u>. ○ yes ○ no

25. The n<u>ei</u>ghbors strolled l<u>ei</u>surely in their yards. ○ yes ○ no

26. Children like to pl<u>ay</u> in the r<u>ai</u>n. ○ yes ○ no

27. Fr<u>ei</u>ght often must be w<u>ei</u>ghed before shipping. ○ yes ○ no

28. The trail hands c<u>oo</u>ked f<u>oo</u>d over an open fire. ○ yes ○ no

29. My neph<u>ew</u> delivers n<u>ew</u>spapers. ○ yes ○ no

30. The soldiers took a br<u>ea</u>k after br<u>ea</u>kfast. ○ yes ○ no

31. He <u>oi</u>led the squeaky wheels on his t<u>oy</u> truck. ○ yes ○ no

> **Write the number of syllables you hear in each word. Then write the vowel pair, vowel digraph, or diphthong that each word contains.**

	Syllables	Vowel Pairs	Vowel Digraphs	Diphthongs
32. juice	_____	_____	_____	_____
33. shower	_____	_____	_____	_____
34. least	_____	_____	_____	_____
35. pheasant	_____	_____	_____	_____
36. retrieve	_____	_____	_____	_____
37. waterproof	_____	_____	_____	_____

Possible score on Unit 2 Pretest is 37. Number correct _____

> **Fill in the circle beside the word that has a vowel sound that matches the sound listed.**

1. long **a** sound   ○ character   ○ matches   ○ daisy
2. long **a** sound   ○ payment   ○ capital   ○ shark
3. long **e** sound   ○ sleigh   ○ steeple   ○ shell
4. long **e** sound   ○ protein   ○ weigh   ○ skies
5. long **o** sound   ○ crawl   ○ lock   ○ coal
6. long **o** sound   ○ touch   ○ tiptoe   ○ morning
7. long **o** sound   ○ tomorrow   ○ crock   ○ moose
8. long **a** sound   ○ sweater   ○ break   ○ wealth
9. long **a** sound   ○ awkward   ○ caution   ○ survey
10. long **a** sound   ○ cast   ○ believe   ○ neigh
11. long **e** sound   ○ relief   ○ express   ○ flies
12. long **i** sound   ○ wield   ○ cries   ○ niece
13. long **u** sound   ○ quit   ○ quilt   ○ suit
14. long **u** sound   ○ puppy   ○ guitar   ○ cruise

> **Next to each word in Column 1, write the letter of the word in Column 2 with the same vowel sound.**

15. ___ balloon   A. naughty
16. ___ shrewd   B. broom
17. ___ biscuit   C. aloud
18. ___ lawyer   D. dew
19. ___ power   E. blood
20. ___ voyage   F. poison
21. ___ flood   G. build

Go to the next page. →

> **Read each sentence. Fill in the circle beside yes** if the underlined vowels have the same sound or beside **no** if they do not.

22. The bad <u>au</u>thor wrote <u>aw</u>kward sentences.   ○ yes   ○ no

23. The w<u>ea</u>ther outlook for the week is bl<u>ea</u>k.   ○ yes   ○ no

24. C<u>ou</u>nt the number of colors in a rainb<u>ow</u>.   ○ yes   ○ no

25. How did a b<u>ee</u>tle get into the gr<u>ee</u>nhouse?   ○ yes   ○ no

26. The tr<u>ai</u>n was delayed for an hour.   ○ yes   ○ no

27. Th<u>ey</u> heard the horse n<u>ei</u>ghing in the barn.   ○ yes   ○ no

28. We saw the racc<u>oo</u>n's f<u>oo</u>tprints in the field.   ○ yes   ○ no

29. The royal p<u>ew</u>ter and j<u>ew</u>elry are in the museum.   ○ yes   ○ no

30. The storm caused h<u>ea</u>vy b<u>ea</u>ch erosion.   ○ yes   ○ no

31. The b<u>oy</u> s<u>oi</u>led his clothes playing football.   ○ yes   ○ no

> **Write the number of syllables you hear in each word. Then write the vowel pair, vowel digraph, or dipthong that each word contains.**

	Syllables	Vowel Pairs	Vowel Digraphs	Dipthongs
32. disobey	_____	_____	_____	_____
33. soapy	_____	_____	_____	_____
34. cloud	_____	_____	_____	_____
35. portray	_____	_____	_____	_____
36. shook	_____	_____	_____	_____
37. treachery	_____	_____	_____	_____

Possible score on Unit 2 Posttest is 37. Number correct _____

Student Progress Checklist

Make as many copies as needed to use for a class list. For individual portfolio use, cut apart each student's section. As indicated by the code, color in boxes next to skills satisfactorily assessed and mark an X by those requiring reteaching. Marked boxes can later be colored in to indicate mastery.

STUDENT PROGRESS CHECKLIST

Code: ■ Satisfactory   ☒ Needs Reteaching

Student: _____

_____

Pretest Score: _____

Posttest Score: _____

Skills

❑ Vowel Pairs *ai, ay*

❑ Vowel Pairs *ee, ei*

❑ Vowel Pairs *oa, oe, ow*

❑ Vowel Digraph *ea*

❑ Vowel Digraphs *au, aw*

❑ Vowel Digraphs *ei, ey*

❑ Vowel Digraph *ie*

❑ Vowel Digraph *oo*

❑ Vowel Digraph *ui*

❑ Diphthongs *oi, oy*

❑ Diphthongs *ou, ow*

❑ Diphthong *ew*

❑ Syllables

Comments / Learning Goals

Student: _____

_____

Pretest Score: _____

Posttest Score: _____

Skills

❑ Vowel Pairs *ai, ay*

❑ Vowel Pairs *ee, ei*

❑ Vowel Pairs *oa, oe, ow*

❑ Vowel Digraph *ea*

❑ Vowel Digraphs *au, aw*

❑ Vowel Digraphs *ei, ey*

❑ Vowel Digraph *ie*

❑ Vowel Digraph *oo*

❑ Vowel Digraph *ui*

❑ Diphthongs *oi, oy*

❑ Diphthongs *ou, ow*

❑ Diphthong *ew*

❑ Syllables

Comments / Learning Goals

Spelling Connections

INTRODUCTION

The Unit Word List is a comprehensive list of spelling words drawn from this unit. The words are grouped by word study elements. To incorporate spelling into your word study program, use the activity in the Curriculum Connections section of each teaching plan.

The spelling lessons utilize the following approach for each set of words.

1. Administer a pretest of the words that have not yet been introduced. Dictation sentences are provided.

2. Provide practice.

3. Reassess. Dictation sentences are provided.

A final test is provided on page 62.

DIRECTIONS

Make a copy of Blackline Master 14 for each student. After administering the pretest for the sounds of the various letters and combinations of letters, give each student a copy of the appropriate word list.

Students can work with a partner to practice spelling the words orally and identifying the appropriate sound in each word. They can also create letter cards to use to form the words on the list. You may want to challenge students to identify other words that have the same sound variant or combination. Students can write words of their own on *My Own Word List* (see Blackline Master 14).

Have students store their list words in an envelope or a plastic zipper bag in their books or notebooks. You may want to suggest that students keep a spelling notebook, listing words with similar patterns. You could also invite students to build word-wall displays in the classroom. Each section of the wall can focus on words with a single word study element. The walls will become a good resource when students are writing.

UNIT WORD LIST

Vowel Pairs *ai, ay, ee, ei, oa, oe, ow*

aim
play
seize
coat
tow
remain
crayon
steeple
tomorrow
foe

Vowel Digraphs *ea, ei, ey, ie, au, aw, oo, ui*

break
leaf
vein
August
scrawl
yield
tie
flood
built
fruit

Diphthongs *oi, oy, ou, ow, ew;* Syllables

corduroy
moist
loud
down
sour
strewn

Name _____

 **S**pelling

UNIT 2 WORD LIST

Vowel Pairs ai, ay, ee, ei, oa, oe, ow

aim
play
seize
coat
tow
remain
crayon
steeple
tomorrow
foe

Vowel Digraphs ea, ei, ey, ie, au, aw, oo, ui

break
leaf
vein
August
scrawl
yield
tie
flood
built
fruit

Diphthongs oi, oy, ou, ow, ew; Syllables

corduroy
moist
loud
down
sour
strewn

My Own Word List

Word Study Games, Activities, and Technology

The following collection of ideas offers a variety of opportunities to reinforce word study skills while actively engaging students. The games, activities, and technology suggestions can easily be adapted to meet the needs of your group of learners. They vary in approach so as to consider sudents' different learning styles.

● MASQUERADE PARTY

Note that a digraph may look like a vowel pair but that this is a masquerade. A digraph does not always follow the long vowel rule. Provide students with posterboard and art materials. Allow each to create a party mask covering the upper part of the face, with a space for eyes cut out. Write a list of words containing vowel pairs and digraphs on the chalkboard. As you point to a word, ask a volunteer to pronounce it. If it contains a digraph, the student should speak from behind the mask. If the word has a vowel pair, the mask should stay on the desk. After a correct response, have the class repeat the word with or without masks, as appropriate.

▲ SILENT PARTNERS

Tell students that a silent partner is someone whom everybody can see is part of a pair but who does not make a sound. A silent partner lets the other partner speak for both. Explain that in vowel pairs the second vowel is a silent partner who keeps quiet while the first vowel says its long sound. Pair the students and provide each set of partners with a list of words containing vowel pairs. Illustrate the idea of the silent partner by modeling two words. For example, write the word *play* on the chalkboard. Point to the *a*, saying, *I am the long a sound in the word* play, then point to the *y*, saying, *I am* y, *long a's silent partner in the word* play. Choose a second word, such as *break*, in which the first vowel is silent. Call on partners to follow your example by writing different words on the board and taking the parts of the speaking partner and the silent partner.

◆ CLOSE ENCOUNTER OF THE VOWEL KIND

Tell students that you found the following alien communication on your computer (or in your mailbox). Ask them to help with your assignment. Challenge them to find the one spelling mistake that might be caused by mispronunciation (*niece* instead of *nice*). Have the class practice reading the message aloud. When you are satisfied, "make contact." You might also have groups prepare original, helpful messages concerning vowel sounds. If possible, have students tape and play back the class communications.

> Good Morning, Teacher! We live on a planet beyond your moon. Don't stare at the ceiling, silly goose, you cannot view us. We are learning English from newspapers so that a space crew can pay a neighborly visit to your school next autumn. We do not want our speech to sound awkward, but vowel noises do not come easily to us. This is not a hoax; we would not deceive you. Please help us learn to pronounce by reading this message aloud. We hope our request does not annoy you. Have an enjoyable, healthy breakfast after daybreak. Try some niece strawberries and broiled rainbow trout.

■ DIPH-SONGS!

Have students write the titles or first lines for as many songs as come to mind. Then have them circle the vowel digraphs and underline the diphthongs in the words. Have the students select their favorite songs and ask a volunteer to write the titles or first lines on the board. As a class activity, circle the vowel digraphs and underline the diphthongs. Then invite them to sing together and snap their fingers whenever they come to a word that contains a vowel digraph or diphthong. After some practice you might suggest that they snap their fingers for digraphs and clap their hands for diphthongs.

✳ PHONETIC BASKETBALL

Play a variation of the playground basketball game "horse." In this game, players take turns trying a variety of shots, such as a jumpshot, a hook, or a layup. If Player 1 makes the shot, Player 2 must make the same shot, or Player 1 gains a letter. No player may try the same shot twice in a row. The first player to spell *horse* wins. Pair students. Player 1 begins by saying a word that contains a vowel pair, vowel digraph, or diphthong. Player 2 must say another word that contains that phoneme, or Player 1 gains a letter. In either case, Player 2 goes first in the next round, and play alternates in succeeding rounds. Play continues until one player spells *horse*. Suggest that one partner be the scorekeeper while the other records phonemes that have been used, to ensure that none is used twice in a row. Encourage students to avoid repetition until most unit phonemes have been used once.

● WORD SEARCH

Challenge students to create word-search puzzles using words containing vowel pairs, vowel digraphs, or diphthongs discussed in any one lesson. Before students begin, you may wish to have them search through any reading materials available to find words containing the selected vowel combinations. After students have completed their puzzles, invite them to exchange papers with a partner and solve each other's puzzles.

▲ SHOPPING SPREE

Have the class play "going on a shopping spree." Tell students that the only things they can buy are items whose names contain a vowel pair, such as raisins, beef, or a boat. One student begins by saying *I am going on a shopping spree to buy raisins*. The student then writes the word *raisins* on the board and underlines the vowel pair. The next student says *I am going on a shopping spree to buy raisins and . . .* Each student adds an item and writes its name on the board. You might have the class pronounce the names of the items as the list grows. You could vary the activity using digraphs and diphthongs.

◆ CHALK RELAY RACE

Write these words on the board: *squeal, feather, seal, leash, pleasant, break, eagle, spread, treasure, neat, east, steak, bread, team, healthy, clean, great, heavy.* Then invite teams of six students to have a chalk relay race. Each team should line up ten feet from the board. At a signal, the first team member goes to the board, writes one word from the list with *ea* that stands for long *e*, then takes the chalk to the next player. The first team to have written six long *e* words from the list wins. The game may be repeated with team members writing words with *ea* standing for the short *e* sound.

■ SENTENCE CHALLENGE

Groups of three or four students can brainstorm lists of words for each sound of the digraphs *ui* and *oo*. Challenge the groups to compose sentences using two or more words from each list. Afterward, encourage the groups to reread their sentences to determine whether details can be added to make the sentences more interesting. This activity can be varied by using other digraphs found in a limited number of words.

✳ PHONEME SHUFFLEBOARD

Use Blackline Master 15 to make a game board featuring words with vowel pairs, vowel digraphs, and/or diphthongs. Make a master copy by writing the various combinations of letters in the spaces provided. You might wish to concentrate on vowel digraphs, for example, or a combination of all the concepts studied. Allow the middle space (worth 25 points) to stay blank. Then make copies to distribute to pairs of students. Explain that partners should sit at a table across from one another and, using a coin or checker, take turns playing "phoneme shuffleboard" (each player starts at the nearest edge of the game board and pushes the token across the board toward the other player). As a player lands on a vowel combination, he or she must say and spell a word containing that phoneme. If a player lands on the middle space, his or her opponent can choose the vowel combination that must be used. Play continues until one player reaches 150 points.

Technology

The following software products are designed to reinforce students' knowledge of grammar.

Grammar Rock   Based on the popular PBS television series, *Grammar Rock* emphasizes grammar, phonics, and spelling. Five videos from the television program are included. Each student's progress can be tracked electronically through 19 multilevel games.
** Creative Wonders
   P. O. Box 9017
   Redwood City, CA 94063-9017
   (800) 543-9778

Grammar Games   An introductory quiz assesses grammar skills and then places children into various activities accordingly. Four games offer practice in fragmented vs. complete sentences, using correct noun and verb forms, and punctuation.

** Davidson & Associates, Inc.
   19840 Pioneer Avenue
   Torrance, CA 90503
   (800) 545-7677

I. M. Meen   Students practice spelling, grammar, and pronunciation as they find and proofread 150 scrolls while navigating through a spooky mazelike dungeon and fighting off evil pirates. (Thirty-six levels of text are included.)
** Simon & Schuster Interactive
   P.O. Box 2002
   Aurora, CO 80040-2002
   (800) 910-0099

Name _____

Phoneme Shuffleboard

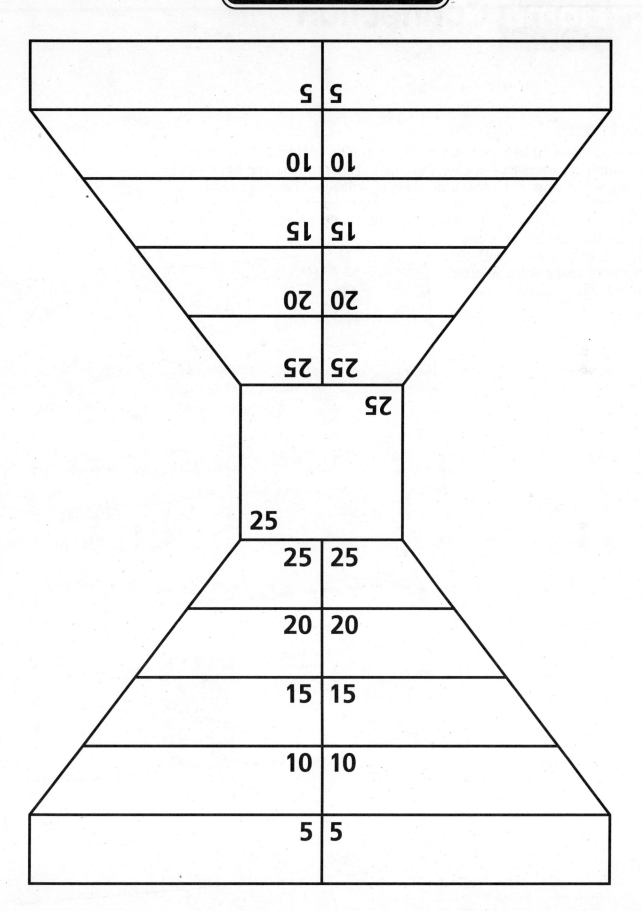

Home Connection

HOME LETTER

A letter is available to be sent home at the beginning of Unit 2. This letter informs family members that students will be learning to read and write words containing vowel pairs and varying numbers of syllables. The suggested home activity revolves around discovering hidden-picture words in a work of art. This activity promotes interaction between child and family members while supporting the student's learning of reading and writing words with the targeted word study skills. A letter is also available in Spanish on page 33q.

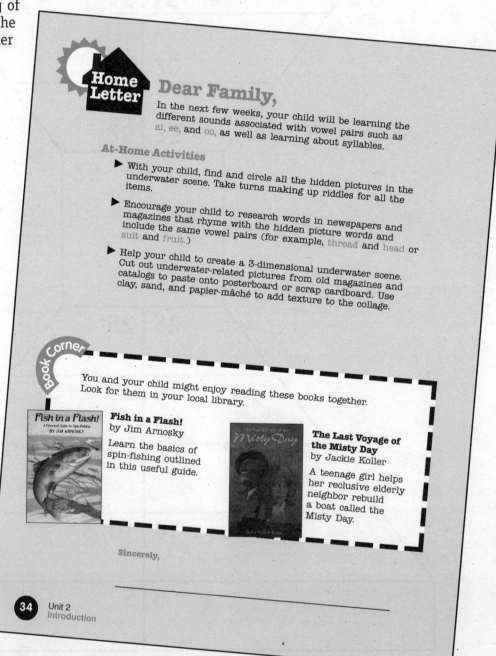

Home Letter

Dear Family,

In the next few weeks, your child will be learning the different sounds associated with vowel pairs such as ai, ee, and oo, as well as learning about syllables.

At-Home Activities

▶ With your child, find and circle all the hidden pictures in the underwater scene. Take turns making up riddles for all the items.

▶ Encourage your child to research words in newspapers and magazines that rhyme with the hidden picture words and include the same vowel pairs (for example, thread and head or suit and fruit.)

▶ Help your child to create a 3-dimensional underwater scene. Cut out underwater-related pictures from old magazines and catalogs to paste onto posterboard or scrap cardboard. Use clay, sand, and papier-mâché to add texture to the collage.

Book Corner

You and your child might enjoy reading these books together. Look for them in your local library.

Fish in a Flash!
by Jim Arnosky

Learn the basics of spin-fishing outlined in this useful guide.

The Last Voyage of the Misty Day
by Jackie Koller

A teenage girl helps her reclusive elderly neighbor rebuild a boat called the Misty Day.

Sincerely,

Carta para la casa

Estimada familia,

En las semanas próximas, su hijo/a va a estudiar los diferentes sonidos asociados con parejas de vocales tales como **ai**, **ee**, y **oo** además de estudiar las sílabas.

Actividades para hacer en casa

▶ Con su hijo/a hallen y encierren en un círculo las imágenes escondidas en la escena submarina. Túrnense en inventar adivinanzas en inglés para cada artículo.

▶ Animen a su hijo/a a investigar palabras en inglés en periódicos y revistas que rimen con las palabras escondidas e incluyan los mismos pares de vocales, por ejemplo, **thread (hilar)** y **head (cabeza)** o **suit (traje)** y **fruit (fruta)**.

▶ Ayuden a su hijo a crear una escena submarina en tercera dimensión. Recorten láminas de escenas submarinas de revistas y catálogos viejos para pegarlas en cartulina o en pedazos de cartón descartados. Usen arcilla, arena o papel maché para añadirle textura a esta combinación de fotos o collage.

Rincón del libro

Quizás a su hijo/a y a ustedes les guste leer estos libros juntos. Búsquenlos en la biblioteca de su localidad.

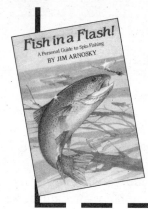

Fish in a Flash!
por Jim Arnosky

Aprendan lo básico sobre la pesca de remolino según se relata en esta útil guía.

The Last Voyage of the Misty Day
por Jackie French Koller

Una adolescente ayuda a su anciano vecino recluido a reconstruir un barco llamado **"Misty Day"**.

Atentamente, _____

Unit 2

Pages 33–34

Vowel Pairs, Digraphs, Diphthongs, Syllables

> ### ASSESSING PRIOR KNOWLEDGE
>
> To assess students' prior knowledge of vowel pairs, digraphs, diphthongs, and syllables, use the pretest on pages 33e–33f.

Unit Focus

USING THE PAGE

- Invite students to look carefully at the illustration of sea life before you ask a volunteer to read the directions aloud.

- After students have had a chance to search for the "hidden treasures" in the illustration, ask volunteers to point out some of the items hidden in the underwater scene.

- Invite a volunteer to read the question asked by the character. Encourage students to talk about what kinds of objects might be found on a real dive. Invite students to make a list of those kinds of objects to compare to the treasures found in the illustration.

- **Critical Thinking** Read aloud the question the character asks on page 33. Have students tell where they might look to find out more about being an underwater archeologist.

BUILDING A CONTEXT

- Challenge students to list on the board all the hidden treasures found in the picture.

- Read the words aloud and have students look for words with similar vowel pairs, digraphs, or diphthongs.

UNIT **2** Vowel Pairs, Digraphs, Diphthongs, Syllables

If you were an undersea archaeologist, what kinds of objects would you expect to find on a dive?

Critical Thinking

There are 13 hidden treasures in this picture. Can you find them?

Unit 2 Introduction **33**

UNIT OPENER ACTIVITIES

LOOK AGAIN

Ask students to pay special attention to the details of underwater life on page 33 and then to compare those details to the hidden treasures in the picture (*boot, foot, needle, thread, bow and arrow, flower, suit, faucet, crayon, guitar, pail steak*). In what way is the comparison between the realistic details and the hidden treasures humorous? Why do students think each treasure has been placed in this underwater scene? (*Each word includes a vowel pair, digraph, or diphthong to be studied in the unit.*)

UNDERWATER WORDS

Write the phrase *underwater life* on the board and invite students to see how many smaller words they can find "hidden" in the phrase. Challenge students to make a list of the words.

AN UNDERSEA EXPEDITION

Invite students to dramatize an underwater expedition. Challenge them to role-play a group of divers in search of a hidden treasure beneath the sea.

33

Dear Family,

In the next few weeks, your child will be learning the different sounds associated with vowel pairs such as ai, ee, and oo, as well as learning about syllables.

At-Home Activities

▶ With your child, find and circle all the hidden pictures in the underwater scene. Take turns making up riddles for all the items.

▶ Encourage your child to research words in newspapers and magazines that rhyme with the hidden picture words and include the same vowel pairs (for example, thread and head or suit and fruit.)

▶ Help your child to create a 3-dimensional underwater scene. Cut out underwater-related pictures from old magazines and catalogs to paste onto posterboard or scrap cardboard. Use clay, sand, and papier-mâché to add texture to the collage.

You and your child might enjoy reading these books together. Look for them in your local library.

Fish in a Flash!
by Jim Arnosky

Learn the basics of spin-fishing outlined in this useful guide.

The Last Voyage of the Misty Day
by Jackie Koller

A teenage girl helps her reclusive elderly neighbor rebuild a boat called the Misty Day.

Sincerely,

_____

BULLETIN BOARD

Invite students to draw real or imaginary sea creatures to display on an underwater mural entitled "Life Beneath the Sea." Each real or imaginary sea creature should have a caption with its name and factual or imaginative information about it.

● The Home Letter on page 34 is intended to acquaint family members with the word study skills students will be studying in the unit. Encourage everyone to complete the activities with a family member. Invite students to look in the local library for the books listed on page 34 and to read them with family members

● The Home Letter can also be found on page 33q in Spanish.

CURRICULUM CONNECTIONS

SOCIAL STUDIES

Invite students to research areas of the world where underwater archaeological expeditions have taken place, such as the search in the Mediterranean Sea for the lost island of Atlantis. Students should give oral presentations about what they have learned.

WRITING

Have students imagine they were members of an underwater expedition. Invite them to write journal entries about their experience, describing what they did and how they felt.

SCIENCE

Challenge students to research what life is like for one kind of sea creature. For example, where do seals live and what are their daily lives like? Encourage students to give an oral presentation of their information.

Lesson 15

Pages 35–36

Vowel Pairs *ai, ay*

INFORMAL ASSESSMENT OBJECTIVE

Can students

✔ recognize that the vowel pairs *ai* and *ay* can stand for the long *a* sound?

Lesson Focus

INTRODUCING THE SKILL

- Write *waist, maintain, play, stay, rain,* and *daytime* on the board and ask the class to read the words aloud.

- Point to *waist* and ask a volunteer to identify the vowels, then say the word aloud. Ask what vowel sound students hear. Help them identify the *ai* in *waist* as a vowel pair, two vowels together that make one long vowel sound. The first vowel has the long sound of its name and the second vowel is silent.

- Call on students to circle the vowel pair in each word and to identify the vowel sound.

- Ask students to write on the board other words that contain the vowel pair *ai* or *ay*.

USING THE PAGES

- Give students help as necessary to complete pages 35 and 36. When they have completed the pages, review what they have learned about the vowel pairs *ai* and *ay*.

- **Critical Thinking** Read aloud the question on page 36 and discuss answers with students.

 Read each sentence. Circle each word that has the long **a** sound. Then draw a line under the letters that stand for that sound.

> **RULE**
> In a **vowel pair,** two vowels come together to make one long vowel sound. The first vowel in the pair has the long sound of its name and the second is silent. The vowel pairs **ai** and **ay** follow the long-vowel rule and can stand for the long **a** sound.
>
> a**i**m pl**ay**

1. I do all of my (painting) in a special studio.
2. The studio is filled with (pails,) (trays,) and other (containers.)
3. The floor is always (stained) with (paint.)
4. I often (stay) in my studio for hours, and sometimes I (paint) all (day.)
5. My last (painting) was a beautiful (sailboat) on the (bay.)
6. (Today) I'm drawing a (train) whizzing through a field of (grain.)
7. Later (today,) Mother and I will (pay) a visit to a friend.
8. I hope we won't be (detained) long; I want to finish my drawing (today.)
9. When time is (available,) I will (paint) a picture for my parents' anniversary.
10. Maybe that will help (explain) to them why I (stay) in my studio so long!

 Circle the word in each row that has the long **a** sound. Then draw a line under the letters that stand for that sound.

11. tramp	tap	star	tram	(stray)
12. drab	(delay)	dance	dash	damp
13. (crayon)	cancel	clatter	capitol	candle
14. rabbit	ran	ranch	(remain)	remark
15. matches	mask	(mail)	marches	mat
16. (plain)	pals	plant	pans	pats
17. watch	arrest	answer	argue	(sway)
18. drama	(dainty)	dam	dad	dare
19. prance	planter	(payment)	padlock	pantry
20. hatch	half	harvest	(hail)	hall

FOCUS ON ALL LEARNERS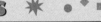

ENGLISH LANGUAGE LEARNERS/ESL

Before beginning to work, read the rule on page 35 with students and make sure they understand the long-vowel rule of vowel pairs. As background for page 36, talk about family vacations students have taken or brainstorm destinations for dream vacations.

VISUAL LEARNERS

INDIVIDUAL Write the words *day, tail,* and *rain* at the top of separate sheets of paper. Post the papers where students can write on them to add rhyming words. Encourage students to write nonsense rhymes using words from the lists.

KINESTHETIC/VISUAL LEARNERS

PARTNER

Materials: newspapers

Have students page through newspapers, looking for words with the vowel pairs *ai* or *ay*. Ask them to match each word they find with another word that has the other vowel pair and list both words.

Complete each sentence with a word from the word bank.

train	away	remain	delayed	always	rain
sway	explained	pails	daybreak	repay	stayed
pain	relay	grains	raisin	sailing	sprained

1. We had fun when we were _____**away**_____ on vacation.

2. We traveled by _____**train**_____ from our home in Phoenix, Arizona.

3. We were _____**delayed**_____ only once during the trip.

4. We _____**stayed**_____ at our aunt and uncle's home in California for a week.

5. We wanted to do so many things that we _____**always**_____ woke up early.

6. One day we even left the house before _____**daybreak**_____.

7. Aunt Flo and Uncle George were going to take us _____**sailing**_____ on the ocean.

8. Aunt Flo gave us our life jackets and _____**explained**_____ how to use them.

9. We enjoyed it when the boat would _____**sway**_____ back and forth in the breeze.

10. On the shore, we built sand castles with our shovels and _____**pails**_____.

11. In the evenings, we played games and held _____**relay**_____ races.

12. During one race, Uncle George tripped and _____**sprained**_____ his ankle.

13. Uncle George insisted that his injury did not cause him much _____**pain**_____.

14. The weather was great; it did not _____**rain**_____ once.

15. We thought about how we could _____**repay**_____ Uncle George and Aunt Flo for the good time we had.

16. We baked them several loaves of _____**raisin**_____ bread as a thank-you present.

17. We added nuts and three kinds of _____**grains**_____ to the batter.

18. We were sorry that we could not _____**remain**_____ for a longer visit.

What are the most important story events?

Critical Thinking

36 Lesson 15
Vowel pairs ai, ay

SPELLING

The following sentences can be used as a pretest for spelling words with vowel pairs *ai, ay, ee, ei, oa, oe, ow*.

1. **aim** — My **aim** is to finish reading by Friday.
2. **play** — I like to **play** duets on the piano.
3. **seize** — Can the dog **seize** the bone?
4. **coat** — The **coat** looks warm.
5. **tow** — Let's **tow** the boat.
6. **remain** — Will you **remain** inside with me?
7. **crayon** — I like the color of that **crayon.**
8. **steeple** — That **steeple** is on the church.
9. **tomorrow** — We have a test **tomorrow.**
10. **foe** — Are you a friend or a **foe?**

WRITING

Portfolio Have students look through art books, then write an essay about an artist or a painting that they admire. Encourage them to include words with *ai* and *ay* in their writing.

SOCIAL STUDIES/MATH

Encourage students to find Arizona and California on a map. Help them figure out the distance between these two states and plot a number of possible train routes a traveler might take.

HEALTH/MATH

Encourage the class to design a first-aid kit to take along on class trips. Ask the school nurse to visit the classroom to advise students on good items to include and the quantity needed. Using drugstore advertisements and other research, students can estimate the cost of outfitting the kit they design.

AUDITORY/KINESTHETIC LEARNERS

LARGE GROUP Give students meaning clues, such as *I am thinking of a word that means a kind of bucket,* for words that have vowel pairs *ai* and *ay*. Have the student who identifies each word write it on the board and circle the vowel pair. Try *subway, train, stay, relay,* and *pail*.

GIFTED LEARNERS

Challenge students to create a list of phrases with two long *a* words spelled *ai* and *ay*. Examples are: *crayon stain, mail delay,* and *dainty tray*.

LEARNERS WHO NEED EXTRA SUPPORT

On the board, build word lists with *ai* and *ay*. For example, spell *pain*, then have students change the *p* to an *m*, the *m* to an *r*, and the *r* to *st* (for *main, rain, stain*). Also try *bay*. **See Daily Word Study Practice, page 183.**

Lesson 16
Pages 37–38

Vowel Pairs ee, ei

INFORMAL ASSESSMENT OBJECTIVE

Can students

✔ recognize that the vowel pairs *ee* and *ei* can stand for the long e sound?

Lesson Focus

INTRODUCING THE SKILL

- Write *st(ee)l* and *c(ei)ling* on the board, leaving blanks for the letters in parentheses. Ask students: *What word means a very strong metal?* and *What word means the top part of a room?* As students answer each question, fill in the missing letters.

- Ask students to read the completed words aloud and to identify the long vowel sound in each one. Help them conclude that the vowel pairs *ee* and *ei* stand for the long e sound in *steel* and *ceiling*.

- Give students a chance to name other words in which *ee* and *ei* stand for long e. Ask them to write the words on the board and circle the vowel pairs.

USING THE PAGES

- Be sure students understand how to complete pages 37 and 38.

- **Critical Thinking** Read aloud the questions on page 38 and discuss answers with students.

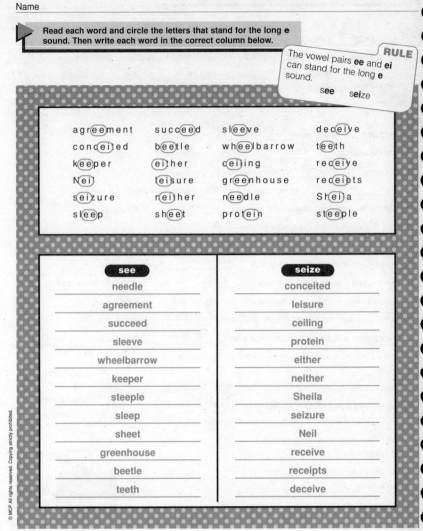

Name _____

Read each word and circle the letters that stand for the long e sound. Then write each word in the correct column below.

RULE
The vowel pairs **ee** and **ei** can stand for the long **e** sound.

see   seize

agr(ee)ment	succ(ee)d	sl(ee)ve	dec(ei)ve
conc(ei)ted	b(ee)tle	wh(ee)lbarrow	t(ee)th
k(ee)per	(ei)ther	c(ei)ling	rec(ei)ve
N(ei)l	l(ei)sure	gr(ee)nhouse	rec(ei)pts
s(ei)zure	n(ei)ther	n(ee)dle	Sh(ei)la
sl(ee)p	sh(ee)t	prot(ei)n	st(ee)ple

see	seize
needle	conceited
agreement	leisure
succeed	ceiling
sleeve	protein
wheelbarrow	either
keeper	neither
steeple	Sheila
sleep	seizure
sheet	Neil
greenhouse	receive
beetle	receipts
teeth	deceive

FOCUS ON ALL LEARNERS

ENGLISH LANGUAGE LEARNERS/ESL

Ask students to read the words at the top of page 37 to be sure they are pronouncing both vowel pairs correctly. Before beginning page 38, ask students about their experiences taking care of houseplants or helping care for a garden.

VISUAL LEARNERS

SMALL GROUP

Materials: chart paper

Encourage small groups of students to look through a textbook for words with the *ee* or *ei* vowel pair. Have them list the words on a sheet of paper. Ask groups to compare their lists and to compile a class list of *ee* words and *ei* words on chart paper.

KINESTHETIC LEARNERS

LARGE GROUP

Have students choose words with the vowel pairs *ee* or *ei* to pantomime for other students to guess. If needed, suggest these words: *needle, wheelbarrow, seize, ceiling, conceited, sleep, beetle, tree.*

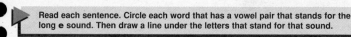

Read each sentence. Circle each word that has a vowel pair that stands for the long e sound. Then draw a line under the letters that stand for that sound.

1. (Sheila) Franklin owns and operates a (greenhouse) in her community.
2. She (agreed) never to move it from its location on a quiet, secluded (street).
3. She enjoys the sight of strong (trees), flowering plants, and young (seedlings).
4. The sides and (ceiling) of her (greenhouse) are glass, which (Sheila) (keeps) shiny.
5. Outside, an enormous (weeping) willow (sweeps) over the sprawling property.
6. Beside it, a (beech) (tree) with gray bark and edible nuts is visible.
7. (Sheila) gathers honey from (beehives) that she (keeps) on her property.
8. She (succeeds) in her business because she is (deeply) devoted to her job.
9. One can often (see) her hauling soil and fertilizer in a large (wheelbarrow).
10. She is always ready to (seize) any chance to improve her business.
11. She works long hours and never (seems) to get (sleepy)!
12. (Sheila) (guarantees) every plant and shrub that she sells.
13. She reminds her customers to always (keep) their (receipts).
14. (Sheila) (receives) many compliments from patrons because she is (neither) (conceited) nor (deceitful).
15. Everyone (agrees) that she runs a great business.
16. Even in her (leisure) time, (Sheila) is glad to lend a helping hand to anyone.

What kind of person is Sheila Franklin? What clues are there in the story that describe her character traits?

Critical Thinking

38 Lesson 16
Vowel pairs ee, ei

SPELLING

Write the vowel pairs *ai, ay, ee, ei, oa, oe, ow* on separate cards and display them on the chalkboard ledge. Then say the spelling words *aim, play, seize,* one at a time. Call on volunteers to hold up the card with the vowel pair they hear and write the word on the board. Continue with other spelling words: *coat, tow, remain, crayon, steeple, tomorrow, foe.*

WRITING

Have students write a list of questions to ask Sheila Franklin in an interview for the town newspaper's Kids' Column. As background for the questions, ask them to write a short paragraph about why Ms. Franklin was chosen to be interviewed.

SCIENCE

Portfolio Ask students to cut pictures of high-protein foods from magazines and display them on a bulletin board. Have them identify the pictures with names that contain an *ei* or *ee* vowel pair to list in their Word Banks. Then have students write a short essay on what protein can do for them.

FINE ARTS

Suggest students examine their school surroundings with the eyes of a landscape architect. How would they change or add to the plantings if they could? Challenge them to draw a simple map of the school building and its site, then find out what kinds of plants can grow in your climate. Have them add trees and other plantings to the map to show their design ideas.

AUDITORY LEARNERS

LARGE GROUP Play 20 questions by having students ask yes or no questions to guess an *ee* or *ei* word you are thinking of. Before they start the questions, tell them whether the word refers to a plant, animal, person, or thing. Try *tree, beetle, wide receiver,* and *ceiling*.

GIFTED LEARNERS

Challenge students to list 20 *ee* or *ei* words in which the vowel pair is missing. Then have partners trade papers and find out who can fill in the vowel pairs to complete the most words correctly.

LEARNERS WHO NEED EXTRA SUPPORT

Materials: picture books and magazines illustrating *ee* and *ei* words

Have students take turns showing their pictures while others identify the picture name. Then help them write the words. **See Daily Word Study Practice, page 183.**

Lesson 17

Pages 39–40

Vowel Pairs oa, oe, ow

INFORMAL ASSESSMENT OBJECTIVE

Can students

✔ recognize that *oa*, *oe*, and *ow* can stand for the long *o* sound?

Lesson Focus

INTRODUCING THE SKILL

- Write *coach*, *tiptoe*, and *shadow* on the board and ask students to read the words aloud. Ask what vowel sound is heard in all three words. *(long o)*

- Circle the two letters in each word that stand for the long *o* sound. Have students recall what a vowel pair is, then explain that *oa* and *oe* are vowel pairs. Explain that *ow* can sometimes be a vowel pair, as it is in *shadow*, and can stand for the long *o* sound.

- Challenge students to think of other words in which *oa*, *oe*, and *ow* stand for the long *o* sound. Have them write their words on the board.

USING THE PAGES

Have students read the directions for completing pages 39 and 40 and be sure they understand what to do. When students have completed the pages, ask what they learned about *oa*, *oe*, and *ow*.

Name _____

> Read each sentence. Circle each word that has the long o sound. Then draw a line under the letters that stand for that sound.

RULE
The vowel pairs **oa** and **oe** can stand for the long **o** sound. The letters **ow** can also stand for the long **o** sound.

c**oa**t   t**oe**   cr**ow**

1. Luis, a person I (know,) is certain that he will (grow) taller during the next few years.
2. He (boasts) that someday he will be as tall as his favorite basketball player.
3. Luis (knows) that he is the best basketball player on our team.
4. He bounces the ball and stands on (tiptoe) when he makes free (throws.)
5. A talented athlete, he (shows) good sportsmanship wherever he (goes.)
6. If he misses a shot or commits a foul, Luis never (moans) or (groans.)
7. Even when he outscores every other player, Luis does not brag and (gloat.)
8. He promises never to (outgrow) his school spirit and always wears our school crest on his (coat.)

> Complete each sentence with a word from the word bank.

9. In our home economics class yesterday, we baked __loaves__ of bread.
10. I forgot my copy of the recipe, so I had to __borrow__ Joan's.
11. We combined the ingredients in large mixing __bowls__.
12. Today, we will __toast__ the bread and prepare a breakfast.
13. We will serve the toast with __poached__ eggs and juice.
14. We will poach the eggs in a __shallow__ pan.
15. Mrs. Harris may also let us make __oatmeal__ or some other cereal.
16. I wonder what we will cook __tomorrow__.
17. Before the class __goes__ on to the next unit, we will have a test.

borrow
loaves
shallow
bowls
oatmeal
toast
goes
poached
tomorrow

Lesson 17
Vowel pairs oa, oe; Letter pair ow   **39**

FOCUS ON ALL LEARNERS

ENGLISH LANGUAGE LEARNERS/ESL

Before beginning page 39, talk with students about the game of basketball and the physical traits and skills that make good players. Be sure they understand how to complete a hidden-word puzzle.

VISUAL/KINESTHETIC LEARNERS

INDIVIDUAL

Materials: newspapers

Encourage students to work independently to find and circle words in the newspapers that contain *oa*, *oe*, and *ow* that stand for the long *o* sound. If they are not sure how a word is pronounced, suggest they check a dictionary.

KINESTHETIC/AUDITORY LEARNERS

 LARGE GROUP

Have students stand on tiptoe every time they hear a word with the long *o* sound. Say these words: *know, peach, oatmeal, tomorrow, delayed, moaning, conceited, available, hoe, groan, goes, sleepy.*

Twenty-four words in which **oa**, **oe**, and **ow** stand for the long **o** sound are hidden in the puzzle. Some go across and others go up and down or diagonally. Circle each word as you find it in the puzzle, then write the words in the correct column below.

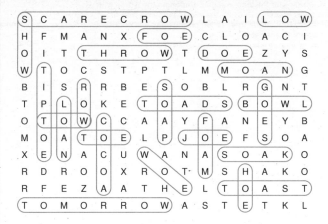

oa	**ow**	**oe**
moan	scarecrow	foe
soap	low	doe
toads	show	toe
loan	throw	hoe
foam	row	goes
cocoa	bowl	Joe
soak	tow	tiptoe
toast	tomorrow	woe

Use a word from the puzzle to complete each sentence below.

1. After ice skating in the cold, we drank some hot _____cocoa_____ to help us.
2. _____Tomorrow_____ we will row the boat on the lake.

40

Lesson 17
Vowels pairs oa, oe; Letter pair ow

CURRICULUM CONNECTIONS

SPELLING

The following sentences can be used as a posttest for spelling words with vowel pairs *ai, ay, ee, ei, oa, oe, ow.*

1. **aim**   I will **aim** my talk at athletes.
2. **play**   Do you like to **play** board games?
3. **seize** The cat tried to **seize** my scarf.
4. **coat**   I need a new **coat** this winter.
5. **tow**   Our car needs a **tow** to the garage.
6. **remain** Sarah will **remain** home today.
7. **crayon** Use a **crayon** to draw the picture.
8. **steeple** I see a bird on the church **steeple.**
9. **tomorrow** I will go **tomorrow.**
10. **foe**   I hope you aren't my **foe!**

WRITING

Portfolio Write the following compound words on the board: *road + side = roadside, in + road = inroad, road + runner = roadrunner.* Invite students to suggest other compound words that contain *road.* Then encourage them to make other compound words using *house, snow, boat,* and *foot* or other words with *oe, oa,* or *ow.*

SOCIAL STUDIES

Challenge students to discover the major grains used for eating and for baking loaves of bread in different world cultures. Where are oats traditional, for instance, and where are rice, quinoa, wheat, millet, barley, bulgur, and corn commonly used?

SCIENCE

Is it a toad or a frog? Do all toads live on land and all frogs live only near water? Or is it the other way around, or neither way? Challenge students to find out about the habitats of toads and frogs and create a poster or chart that explains how you might tell them apart.

AUDITORY/KINESTHETIC LEARNERS

LARGE GROUP

Write *rainbow, soak, float, foam, show, groan, goal, stowaway, throat, shallow, minnows, coast, elbow, boast, toast, shallow, slow, toe, tow,* and *boat* on the board. Have students choose a word and use it in a sentence as part of a group story called "An Adventure at Sea."

GIFTED LEARNERS

Challenge students to make up their own word search using new words with *oa, oe,* and *ow* standing for the long *o* sound.

LEARNERS WHO NEED EXTRA SUPPORT

Help students successfully begin the practice by working with them to complete the top of page 39. Have them take turns reading the sentences and identifying words with long *o* spelled *oa, oe,* or *ow.*
See Daily Word Study Practice, page 183.

Lesson 18

Pages 41–42

Vowel Digraph *ea*

INFORMAL ASSESSMENT OBJECTIVES

Can students

✔ recognize that the vowel digraph *ea* can stand for the long *a* sound, the long *e* sound, and the short *e* sound?

✔ recognize and identify the vowel digraph *ea* in words in context?

Lesson Focus

INTRODUCING THE SKILLS

- Write this sentence on the board: *I like to <u>eat breakfast</u> at <u>daybreak</u>.* Say the sentence aloud, pointing to the underlined words as you do so.

- Ask students what pair of vowels each underlined word contains. *(ea)*

- Have the class say the words aloud. Ask whether the letters *ea* stand for the same sound in each word.

- Help students conclude that the vowel digraph *ea* can stand for three sounds: long *e* as in *eat*, short *e* as in *breakfast*, and long *a* as in *daybreak*.

- Have students suggest additional *ea* words that contain the long *a*, long *e*, and short *e* sounds.

USING THE PAGES

- After students have completed the pages, encourage them to tell what they have learned about the vowel digraph *ea*.

- **Critical Thinking** Read aloud the question on page 42 and discuss answers with students.

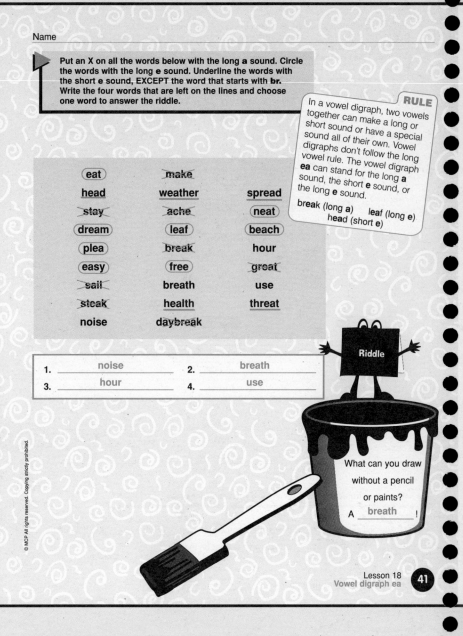

Name

Put an X on all the words below with the long **a** sound. Circle the words with the long **e** sound. Underline the words with the short **e** sound, EXCEPT the word that starts with **br.** Write the four words that are left on the lines and choose one word to answer the riddle.

RULE

In a vowel digraph, two vowels together can make a long or short sound or have a special sound all of their own. Vowel digraphs don't follow the long vowel rule. The vowel digraph **ea** can stand for the long **a** sound, the short **e** sound, or the long **e** sound.

break (long a) leaf (long e)
head (short e)

eat	make	
head	weather	spread
stay	ache	neat
dream	leaf	beach
plea	break	hour
easy	free	great
sail	breath	use
steak	health	threat
noise	daybreak	

Riddle

1. _____noise_____   2. _____breath_____
3. _____hour_____   4. _____use_____

What can you draw without a pencil or paints?

A _____breath_____ !

Lesson 18
Vowel digraph ea   **41**

FOCUS ON ALL LEARNERS

ENGLISH LANGUAGE LEARNERS/ESL

Pair fluent English speakers with second-language learners. Encourage students to review the words in the box on page 41 by defining each word, telling which sound the *ea* stands for, and using each of the words in oral sentences.

VISUAL LEARNERS

LARGE GROUP

Write these words on the board: *squeal, feather, seal, leash, pleasant, break, eagle, spread, treasure, neat, east, steak.* Invite teams to have a chalk relay race. At a signal, the first team member goes to the board, writes one word from the list that contains the sound of long *e*, then takes the chalk to the next player. The first team to write five long *e* words wins.

KINESTHETIC LEARNERS

LARGE GROUP

The class can play a game called "1-2-3." Ask a volunteer to read a list of words that contain the vowel digraph *ea*. Have students hold up one finger if they hear the long *a* sound in a word, two for the long *e* sound, and three for the short *e* sound.

**Complete each sentence with a word from the word bank.
Then write each word you used in the correct column below.**

1. "It's my _____pleasure_____," I told Jan, "to help you with your laundry."

2. I held the basket as Jan _____reached_____ in and removed the clothes.

3. She dropped the clothes into the washing machine and added the soap and _____bleach_____.

4. Turning to _____leave_____ the laundry room, I saw a sock on the floor.

5. I picked it up and pulled off a loose _____thread_____ that hung from the sock.

6. We took a short _____break_____ before we tackled our next chore.

7. Jan held the bucket very _____steady_____ as I filled it with hot water.

8. "Are you _____ready_____?" she asked as I shut off the water.

9. We scrubbed the walls, the floor, and even _____underneath_____ the cupboards.

10. "This was a _____great_____ day," said Jan.

11. "Everything looks so _____neat_____ and tidy."

12. "I think we should go out for a _____steak_____ dinner!"

Word Bank:
bleach
break
great
leave
neat
pleasure
reached
ready
steady
steak
thread
underneath

Imagine that you are the narrator. What would you say to Jan's suggestion about dinner?

Critical Thinking

ea as in **break**	ea as in **leaf**	ea as in **head**
break	reached	pleasure
great	bleach	thread
steak	leave	steady
	underneath	ready
	neat	

42 Lesson 18
Vowel digraph ea

AUDITORY/VISUAL LEARNERS

Write the following words on the board: *increased, great, health, break, leaf, leash, underneath, breakfast.* Then call on volunteers to read each word aloud, circle the vowel digraph *ea*, tell whether the *ea* stands for the long *a* sound, the long *e* sound, or the short *e* sound, and use the words in oral sentences.

GIFTED LEARNERS

Challenge students to write a description of a fantasy breakfast to which they have invited at least three of their real or fictional heroes. Challenge them to use as many words as possible that include the vowel digraph *ea* in their descriptions.

LEARNERS WHO NEED EXTRA SUPPORT

Materials: two sets of word cards

Ask students to work with partners to play a memory game using word cards with words containing the vowel digraph *ea*. Possible words to use may include *steak, health, leash, sweater, break, eat, great, beach, heavy,* and *seat.* **See Daily Word Study Practice, page 184.**

CURRICULUM CONNECTIONS

SPELLING

The following sentences can be used as a pretest for spelling words with vowel pairs *ea, ei, e;y, ie, au, aw, oo, ui.*

1. **break**   Be careful not to **break** the cup.
2. **leaf**   That **leaf** is beautiful.
3. **vein**   I can see a **vein** in my hand.
4. **August**   My birthday is in **August.**
5. **scrawl**   I'll **scrawl** my name on the card.
6. **yield**   A car should **yield** to a walker.
7. **tie**   **Tie** a bow with the ribbon.
8. **flood**   The water will **flood** the land.
9. **built**   We **built** a tree house.
10. **fruit**   Grapes are my favorite **fruit.**

WRITING

Portfolio   Invite students to write a description of their favorite kind of weather. Challenge students to use words with the vowel digraph *ea* in their descriptions.

SOCIAL STUDIES

Tell students this information about the Spanish ship *Atocha*: It left Spain in 1622, headed for Central America and the West Indies. As it sailed into the Straits of Florida, the winds of a hurricane threw the ship onto a reef, where it sank in minutes. Three hundred years later, treasure hunters found the ship on the ocean floor. Challenge students to research information about other sunken ships and the treasure hunters who recover treasures from these vessels.

ART

Invite students to look through magazines and newspapers and create a collage of pictures and captions with words that contain the vowel digraph *ea.*

Lesson 19

Pages 43–44

Vowel Digraphs ei, ey, and Vowel Digraphs au, aw

Lesson Focus

INTRODUCING THE SKILLS

- Write *they* and *weigh* on the board and have the class read the words aloud.
- Ask students what long vowel sound they heard in each word. *(long a)*
- Point to each word and ask what vowel digraph stands for the long *a* sound.
- Help students conclude that the vowel digraphs *ey* and *ei* stand for the long *a* sound.
- Repeat the procedure, using *awful* and *sauce* for the vowel digraphs *au* and *aw*.

USING THE PAGES

Give students help as necessary to complete pages 43 and 44. After they have completed the pages, encourage them to review their work with a partner and discuss what they have learned about the vowel digraphs *ei, ey, au,* and *aw*.

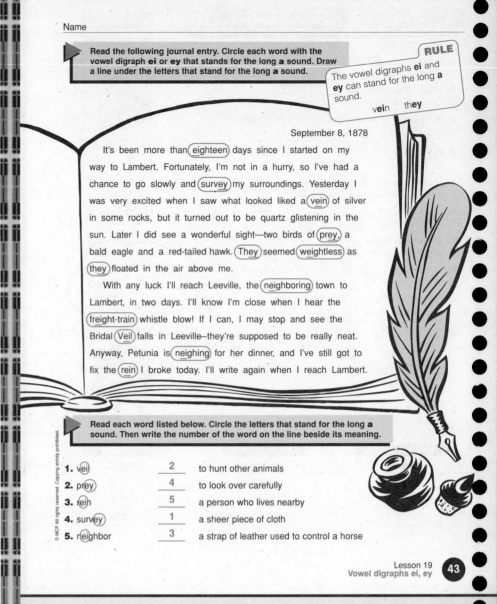

Name

Read the following journal entry. Circle each word with the vowel digraph **ei** or **ey** that stands for the long **a** sound. Draw a line under the letters that stand for the long **a** sound.

RULE
The vowel digraphs **ei** and **ey** can stand for the long **a** sound.
vein   they

September 8, 1878

It's been more than (eighteen) days since I started on my way to Lambert. Fortunately, I'm not in a hurry, so I've had a chance to go slowly and (survey) my surroundings. Yesterday I was very excited when I saw what looked liked a (vein) of silver in some rocks, but it turned out to be quartz glistening in the sun. Later I did see a wonderful sight—two birds of (prey), a bald eagle and a red-tailed hawk. (They) seemed (weightless) as (they) floated in the air above me.

With any luck I'll reach Leeville, the (neighboring) town to Lambert, in two days. I'll know I'm close when I hear the (freight-train) whistle blow! If I can, I may stop and see the Bridal (Veil) falls in Leeville—they're supposed to be really neat. Anyway, Petunia is (neighing) for her dinner, and I've still got to fix the (rein) I broke today. I'll write again when I reach Lambert.

Read each word listed below. Circle the letters that stand for the long **a** sound. Then write the number of the word on the line beside its meaning.

1. v(ei)l — **2** — to hunt other animals
2. pr(ey) — **4** — to look over carefully
3. r(ei)n — **5** — a person who lives nearby
4. surv(ey) — **1** — a sheer piece of cloth
5. n(ei)ghbor — **3** — a strap of leather used to control a horse

Lesson 19
Vowel digraphs ei, ey **43**

FOCUS ON ALL LEARNERS

ENGLISH LANGUAGE LEARNERS/ESL

Before students complete page 43, discuss what life might have been like for a traveler on horseback in 1878. Then read the journal entry together and pick out the unusual images, such as *quartz glistening in the sun* or *two birds of prey*. Be sure students are able to visualize what the writer is describing.

VISUAL LEARNERS

PARTNER Challenge students to create word-search puzzles using words with the digraphs *au* and *aw*. Before beginning, students may search through reading materials to find *au* and *aw* words. Invite students to exchange papers with a partner and solve each other's puzzle.

KINESTHETIC LEARNERS

LARGE GROUP Divide a sheet of chart paper into four equal parts and write *Vein, They, Autumn,* and *Draw* as headings for each column. Display the chart on the board and challenge students to come to the board and write as many words as possible with the same digraph and sound in each column. Invite volunteers to use each word in a sentence.

Complete each sentence with a word from the word bank.

RULE
The vowel digraphs **au** and **aw** both stand for the same vowel sound.
August   dr**aw**

1. Every _____ autumn _____ the school yearbook staff begins its work.

2. Working _____ awfully _____ hard, the student photographers take pictures.

3. Sometimes they have to be _____ cautious _____ when waiting for good shots.

4. They often take pictures as students _____ audition _____ for the school play.

5. After the photographs are developed, they are stored in _____ drawers _____ .

6. Every year, an _____ author _____ is chosen to write an essay for the yearbook.

7. An artistic student is selected to _____ draw _____ the cover design for the yearbook.

8. When the books are distributed, everyone eagerly collects _____ autographs _____ .

9. The students willingly _____ scrawl _____ messages in each other's books.

Word Bank:
audition
author
autographs
autumn
awfully
cautious
draw
drawers
scrawl

Write the number of each word on the line beside its meaning.

10. shawl	15	a small, round shallow dish
11. cautious	13	to melt; to become unfrozen
12. applaud	14	not graceful; clumsy
13. thaw	12	to express approval by clapping
14. awkward	18	a large pot or kettle
15. saucer	17	to bite, chew, or wear away
16. withdraw	16	to take or pull out
17. gnaw	10	a cloth worn as a covering for the shoulders
18. cauldron	11	to be very careful

44
Lesson 19
Vowel digraphs au, aw

44

CURRICULUM CONNECTIONS

SPELLING

Materials: bag, paper slips

Place slips of paper in a bag, with the spelling words *break, leaf, vein, August, scrawl, yield, tie, flood, built, fruit*. Invite students to pick a word to act out while classmates guess. Suggest that students use props if necessary. The student who guesses correctly, spells the word aloud, and writes it on the board.

WRITING

Challenge students to create nonsense sentences that contain words with the digraphs *ei, ey, au,* and *aw*, such as *They said the awful author gnawed the bone.* Invite students to read their sentences to their classmates and encourage volunteers to identify the words with the digraphs.

SCIENCE

Portfolio Ask students to research the following information and write a paragraph about one of these animals: moose, reindeer, bald eagle, red-tailed hawk, or elk.

Animal name   Where does it live?
What does it eat?   What does it do in winter?
Does it live alone or in groups?

ART

Invite students to make a poster advertising the sale of your school's yearbook. Explain that students can make up the name and any information about the yearbook if your school doesn't actually have one.

AUDITORY/VISUAL LEARNERS

PARTNER Have pairs of students divide a sheet of paper into two columns labeled *ei* and *ey*. Have students take turns dictating to each other words in which *ei* and *ey* stand for the long *a* sound. The partner who is listening should write each word in the correct column.

GIFTED LEARNERS

Challenge students to imagine they are pioneers or ranchers heading west on horseback or in a wagon train across the American frontier. Invite students to write several journal entries, describing what life was like for them during their journey.

LEARNERS WHO NEED EXTRA SUPPORT

Materials: two sets of word cards

Ask students to work with partners to play a memory game using word cards with words that contain the vowel digraphs *ei, ey, au,* and *aw*. Suggested words include *withdraw, reindeer, autumn, survey, eight, neighbor, draw, author, saucer,* and *obey*. **See Daily Word Study Practice, page 184.**

Lesson 20
Pages 45–46

Vowel Digraph ie

Lesson Focus

INTRODUCING THE SKILL

- Write the following sentences on the board, omitting the underlines: *The thief shrieked and ran away. Mr. Jones got pie on his tie.* Ask volunteers to read the sentences and to underline the words that contain *ie*.

- Have students say the underlined words aloud to compare the vowel sounds. Ask if the *ie* words in the first sentence have the same long vowel sound as the *ie* words in the second sentence. *(no)* Help them see that *ie* can stand for the long e in *thief* and *shrieked* as well as for the long *i* in *pie* and *tie*.

- Encourage students to create their own sentences with *ie* words and to write them on the board. Challenge the class to identify the vowel sound *ie* stands for.

USING THE PAGES

- If necessary, help students complete pages 45 and 46.

- **Critical Thinking** Read aloud the question on page 46 and discuss answers with students.

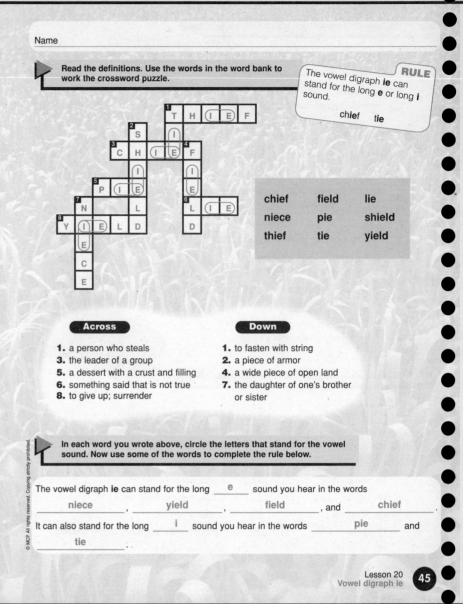

Name

Read the definitions. Use the words in the word bank to work the crossword puzzle.

RULE The vowel digraph **ie** can stand for the long **e** or long **i** sound.
chief   tie

chief	field	lie
niece	pie	shield
thief	tie	yield

Across
1. a person who steals
3. the leader of a group
5. a dessert with a crust and filling
6. something said that is not true
8. to give up; surrender

Down
1. to fasten with string
2. a piece of armor
4. a wide piece of open land
7. the daughter of one's brother or sister

In each word you wrote above, circle the letters that stand for the vowel sound. Now use some of the words to complete the rule below.

The vowel digraph **ie** can stand for the long ___e___ sound you hear in the words
___niece___ , ___yield___ , ___field___ , and ___chief___
It can also stand for the long ___i___ sound you hear in the words ___pie___ and
___tie___ .

Lesson 20
Vowel digraph ie **45**

FOCUS ON ALL LEARNERS

ENGLISH LANGUAGE LEARNERS/ESL

Read the words in the boxes at the top of both pages with students to be sure they are familiar with the pronunciation and meaning of each word. Before they begin page 46, talk about dog training.

VISUAL LEARNERS

PARTNER **Materials:** index cards

Have pairs play "*ie* concentration." On four index cards each, they write *long e* and *long i*. On four each they write words in which *ie* stands for long *e* and in which *ie* stands for long *i*. With the cards mixed up and face down, they try to match a word card with its digraph.

KINESTHETIC LEARNERS

LARGE GROUP **Materials:** markers or colored chalk

Have students write the following words on paper or on the board, using different colored markers or chalk for the vowel digraph *ie*. Say *chief, lied, field, believe, tried, untie, relief, shield,* and *cried.*

> Complete each sentence with a word from the word bank.

achieve believed brief disbelief field
niece grief lie pieces relief pies
satisfied shrieked thief tried untie

1. The pet club held its _____ brief _____ weekly meeting after school.

2. Jason announced that his dog, Trooper, was misbehaving and giving him _____ grief _____.

3. Jason explained that Trooper was a _____ thief _____ because he stole dog treats from a kitchen cabinet.

4. He added, "Trooper always tried to _____ untie _____ my shoelaces, too!"

5. "He runs away from me when we walk across the grassy _____ field _____."

6. "I can't even get him to _____ lie _____ down."

7. Jason's mother wasn't happy with Trooper because he ate one of her prize _____ pies _____.

8. The club members _____ shrieked _____ with laughter as they imagined Trooper in action.

9. Mr. Andrews, the club sponsor, shook his head in _____ disbelief _____.

10. "How might Jason _____ achieve _____ success in dealing with his dog?" asked Mr. Andrews.

11. Then everybody _____ tried _____ to offer solutions to Jason's problem.

12. Mr. Andrews's _____ niece _____, Elinor, thought Trooper needed more exercise.

13. Annie said she _____ believed _____ that the dog was seeking attention.

14. Steven suggested that Jason give Trooper small _____ pieces _____ of treats whenever the dog was good.

15. Jason was _____ satisfied _____ that he had some ideas to try.

16. With a sigh of _____ relief _____, Jason thanked the club members for their help.

What advice would you give Jason in dealing with his dog?

DOG TREATS

Critical Thinking

(46) Lesson 20
Vowel digraph ie

AUDITORY LEARNERS

PARTNER Have each student write sentences that contain words with the letters *ie* standing for the long *e* and long *i* sounds, then read their sentences to a partner, leaving out the word with *ie*. The listening partner names the missing word and uses it in another sentence.

GIFTED LEARNERS

Challenge students to write sentences using as many words with the vowel digraph *ie* as possible. An example is *The thief shrieked in disbelief when the chief untied the briefcase lying in the field.*

LEARNERS WHO NEED EXTRA SUPPORT

Materials: word cards with *ie* words

Have students work with a partner to sort the word cards according to the long *e* or long *i* vowel sound. **See Daily Word Study Practice, page 184.**

CURRICULUM CONNECTIONS

SPELLING

Write these word parts on the board for *break, leaf, vein, August, scrawl, yield, tie, flood, built, fruit* and have students write the missing letters: br_ _k, l_ _f, v_ _n, _ _gust, scr_ _l, y_ _ld, t_ _, fl_ _d, b_ _lt, fr_ _t.

WRITING

Portfolio Challenge students to write a detective story about a police chief looking for a thief. Encourage them to use *ie* words to describe the crime.

SOCIAL STUDIES

Explain that knights in the Middle Ages carried shields decorated with coats of arms. The coat of arms contained symbols that represented the knight's family, home, occupation, and brave deeds. Suggest that students design shields with their own coats of arms. Display the shields and encourage students to explain the symbols used.

SCIENCE

Challenge students to find out how domesticated dogs can be more than pets to their human owners. They might find out about these working dogs: sheepherders, guide dogs, dogs trained to help deaf and physically disabled people, mountain rescue dogs, and drug-sniffing dogs. Ask students to find out how these hard workers are trained for their jobs.

Vowel Digraph oo

INFORMAL ASSESSMENT OBJECTIVES

Can students

✔ recognize that the vowel digraph *oo* can stand for the vowel sounds in *moon, look,* and *flood*?

✔ identify and write words with the vowel digraph *oo*?

Lesson Focus

INTRODUCING THE SKILL

- On the board write *moon, look,* and *flood*. Underline the letters *oo* in each word and say that *oo* is a vowel digraph.

- Read each word. Help students conclude that the digraph *oo* can stand for different sounds—/oo/, /o͞o/, /u/.

- Say several *oo* words, such as *spoon, shook, blood, stoop, wood, scoop, boot, foot,* and *rooster*. Call on volunteers to repeat each word and indicate the word on the board in which the vowel sound is the same.

USING THE PAGES

- Be sure students understand how to complete pages 47 and 48.

- **Critical Thinking** Read aloud the question on page 48 and discuss answers with students.

Name _____

▶ Write the correct name for each picture. Then circle the letters that stand for the vowel sound that you hear in that name.

> **RULE** The vowel digraph **oo** stands for the vowel sound you hear in **moon** and **cook**.

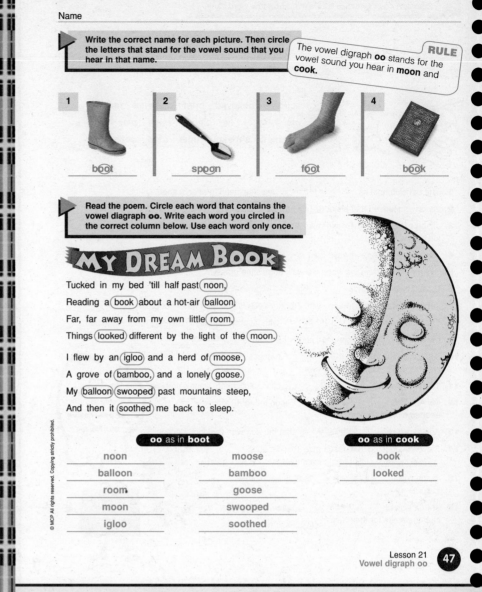

1. boot
2. spoon
3. foot
4. book

▶ Read the poem. Circle each word that contains the vowel diagraph **oo**. Write each word you circled in the correct column below. Use each word only once.

MY DREAM BOOK

Tucked in my bed 'till half past (noon,)
Reading a (book) about a hot-air (balloon,)
Far, far away from my own little (room,)
Things (looked) different by the light of the (moon.)

I flew by an (igloo) and a herd of (moose,)
A grove of (bamboo,) and a lonely (goose.)
My (balloon) (swooped) past mountains steep,
And then it (soothed) me back to sleep.

oo as in **boot**		oo as in **cook**
noon	moose	book
balloon	bamboo	looked
room	goose	
moon	swooped	
igloo	soothed	

FOCUS ON ALL LEARNERS

ENGLISH LANGUAGE LEARNERS/ESL

PARTNER

Materials: index cards

Encourage students to make word and picture cards for words containing the vowel digraph *oo*. Have students write the word on one card and draw a picture of that object on another card. Pairs of students can match pictures with words.

VISUAL LEARNERS

Display the following hink-pink: *A person who steals something to read is a* <u>book crook</u>. Challenge students to work independently to write other hink-pinks using rhyming words with the vowel digraph *oo*.

KINESTHETIC LEARNERS

LARGE GROUP

Divide the class into two teams to play "word race" and call one student from each team to the board. Read a word with the vowel digraph *oo* aloud and have students correctly use each word in a sentence and then write the word on the chalkboard in the correct column—*oo* as in *boot*; *oo* as in *cook*; or *oo* as in *flood*.

▶ Circle the word that completes each sentence. Write it on the line.

RULE
The vowel digraph **oo** can stand for three different vowel sounds, as in the words **moon**, **cook**, and **flood**.

1. We are planning our special __classroom__ picnic.

(classroom)   foolish   driftwood

2. Tony, our class president, writes our plans in his __notebook__ .

checkbook   (notebook)   woodwork

3. Ms. O'Rourke announces a __foolproof__ plan for the picnic's success.

flood   (foolproof)   bookcase

4. She assigns each __schoolchild__ a special responsibility.

(schoolchild)   footprint   bloodhound

5. Someone has to bring the forks and __spoons__ .

books   (spoons)   pools

6. Everyone will bring some __food__ .

stood   fool   (food)

7. The class decides to have the picnic near the __brook__ .

book   boot   (brook)

8. It is located in a beautiful __wooded__ area near the school.

(wooded)   barefoot   cooked

9. "All the shady trees will keep us __cool__ ," says Tony.

good   pool   (cool)

10. It will be easy for our class to __troop__ to the picnic area.

(troop)   hoop   smooth

Do you agree that Ms. O'Rourke's plan is foolproof? Support your answer.

Critical Thinking

48   Lesson 21
Vowel digraph oo

SPELLING

Write these words on the chalkboard and ask students to choose one word to finish each sentence.

flood   leaf   fruit   built   break

1. That _____ came from the tree. *(leaf)*
2. Pineapple is my favorite _____. *(fruit)*
3. Don't _____ my favorite glass! *(break)*
4. We _____ a tree house in our yard. *(built)*
5. If it keeps raining, we will have a _____. *(flood)*

Invite student teams to create similar sentences using the spelling words *yield, scrawl, vein, tie,* and *August.*

WRITING

Portfolio   Invite students to write an advertisement about a book they loved to read because it carried them to a faraway place.

MATH

Encourage students to research hot-air balloons, answering questions such as these. *When was the first hot-air balloon launched? How far did it go? What records have been set?* Then have groups of students compile their information on charts that compare the statistics of early balloon trips to modern-day balloon trips.

LANGUAGE ARTS/ART

Invite students to create a class book of hink-pinks by writing and illustrating on separate sheets of paper the ones created in the Visual Learners activity. Encourage students to write and illustrate new hink-pinks for other sounds.

AUDITORY LEARNERS

LARGE GROUP   Invite the class to play "context clues." Write the words *notebooks, footprints, flood, woolen, booth,* and *driftwood* on the board. Then read aloud sentences such as *I put on a* (woolen) *hat to keep me warm,* leaving out the word in parentheses. Have students complete each sentence with a word from the board.

GIFTED LEARNERS

Challenge students to create an itinerary of places they would like to visit in a magical hot-air balloon. Students can draw a map for a magical journey they would like to take.

LEARNERS WHO NEED EXTRA SUPPORT

Help students make a chart with three columns for *oo* as in *boot; oo* as in *cook;* or *oo* as in *flood.* Then have pairs of students choose ten *oo* words and place the words in the correct columns on the chart. **See Daily Word Study Practice, page 184.**

Lesson 22

Pages 49–50

Vowel Digraph ui

✳ ∙ ● ∙ ◆ ∙ ■ ∙ ● ∙ ✳ ∙ ● ∙ ◆ ∙ ■ ∙ ●

INFORMAL ASSESSMENT OBJECTIVE

Can students

✔ recognize that the vowel digraph *ui* can stand for the vowel sound in *built* and for the vowel sound in *fruit*?

Lesson Focus

INTRODUCING THE SKILL

- Write the following sentence on the board: *Steve had a juicy steak, some bruised fruit, and a biscuit for lunch.* Ask students to read the sentence aloud and to identify the words that contain the vowel digraph *ui*.

- Call on a volunteer to circle the *ui*'s and say the words aloud. Help students conclude that the digraph *ui* can stand for the sound of long *u*, as in *raccoon*, or for the sound of short *i*, as in *twig*.

- Challenge the class to think of another sentence that contains words with the vowel digraph *ui*.

USING THE PAGES

- Help students complete pages 49 and 50 if they need assistance. Then go over the lesson together and encourage students to ask questions.

- **Critical Thinking** Read aloud the question on page 50 and discuss answers with students.

49

Name _____

Write **i** beside each word that has the same vowel sound you hear in **built**. Write **oo** beside each word that has the same vowel sound you hear in **fruit**.

> **RULE**
> The vowel digraph **ui** can stand for the vowel sound you hear in **fruit** or the vowel sound you hear in **built**.

1. _oo_ cruise
2. _i_ build
3. _i_ guilty
4. _i_ guitar
5. _oo_ suit
6. _oo_ juice
7. _i_ building
8. _oo_ bruise
9. _oo_ pursuit
10. _oo_ recruit
11. _oo_ nuisance
12. _i_ biscuits

Complete each sentence with a word from the word bank.

13. The museum has _____built_____ a special room for exhibiting folk art.

14. There is an elaborately carved _____guitar_____ there, along with several other musical instruments.

15. On the wall there is an unusual painting of a man wearing a two-piece purple _____suit_____.

16. One exhibit features carved wooden _____fruits_____, such as apples and bananas.

17. The museum is hoping to _____recruit_____ volunteers to conduct tours.

18. I wish that I had some paintings that were _____suitable_____ to exhibit.

19. Someday there will be a separate _____building_____ just for folk art.

| suitable |
| recruit |
| built |
| suit |
| fruits |
| building |
| guitar |

Lesson 22
Vowel digraph ui **49**

FOCUS ON ALL LEARNERS ✳ ∙ ● ∙ ◆ ∙ ■ ∙ ◆

ENGLISH LANGUAGE LEARNERS/ESL

Help students hear the difference in the vowel sounds of *fruit* and *built*. Provide cards with *fruit* and *built* for them to refer to as they work. Complete several items at the top of page 49 together before having them complete the page on their own.

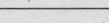

VISUAL LEARNERS

PARTNER Begin a list of *ui* words on the board with *build, cruise, nuisance,* and *suit* and have students brainstorm additional words. When at least 12 words have been listed, have students work in pairs to sort the words by *i* or *oo* vowel sound.

KINESTHETIC/AUDITORY LEARNERS

LARGE GROUP Write the words *built* and *fruit* on separate sheets of paper and tape each sheet in a different corner of the classroom. Then read aloud words with the vowel digraph *ui*. Encourage students to go to the corner whose word contains the same sound as the word you say.

> **Fill in the circle next to the word that completes each sentence. Write it on the line.**

1. My parents went on a ___cruise___ to St. Thomas.
   ○ bruise ● cruise ○ quilt

2. They stayed in a hotel that had been ___built___ a century ago.
   ○ cruised ● built ○ recruited

3. Their room in that ___building___ was simple but very comfortable.
   ● building ○ pursuing ○ cruising

4. During the day their favorite ___pursuit___ was taking long walks.
   ● pursuit ○ recruit ○ cruise

5. The hot Caribbean weather was ___suitable___ for outdoor activities.
   ● suitable ○ built ○ cruising

6. They walked the crowded streets, often buying ___fruits___ from sidewalk vendors.
   ○ quilts ● fruits ○ cruising

7. My mother said the oranges were always ___juicy___ and sweet.
   ● juicy ○ guilty ○ recruited

8. She never saw a ___bruise___ on a banana!
   ● bruise ○ cruise ○ pursuit

9. They liked to stop at an outdoor restaurant that served wonderful ___biscuits___ .
   ○ suits ● biscuits ○ quilts

10. My father enjoyed watching street musicians playing ___guitars___ and steel drums.
    ● guitars ○ suits ○ cruises

11. They said they felt ___guilty___ having so much fun without me.
    ○ rebuilt ○ bruised ● guilty

12. I hope I don't make a ___nuisance___ of myself by asking so many questions about their trip!
    ○ recruit ● nuisance ○ bruise

> **What questions would you ask about this trip?**

Critical Thinking

50 Lesson 22
Vowel digraph ui

Lesson 23

Pages 51–52

 **R**eading  **W**riting

Reviewing Vowel Pairs ai, ay and ei, ee; Vowel Digraphs ea, ey, ei, ie, au, aw, oo, ui

* ◆ • ● ■ ◆ • ● ✦ ◆ • ✦ ◆ ■ ◆ • ●

INFORMAL ASSESSMENT OBJECTIVES

Can students

✔ read an article containing words with vowel pairs *ai, ay, ei,* and *ee* and vowel digraphs *ea, ey, ei, ie, au, aw, oo, ui*?

✔ write a description using such words?

Lesson Focus

READING

- On the board, write the words *break, head, meat, eight, they, rain, clay, field, pie, cause, awful, sleep, ceiling, build, soon, flood, fruit, boots, hook, guitar, juice, wood,* and *balloon.*

- Call on a volunteer to give an oral hint for one of the words, such as *This word refers to something you drink. (juice)* Invite students to guess the word.

- Challenge the student who guesses the word first to come to the board, identify the vowel pair or vowel digraph and its sound, and then give a hint for another word.

WRITING

Explain to students that on page 52 they will design a flag for their school and will write a description of their flag. Students can use information they know about flags as well as information they learned from reading page 51.

 Reading ▶ **Read the following article. Then answer the question at the end of the story.**

FLYING SYMBOLS

Since ancient times flags have been used to identify tribes, armies, and nations. The first flags might have been cloth streamers tied to poles with carved symbols on top. Eventually the cloth became more rectangular and the symbols were sewn with needle and thread or painted on the cloth.

Flags have flown from chariots, elephants, horses, ships, and military vehicles. Signals of distress or surrender in battle, an upcoming storm, or a special ceremony can also be communicated with flags. For example, the British navy invented a series of code flags in the 1700s and 1800s. By 1889 there was a separate flag for each letter and number. With these flags, complicated messages are still passed from ship to ship today.

National flags frequently include symbols to express important ideas. The flag of Canada, for example, has a maple leaf to represent the red maple trees in that country. The flag of the United States of America has stars to represent the 50 states. The shape of many modern flags is rectangular, but there are exceptions to this rule. The Swiss flag is square, the flag of Quatar is a thin banner, and the flag of Nepal is a pennant shape. Whatever the design, citizens of a country are very loyal to their flag.

What symbol would you choose to decorate your own personal flag? What does it mean to you?

_____
_____
_____
_____
_____

FOCUS ON ALL LEARNERS ✦ ● ◆ ■ ◆

ENGLISH LANGUAGE LEARNERS/ESL

Materials: index cards

Encourage students to make word and picture cards for words containing vowel pairs *ai, ay, ei,* and *ee* and vowel digraphs *ea, ey, ei, ie, au, aw, oo,* and *ui.* Have students write the word on one card and draw a picture of that object on another card. Pairs of students can match pictures with words.

VISUAL LEARNERS

SMALL GROUP

Groups of students can brainstorm lists of words for each sound of the digraphs *ea, ey, ei, ie, au, aw, oo,* and *ui.* Challenge each group to create sentences using two or more words from each list.

KINESTHETIC LEARNERS

LARGE GROUP

Draw a baseball diamond on the board and write a vowel pair or digraph in the middle. A player writes a word with that vowel pair or digraph. If that word is spelled correctly, the next player comes to bat. Repeat the game with different pairs and digraphs.

Writing

Your class needs to design a flag to be flown at an all-school field day. Use the following helpful hints and words from the word bank to write a description of your flag.

Think about:
- shape
- colors
- material
- symbols

plain	crayon	green
either	coat	rainbow
thread	team	great
draw	eight	shield

Helpful Hints

CURRICULUM CONNECTIONS

SPELLING

The following sentences can be used as a posttest for spelling words with vowel digraphs *ea, ei, ey, ie, au, aw, oo, ui.*

1. **break**   I hope the chair doesn't **break.**
2. **leaf**   Look at the falling **leaf.**
3. **vein**   A **vein** in a leaf carries food.
4. **August**   We go on vacation in **August.**
5. **scrawl**   Don't **scrawl** your name carelessly.
6. **yield**   The trees **yield** large apples.
7. **tie**   Let's **tie** the boat to the dock.
8. **flood**   I hope the river doesn't **flood.**
9. **built**   She **built** a house for her dog.
10. **fruit**   Most **fruit** taste great!

SOCIAL STUDIES

Encourage students to research flags from different countries and give an oral presentation about the history of one country's flag.

MUSIC/FINE ARTS

Invite students to draw and cut out large paper flags from different countries and then display their flags in a "parade of flags," complete with marching music.

AUDITORY LEARNERS

SMALL GROUP Challenge groups of students to choose a category such as sports or animals, write the category at the top of a sheet of paper, and list the letters *ai, ay, ei, ee, ea, ey, ei, ie, au, aw, oo,* and *ui* down the left side. For each pair of letters, challenge students to think of at least one word that fits the category.

GIFTED LEARNERS

Challenge pairs of students to create a series of code flags and to present them to their classmates in a dramatization. Encourage the rest of the class to try to figure out the meanings of the code flags.

LEARNERS WHO NEED EXTRA SUPPORT

Write the following on the board: *holiday, raisin, treasure, break, fried, sleepy, build, soon, ceiling.* Ask volunteers to read each word aloud, circle the vowel pair or digraph, and name the sound the digraph stands for. Challenge students to use the words in oral sentences. **See Daily Word Study Practice, pages 183–184.**

Lesson 24

Pages 53–54

Diphthongs *oi, oy*

INFORMAL ASSESSMENT OBJECTIVE

Can students

✓ recognize that the diphthongs *oi* and *oy* stand for the sound of *oy* in *boy*?

Lesson Focus

INTRODUCING THE SKILL

- Write *boy* and *boil* on the board and point to each word as you read it. Help students hear how the letters *o* and *y* in *boy* blend together to produce one vowel sound. Tell students that this blended sound is called a diphthong.

- Point to *boil* and ask a volunteer to pronounce it. Help students identify the *oi* as a diphthong.

- Now write *enjoy, foil, soybean, moist,* and *employ* on the board. Have students read the words and identify the diphthongs.

USING THE PAGES

Be sure students understand how to complete pages 53 and 54. Point out that at the top of page 54, there are two steps: identifying the meaning of each word and circling the diphthong. To complete the bottom of page 54, students should use those same words. When students have completed the pages, encourage them to review what they know about the diphthongs *oi* and *oy*.

Name _____

▶ Complete each sentence with a word from the word bank.

> **RULE**
> A **diphthong** is two letters blended together as one vowel sound. The diphthongs **oi** and **oy** stand for the same vowel sound.
>
> **oil**   **toy**

1. Beth said she would ___enjoy___ helping with the gardening.

2. Wearing ___corduroy___ overalls, she walked out to the yard.

3. Beth knelt down to touch the ___soil___.

4. It was still ___moist___ from last night's rain.

5. She noticed that bugs had nearly ___destroyed___ some flowers.

6. When she saw a large, squirming insect, Beth ___recoiled___ in disgust.

7. Then she moved her hand swiftly to catch the ___annoying___ creature.

8. Beth enjoyed her work and was ___disappointed___ when it began to rain.

Word Bank:
annoying
corduroy
destroyed
disappointed
enjoy
moist
recoiled
soil

▶ In the puzzle, circle 12 words containing the diphthongs **oi** and **oy.** Then write the words on the lines below.

boy	oil
soil	joy
toy	join
point	moist
spoil	Roy
noise	royal

```
B  M  I  O  S  T  O  Y
B  O  L  T  P  O  I  N  T
O  Y  T  A  M  I  Y  M  S
A  E  N  B  L  U  R  E  P
L  N  O  I  L  J  E  D  O
A  J  I  L  M  O  O  D  I
W  O  S  E  R  O  Y  A  L
R  I  N  E  O  I  A  N  E
A  Z  N  A  Y  S  D  T  Z  A
Z  E  N  O  T  S  M  A
```

FOCUS ON ALL LEARNERS

ENGLISH LANGUAGE LEARNERS/ESL

Pair fluent English speakers with second-language learners to work together to review the words found in the puzzle on page 53. Encourage students to use each of the 12 words in oral sentences before actually completing the puzzle.

VISUAL LEARNERS

INDIVIDUAL   Suggest students make word-scramble puzzles. After listing five or more words that contain the diphthongs *oi* or *oy*, on the back of the paper, they can rewrite each word in scrambled form (oby for boy). Students can trade papers for unscrambling.

KINESTHETIC/VISUAL LEARNERS

PARTNER

Materials: index cards

Have pairs make letter cards and take turns arranging them to spell words with the *oi* and *oy* diphthongs. One partner suggests a word that the other constructs.

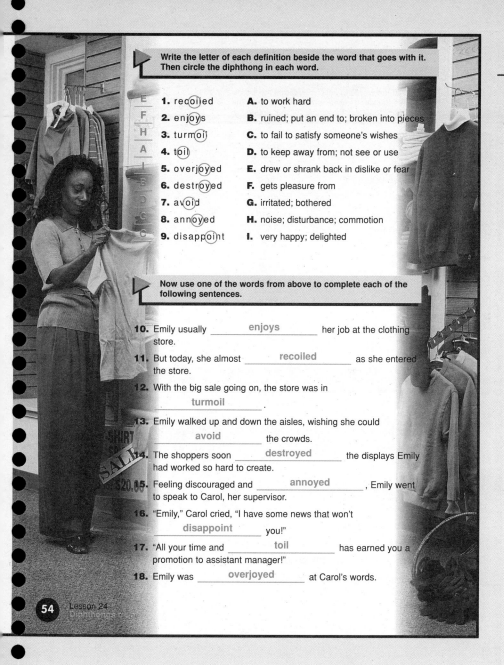

Write the letter of each definition beside the word that goes with it. Then circle the diphthong in each word.

1. recoiled   **A.** to work hard
2. enjoys   **B.** ruined; put an end to; broken into pieces
3. turmoil   **C.** to fail to satisfy someone's wishes
4. toil   **D.** to keep away from; not see or use
5. overjoyed   **E.** drew or shrank back in dislike or fear
6. destroyed   **F.** gets pleasure from
7. avoid   **G.** irritated; bothered
8. annoyed   **H.** noise; disturbance; commotion
9. disappoint   **I.** very happy; delighted

Now use one of the words from above to complete each of the following sentences.

10. Emily usually ___enjoys___ her job at the clothing store.
11. But today, she almost ___recoiled___ as she entered the store.
12. With the big sale going on, the store was in ___turmoil___.
13. Emily walked up and down the aisles, wishing she could ___avoid___ the crowds.
14. The shoppers soon ___destroyed___ the displays Emily had worked so hard to create.
15. Feeling discouraged and ___annoyed___, Emily went to speak to Carol, her supervisor.
16. "Emily," Carol cried, "I have some news that won't ___disappoint___ you!"
17. "All your time and ___toil___ has earned you a promotion to assistant manager!"
18. Emily was ___overjoyed___ at Carol's words.

54   Lesson 24

SPELLING

The following sentences can be used as a pretest for spelling words with diphthongs *oi, oy, ou, ow, ew*..

1. **corduroy**   These pants are **corduroy**.
2. **moist**   The skin lotion feels **moist**.
3. **loud**   That music is **loud**.
4. **down**   My cat is **down** in the basement.
5. **sour**   The milk is **sour**.
6. **strewn**   The papers are **strewn** all over.

WRITING

Portfolio Have students write what being overjoyed means to them. Their narrative can be realistic or imaginative; it can describe when they felt overjoyed or when they did something that gave someone else joy, like helping someone who felt disappointed or annoyed. Have them identify the words with an *oi* or *oy* diphthong.

SCIENCE

Suggest students use library books to learn more about poisonous plants and animals. Have each student choose one and create a "beware" poster explaining how it is dangerous. Display the posters and have students tell what they learned.

MATH

Invite students to explore probability by tossing diphthong coins. Ask them to mark the sides of two quarters *oi* and *oy*, then toss the coins 50 times and record the results. Encourage students to chart the results on a table. Then ask students to think of words for each diphthong. They can try to match the number of words with the numbers recorded in the table.

AUDITORY LEARNERS

LARGE GROUP Read these clues to help students identify the words *oyster, decoy, moist, poison, voyage, noise*: 1. *It could kill a person; 2. slightly wet; 3. a long trip; 4. an animal that forms pearls; 5. a loud sound; 6. an artificial bird used to attract other birds.*

GIFTED LEARNERS

Challenge students to create a crossword puzzle using as many words as possible that contain the diphthongs *oi* and *oy*.

LEARNERS WHO NEED EXTRA SUPPORT

Materials: colored chalk

Write *enjoy, annoy, oil, soil, join, royal,* and *moist* on the board. Have students read each word aloud, then rewrite it, using colored chalk to write the diphthongs. **See Daily Word Study Practice, pages 184–185.**

Lesson 25
Pages 55–56

Diphthongs ou, ow

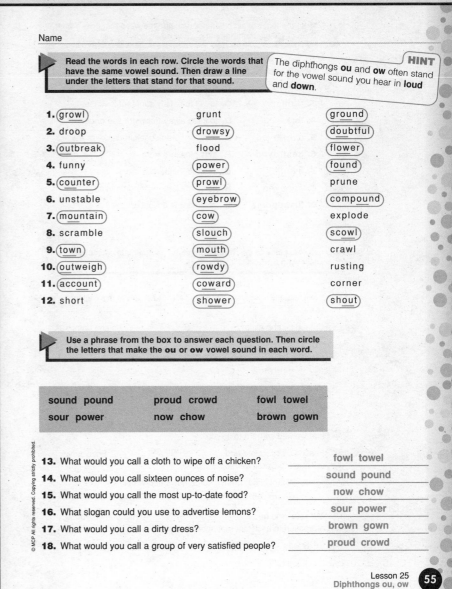

INFORMAL ASSESSMENT OBJECTIVE

Can students

✔ recognize that the diphthongs *ou* and *ow* stand for the sound of *ow* in *down*?

Lesson Focus

INTRODUCING THE SKILL

- Write the words *cowboy, pound, rowdy,* and *trout* on the board. Call on a volunteer to read the words aloud, then challenge the class to make up a sentence that contains all four words.

- Ask a volunteer to write the sentence on the board. Have the class recall what a diphthong is, then have the volunteer point to all the words in the sentence that contain the *ou* or *ow* diphthong. Ask what sound *ou* and *ow* stand for in the words.

- Help students conclude that *ou* and *ow* contain the same vowel sound heard in *loud* and *down*.

- Encourage students to name other words with *ou* and *ow*. Write their words on the board.

USING THE PAGES

- Help students if they need it as they complete pages 55 and 56. Then have partners correct their pages together by comparing their work.

- **Critical Thinking** Read aloud the question on page 56 and discuss answers with students.

Name

▶ Read the words in each row. Circle the words that have the same vowel sound. Then draw a line under the letters that stand for that sound.

> **HINT**
> The diphthongs **ou** and **ow** often stand for the vowel sound you hear in **loud** and **down**.

1. (growl)	grunt	(ground)
2. droop	(drowsy)	(doubtful)
3. (outbreak)	flood	(flower)
4. funny	(power)	(found)
5. (counter)	(prowl)	prune
6. unstable	(eyebrow)	(compound)
7. (mountain)	(cow)	explode
8. scramble	(slouch)	(scowl)
9. (town)	(mouth)	crawl
10. (outweigh)	(rowdy)	rusting
11. (account)	(coward)	corner
12. short	(shower)	(shout)

▶ Use a phrase from the box to answer each question. Then circle the letters that make the **ou** or **ow** vowel sound in each word.

sound pound	proud crowd	fowl towel
sour power	now chow	brown gown

13. What would you call a cloth to wipe off a chicken? — fowl towel

14. What would you call sixteen ounces of noise? — sound pound

15. What would you call the most up-to-date food? — now chow

16. What slogan could you use to advertise lemons? — sour power

17. What would you call a dirty dress? — brown gown

18. What would you call a group of very satisfied people? — proud crowd

Lesson 25
Diphthongs ou, ow **55**

FOCUS ON ALL LEARNERS

ENGLISH LANGUAGE LEARNERS/ESL

Work with students to begin the top section of page 55. Read the choices for the first two numbered items so students can hear the sounds before answering. Let students read aloud subsequent items until they feel comfortable continuing on their own.

VISUAL LEARNERS

LARGE GROUP

Ask a volunteer to write the alphabet on the board. One student points to a letter and challenges another to name a word that begins with the letter and contains the diphthong *ou* or *ow*. If the student can't within 30 seconds, the first student must name the word.

KINESTHETIC LEARNERS

LARGE GROUP

Play Simon says. Give students a command to carry out only if it contains a word with the diphthong *ou* or *ow*. Try *make a scowl, howl with laughter, touch your nose, smile, grin with your mouth, look thoughtful, crowd together, sit with a slouch,* and *don't act rowdy.*

Circle the word that completes each sentence. Write it on the line.

1. The weather was dreary, and it rained __throughout__ the day.
   - about
   - (throughout)
   - around

2. Dennis and Aimee felt tired and __drowsy__ .
   - (drowsy)
   - soundly
   - rowdy

3. In poor spirits, they __slouched__ wearily on the sofa.
   - pouched
   - couched
   - (slouched)

4. "What can we do to perk up?" Dennis wondered __aloud__ .
   - (aloud)
   - about
   - allow

5. "Let's dress as __clowns__ and have a circus!" said Aimee.
   - clouds
   - (clowns)
   - cowards

6. Dennis __howled__ with laughter at the idea.
   - (howled)
   - glowered
   - growled

7. "I can wear my trick __flower__ that sprays water," he said.
   - powder
   - power
   - (flower)

8. "There's that big __brown__ tie I can wear, too!"
   - gown
   - (brown)
   - hound

9. "And I'll wear that funny green wig you __found__ ," said Aimee.
   - round
   - (found)
   - sound

10. She added, "We can paint wide smiles around our __mouths__ ."
    - (mouths)
    - prows
    - shouts

Critical Thinking

Which child will be a funnier clown? Why?

56 Lesson 25
Diphthongs ou, ow

SPELLING

Write the dipthongs *oi, oy, ou, ow, ew* on the chalkboard. Then say the spelling words *corduroy, moist,* and *loud,* one at a time. Call on volunteers to point to the diphthong they hear and write the word on the board. Continue with the remaining spelling words *down, sour,* and *strewn.* Then invite volunteers to write other words that contain the same diphthongs and use each word in a sentence.

WRITING

Portfolio Challenge pairs of students to write "clowning around" stories with as many *ou* and *ow* words as possible. Suggest they brainstorm a list of words before they begin. Encourage students to share their stories with their classmates.

MATH

Explain to students that numeration systems give people ways to count and name numbers. Challenge them to find out more about the systems people have used for counting through the ages. Have students work in small groups to prepare short oral reports on different systems used for counting.

FINE ARTS

Portfolio Invite students to make up and illustrate phrases that include both diphthongs *ou* and *ow,* such as *a pound of howling trout* or *clowns with big mouths.* Encourage students to be outrageous in their creations. Provide chart paper for their illustrations and display them on a diphthong word wall.

AUDITORY LEARNERS

LARGE GROUP Write *found, flowers, growl, shout,* and *sour* on the board. Read these sentences for students to complete: *I ___ my missing hat. A bouquet of ___ is a great present. I like the ___ taste of lemons. The crowd gave a victory ___. The dog has a ferocious ___!*

GIFTED LEARNERS

Challenge students to create a handbook for dreary weather, listing things to do during a day when they're stuck indoors. Each item must contain at least one word with the diphthongs *ou* or *ow.*

LEARNERS WHO NEED EXTRA SUPPORT

Help students make a chart with two columns—one for *ou* as in *loud* and one for *ow* as in *down.* Then have them choose ten words from the answer words at the top of page 55 and place the words in the correct columns on the chart. **See Daily Word Study Practice, pages 184–185.**

56

Lesson 26
Pages 57–58

Diphthong ew and Syllables

✱ ⬦ ・ ◆ ■ ◆ ● ✱ ⬦ ・ ◆ ■ ◆ ●

INFORMAL ASSESSMENT OBJECTIVES

Can students

✔ recognize that the diphthong *ew* stands for the vowel sound in *new*?

✔ determine the number of syllables in a word?

Lesson Focus

INTRODUCING THE SKILLS

- Write *new* on the board and say it, emphasizing the *ew* sound. Ask students what two letters stand for the vowel sound they hear in *new*. (ew)

- Have students generate additional words that contain the diphthong *ew*. Call on volunteers to write the words on the board and to say them aloud.

- Help students recall that the number of syllables in a word is determined by the number of vowel sounds. Say *mildew, new, autumn, newspaper*, and *foundation* and ask the class for the number of syllables in each word.

USING THE PAGES

- Be sure students understand how to complete page 58. You might want to work several items together as a group.

- **Critical Thinking** Read aloud the question on page 57 and discuss answers with students.

Name _____

 Complete each sentence with a word from the word bank.

RULE The diphthong **ew** stands for the vowel sound you hear in **new**. This is nearly the same vowel sound you hear in **spool**.

anew	crew	outgrew	drew	shrewd
few	jewelry	pewter	jewels	strewn
knew	nephew	renew	newspapers	

1. Ron Richter owns a _____**jewelry**_____ shop.
2. He is known in town as a _____**shrewd**_____ businessperson.
3. His _____**nephew**_____, Calvin, works in the store each weekend.
4. Ron also employs a _____**few**_____ other workers.
5. Ron takes great pride in this dedicated _____**crew**_____ of workers.
6. The shop is filled with gold, silver, and _____**pewter**_____ objects.
7. In the front windows, gems and _____**jewels**_____ sparkle and shine.
8. Every week the glass cases are filled _____**anew**_____ with gleaming watches, bracelets, and rings.
9. Each Sunday, Ron advertises a sale in all the _____**newspapers**_____.
10. Last Sunday's advertisement _____**drew**_____ large crowds to the shop.
11. Ron _____**knew**_____ that his business would do well that day.
12. He was so busy that empty boxes were _____**strewn**_____ around his office at the end of the day.
13. If business continues to boom, Ron might not _____**renew**_____ the lease on his shop.
14. His business already _____**outgrew**_____ one shop, and he might move again to an even bigger shop.

Why might Ron move his jewelry store to another location?

 Critical Thinking

Lesson 26
Diphthong ew **57**

FOCUS ON ALL LEARNERS ✱ ・ ◆ ・ ■ ◆

ENGLISH LANGUAGE LEARNERS/ESL

Pair fluent English speakers with second-language learners to work together to complete page 58. Suggest they say each word aloud quietly and slowly so that each syllable is distinct.

VISUAL/AUDITORY LEARNERS

 **LARGE GROUP**

Change *ew* words. Say *Start with* dew *and change the first letter to make a word that means "not many."* Add the suffix *-er. Change the first and last letters to make a gem. Add -ry to the end. Erase the first letter and the last three letters. What is left?* (ewe)

KINESTHETIC/VISUAL LEARNERS

INDIVIDUAL

Have students look through reading materials in the classroom to collect multisyllabic words and write sentences on the board using them; for example, *I appreciated the mysterious disappearance of my ignominious homework assignment.*

> Say each word. Write the number of vowels you see and the number of vowel sounds you hear.

	Vowels Seen	Vowel Sounds Heard			Vowels Seen	Vowel Sounds Heard
1. remainder	4	3		24. exhaust	3	2
2. proceed	3	2		25. lawbreaker	4	3
3. mountain	4	2		26. obey	3	2
4. loafer	3	2		27. convey	3	2
5. woeful	3	2		28. loaded	3	2
6. abstain	3	2		29. lawnmower	3	3
7. retreat	3	2		30. greedily	4	3
8. vein	2	1		31. receipt	3	2
9. daybreak	4	2		32. authentic	4	3
10. laundry	3	2		33. roommate	4	2
11. sprawl	1	1		34. proof	2	1
12. occupied	4	3		35. bounty	3	2
13. toadstool	4	2		36. groan	2	1
14. countless	3	2		37. misunderstood	5	4
15. likelihood	5	3		38. woodpile	4	2
16. fried	2	1		39. flaunt	2	1
17. loosen	3	2		40. building	3	2
18. spoon	2	1		41. wheelbarrow	4	3
19. relieved	4	2		42. guilty	3	2
20. yield	2	1		43. suited	3	2
21. applied	3	2		44. billow	2	2
22. outgrow	3	2		45. noise	3	1
23. ounce	3	1		46. acquainted	5	3

58 Lesson 26
Syllables

SPELLING

Ask students to use the spelling words to give and spell aloud the opposite of each of the following:

1. dry *(moist)*
2. soft *(loud)*
3. up *(down)*
4. sweet *(sour)*
5. carefully placed *(strewn)*

WRITING

Portfolio Challenge students to write a haiku. Explain that this poetic form contains three lines, with a specific syllable count for each line. Here is an example.

Falling from the trees [5 syllables]

Floating on the gentle wind [7]

Colors in the grass [5]

Haiku express a mood by combining something physical, such as a sight or sound, with a feeling or season.

SCIENCE

Suggest students look through books about jewelry. Then challenge them to choose one kind of material, such as gold or silver, and research how it is transformed into jewelry. Encourage them to share their information with their classmates.

MUSIC

Invite students to write favorite song titles on the board and identify the vowel digraphs, diphthongs, or number of syllables in the words. Some students could look at vocal sheet music and note the connection between the notes in the melody and the syllables in the words.

Technology
AstroWord Multisyllabic Words .
©1998 Silver Burdett Ginn Inc.
Division of Simon & Schuster.

SMALL GROUP
AUDITORY LEARNERS

Invite pairs of students to take turns composing oral sentences that contain at least one word with the diphthong *ew*. Have the partner who is listening write the *ew* word, say it aloud, and circle the diphthong.

GIFTED LEARNERS

Suggest that students find out about the word history of *diphthong*. How does the meaning of its Greek roots relate to the use of the words in these phonics lessons? Encourage them to add words with the diphthong *ew* to their personal Word Bank.

LEARNERS WHO NEED EXTRA SUPPORT

Review with students the diphthongs in this lesson and in previous lessons. Encourage them to add troublesome words to a vocabulary notebook they may be keeping. **See Daily Word Study Practice, pages 184–185, 193.**

Lesson 27

Reading **Writing**

Reviewing Dipthongs *oi*, *oy*, *ou*, *ow*, *ew*

INFORMAL ASSESSMENT OBJECTIVES

Can students

✔ read a report containing words with diphthongs *oi*, *oy*, *ou*, *ow*, and *ew*?

✔ write a narrative using such words?

✔ determine the number of syllables in a word?

Lesson Focus

READING

- Write the words *oil, toy, loud, down,* and *new* at the top of the board. Have students circle the diphthong in each word and identify the sound.

- Then say the words *lawbreaker, misunderstood, vein, noise,* and *exhaust*. Ask volunteers to identify the number of syllables in each word.

- Tell students that as they read the report on page 59, they will come across words with the diphthongs *oi, oy, ou, ow,* and *ew* as well as words with different numbers of syllables.

WRITING

Students may use information they learned from reading page 59. As they write their descriptions, encourage them to use words in the word box.

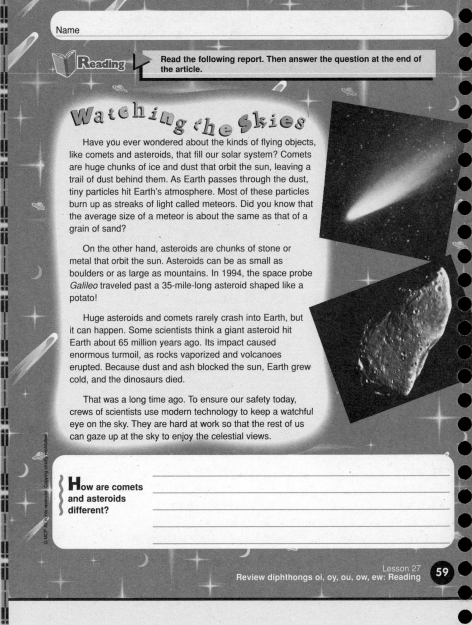

Name

Reading | Read the following report. Then answer the question at the end of the article.

Watching the Skies

Have you ever wondered about the kinds of flying objects, like comets and asteroids, that fill our solar system? Comets are huge chunks of ice and dust that orbit the sun, leaving a trail of dust behind them. As Earth passes through the dust, tiny particles hit Earth's atmosphere. Most of these particles burn up as streaks of light called meteors. Did you know that the average size of a meteor is about the same as that of a grain of sand?

On the other hand, asteroids are chunks of stone or metal that orbit the sun. Asteroids can be as small as boulders or as large as mountains. In 1994, the space probe *Galileo* traveled past a 35-mile-long asteroid shaped like a potato!

Huge asteroids and comets rarely crash into Earth, but it can happen. Some scientists think a giant asteroid hit Earth about 65 million years ago. Its impact caused enormous turmoil, as rocks vaporized and volcanoes erupted. Because dust and ash blocked the sun, Earth grew cold, and the dinosaurs died.

That was a long time ago. To ensure our safety today, crews of scientists use modern technology to keep a watchful eye on the sky. They are hard at work so that the rest of us can gaze up at the sky to enjoy the celestial views.

How are comets and asteroids different?

FOCUS ON ALL LEARNERS

ENGLISH LANGUAGE LEARNERS/ESL

Before beginning page 59, encourage a discussion about comets and asteroids. Then invite students to search the report and pick out all the words that contain the diphthongs *oi, oy, ou, ow,* and *ew*.

VISUAL LEARNERS

PARTNER

Materials: index cards, felt markers

Prepare double sets of word cards for the following words: *account, crew, jewels, voyage, mountains, join, enjoy, found, route, destroy*. Place the cards face down in a stack on a desk and have partners play a memory game by finding two matching words.

KINESTHETIC LEARNERS

LARGE GROUP

List the diphthongs *oi, oy, ou, ow,* and *ew* on the board and give each team of five students a sheet of paper. The first team member writes a word with the first diphthong and passes the paper to the second team member. The first team to correctly write five words, one for each diphthong, is the winner.

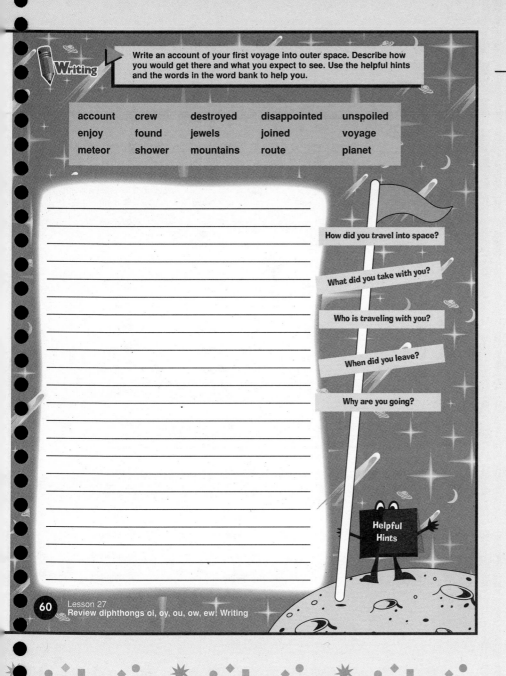

Writing

Write an account of your first voyage into outer space. Describe how you would get there and what you expect to see. Use the helpful hints and the words in the word bank to help you.

account	crew	destroyed	disappointed	unspoiled
enjoy	found	jewels	joined	voyage
meteor	shower	mountains	route	planet

How did you travel into space?

What did you take with you?

Who is traveling with you?

When did you leave?

Why are you going?

Helpful Hints

CURRICULUM CONNECTIONS

SPELLING

The following sentences can be used as a posttest for spelling words with diphthongs *oi, oy, ou, ow, ew.*.

1. **corduroy**   I have a **corduroy** shirt.
2. **moist**   The towel feels **moist.**
3. **loud**   What was that **loud** noise?
4. **down**   The party is **down** in the basement.
5. **sour**   Do you like really **sour** candy?
6. **strewn**   My socks are **strewn** all over the room.

SCIENCE

Challenge students to research a specific comet and present an oral report complete with accompanying illustrations about that comet.

FINE ARTS

Invite students to create a collage, a panorama, or a multimedia illustration of the solar system, including pictures of comets, meteors, and asteroids as well as the planets and stars. Students who have researched a specific comet may choose to add their illustrations to this display.

AUDITORY LEARNERS

Materials: index cards

Write the words *jewels, new, unspoiled, found, mountain, flowers,* and *crew* on the board. Write these subjects on index cards: *a voyage on a ship, a garden, exploring under the ocean, a trip in a time-traveling capsule.* Invite students to select a card and tell a story using the words on the board.

GIFTED LEARNERS

Invite students to "discover" their own comets, name their discoveries after themselves, and write an imaginative historical and scientific account of the comet.

LEARNERS WHO NEED EXTRA SUPPORT

Display a series of word cards containing words with the diphthongs *oi, oy, ou, ow,* and *ew.* Ask volunteers to read each word aloud, point out the diphthong, and use the word in a sentence. Sample words might include *spoil, new, how, ground,* and *loyal.* **See Daily Word Study Practice, pages 184–185.**

Lesson 28

Pages 61–62

Unit Checkup

Reviewing Vowel Pairs, Digraphs, Diphthongs, Syllables

Can students

✔ identify and write words with vowel pairs *ai, ay, ee, ei, oa, oe;* letter pair *ow;* and vowel digraphs *ea, ei, ey, ie, oo, ui?*

✔ identify and write words with the diphthongs *oi, oy, ou, ow,* and *ew?*

Lesson Focus

PREPARING FOR THE CHECKUP

- On the board, write these headings: vowel pairs *ai, ay, ee, ei, oa, oe;* letter pair *ow;* vowel digraphs *ea, ei, ey, ie, oo, ui;* diphthongs *oi, oy, ou, ow, ew.*

- Call on volunteers to come to the board and suggest and write words to go under each heading.

- Read the following words aloud and ask a volunteer to count the number of syllables in each word: *lawnmower, exhaust, proceed, sprawl, fried, loosen.*

USING THE PAGES

Make sure students understand the directions for pages 61 and 62. After students have completed the pages, assign small groups one topic in this unit (vowel pairs, digraphs, diphthongs, or syllables). Encourage them to discuss what they have learned about their topic. Invite volunteers from each group to summarize their discussions for the class.

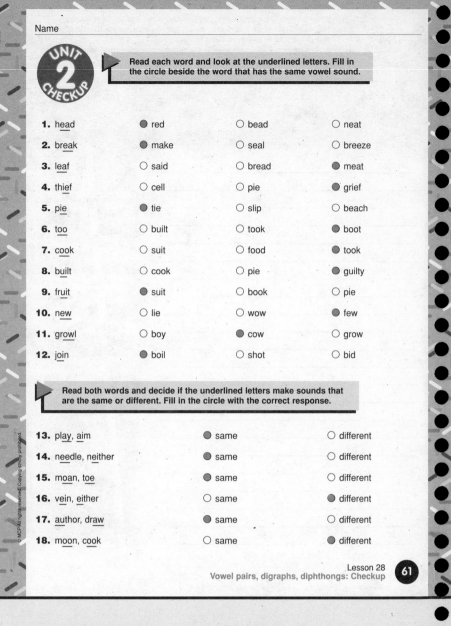

Name _____

UNIT 2 CHECKUP

Read each word and look at the underlined letters. Fill in the circle beside the word that has the same vowel sound.

1. head — ● red — ○ bead — ○ neat
2. break — ● make — ○ seal — ○ breeze
3. leaf — ○ said — ○ bread — ● meat
4. thief — ○ cell — ○ pie — ● grief
5. pie — ● tie — ○ slip — ○ beach
6. too — ○ built — ○ took — ● boot
7. cook — ○ suit — ○ food — ● took
8. built — ○ cook — ○ pie — ● guilty
9. fruit — ● suit — ○ book — ○ pie
10. new — ○ lie — ○ wow — ● few
11. growl — ○ boy — ● cow — ○ grow
12. join — ● boil — ○ shot — ○ bid

Read both words and decide if the underlined letters make sounds that are the same or different. Fill in the circle with the correct response.

13. play, aim — ● same — ○ different
14. needle, neither — ● same — ○ different
15. moan, toe — ● same — ○ different
16. vein, either — ○ same — ● different
17. author, draw — ● same — ○ different
18. moon, cook — ○ same — ● different

Lesson 28
Vowel pairs, digraphs, diphthongs: Checkup **61**

FOCUS ON ALL LEARNERS

ENGLISH LANGUAGE LEARNERS/ESL

Before students begin page 62, write the word *machine* on the board. Talk about what a machine is and ask students to give examples of machines that make life easier today, such as washing machines or hair dryers.

VISUAL LEARNERS

PARTNER Invite students to play "guess the word" with the review answers. One player picks a word and gives a clue about it, such as *I am thinking of a word that has two syllables, starts with an s, and means "to look for."* The other player searches the review answers and finds the word *survey.*

KINESTHETIC LEARNERS

LARGE GROUP Ask students to label sections of the chalkboard with the following headings: *Vowel Pairs, Vowel Digraphs, Diphthongs.* Then invite volunteers to write words from the review pages under the correct headings on the board.

Read the words in the box. Then read the article and write the correct word from the word bank on the line to complete each sentence.

leisure	brooks	built	cheaper	field	foreign	great
loud	recruited	stayed	succeed	thread	tried	

A WORKING FACTORY

People who lived in the United States during the first half of the 19th century saw a __great__ many changes in their way of life. These changes included new machinery to make products like textiles __cheaper__ and faster than they could be made by hand. Using giant spools of __thread__ and huge looms, factories __tried__ to make cloth quickly to meet demand.

The first textile plant in the United States was __built__ on a __field__ in Rhode Island, near a river that supplied water power for the machines. Soon it seemed that factories were springing up beside every possible water source, from large __brooks__ to rivers!

Factory work was hard, and working conditions included very few windows and very __loud__ machinery. Men, women, and children were __recruited__ from local farms and __foreign__ countries to work 18 hours a day, 6 days a week. These workers had no time for __leisure__. Often, they were paid less than two dollars a week! Factory life was hard, but most workers __stayed__ because those jobs were their chance to __succeed__.

1. What was an important change to American life in the mid-1800s?

_____

_____

2. Why do you think children worked in factories?

_____

_____

62 Lesson 28
Vowel pairs, digraphs, diphthongs: Checkup

AUDITORY LEARNERS

PARTNER Invite students to sit in a circle and play "say it!" The first group member announces a vowel pair such as *oa*. The student sitting next to the first player says a word that uses that vowel pair, such as *coat* or *boat*. Then that student announces another vowel pair or vowel digraph and so on around the circle.

GIFTED LEARNERS

Invite students to try writing a humorous poem or story using as many words as possible from one category, such as a poem filled with words that include the vowel pair *ee*.

LEARNERS WHO NEED EXTRA SUPPORT

Work with students to review the unit by completing the pages with them orally, letting them read the items and answer choices aloud to you. **See Daily Word Study Practice, pages 183–185, 193.**

ASSESSING UNDERSTANDING OF UNIT SKILLS ✳ ● ◆ ■ ◆ ●

Student Progress Assessment You may wish to review the observational notes you made as students worked through the activities in the unit. Your notes will help you evaluate the progress students made with vowel pairs, digraphs, diphthongs, and syllables.

Portfolio Assessment Review the materials students have collected in their portfolios. You may wish to have interviews with students to discuss their written work and the progress they have made since the beginning of the unit. As you review students' work, evaluate how well they use the unit skills.

Daily Word Study Practice For students who need additional practice with any of the topics in this unit, quick reviews are provided on pages 183–185, 193 in Daily Word Study Practice.

Word Study Posttest To assess students' mastery of the skills covered in this unit, use the posttest on pages 33g–33h.

SPELLING CUMULATIVE POSTTEST

Use the following words and dictation sentences.
1. **aim** Don't **aim** that ball at me.
2. **play** Can you **play** the guitar?
3. **seize** **Seize** the chance to go fishing.
4. **coat** Is that a new **coat?**
5. **tow** I can **tow** your wagon.
6. **remain** Dad can **remain** with the baby.
7. **crayon** Red is my favorite color **crayon.**
8. **steeple** Look at that tall **steeple.**
9. **tomorrow** **Tomorrow** is Tuesday.
10. **foe** I want to be your friend, not your **foe.**
11. **break** Don't **break** that vase.
12. **leaf** I see a beautiful **leaf.**
13. **vein** The **vein** in my hand is blue.
14. **August** My favorite month is **August.**
15. **scrawl** Do you **scrawl** your signature?
16. **yield** A bank account can **yield** interest.
17. **tie** Will you help me **tie** this package?
18. **flood** Will the river **flood** this year?
19. **built** We **built** a play house for my sister.
20. **fruit** Eating **fruit** is good for you.
21. **corduroy** **Corduroy** keeps you warm.
22. **moist** The air feels **moist.**
23. **loud** The baby has a **loud** cry.
24. **down** Dad is **down** in the basement.
25. **sour** This orange tastes too **sour.**
26. **strewn** Your clothes are **strewn** all over.

Teacher Notes

Assessment Strategy Overview

Throughout Unit 3, assess students' ability to recognize and define prefixes, roots, base words, and suffixes and to combine sentences using conjunctions. There are various ways to assess students' progress. You may also want to encourage students to evaluate their own work and participate in setting goals for their own learning.

FORMAL ASSESSMENT

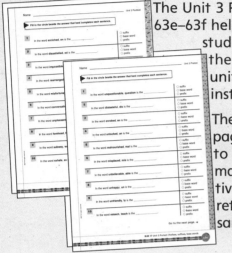

The Unit 3 Pretest on pages 63e–63f helps to assess a student's knowledge at the beginning of the unit and to plan instruction.

The Unit 3 Posttest on pages 63g–63h helps to assess mastery of unit objectives and to plan for reteaching, if necessary.

INFORMAL ASSESSMENT

The Reading & Writing pages and Unit Checkup in the student book are an effective means of evaluating students' performance.

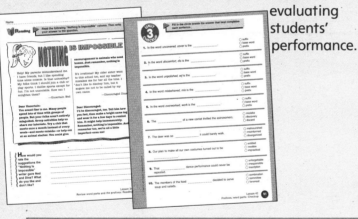

PORTFOLIO ASSESSMENT

 This logo appears throughout the teaching plans. It signals opportunities for collecting students' work for individual portfolios. You may also want to collect the following pages.

❖ Unit 3 Pretest and Posttest, pages 63e–63h

❖ Unit 3 Reading & Writing, pages 75–76, 89–90

❖ Unit 3 Checkup, pages 91–92

STUDENT PROGRESS CHECKLIST

Use the checklist on page 63i to record students' progress. You may want to cut the sections apart to place each student's checklist in his or her portfolio.

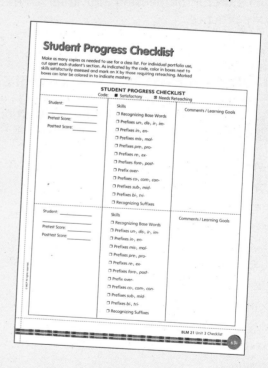

Skill	Reading & Writing Pages	Unit Checkup
Prefixes *un-, dis-, ir-, in-, im-*	75–76	91–92
Prefixes *in-, en-*	75–76	91–92
Prefixes *mis-, mal-*	75–76	91–92
Prefixes *pre-, pro-*	75–76	91–92
Prefixes *re-, ex-*	89–90	91–92
Prefixes *fore-, post-*	89–90	91–92
Prefix *over-*	89–90	91–92
Prefixes *co-, com-, con-*	89–90	91–92
Prefixes *sub-, mid-*	89–90	91–92
Prefixes *bi-, tri-*	89–90	91–92
Recognizing Word Parts	75–76, 89–90	91–92

63c

Administering and Evaluating the
Pretest and Posttest

DIRECTIONS

To help you assess students' progress in learning Unit 3 skills, tests are available on pages 63e–63h. Administer the Pretest before students begin the unit. The results of the Pretest will help you identify each student's strengths and needs in advance, allowing you to structure lesson plans to meet individual needs. Administer the Posttest to assess students' overall mastery of skills taught in the unit and to identify specific areas that will require reteaching.

PERFORMANCE ASSESSMENT PROFILE

The following chart will help you identify specific skills as they appear on the tests and enable you to identify and record specific information about an individual's or the class's performance on the tests.

Depending on the results of the tests, refer to the Reteaching column for lesson-plan pages where you can find activities that will be useful for meeting individual needs or for daily word study practice.

PERFORMANCE ASSESSMENT PROFILE

Skill	Pretest Questions	Posttest Questions	Reteaching Focus on All Learners	Daily Word Study Practice
Base Words	1, 10	3, 9	65–66, 75–76	185
Prefixes *un-, dis-, ir-, in-, im-*	2, 8, 11, 23	11, 23	67–68, 75–76	185
Prefixes *in-, en-*	3	1	69–70, 75–76	185
Prefixes *mis-, mal-*	5, 6	5	71–72, 75–76	185
Prefixes *pre-, pro-*	12, 13, 19	13, 19	73–76	185
Prefixes *re-, ex-*	14, 20	4, 10, 14, 20	77–78, 89–90	186
Prefixes *fore-, post-*	18, 25	8, 18, 25	79–80, 89–90	186
Prefix *over-*	22	22	81–82, 89–90	186
Prefixes *co-, com-, con-*	17, 24	6, 17, 24	83–84, 89–90	186–187
Prefixes *sub-, mid-*	16, 21	12, 16, 21	85–86, 89–90	186–187
Prefixes *bi-, tri-*	15	15	87–90	186–187
Suffixes	7, 9	2, 7		

Fill in the circle beside the answer that best completes each sentence.

1

In the word **unquestionable**, **question** is the _____.

○ suffix
○ base word
○ prefix

2

In the word **distasteful**, **dis** is the _____.

○ suffix
○ base word
○ prefix

3

In the word **enrobed**, **en** is the _____.

○ suffix
○ base word
○ prefix

4

In the word **unlocked**, **un** is the _____.

○ suffix
○ base word
○ prefix

5

In the word **malnourished**, **mal** is the _____.

○ suffix
○ base word
○ prefix

6

In the word **misplaced**, **mis** is the _____.

○ suffix
○ base word
○ prefix

7

In the word **unbelievable**, **able** is the _____.

○ suffix
○ base word
○ prefix

8

In the word **unhappy**, **un** is the _____.

○ suffix
○ base word
○ prefix

9

In the word **unfriendly**, **ly** is the _____.

○ suffix
○ base word
○ prefix

10

In the word **reteach**, **teach** is the _____.

○ suffix
○ base word
○ prefix

Go to the next page. →

Name _____ Unit 3 Pretest

> **Fill in the circle beside the answer that best completes each sentence.**

11. Karen could not find her shoes because her room was so _____.
    ○ unhappy   ○ disorganized   ○ enrobed

12. Brushing your teeth regularly _____ healthy teeth and gums.
    ○ promotes   ○ discourages   ○ combines

13. The weather report _____ a thunderstorm on Saturday.
    ○ costars   ○ predicts   ○ prepares

14. Marta and I were _____ after hiking Mount Monadnock.
    ○ exchanged   ○ exhausted   ○ rebuilt

15. A _____ is a geometric figure with three sides.
    ○ bisected   ○ tricycle   ○ triangle

> **Match the words to their definitions. In the space by each word, write the letter of its definition.**

16. _____ midair   **a.** to go forward
17. _____ cooperate   **b.** to join together
18. _____ forenoon   **c.** to rank below
19. _____ proceed   **d.** not possible
20. _____ rebuild   **e.** in the middle of the air
21. _____ subordinate   **f.** to operate together
22. _____ overcook   **g.** before noon
23. _____ impossible   **h.** to cook too much
24. _____ combine   **i.** to put off until later
25. _____ postpone   **j.** to build again

Possible score on Unit 3 Pretest is 25. Number correct _____

© MCP All rights reserved. Copying of this page permitted.

BLM 18 Unit 3 Pretest: Prefixes, suffixes, base words

63f

> ▶ **Fill in the circle beside the answer that best completes each sentence.**

1 In the word **enriched**, **en** is the _____.
- ○ suffix
- ○ base word
- ○ prefix

2 In the word **dissatisfied**, **ed** is the _____.
- ○ suffix
- ○ base word
- ○ prefix

3 In the word **impossible**, **possible** is the _____.
- ○ suffix
- ○ base word
- ○ prefix

4 In the word **rearranged**, **re** is the _____.
- ○ suffix
- ○ base word
- ○ prefix

5 In the word **misfortune**, **mis** is the _____.
- ○ suffix
- ○ base word
- ○ prefix

6 In the word **conversation**, **con** is the _____.
- ○ suffix
- ○ base word
- ○ prefix

7 In the word **unpleasantly**, **ly** is the _____.
- ○ suffix
- ○ base word
- ○ prefix

8 In the word **forehead**, **fore** is the _____.
- ○ suffix
- ○ base word
- ○ prefix

9 In the word **subway**, **way** is the _____.
- ○ suffix
- ○ base word
- ○ prefix

10 In the word **exhale**, **ex** is the _____.
- ○ suffix
- ○ base word
- ○ prefix

Go to the next page. →

> ► **Fill in the circle beside the answer that best completes each sentence.**

11. Katie was _____ when she missed the winning goal in overtime.
○ encouraged   ○ discouraged   ○ excited

12. At night when the clock strikes 12, it's _____.
○ forenoon   ○ midway   ○ midnight

13. Our teacher helped us to _____ for the spelling bee.
○ costar   ○ predict   ○ prepare

14. Matthew wants to _____ his new blue sweater for a red one.
○ exchange   ○ extreme   ○ revisit

15. Alice likes to ride her _____ to school.
○ triple   ○ bicycle   ○ bicentennial

> ► **Match the words to their definitions. In the space by each word, write the letter of its definition.**

16. _____ midstream   **a.** to move forward

17. _____ costar   **b.** to rival

18. _____ forewarn   **c.** to take away from

19. _____ propel   **d.** to make something better

20. _____ recall   **e.** in the middle of a stream

21. _____ subtract   **f.** to star together

22. _____ overcharge   **g.** to warn about before

23. _____ improve   **h.** to charge too much

24. _____ compete   **i.** after the war

25. _____ postwar   **j.** to remember

Possible score on Unit 3 Posttest is 25. Number correct _____

Student Progress Checklist

Make as many copies as needed to use for a class list. For individual portfolio use, cut apart each student's section. As indicated by the code, color in boxes next to skills satisfactorily assessed and mark an X by those requiring reteaching. Marked boxes can later be colored in to indicate mastery.

STUDENT PROGRESS CHECKLIST
Code: ■ Satisfactory   ☒ Needs Reteaching

Student: _____ _____ Pretest Score: _____ Posttest Score: _____	Skills	Comments / Learning Goals
	❑ Recognizing Base Words	
	❑ Prefixes *un-, dis-, ir-, im-*	
	❑ Prefixes *in-, en-*	
	❑ Prefixes *mis-, mal-*	
	❑ Prefixes *pre-, pro-*	
	❑ Prefixes *re-, ex-*	
	❑ Prefixes *fore-, post-*	
	❑ Prefix *over-*	
	❑ Prefixes *co-, com-, con-*	
	❑ Prefixes *sub-, mid-*	
	❑ Prefixes *bi-, tri-*	
	❑ Recognizing Suffixes	
Student: _____ _____ Pretest Score: _____ Posttest Score: _____	Skills	Comments / Learning Goals
	❑ Recognizing Base Words	
	❑ Prefixes *un-, dis-, ir-, im-*	
	❑ Prefixes *in-, en-*	
	❑ Prefixes *mis-, mal-*	
	❑ Prefixes *pre-, pro-*	
	❑ Prefixes *re-, ex-*	
	❑ Prefixes *fore-, post-*	
	❑ Prefix *over-*	
	❑ Prefixes *co-, com-, con-*	
	❑ Prefixes *sub-, mid-*	
	❑ Prefixes *bi-, tri-*	
	❑ Recognizing Suffixes	

Spelling Connections

INTRODUCTION

The Unit Word List is a comprehensive list of spelling words drawn from this unit. The words are grouped according to prefixes. To incorporate spelling into your word study program, use the activity in the Curriculum Connections section of each teaching plan.

The spelling lessons utilize the following approach for each set of words.

1. Administer a pretest of the words that have not yet been introduced. Dictation sentences are provided.

2. Provide practice.

3. Reassess. Dictation sentences are provided.

A final test is provided in Lesson 42 on page 92.

DIRECTIONS

Make a copy of Blackline Master 22 for each student. After administering the pretest, give each student a copy of the appropriate word list.

Students can work with a partner to practice spelling the words orally and identifying the prefix in each word. They can also make and use letter cards to form the words on the list. You may want to challenge students to identify other words that have the same or different prefixes. Students can write words of their own on *My Own Word List* (see Blackline Master 22).

Have students store their list words in envelopes or plastic zipper bags in the backs of their books or notebooks. Alternatively, you may want to suggest that students keep a spelling notebook, listing words with similar patterns. You could also invite students to build word-wall displays in the classroom. Each section of the wall can focus on words with a single word study element. The walls will become a good spelling resource when students are writing.

UNIT WORD LIST

Units of Meaning; Prefixes *un-, dis-, ir-, in-, im-; in-, en-; mis-, mal-; pro-*

unhappy
disapprove
irregular
inexpensive
impractical
indent
entangle
misbehave
maltreat
proceed

Prefixes *re-, ex-; over-; co-, com-, con-; sub-, mid-; tri-*

recite
return
export
overeager
coauthor
combine
conspire
subway
midnight
tripod

Name _____

 Spelling

UNIT 3 WORD LIST

Units of Meaning; Prefixes un, dis, ir, in, im; in, en; mis, mal; pro

unhappy
disapprove
irregular
inexpensive
impractical
indent
entangle
misbehave
maltreat
proceed

Prefixes re, ex; over; co, com, con; sub, mid; tri

recite
return
export
overeager
coauthor
combine
conspire
subway
midnight
tripod

My Own Word List

Word Study Games, Activities, and Technology

The following collection of ideas offers a variety of opportunities to reinforce word study skills while actively engaging students. The games, activities, and technology suggestions can easily be adapted to meet the needs of your group of learners. They vary in approach so as to consider students' different learning styles.

● A ZOO EXHIBIT

Invite students to sketch an outline of a zoo. Their drawing should include the location of an entrance and different exhibits, such as mammals, birds, rare animals, and reptiles. Then they can list their favorite animals and draw them in the appropriate exhibits. After students have finished, have partners work together to describe each animal with words that include prefixes and suffixes discussed in this unit.

▲ IDENTIFYING WORDS

Write the following words on the chalkboard, omitting the slash lines: *dis/continue, in/scribe, en/tangle/ment, re/ject/ion, pre/dict/ion, im/poss/ible, un/cook/ed, mis/lead/ing*. Have volunteers come to the board, identify the various word parts of each word, and separate the parts. Ask others to define the meanings of the roots and base words. Encourage students to consult the dictionary and to suggest how the addition of prefixes and suffixes affect word meanings.

◆ WORD SEARCH

Provide pairs of students with a newspaper or magazine and ask them to find words beginning with the prefixes *un-, dis-, ir-, in-,* and *im-*. Have partners copy the words onto a sheet of paper and divide them into prefix, base or root, and suffix. Ask the pairs to use their words in a paragraph and share it with the class. You might combine student-generated word lists and use them as the basis for a word wall.

■ OPPOSITES SOMETIMES ATTRACT

Write the following words in pairs on the chalkboard: *promotion, demotion; exhale, inhale; encourage, discourage; prepaid, unpaid; reconstruct, deconstruct; subway, midway*. Discuss with the class the words' definitions and the ways prefixes affect meaning. Invite the class to use each of these words in a sentence. Have partners demonstrate their paired words, using magnets or paper models of magnets.

✳ TREASURE HUNT

Invite students to create maps showing the route to a hidden treasure. Tell them to include at least six obstacles that must be avoided in order to reach the treasure. Have partners exchange and solve each other's puzzles. To avoid an obstacle, players must use the clue (definition) that is given and a suggested prefix to identify a word. Allow mapmakers and players to consult a dictionary as necessary. Here are examples of clues.

The road ahead cannot be traveled over. It is *im*(passable).

You cannot get through the high, thick vegetation. It is *over*(grown).

This stream becomes treacherous halfway across. Be careful in *mid*(stream).

● FOLLOW THE DIRECTIONS

Invite students to complete the directions for replacing the ink cartridge in a ballpoint pen. They can choose appropriate prefixes from the following list, which you can write on the board: *re-, re-, re-, in-, in-, dis-, dis-, un-, en-.*

1. [___]assemble the ballpoint pen tube by [__]screwing the top from the base.
2. [__]move the old ink cartridge, and [___]card it in the wastebasket.
3. [__]sert the ink [__]fill into the base of the ballpoint pen tube.
4. [___]assemble the pen tube by screwing the top onto the base.
5. [__]scribe a word on a piece of paper to [__]sure the pen is working correctly.

▲ PONY EXPRESS

Invite students to play a game of "pony express." Write St. Joseph, Missouri, and Sacramento, California, at opposite ends of the board. At regularly spaced intervals in between, write any six prefixes discussed in this unit, such as *dis-, en-, mal-, pre-, fore-,* and *co-.* Tell students that these are relay stations along the mail route. At each station the pony express will change riders (students) and mounts (prefixes). Have teams of six compete in turn. Each team member stands by a relay station. The first rider writes two words containing the prefix *dis-,* walks to the second relay station, and hands the chalk to the next rider, who writes two words containing *en-,* and so on. The team that delivers the mail (writes 12 correct words) in the shortest time wins.

◆ SUBWAY STORY

Write *subway, mistake, misread, discouraged, midway, consequently, inform, redirect, overheard,* and *comfortably* on the chalkboard. Have pairs of students write and illustrate a story about a trip on the subway during which they became lost but in the end happily reached their destination. Challenge them to use as many of the listed words as they can as well as other words with unit prefixes.

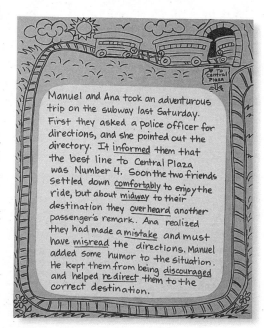

Manuel and Ana took an adventurous trip on the subway last Saturday. First they asked a police officer for directions, and she pointed out the directory. It informed them that the best line to Central Plaza was Number 4. Soon the two friends settled down comfortably to enjoy the ride, but about midway to their destination they overheard another passenger's remark. Ana realized they had made a mistake and must have misread the directions. Manuel added some humor to the situation. He kept them from being discouraged and helped redirect them to the correct destination.

■ TREE ROOTS

Tell students that a taproot is the primary root of a tree. Invite them to draw a picture of a vertical tree trunk and an irregular horizontal line to indicate the ground. Tell them to add a taproot extending from the trunk below ground. Then they should label the taproot with one of the root-word parts discussed in this unit, for example, *ject, scrib, dict*. Challenge students to find words that contain this root. They can write each word on horizontal lines representing smaller roots that spread out from the main root. A group of students may wish to construct a cardboard model of a root system with one or more featured root words.

✳ RHYMING DEFINITIONS

Challenge students to make up their own rhyming definitions. One word in each answer must begin with a prefix discussed in this unit, the other can be any word that rhymes. You might allow students to consult a thesaurus. After students have finished, ask volunteers to say the answer word and read their definition to the class.

● PREFIX WORD WHEEL

Use Blackline Master 23 to make a word-wheel game board featuring prefixes discussed in this unit and make copies to distribute to pairs of students. Explain that partners should sit at a table across from one another. After placing the word wheel between them and positioning a pencil on the wheel, students can take turns spinning the pencil. Each player must say and spell a word containing the prefix that the pencil points to when it stops spinning. Every correct response earns one point; words may not be repeated. Partners can take turns recording correct responses to avoid repetition. Play continues until one player reaches 20 points.

Technology

The following software products are designed to stimulate word play and provide opportunities to "crack the code."

Reading Blaster   Students in grades 3 through 6 will be challenged by hundreds of word-skill games in this program. Skills practiced include spelling, alphabetizing, synonyms, antonyms, and following directions.
** Davidson & Associates, Inc.
   19840 Pioneer Avenue
   Torrance, CA 90503
   (800) 545-7677

Top Secret Decoder   Practice in logical thinking skills and language is provided for older children through this program, which teaches them how to encode, print, and decode their own written messages through 16 coding tools.
** Houghton Mifflin Interactive
   120 Beacon Street
   Somerville, MA 02143
   (800) 829-7962

Prefix Word Wheel

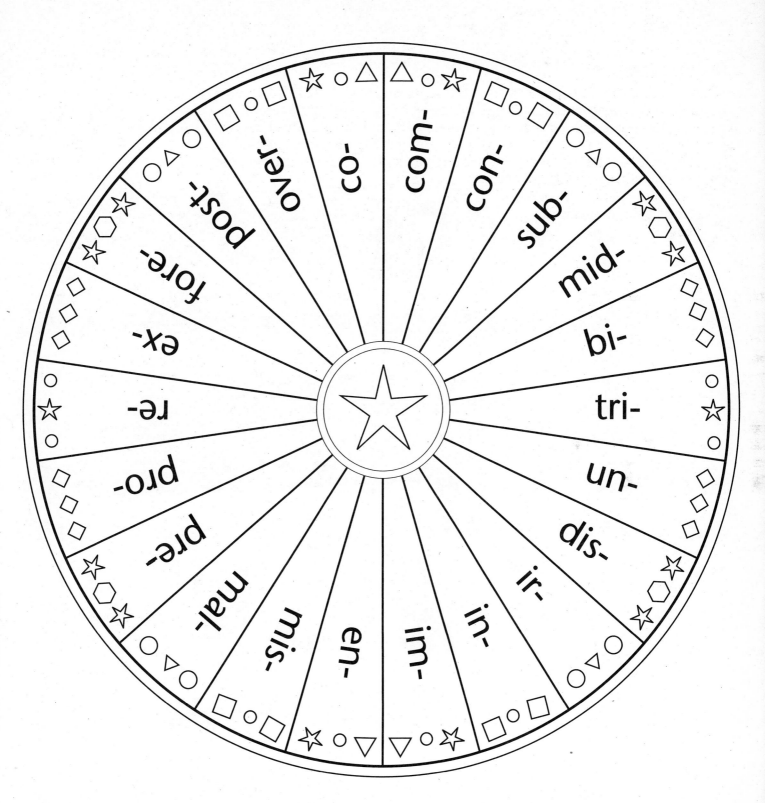

Home Connection

HOME LETTER

A letter is available to be sent home at the beginning of Unit 3. This letter informs family members that students will be learning to identify and use prefixes. The suggested home activity revolves around reading a coded message and identifying the prefixes in the message. This activity promotes interaction between child and family members while supporting the student's learning of reading and writing words with the targeted word study skills. A letter is also available in Spanish on page 63q.

Home Letter

Dear Family,

During the next few weeks your child will be learning to identify and use prefixes. Prefixes are word parts that are added to base words and word roots: **Un** is a prefix, as in **un**usual; other prefixes include **mis**, as in **mis**understand, **sub**, as in **sub**marine, and **en**, as in **en**rich.

At-Home Activities

Here are some activities you and your child could do together:

▶ Reread the coded message on the other side of this paper, and identify the prefixes in the message.

▶ With your child, create posters with a coded message. You could encode reminders for family members to take the trash outside or not to put an empty jug of milk back in the refrigerator.

▶ Identify the prefixes you see in newspaper headlines, magazine covers, or other printed materials.

Book Corner

You and your child might enjoy reading these books together. Look for them in your local library.

Loads of Codes and Secret Ciphers
by Paul B. Janeczko

Along with the codes and ciphers are historical trivia and information on how to break codes and build simple devices for transmitting secret messages.

From the Mixed-Up Files of Mrs. Basil E. Frankweiler
by E. L. Konigsburg

Two runaways find themselves wrapped up in a mystery about a statue at the New York Metropolitan Museum.

Sincerely,

_____

64   Unit 3
Introduction

Carta para la casa

Estimada familia,

En las semanas próximas, su hijo/a va a aprender a identificar y a usar los prefijos. En inglés, los prefijos son partes de palabras que se agregan a las palabras base y a raíces de palabras: **Un** es un prefijo, como en **unusual** (**inusual**); otros prefijos incluyen **misunderstand** (**no comprender**), **submarine** (**submarino**) y **enrich** (**enriquecer**).

Actividades para hacer en casa

He aquí algunas actividades que su hijo/a y ustedes pueden realizar juntos.

▶ Vuelvan a leer el mensaje en clave al dorso de esta hoja, e identifiquen los prefijos en este mensaje.

▶ Juntos con su hijo/a confeccionen carteles con un mensaje en clave. Pueden poner recordatorios en clave para que los familiares saquen la basura o para que recuerden no colocar envases de leche vacíos en el refrigerador.

▶ Identifiquen los prefijos que vean en los titulares de los periódicos, o en las portadas de revistas u otro material de lectura.

Quizás a su hijo/a y a ustedes les guste leer estos libros juntos. Búsquenlos en la biblioteca de su localidad.

Loads of Codes and Secret Ciphers
por Paul B. Janeczko

Además de códigos y claves hay muchos datos históricos triviales, así como información sobre cómo romper códigos y sobre cómo crear dispositivos simples para transmitir mensajes secretos.

From the Mixed-Up Files of Mrs. Basil E. Frankweiler
por E. L. Konigsburg

Dos fugitivos se ven involucrados en un misterio acerca de una estatua en el Museo Metropolitano de Nueva York.

Atentamente, _____

Prefixes, Suffixes, Roots, and Base Words

ASSESSING PRIOR KNOWLEDGE

To assess students' prior knowledge of prefixes, suffixes, roots, and base words, use the pretest on pages 63e–63f.

Unit Focus

USING THE PAGE

- Invite students to consider the coded message on page 63. Point out that if they can decode all the sentences they will "uncover" a secret in an old trunk. Ask them to recall any rebus puzzles they have solved in the past.

- Invite students to suggest words for each of the pictures in the first sentence. Remind students that in a rebus puzzle, plus and minus signs refer to adding or deleting letters.

- Proceed through the page, helping students with difficult rebuses.

- **Critical Thinking** Read aloud the question the character asks at the bottom of page 63. Ask students to share their ideas for alternative rebuses.

BUILDING A CONTEXT

Point out that many of the words on page 63 have prefixes which change the meaning of the base word or root. Have students identify some of these words and describe the meaning of each prefix. (*midway, uncover, misread, impossible, rearrange, prejudge, postpone, proceed*) Invite students to recall other words with the same prefixes.

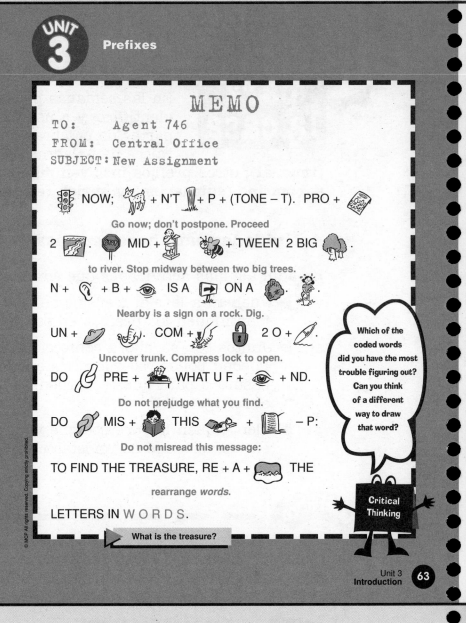

MEMO

TO: Agent 746
FROM: Central Office
SUBJECT: New Assignment

NOW; + N'T + P + (TONE – T). PRO +

Go now; don't postpone. Proceed

2 . MID + + TWEEN 2 BIG .

to river. Stop midway between two big trees.

N + + B + IS A ON A .

Nearby is a sign on a rock. Dig.

UN + . COM + 2 O + .

Uncover trunk. Compress lock to open.

DO PRE + WHAT U F + + ND.

Do not prejudge what you find.

DO MIS + THIS + – P:

Do not misread this message:

TO FIND THE TREASURE, RE + A + THE

rearrange words.

LETTERS IN W O R D S.

Which of the coded words did you have the most trouble figuring out? Can you think of a different way to draw that word?

Critical Thinking

What is the treasure?

UNIT OPENER ACTIVITIES

GET THE MESSAGE

Challenge students to use a rebus code to write a short or long secret message. Have them try out their codes with a small group and revise them to make them clearer. Then display each rebus message in the classroom.

WHAT A TREASURE!

Invite students to imagine their own treasure. What would they like to discover in a secret old trunk? Have students write a few paragraphs about what they would find.

A TREASURE MAP

Students can make their own maps with secret directions by creating a personal alphabet code. Demonstrate how to write out the alphabet with a blank under each letter. Have each student write their own alphabets and then choose a letter to begin their "secret code" by writing an *A* under any letter but *A* and writing out the rest of the 25 letters in order. Students can then proceed to hide an object in the classroom, write coded instructions on how to find it, and trade treasure maps with a partner.

> Add a prefix from the soccer ball to each base word. Write the new word on the line.

un dis
ir in
im

1. Tammy's soccer team has won every game and seems to be _____**unbeatable**_____ this year.
(beatable)

2. There has been _____**incredible**_____ improvement since last season.
(credible)

3. Last year there were many _____**disadvantages**_____.
(advantages)

4. Practice was held at a time that was _____**inconvenient**_____ for the players.
(convenient)

5. Coach Lawson was very busy and her directions were _____**unclear**_____
(clear)

6. Players were often _____**uncertain**_____ what to do.
(certain)

7. Because of their poor record, the players were _____**inattentive**_____ at practice.
(attentive)

8. Some players acted in a very _____**immature**_____ way.
(mature)

9. They were _____**irresponsible**_____ and inconsiderate.
(responsible)

10. No one is _____**unhappy**_____
(happy)
with the way this year's season is progressing.

11. Coach Lawson won't look for any new players next season because she thinks they are all _____**irreplaceable**_____.
(replaceable)

12. She believes that it is _____**impossible**_____
(possible)
to have a better team!

68 Lesson 30
Prefixes un-, dis-, ir-, in-, im-

68

Lesson 31

Pages 69–70

Prefixes in-, en-

INFORMAL ASSESSMENT OBJECTIVES

Can students

✔ recognize and identify the meanings of the prefixes *in* and *en*?

✔ read words that contain the prefixes *in* and *en*?

Lesson Focus

INTRODUCING THE SKILL

- Write the following sentences on the board

  1. I inflate the bike tire.
  2. We will enclose the yard with a fence.

- Ask a volunteer to read each sentence aloud, underline the word with a prefix, and circle the prefix. *(in-, en-)*

- Have the class repeat the first sentence and tell you the meaning of *inflate*. *(to cause to puff up or make bigger)*

- Invite the class to read the second sentence and define the word *enclose*. *(to cause to be surrounded)*

- Explain that the prefix *en-* can mean *cause to be* or *make*.

USING THE PAGES

- If students need help completing pages 69 and 70, have them first read the page aloud.

- **Critical Thinking** Read aloud the question on page 69 and discuss answers with students.

69

Fill in the circle beside the word that completes each sentence. Write the word on the line.

> **RULE**
> **In** and **en** are prefixes that can mean *cause to be* or *make*.
> **in**dent = to begin a line in from the margin
> **en**tangle = to cause something to be tangled

1. Our class just completed a bulletin-board display for the school, _____**entitled**_____ "Save Our Environment."
   - ○ entangled
   - ● entitled
   - ○ enlarged

2. We _____**included**_____ pictures of various endangered animals.
   - ● included
   - ○ intended
   - ○ invented

3. Most of the _____**information**_____ was gathered from the Internet.
   - ○ independence
   - ● information
   - ○ inscription

4. We found out that there are hundreds of _____**endangered**_____ birds, plants, and animals.
   - ○ entangled
   - ○ enriched
   - ● endangered

5. Our goal was to _____**encourage**_____ younger students to begin thinking about the environment.
   - ● encourage
   - ○ enrich
   - ○ enlarge

6. People need to be reminded that they _____**inhabit**_____ this earth with millions of other species.
   - ● inhabit
   - ○ inhale
   - ○ include

7. Many organizations help us _____**increase**_____ our knowledge of animals that are at risk.
   - ○ income
   - ● increase
   - ○ indoors

Critical Thinking

Do you think it is important to know about endangered species and to help solve the problem? Give reasons for your answer.

Lesson 31
Prefixes in-, en-
69

FOCUS ON ALL LEARNERS

ENGLISH LANGUAGE LEARNERS/ESL

Before beginning page 69, talk with students about animals that are endangered or extinct. Encourage students to use the word *endangered*.

VISUAL LEARNERS

INDIVIDUAL Challenge students to write a story using the words *inflated, entangled, enrobed, encaged, enchained* and *inscribed*. Suggest that they look at the pictures on page 70 to get ideas for their stories. Have students share their completed work with the class.

KINESTHETIC LEARNERS

LARGE GROUP Write the base words *rich* and *dent* on the board as well as these sentences, omitting answers: *Our friendship will ___our lives. (enrich) _the first line of a paragraph. (Indent)* Ask volunteers to complete each sentence by adding a prefix to one of the base words.

▶ **Write the letter of the phrase that tells the meaning of the word.**

f **1.** entangled   **a.** put in a cage

b **2.** inhale   **b.** breathe in

e **3.** enchain   **c.** live in or on

h **4.** enrobe   **d.** write on stone or paper

c **5.** inhabit   **e.** fasten something in place with a chain

d **6.** inscribe   **f.** get twisted up or caught in

a **7.** encage   **g.** add to or grow

g **8.** increase   **h.** dress in a long, loose garment

▶ **Look closely at the pictures and read their names. Then use the names to answer the questions.**

king   cat   lion

bike   tire   bracelet

9. Which one is being *inflated*?
    tire

10. Which one is *encaged*?
    lion

11. Which one is *enrobed*?
    king

12. Which one is *enchained*?
    bike

13. Which one is *entangled*?
    cat

14. Which one is being *inscribed*?
    bracelet

70   Lesson 31
Prefixes in-, en-

SPELLING

Write these words on a word wall and ask students to choose one to write a definition and a sentence for each: *unhappy, disapprove, irregular, inexpensive, impractical, indent, misbehave, maltreat, proceed, entangle.*

WRITING

Portfolio Engage students in a discussion about the meaning of *inscribe*. Ask them to describe inscriptions they have seen or read. Invite students to consider what kinds of words are inscribed on objects such as statues, gravestones, coins, medallions, trophies, coins, and artwork. Ask them to write sample inscriptions to commemorate important events in their own lives.

SCIENCE/SOCIAL STUDIES

Have students research, on the Internet or through local organizations, the leading environmental threats in their own area. Help them gather information about the plant, animal, or environment that is at risk to see what they could do to become involved, either as individuals or as a class.

FINE ARTS

Challenge students to create posters about the endangered animal that interests them the most. Explain that the posters should contain an illustration of the animal and some persuasive writing that would help convince others to work for the cause.

 AstroWord Prefixes. ©1998 Silver Burdett Ginn, Inc. Division of Simon & Schuster.

 ## AUDITORY/KINESTHETIC LEARNERS

Materials: index cards

Distribute two index cards to each student. Have students write *en* or *in* in large letters on separate cards. As you name words that contain the prefixes *en-* or *in-*, have students hold up the card that represents the sound they hear.

GIFTED LEARNERS

Challenge students to look up *en-* and *in-* words in the dictionary and write sentences using as many words beginning with *en-* or *in-* as they can.

LEARNERS WHO NEED EXTRA SUPPORT

Materials: index cards

Help students make word cards for *rich, title, different, courage,* and *tangled* and cards for *en-* and *in-*. Have students put cards together to create words with prefixes and use them in sentences. **See Daily Word Study Practice, page 185.**

Lesson 32

Pages 71–72

Prefixes mis-, mal-

INFORMAL ASSESSMENT OBJECTIVES

Can students

✔ identify the meanings of the prefixes *mis-* and *mal-*?

✔ read and comprehend words with the prefixes *mis-* and *mal-*?

Lesson Focus

INTRODUCING THE SKILL

- Write *adjusted* and *inform* on the board and challenge students to use each word in a sentence.

- Say the sentence *The child couldn't get used to the school so she was maladjusted.* Then call on a volunteer to underline the prefix *mal-* in front of *adjusted* and to tell the meaning of *maladjusted.* (adjusted badly)

- Help students conclude that the prefix *mal-* means "bad" or "badly." Encourage them to suggest and define other words with *mal-*.

- Follow the same procedure, using the word *inform* and the prefix *mis-*.

USING THE PAGES

- Give students help as necessary to complete pages 71 and 72. Then review the prefixes *mis-* and *mal-* as you correct the pages together.

- **Critical Thinking** Have students respond to the questions on pages 71 and 72 and discuss their answers.

Name _____

▶ Circle each word below in which **mis** or **mal** is used as a prefix.

> **RULE**
> **Mis** and **mal** are prefixes that usually mean *bad* or *badly*.
> **mis**behave = behave badly
> **mal**treat = treat badly

(mismatch)　(maladjusted)　(mistrusts)　mister

missile　　　mail　　　　(malformed)　(mistake)

misty　　　　mallet　　　(mistreated)　(malnutrition)

(malnourished)　(misfortune)　(misled)　(miscalculated)

▶ Use one of the words circled to complete each sentence. Write the word on the line.

1. Samson, the wildcat, had the ___misfortune___ of being captured.
2. He ___miscalculated___ his own strength.
3. He was ___misled___ into thinking he could run so fast he'd never get caught.
4. However, because Samson's front paw was ___malformed___, he could not move quickly.
5. He made the ___mistake___ of being overconfident.
6. After his capture the biologists noticed that Samson was thin and suffered from ___malnutrition___.
7. They took him to the zoo, where he would not be ___mistreated___ by people.
8. At the zoo, Samson adjusted so well to the other animals that no one could say he was ___maladjusted___.
9. Samson now gets plenty of food and is no longer ___malnourished___.
10. People have become his friends, and Samson no longer ___mistrusts___ anyone.

> How do you think Samson's capture affected his life?

Critical Thinking

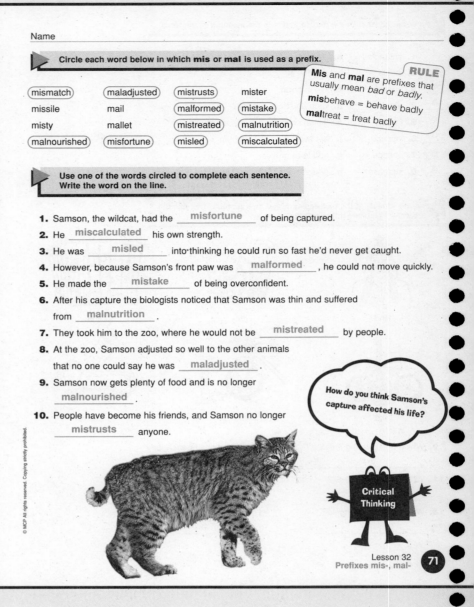

Lesson 32
Prefixes mis-, mal-

71

FOCUS ON ALL LEARNERS

ENGLISH LANGUAGE LEARNERS/ESL

Before beginning page 71, help students identify the *mis-* and *mal-* words at the top of the page. Be sure they know the meaning of each base word or word root.

VISUAL LEARNERS

SMALL GROUP Post two charts, one labeled *mis*, the other *mal*. Write *fortune, match, nutrition, adjusted, calculated,* and *behaved* on the board. Ask volunteers to add the correct prefix to make each word its opposite and write it in the appropriate column.

KINESTHETIC/VISUAL LEARNERS

LARGE GROUP Ask students to brainstorm words with *mis-* and *mal-* and write their suggestions on the board. After at least six words have been generated, call on volunteers to choose a word, circle the prefix, and use the word in a sentence.

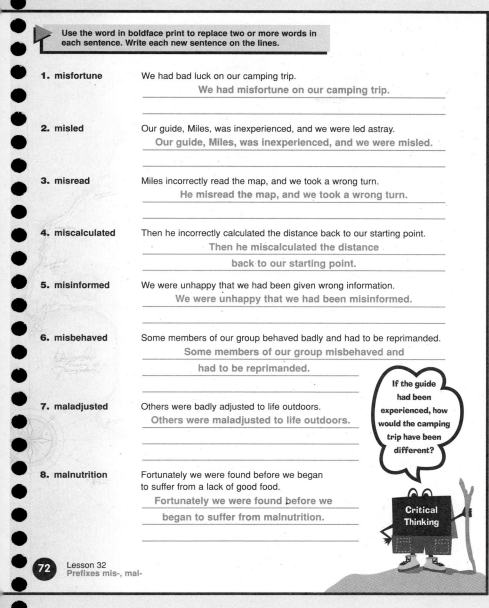

Use the word in boldface print to replace two or more words in each sentence. Write each new sentence on the lines.

1. **misfortune**   We had bad luck on our camping trip.

    We had misfortune on our camping trip.

2. **misled**   Our guide, Miles, was inexperienced, and we were led astray.

    Our guide, Miles, was inexperienced, and we were misled.

3. **misread**   Miles incorrectly read the map, and we took a wrong turn.

    He misread the map, and we took a wrong turn.

4. **miscalculated**   Then he incorrectly calculated the distance back to our starting point.

    Then he miscalculated the distance

    back to our starting point.

5. **misinformed**   We were unhappy that we had been given wrong information.

    We were unhappy that we had been misinformed.

6. **misbehaved**   Some members of our group behaved badly and had to be reprimanded.

    Some members of our group misbehaved and

    had to be reprimanded.

7. **maladjusted**   Others were badly adjusted to life outdoors.

    Others were maladjusted to life outdoors.

8. **malnutrition**   Fortunately we were found before we began to suffer from a lack of good food.

    Fortunately we were found before we

    began to suffer from malnutrition.

> **If the guide had been experienced, how would the camping trip have been different?**
>
> Critical Thinking

72   Lesson 32
Prefixes mis-, mal-

AUDITORY/KINESTHETIC LEARNERS

INDIVIDUAL

Students write the word that completes each sentence you read by adding *mis-* or *mal-* to a word in the sentence. *A badly nourished person is ___. If I haven't calculated well, I have ___. A machine that doesn't function well ___. An adventure that goes badly is a ___.*

GIFTED LEARNERS

Challenge students to write two paragraphs, one about a lucky person and one about an unlucky person. Have them use base words like *fortune, treated, adjusted, lead, behaved* and the same words with the prefixes *mis-* and *mal-* to contrast the two characters.

LEARNERS WHO NEED EXTRA SUPPORT

Help students begin page 71 by working together to identify the words with *mis-* and *mal-*. Be sure students know what each means before they begin using the words to complete sentences. **See Daily Word Study Practice, page 185.**

SPELLING

Write the prefixes *ir, dis, pro, mis, in, mal, en, un,* and *im* on separate cards and display them on the chalk ledge. Then say the list words *unhappy, disapprove, irregular, inexpensive, impractical, indent, misbehave, maltreat, proceed,* and *entangle,* one at a time. Call on volunteers to hold up the card with the prefix they hear and write the word on the board.

WRITING

Portfolio Challenge students to write a story about a trip in which the participants misread a map and end up in a strange, even fantastical, place. Encourage them to use words with the prefixes *mis-* and *mal-* in their stories.

SCIENCE

Write the sentences below on the board. Ask students to use reference books to find the misinformation in each. Then have them write a correct statement. *1. A walking stick is a stick that walks.* (A walking stick is an insect or a cane.) *2. A sea lion is a lion that lives in the sea.* (A sea lion is a member of the seal family, not the cat family.) *3. A firefly is a large fly.* (A firefly is a winged beetle.)

HEALTH

Point out that many people in the world are malnourished because they do not have access to the quantity and quality of food that most Americans have. Encourage students to research the agencies that feed the hungry locally, nationally, and internationally.

Technology

AstroWord Prefixes. ©1998 Silver Burdett Ginn, Inc. Division of Simon & Schuster.

Lesson 33

Pages 73–74

Prefixes pre-, pro-

INFORMAL ASSESSMENT OBJECTIVES

Can students

✔ identify the meanings of the prefixes *pre-* and *pro-*?

✔ read and comprehend words with the prefixes *pre-* and *pro-*?

Lesson Focus

INTRODUCING THE SKILL

- Write this sentence on the board: *The wind propelled the model plane through the air.* Ask a volunteer to circle the prefix in *propelled* and explain what it means. (*before* or *forward*)

- Explain that *pro-* has another meaning. Say the sentence *Some states have strong proenvironment laws.* Ask students what *pro-* means in *proenvironment.* (in favor of)

- Repeat the procedure using the prefix *pre-* and the sentence *Meg knew what the movie was about because she had seen a preview.*

USING THE PAGES

- Help students as needed as they complete pages 73 and 74. Correct pages as a group as you review the lesson.

- **Critical Thinking** Read aloud the question on page 74 and discuss answers with students.

Name _____

▶ Read each definition below. Choose a word from the word bank that fits the definition and write the word on the line.

RULES

Pre and **pro** are prefixes that usually mean *before.* **Pro** can also mean *forward.*

precook = to cook before

prospective = likely to happen in the future

proceed = to move ahead; to go forward

produce	predict	promoted	proceed
prejudge	prospective	premature	preconceived

1. __promoted__ — put forward in rank
2. __preconceived__ — formed in one's mind ahead of time
3. __prejudge__ — decide in advance before enough is known to judge fairly
4. __produce__ — to bring forth
5. __predict__ — to tell what one thinks will happen in the future
6. __prospective__ — expected or likely
7. __proceed__ — to move along
8. __premature__ — too hasty or too early

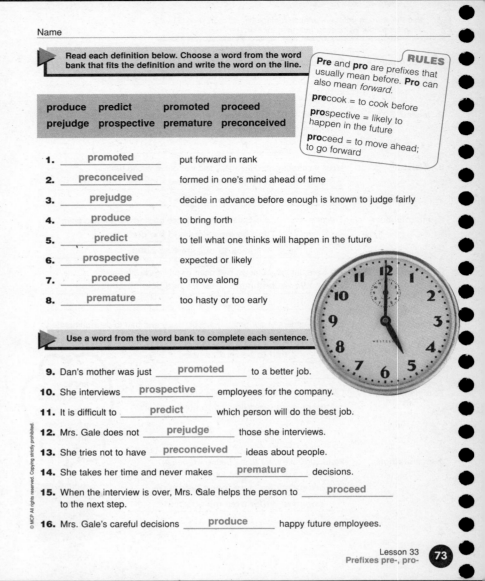

▶ Use a word from the word bank to complete each sentence.

9. Dan's mother was just __promoted__ to a better job.
10. She interviews __prospective__ employees for the company.
11. It is difficult to __predict__ which person will do the best job.
12. Mrs. Gale does not __prejudge__ those she interviews.
13. She tries not to have __preconceived__ ideas about people.
14. She takes her time and never makes __premature__ decisions.
15. When the interview is over, Mrs. Gale helps the person to __proceed__ to the next step.
16. Mrs. Gale's careful decisions __produce__ happy future employees.

FOCUS ON ALL LEARNERS

ENGLISH LANGUAGE LEARNERS/ESL

Be sure students understand the concepts of before and forward. Help them read and define the listed words at the top of each page.

VISUAL LEARNERS

PARTNER Have each pair challenge another, predicting which team can write the most *pre-* and *pro-* words in a given time. One student in each pair writes *pre-* words, the other *pro-* words.

KINESTHETIC LEARNERS

LARGE GROUP **Materials:** prefix cards for *pre-* and *pro-*

List *caution, heat, motion, paid, claim, mature, test, occupy,* and *long* on the board. Have students match one prefix card with a word to make a new word, then write the new word next to its base word.

► Circle each word in which **pre** or **pro** is used as a prefix.

(prepaid)   (prohibited)   (prepared)   (prolong)
pretty   problem   (precocious) (preoccupied)
(prospective) (premature)   (protested)   prowl
(proclaimed) (procrastinated) precious   (proposed)

► Write a word you circled to complete each sentence. Use each word only once.

1. Dad ____proposed____ a wonderful idea.

2. He suggested that we ____prolong____ our vacation and stay another day.

3. No one ____protested____ when Dad brought up the idea.

4. However, our decision was ____premature____ .

5. We had ____procrastinated____ too long.

6. The hotel was full, so we were ____prohibited____ from staying.

7. We were disappointed as we ____prepared____ to leave.

8. We wished that we had ____prepaid____ for our room.

9. Dad ____proclaimed____ that we would plan more carefully next year.

10. We hope that our ____prospective____ vacation will have a happier ending!

What do you think the family decided to do next?

Critical Thinking

SPELLING

The following sentences can be used as a spelling posttest.

1. **unhappy**   The **unhappy** baby cried.
2. **disapprove** I **disapprove** of big dogs.
3. **irregular**   The paper is slanted and **irregular**.
4. **inexpensive** The tickets were **inexpensive**.
5. **impractical** My party hat is **impractical**.
6. **indent**   **Indent** the first paragraph.
7. **misbehave**   Students never **misbehave**.
8. **maltreat**   He never will **maltreat** the bird.
9. **proceed**   We will **proceed** to lunch.
10. **entangle**   Don't **entangle** the rope.

WRITING

Portfolio Challenge students to write a how-to article about preparing to take a test. Articles can be serious or humorous but should include sound suggestions. Ask them to use words with the prefixes *pre-* and *pro-*.

MATH

Suggest students plan the dream class trip anywhere in the world. Have them gather information about fares, room rates, ticket prices, and so on, then figure out how much it would cost them to prepay all their expenses.

Technology

AstroWord Prefixes. ©1998 Silver Burdett Ginn, Inc. Division of Simon & Schuster.

● ■ ◆ ● ✳ ● ◆ ■ ● ● ● ✳ ● ◆ ■ ● ●

AUDITORY/KINESTHETIC LEARNERS

LARGE GROUP Write *proceed, prepaid, predict,* and *protect* on the board. Tell a group oral story about a series of profuse predictions. Each student in turn adds a sentence that builds on the one before. Encourage students to use the words on the board and others with the prefix *pre-* or *pro-*.

GIFTED LEARNERS

In the word *prefix*, is *pre-* a prefix? Have students find out about the roots of *prefix* and any other trivia they can discover about this word part.

LEARNERS WHO NEED EXTRA SUPPORT

Help the student successfully begin page 73 by making sure he or she is familiar with the words in the box. Define unfamiliar words. **See Daily Word Study Practice, page 185.**

Lesson 34

Pages 75–76

 Reading Writing

Reviewing Prefixes

un-, dis-, ir-, im-, in-, en-,
mis-, mal-, pre-, pro-

INFORMAL ASSESSMENT OBJECTIVES

Can students

✔ review an advice column containing words with the prefixes *un-, dis-, ir-, im-, in-, en-, mis-, mal-, pre-,* and *pro-*?

✔ write replies to two letters written to the advice column, using prefixed words?

Lesson Focus

READING

● Write the following words on the board and have students take turns reading them aloud and using them in sentences.

1. misjudge	2. imperfect
3. entrap	4. incapable
5. irregular	6. malnutrition
7. uninvited	8. discount
9. proclaim	10. predict

● Challenge the class to create additional word lists to demonstrate the prefixes they have learned.

WRITING

Explain that on page 76, students will write replies to two letters. They can use their own common sense as well as information they learned from reading the editor's replies to the letters on page 75. Point out that students should use words from the word box when writing their replies.

Name _____

  Reading ▶ **Read the following "Nothing Is Impossible" column. Then write your answer to the question.**

NOTHING IS IMPOSSIBLE

Help! My parents misunderstand me. I have friends, but I like spending time alone outside. Is that unhealthy? My folks think I should join a club or play sports. I dislike sports except for fun. I'm not unsociable. How can I enlighten them?

—Uncertain Ned

Dear Uncertain:
You sound fine to me. Many people spend lots of time with groups of people. But your folks aren't entirely misguided. Group activities help us share our interests. Try a club that meets once a month instead of every week—and meets outside—or help out at an animal shelter. You could give encouragement to animals who need homes. Just remember, nothing is impossible.

It's irrational! My older sister went to this school too, and my teacher mistakes me for her all the time. I don't like to disobey him, but it angers me not to be called by my own name.

—Discouraged Dina

Dear Discouraged:
I'd be discouraged, too. Tell him how you feel, then make a bright name tag and wear it for a few days to remind him. It might help immeasurably. Remember, nothing is impossible. And remember too, we're all a little imperfect–even me!

How would you rate the suggestions the "Nothing Is Impossible" writer gave Ned and Dina? What do you like and don't like?

_____
_____
_____
_____
_____
_____

FOCUS ON ALL LEARNERS

ENGLISH LANGUAGE LEARNERS/ESL

Before students begin page 75, talk about asking for and giving advice. Have students ask questions and discuss the process of writing to the editor.

VISUAL LEARNERS

 PARTNER Invite pairs of students to make crossword puzzles using words with the prefixes *un-, dis-, ir-, im-, in-, en-, mis-, mal-, pre-,* and *pro-.* Clues may contain the base word. Encourage students to exchange papers with another pair and solve one another's puzzle.

KINESTHETIC LEARNERS

SMALL GROUP Ask students to choose a word that describes an emotion and contains a prefix or suffix, such as *joyful, disappointed,* or *sadness.* Have students take turns acting out the word they chose for others to guess.

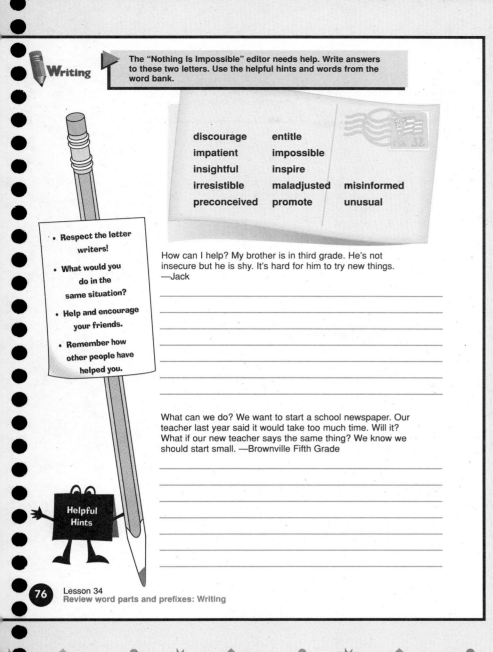

Writing The "Nothing Is Impossible" editor needs help. Write answers to these two letters. Use the helpful hints and words from the word bank.

discourage   entitle
impatient   impossible
insightful   inspire
irresistible maladjusted   misinformed
preconceived promote   unusual

- Respect the letter writers!
- What would you do in the same situation?
- Help and encourage your friends.
- Remember how other people have helped you.

Helpful Hints

How can I help? My brother is in third grade. He's not insecure but he is shy. It's hard for him to try new things. —Jack

_____
_____
_____
_____
_____

What can we do? We want to start a school newspaper. Our teacher last year said it would take too much time. Will it? What if our new teacher says the same thing? We know we should start small. —Brownville Fifth Grade

_____
_____
_____
_____
_____
_____
_____

76
Lesson 34
Review word parts and prefixes: Writing

SPELLING

The following sentences can be used as a pretest for this set of spelling words.

1. **recite**   Our class will **recite** a poem.
2. **export**   We **export** corn to Europe.
3. **return**   I waited for my friend to **return.**
4. **overeager** The **overeager** puppy jumped on me.
5. **coauthor**   My **coauthor** wrote about basketball.
6. **combine**   **Combine** dirt and water to make mud.
7. **conspire**   We will **conspire** to surprise Sam on his birthday.
8. **midnight**   The storm began at **midnight.**
9. **subway**   I took the **subway** to school.
10. **tripod**   Can you attach the camera to a **tripod?**

SCIENCE/SOCIAL STUDIES

Ask students to imagine what kind of training someone might need to write an advice column that dealt with serious life problems. Ask students to research how the fields of sociology and psychology would relate to giving people advice.

FINE ARTS

Portfolio Have students design a logo and design for their own advice column. Display examples from various magazine and newspaper columns. Students can create a title for their column using their own name or a pseudonym.

AUDITORY/KINESTHETIC LEARNERS

SMALL GROUP

Divide the class into groups and assign each group one or more prefixes from the previous lessons. Have students use the dictionary to find and list as many words as they can with their prefixes. Then have them hold a "read-in" to share their lists.

GIFTED LEARNERS

Challenge students to write an example of an advice column for a particular population, for example, pet owners, student athletes, or babysitters.

LEARNERS WHO NEED EXTRA SUPPORT

Introduce some of the difficult words in the article before students begin page 75: _column, unsociable, enlighten, irrational, immeasurably._ **See Daily Word Study Practice, on page 185.**

Lesson 35

Pages 77–78

Prefixes re-, ex-

INFORMAL ASSESSMENT OBJECTIVES

Can students

✔ identify the meanings of the prefixes *re-* and *ex-*?

✔ read and comprehend words with the prefixes *re-* and *ex-*?

Lesson Focus

INTRODUCING THE SKILL

- Write *reread* and *reverse* on the board and have students read them.

- Ask a volunteer to define *reread* and use it in a sentence. Circle the prefix and have students explain what it means. *(again)*

- Explain that *re-* can have another meaning. Point to *reverse* and ask students to define the word. *(the back or opposite side)*

- Follow the same procedure for the prefix *ex-*. Help students understand that *ex-* can mean "out of" *(export)* or "from" *(exhale).*

USING THE PAGES

- Explain that on page 78 students will read about two sisters who are moving. Suggest students think about their own moving experiences as they complete the page.

- **Critical Thinking** Read aloud the Think! question on page 78 and discuss answers with students.

Name _____

Find the twelve words with the prefix **re** or **ex** in the puzzle. The words appear horizontally, vertically, and diagonally. Use the word bank to help you.

RULES

Re is a prefix that means *again* or *back*. **Ex** is a prefix that means *out of* or *from*.

rewrite = to write again

return = to go back to

export = to send goods out of or from a country

```
E Q R E C A L L X C D S E P
X X E E C R E F L E C T T R
C M C W T E F M E Y T A E E
L Q I U E R G E H R B A X C
A E T W S Q A X E E L A C O
I X E D P E X C H A N G E N
M H B K H X M I E P S V E S
Q A C R E H O T S P R J D T
W V Z L K A B E R E C T I R
R S T A R U L I V A P B T U
D T L N G S B R G R H K E C
T A E X C T A E X C E R P T
```

exceed	excerpt	exchange
exclaim	excuse	exhaust
reappear	recall	recite
reconstruct	reflect	retrace

Use one of the words you circled above to match each definition below. Write the word on the line beside its definition.

1. ___excuse___ — to forgive
2. ___exhaust___ — to use up the strength of
3. ___retrace___ — to go back over
4. ___exceed___ — to go beyond
5. ___recall___ — to remember from the past
6. ___exclaim___ — to cry or speak out suddenly and loudly
7. ___excerpt___ — a part from a book, play, or speech
8. ___recite___ — to repeat or say over again from memory
9. ___exchange___ — to give up one thing for another
10. ___reappear___ — to show up again
11. ___reconstruct___ — to build over
12. ___reflect___ — to give back a picture

FOCUS ON ALL LEARNERS ✳ ● ◆ ▪ ◆

ENGLISH LANGUAGE LEARNERS/ESL

Pair students with more English-proficient partners and encourage them to work together to complete the pages.

VISUAL LEARNERS

PARTNER Write these scrambled words on the board, omitting the words in parentheses: *udlceex (exclude)*, *haxeel (exhale)*, *edtxne (extend)*, *rcllae (recall)*, *ilever (relive)*, *ewsrah (rewash)*. Pairs unscramble each word and use it in a sentence. Each word begins with a prefix.

KINESTHETIC/AUDITORY LEARNERS

LARGE GROUP

Materials: colored chalk

Read the following words: *excite, recite, excerpt, reappear, exchange, retrace, replace, explain*. Have students write them on the board, using colored chalk for the prefix.

Circle each word in which **re** or **ex** is used as a prefix.

(reassure)	(exciting)	really	(relocate)
reading	(explain)	(expect)	reach
(rewash)	(reprint)	reason	(expressed)
ready	(replaced)	(rearrange)	(reflected)
(retrace)	(recreate)	(exchange)	(recalled)

MOVING

Write a word you circled to complete each sentence. Use each word only once.

1. Amanda was thrilled when she learned that her family had to _____**relocate**_____ to a new state.

2. Amanda was not sure what to _____**expect**_____ in her new home.

3. But she anticipated many _____**exciting**_____ adventures.

4. Amanda _____**recalled**_____ the last time she had moved.

5. She was eager to make new friends, but knew that her other friends could not be _____**replaced**_____.

6. Amanda's sister _____**expressed**_____ concern and anger about the move.

7. Her unhappiness was _____**reflected**_____ in her face.

8. Amanda tried to _____**explain**_____ why she was so delighted.

9. She tried to _____**reassure**_____ her sister that things would work out.

10. Amanda reminded her sister that they could _____**expect**_____ letters from their old friends.

Why do you think Amanda's sister is concerned about moving?

Critical Thinking

78 Lesson 35
Prefixes re-, ex-

SPELLING

Write the prefixes *ex, over, sub, con, com, tri, re, co,* and *mid* on separate cards and display them on the chalk ledge. Then say the list words *recite, export, return, overeager, coauthor, combine, conspire, midnight, subway,* and *tripod,* one at a time. Call on volunteers to hold up a card with the prefix they hear and write the word on the board.

WRITING

Portfolio Challenge students to write a story about someone their age who is upset to find out his or her family is relocating. They could answer such questions as Where are they moving? Why are they moving? What specific worries does their character have?

SCIENCE

How do people remember facts? Encourage students to research how human memory works. Students might find it useful to develop a list of mnemonic devices to post in the classroom.

LANGUAGE ARTS

Review the writing process with students. Ask them to choose a favorite short piece of their writing that is in the first draft stage, reread the passage, and think how they could revise it. They could ask a partner for suggestions as well. Suggest students use the ideas to rewrite the passage. Let interested students read both versions to the class.

Technology

AstroWord Prefixes. ©1998 Silver Burdett Ginn, Inc. Division of Simon & Schuster.

AUDITORY LEARNERS

LARGE GROUP Write these on the board: *appear, change, count, ex-, re-.* Have students solve these riddles by combining the base words with prefixes: *This happens if things appear again. This is giving one thing and getting another. You do this if you count your coins again.*

GIFTED LEARNERS

Challenge students to create a Word Bank of base words and word roots to which many different prefixes and suffixes can be added.

LEARNERS WHO NEED EXTRA SUPPORT

Materials: word cards with words from the lesson

Have students make and distribute the cards. Have students take turns reading their words aloud and using them in a sentence. **See Daily Word Study Practice, page 186.**

Lesson 36

Pages 79–80

Prefixes fore-, post-

INFORMAL ASSESSMENT OBJECTIVES

Can students

✔ identify the meaning of the prefixes *fore-* and *post-*?

✔ use words containing the prefixes *fore-* and *post-* in context?

Lesson Focus

INTRODUCING THE SKILL

- Write these sentences on the board: *The weather forecast for tomorrow calls for rain. We went to the postgame victory party.*

- Ask students to read the first sentence and discuss the meaning of *forecast.* Circle the prefix *fore-* and help students understand that *fore-* means "front" or "before."

- Have students read the second sentence and discuss the meaning of *postgame.* Circle the prefix *post-*. Ask students to use the context of the sentence to help them decide what the prefix *post-* means. *(after)*

- Encourage students to suggest other words with the prefixes *fore-* and *post-* and to use the words in sentences. Write the words on the board.

USING THE PAGES

Provide guidance as needed as students complete pages 79 and 80. After they have completed the pages, encourage them to discuss what they have learned about the prefixes *fore-* and *post-*.

Name _____

▶ **Write the letter of each word on the line beside its definition.**

_e_ **1.** A time before midday

_d_ **2.** Put off until later

_b_ **3.** An ability to see ahead and know about something before it happens

_g_ **4.** First in importance

_a_ **5.** A message added after the signature of a letter

_f_ **6.** To predict what is coming before it happens

_c_ **7.** Generations after us; people of the future

a. postscript

b. foresight

c. posterity

d. postpone

e. forenoon

f. forecast

g. foremost

▶ **Write a word from the list above to complete each sentence.**

8. Our class wrote letters to save for _____posterity_____.

9. We planned to seal them in a time capsule in the _____forenoon_____ on Friday.

10. The idea of describing our present lives was _____foremost_____ in our minds.

11. We also wanted to _____forecast_____ what would happen in the future.

12. Mark didn't use _____foresight_____ in planning his time wisely.

13. He was adding a _____postscript_____ to his letter as the clock struck 12.

14. We were disappointed when our teacher said we had to _____postpone_____ the project until Monday.

Lesson 36
Prefixes fore-, post-
79

FOCUS ON ALL LEARNERS

ENGLISH LANGUAGE LEARNERS/ESL

Before beginning page 79, be sure students understand the concepts of before and after. Discuss what they do before they come to school in the morning and what activities they plan to do after school.

VISUAL LEARNERS

PARTNER Have students work in pairs to make their own glossary of words by combining word roots or base words with *fore-* and *post-*. Suggest they start with *tell, date, pone, war, sight,* and *man,* then peruse a dictionary to discover other words containing these prefixes.

KINESTHETIC LEARNERS

LARGE GROUP Write *Before* and *After* on the board as column headings. Give a meaning for each word below and have students write the word in the right column on the board. Try *postpone, postgame, forehand, forecast, forearm,* and *postseason.*

Answer each question with a word from the word bank. Then use the words to complete the crossword puzzle.

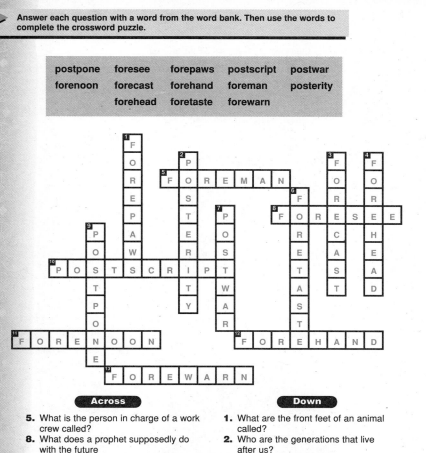

Word Bank:
postpone foresee forepaws postscript postwar
forenoon forecast forehand foreman posterity
forehead foretaste forewarn

Across

5. What is the person in charge of a work crew called?
8. What does a prophet supposedly do with the future?
10. What do the letters *P.S.* at the end of a letter stand for?
11. What period of the day is 11 o'clock in the morning?
12. What is the name of a type of stroke used in tennis?
13. What means "to caution in advance"?

Down

1. What are the front feet of an animal called?
2. Who are the generations that live after us?
3. What does a weather person do?
4. What do hair bangs cover?
6. What is a sample of what is to come?
7. What do you call the period of time after war?
9. Which word means "put off an event until a later date"?

Lesson 36
Prefixes fore-, post-

SPELLING

Write the list words *recite, export, return, overeager, coauthor, combine, conspire, midnight, subway, tripod,* on tagboard strips and cut the words into prefixes and root or base words. Put the pieces in an envelope. Prepare a set for each group of students. Ask groups to put the words together to spell words. Have students write their words on the board.

WRITING

Portfolio Invite students to write a letter to a friend or relative, describing a favorite school activity, and to add a postscript to the letter.

SCIENCE

Invite students to give weather forecasts to the class. Encourage them to watch several TV weather forecasts before writing their own scripts. Display a large map of the United States covered with an acetate sheet or copy an outline of the map on the board. Be sure to give students time to practice before presenting their forecasts.

SOCIAL STUDIES

Suggest students use classroom or library reference materials to find out about the postwar economic and recovery programs that helped Europe recover from World War II.

Technology

 AstroWord Prefixes. ©1998 Silver Burdett Ginn, Inc. Division of Simon & Schuster.

 AUDITORY LEARNERS

SMALL GROUP Invite students to work in small groups to plan a sports telecast and act it out for the class. Suggest that they use the words *postpone, postgame, forehand, forecast, forearm,* and *postseason.*

GIFTED LEARNERS

Suggest students write a stand-up comedy routine based on a confusion of the meanings of the prefixes *fore-* and *post-*. Ask them to use as many words with these prefixes as they can. Provide time for volunteers to share their routines with the class.

LEARNERS WHO NEED EXTRA SUPPORT

Before they complete the crossword puzzle, review with students the definitions of the words in the box. Encourage them to add unfamiliar words to a vocabulary notebook they may be keeping. **See Daily Word Study Practice, page 186.**

Lesson 37

Pages 81–82

Prefix over-

Lesson Focus

INTRODUCING THE SKILL

- Read these sentences aloud, omitting the words in parentheses: *We broke down on the highway when the radiator (overheated). The (overripe) peaches need to be picked quickly.* Have students complete each sentence with a word that begins with *over.*

- Have volunteers repeat each sentence, filling in the correct word. Then ask students to define both words.

- Write the words on the board and circle the prefix *over-.* Help students understand that *over-* can mean "too much" as in *overheated* and "too" as in *overripe.*

USING THE PAGES

- Before they begin working, have students read the rule at the top of page 81 and ask volunteers for examples of *too* and *too much.*

- **Critical Thinking** Read aloud the questions on pages 81 and 82 and discuss answers with students.

Name _____

Choose a word from the word bank that completes each sentence and write it on the line. Use each word only once.

overdo	overtired	overcrowded
overconfident	overflowed	overpriced
overgenerous	overheard	overspent
overview	oversweet	

RULE

When **over** is used as a prefix, it means *too* or *too much.* If an adjective begins with **over**, it usually means *too.* If a verb begins with **over**, the prefix usually means *too much.*

overeager = too eager

overspend = to spend too much

1. The packed gymnasium was ___overcrowded___ the night of the big game.
2. Some of the crowd even ___overflowed___ into the hallway.
3. The vendors had ___overpriced___ their popcorn and hot dogs.
4. Some of the soft drinks were ___oversweet___ and warm.
5. However, the fans didn't seem to mind if they ___overspent___ for snacks.
6. The players knew they could win but were not ___overconfident___.
7. They warmed up but were careful not to ___overdo___.
8. They had trained long and hard and hoped not to become ___overtired___.
9. After the victory the sports announcers were ___overgenerous___ with their praise.
10. They gave their listeners an exciting ___overview___ of the game.
11. We even ___overheard___ one announcer calling it the game of the century!

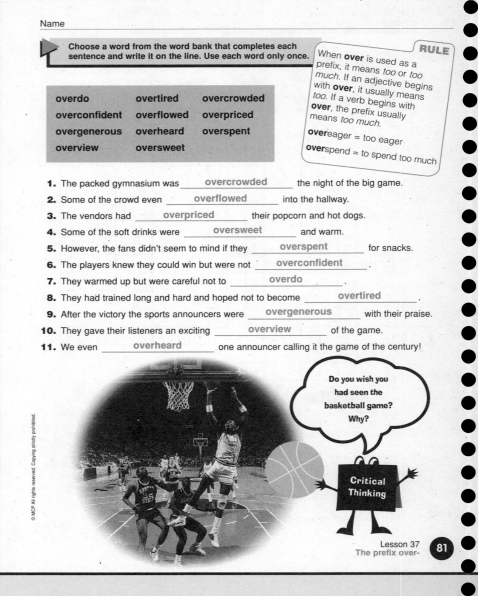

Do you wish you had seen the basketball game? Why?

Critical Thinking

Lesson 37
The prefix over-

81

FOCUS ON ALL LEARNERS

ENGLISH LANGUAGE LEARNERS/ESL

SMALL GROUP

Pair fluent English speakers with second-language learners. Encourage them to review the words in the box on page 81, dividing each word into the prefix and the base word, then use each word in an oral sentence before actually completing the page.

VISUAL LEARNERS

LARGE GROUP

Write *dress, spend, exercise, load, throw, reach, do, flow, pay, charge,* and *cook* on the board. Have volunteers select a word and prepare a riddle for the class, the answer is the word they chose combined with the prefix *over-.*

KINESTHETIC LEARNERS

PARTNER Have volunteers singly or in pairs pantomime the meanings of words with the prefix *over-* for the group to figure out. Remind mimes that because of the meaning of *over-,* their gestures or physical actions might need to be exaggerated.

Fill in the circle beside the word that completes the sentence. Write the word on the line.

1. Mr. Taylor was _____overconfident_____ when he opened his new restaurant.
   ○ overprotect ● overconfident ○ overdone

2. It was located in an _____overpopulated_____ area, so he anticipated a great deal of business.
   ○ overeat ○ overcharge ● overpopulated

3. On the day of the grand opening, the restaurant was _____overcrowded_____.
   ● overcrowded ○ overflow ○ overeager

4. It was very warm, and many of the customers became _____overheated_____.
   ○ overhead ● overheated ○ overage

5. The hostess was _____overtalkative_____ and annoyed some of the patrons.
   ● overtalkative ○ overhear ○ overthrown

6. The waitresses were _____overworked_____ taking care of so many customers.
   ○ overspent ● overworked ○ overbalanced

7. Much of the food was _____overcooked_____ and unappetizing.
   ○ overthrow ● overcooked ○ oversee

8. The customers couldn't finish their orders because the portions were _____overgenerous_____.
   ○ overlay ● overgenerous ○ oversleep

9. People felt the meals were _____overpriced_____ and were disappointed with Mr. Taylor's new establishment.
   ○ overtook ○ overwork ● overpriced

10. Some customers stopped coming, so the restaurant was _____overstocked_____ with food.
    ○ overhang ○ overtake ● overstocked

11. Mr. Taylor was discouraged when he _____overheard_____ so many complaints.
    ○ overload ● overheard ○ overcast

12. He _____overreacted_____ and talked about closing the restaurant.
    ○ overdo ● overreacted ○ overcharge

What advice would you give Mr. Taylor?

Critical Thinking

82 Lesson 37
The prefix over-

AUDITORY LEARNERS

PARTNER Pairs have conversations in which they use at least one word with the prefix *over-* each time it's their turn to speak. Have them keep a list of the words they use to share later with the class.

GIFTED LEARNERS

Challenge students to create a news story that uses at least 20 words with the prefix *over-*. They may write their stories or give oral presentations in the form of a newscast.

LEARNERS WHO NEED EXTRA SUPPORT

Before students begin page 81, help them read the words in the box. Cover the prefix *over-* and have them define the base word, then define the word with *over-* added. **See Daily Word Study Practice, page 186.**

CURRICULUM CONNECTIONS

SPELLING

Write the list words *recite, export, return, overeager, coauthor, combine, conspire, midnight, subway, tripod,* on the chalkboard and ask students to use one in a sentence.

WRITING

Portfolio What would a food critic have said about Mr. Taylor's restaurant? Invite students to imagine they are a food critic writing a review of the restaurant described on page 82. Suggest they reread the page and use that information as well as information of their own. Remind them that reviews include positive comments as well as criticism.

MATH

Careful shoppers can avoid overpaying. Have students study supermarket advertising supplements to make comparisons. Suggest they work in small groups to find out prices for a dozen eggs, a loaf of bread, a gallon of milk, a head of lettuce, a pound of ground beef, and a pound of apples; then use those prices to determine which store had the lowest overall prices, and which had the highest. If you had $5.00 to spend, what would you buy?

HEALTH

Exercise is good for you, isn't it? How do you know if you're overdoing it? Have students find out how much exercise is enough for an average student their age. Suggest they look in health books for answers and invite a gym teacher or coach to visit to help the class develop a good plan.

Technology

AstroWord Prefixes. ©1998 Silver Burdett Ginn, Inc. Division of Simon & Schuster.

Lesson 38

Pages 83–84

Prefixes co-, com-, con-

INFORMAL ASSESSMENT OBJECTIVES

Can students

✔ recognize and identify the meanings of the prefixes *co-, com-,* and *con-*?

✔ use words containing the prefixes *co-, com-,* and *con-* in context?

Lesson Focus

INTRODUCING THE SKILL

- Write *author, motion,* and *course* on the board and ask students to define them.

- Challenge students to add the prefixes *co-, com-,* and *con-* to each word to make new words that mean the following.

1. an author who writes a book with someone else (*coauthor*)
2. a lot of motion or movement together with other activity (*commotion*)
3. a place where two courses or paths come together (*concourse*)

- Tell students that the prefixes *co, com,* and *con* all mean "with" or "together." Encourage them to brainstorm other words with *co-, com-,* and *con-*.

USING THE PAGES

- Have students review their work with a partner after they have completed pages.

- **Critical Thinking** Read aloud the question on page 84 and discuss the answers with students.

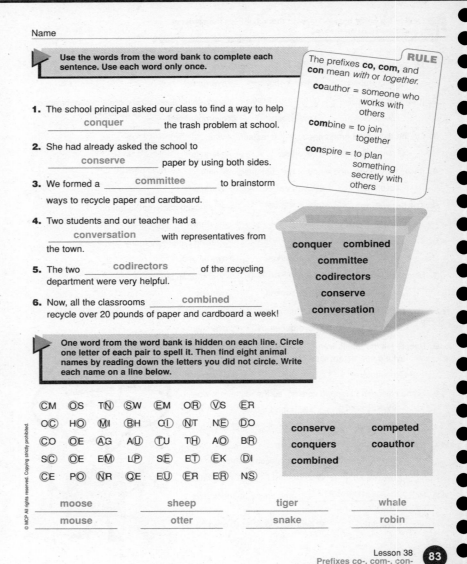

Name _____

Use the words from the word bank to complete each sentence. Use each word only once.

> **RULE**
> The prefixes **co, com,** and **con** mean *with* or *together.*
> **co**author = someone who works with others
> **com**bine = to join together
> **con**spire = to plan something secretly with others

1. The school principal asked our class to find a way to help ____conquer____ the trash problem at school.

2. She had already asked the school to ____conserve____ paper by using both sides.

3. We formed a ____committee____ to brainstorm ways to recycle paper and cardboard.

4. Two students and our teacher had a ____conversation____ with representatives from the town.

5. The two ____codirectors____ of the recycling department were very helpful.

6. Now, all the classrooms ____combined____ recycle over 20 pounds of paper and cardboard a week!

conquer combined
committee
codirectors
conserve
conversation

One word from the word bank is hidden on each line. Circle one letter of each pair to spell it. Then find eight animal names by reading down the letters you did not circle. Write each name on a line below.

CM OS TN SW EM OR VS ER
OC HO MI BH CI NT NE DO
CO OE AG AU TU TH AO BR
SC OE EM LP SE ET EK DI
CE PO NR QE EU ER ER NS

conserve   competed
conquers   coauthor
combined

moose _____   sheep _____   tiger _____   whale _____
mouse _____   otter _____   snake _____   robin _____

FOCUS ON ALL LEARNERS

ENGLISH LANGUAGE LEARNERS/ESL

Before beginning page 83, engage students in a discussion about their favorite TV show or movie actors and introduce the word *costars.* Have students find the base word in *costars* and try to guess how the prefix *co-* changes the word *star.*

VISUAL LEARNERS

INDIVIDUAL

Invite each student to select one word for each prefix *co-, com-,* and *con-* and write a definition for each word along with a scrambled form of the word. They can exchange papers with a partner and use the definitions to unscramble each other's words.

KINESTHETIC LEARNERS

LARGE GROUP

Materials: index cards

Divide the class into three groups and assign one of these prefixes to each group: *com-, con-, co-.* Tell students in each group to write words with their prefixes on cards. Combine the cards. Have volunteers pick a card, identify the prefix, and use the word in a sentence.

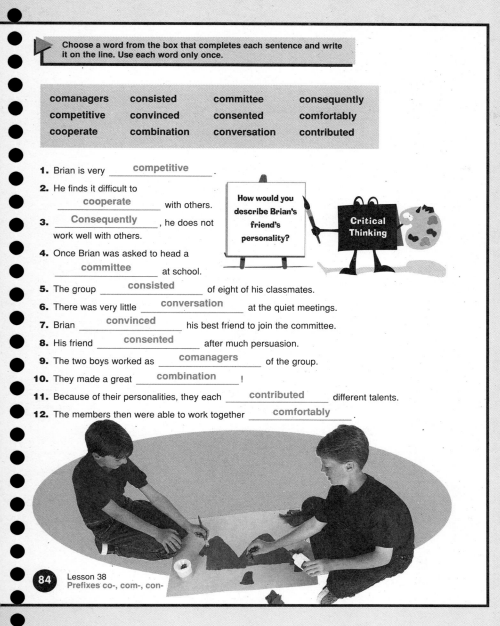

Choose a word from the box that completes each sentence and write it on the line. Use each word only once.

comanagers	consisted	committee	consequently
competitive	convinced	consented	comfortably
cooperate	combination	conversation	contributed

1. Brian is very _____competitive_____

2. He finds it difficult to _____cooperate_____ with others.

3. _____Consequently_____ , he does not work well with others.

4. Once Brian was asked to head a _____committee_____ at school.

5. The group _____consisted_____ of eight of his classmates.

6. There was very little _____conversation_____ at the quiet meetings.

7. Brian _____convinced_____ his best friend to join the committee.

8. His friend _____consented_____ after much persuasion.

9. The two boys worked as _____comanagers_____ of the group.

10. They made a great _____combination_____ !

11. Because of their personalities, they each _____contributed_____ different talents.

12. The members then were able to work together _____comfortably_____ .

How would you describe Brian's friend's personality?

Critical Thinking

84 Lesson 38
Prefixes co-, com-, con-

AUDITORY/KINESTHETIC LEARNERS

SMALL GROUP

Have small groups sit in a circle and compose aloud a story using words with the prefixes *co-*, *com-*, and *con-*. Suggest that each student write a sentence, recite it, and then pass it to the next person.

GIFTED LEARNERS

Challenge students to contact the director of recycling in their own town or county to find out how the class or school could help in a recycling effort.

LEARNERS WHO NEED EXTRA SUPPORT

Materials: index cards, markers

Have small groups of students make word cards for words from the lesson. Help them cut apart the words just after the prefixes *co-*, *com-*, or *con-*. Mix up the pieces and have students put the words back together. **See Daily Word Study Practice, pages 186-187.**

CURRICULUM CONNECTIONS

SPELLING

Materials: small cards or tiles with letters of the alphabet in a paper bag

Draw a square on the board for each letter in one of the list words: *recite, export, return, overeager, coauthor, combine, conspire, midnight, subway, tripod*. Have a student choose a card from the bag and ask, for example, "Is there a *c*?" If that letter is in the word, write it in place, and ask the player to guess the word. If the letter is not in the word, or the player can not guess the word, let the next player pick another letter. Continue until all the words have been spelled.

WRITING

Portfolio Have students choose a partner and become coauthors. Suggest each pair work together to write a letter to the other students at the school, trying to convince them to work harder to recycle their cans, jars, and paper from school lunches.

SCIENCE

Challenge students to research the ways in which different animal species cooperate with each other. Have small groups of students use encyclopedias and other reference books to read about such animals as the grouper fish, which makes regular visits to a "cleaner" fish, which eats pests and dead skin from the grouper's body. Another example is the *plover*, a bird that lands inside a crocodile's open mouth to pick bits of leftover food from between the crocodile's teeth.

Technology

AstroWord Prefixes. ©1998 Silver Burdett Ginn, Inc. Division of Simon & Schuster.

Lesson 39

Pages 85–86

Prefixes sub-, mid-

Can students

✔ identify the meanings of the prefixes *sub-* and *mid-*?

✔ use words containing the prefixes *sub-* and *mid-* in context?

Lesson Focus

INTRODUCING THE SKILL

- Write *subway* and *midnight* on the board and ask students to define them. Underline the prefix *sub-* and ask a volunteer to give the meaning of *sub-* in the word *subway*. *(under* or *below)*

- Tell students that *sub-* has another meaning. Write *subtropical* on the board. Help students identify the meaning of *sub-* as "not quite." *Subtropical* mean "nearly tropical."

- Underline the prefix *mid-* and ask a volunteer to explain what *mid-* means in the word *midnight*. *(middle part* or *in the middle)*

- Have students suggest other words they know with the prefixes *sub-* or *mid-*. Write their words on the board.

USING THE PAGES

Have students read the directions for the three practices. Make sure they know that they will draw four items to complete the picture on page 85. When they have completed the pages, have them go over their work with partners.

Name _____

▶ Read each definition. Then add the prefix **mid** or **sub** to the beginning of the word to make a word that fits the definition.

> **RULES**
> **Sub** can mean *under, below,* or *not quite.* **Mid** can mean the *middle part.*
> **sub**way = underground way or passage
> **mid**night = middle part of the night

1. a ship that goes under sea: __sub__ marine
2. halfway; in the middle: __mid__ way
3. a person below another in rank: __sub__ ordinate
4. put down or overcome by superior force; conquer: __sub__ due
5. air above the ground; in the middle of the air: __mid__ air
6. existing below the conscious; not fully recognized in the mind: __sub__ conscious
7. middle of the week; Wednesday: __mid__ week
8. middle of a stream: __mid__ stream

▶ Follow the directions to finish the picture below.

9. Draw a **submarine** in **midocean**.
10. Draw a jogger who is **midway** over the bridge.
11. Draw a large fish in **midstream**.
12. Draw an airplane in **midair**.

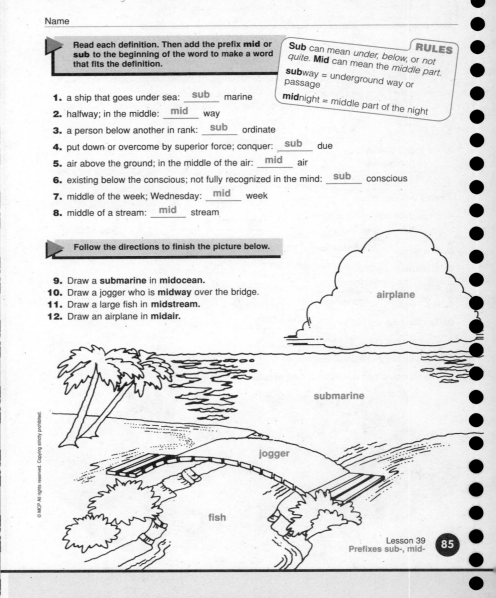

airplane

submarine

jogger

fish

Lesson 39
Prefixes sub-, mid-

FOCUS ON ALL LEARNERS

ENGLISH LANGUAGE LEARNERS/ESL

SMALL GROUP

Before students begin, be sure they understand what *under* and *middle* mean by asking them to demonstrate placing an object under something else and then in the middle of something else. Then add the prefixes *mid-* and *sub-* to words for them to define.

VISUAL LEARNERS

PARTNER

Play "Time is up." Ask pairs to list as many words as possible with *mid-* and *sub-* in two columns on a paper. Give them five minutes, then call *Time is up!* Have students tally the number of words and compare their lists with their classmates' lists.

KINESTHETIC LEARNERS

PARTNER

Materials: slips of paper

Have partners write words from the lesson on slips of paper and prefixes and base words or roots on separate slips. Then have students spread the slips out face down and take turns drawing to make a match.

> **Answer each question by circling the correct answer.**

1. Which day occurs **midweek**?
   - Sunday
   - Friday
   - (Wednesday)

2. Which animal would you look for in **midstream**?
   - robin
   - mouse
   - fish

3. Which of these travels **underwater**?
   - ship
   - (submarine)
   - subway train

4. When is **midday**?
   - (noon)
   - 10 A.M.
   - 2 P.M.

5. Which one is in a body's **midriff** area?
   - leg
   - neck
   - (waistline)

6. Which one is an **underground railroad**?
   - subsoil
   - subset
   - (subway)

7. When is **midnight**?
   - (12 o'clock at night)
   - 10 o'clock at night
   - 6 o'clock at night

8. Which word means the opposite of **subtract**?
   - divide
   - (add)
   - multiply

9. What happens to a storm that **subsides**?
   - (It dies down.)
   - It causes damage.
   - It comes back again.

10. What is an **undercover investigation**?
    - one done inside
    - one done in secret
    - one done alone

11. Where is the **midpoint**?
    - the beginning
    - (the middle)
    - the end

12. Which word means "**to go underwater**"?
    - (submerge)
    - subtract
    - subscribe

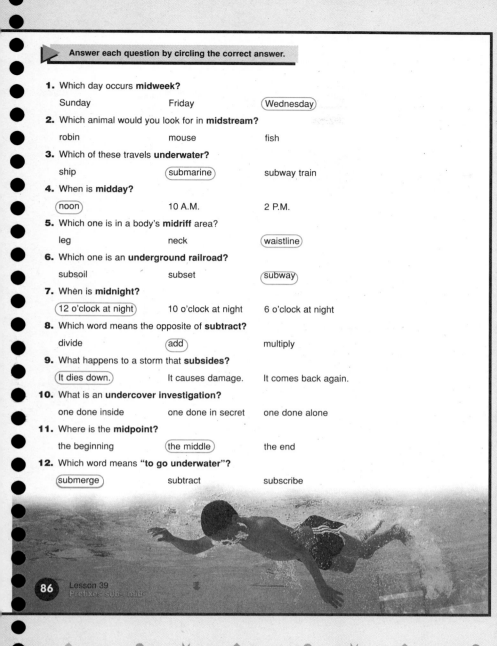

86 Lesson 39
Prefixes sub-, mid-

AUDITORY LEARNERS

LARGE GROUP

Have each student choose a word from the lesson and make up a sentence to give orally to the class, leaving out the word. Listeners name the missing word.

GIFTED LEARNERS

Have students choose a secret object and use words with the prefixes *sub-* and *mid-* to write directions for finding and identifying the object. Encourage them to share their directions with classmates who try to discover the object.

LEARNERS WHO NEED EXTRA SUPPORT

Materials: index cards

Help students make word cards to create words with the prefixes *sub-* and *mid-*. Use the words they make in sentences and ask them to define the word. **See Daily Word Study Practice, pages 186–187.**

SPELLING

Write the list words *recite, export, return, overeager, coauthor, combine, conspire, midnight, subway, tripod* on the board. Have students write a paragraph which includes as many of the words as possible. Compare the paragraphs of volunteers to look at the various subjects coming from one set of words.

WRITING

Portfolio Sometimes the middle is not an exciting place, neither here nor there. Invite students to write a high-adventure story that takes place in one of these middles: midair, midstream, midocean. Encourage students to use creativity in writing their adventures.

FINE ARTS

Portfolio Invite students to make a calendar for a month that will remind them of their assignments, midweek tests, and out-of-school activities. Suggest they make a special symbol to show midweek and personalize the calendars any other way they want.

MATH/LANGUAGE ARTS

Invite students to write word problems using words with the prefixes *sub-, mid-,* and other prefixes they've studied. For example, a problem might ask about a point midway between two other points, or about the weight of a submarine, or about a disappearing number.

AstroWord Prefixes. ©1998 Silver Burdett Ginn, Inc. Division of Simon & Schuster.

Lesson 40

Pages 87–88

Prefixes bi-, tri-

Lesson Focus

INTRODUCING THE SKILL

Materials: pictures of a bicycle and a tricycle

- Write the word *cycle* on the board and ask students what a cycle is. Then hold up the picture of the bicycle and ask how many wheels it has. *(two)*
- Write the prefix *bi-* in front of *cycle* and have students determine that *bi-* means "two."
- Repeat the procedure with the picture of the tricycle and help students understand that the prefix *tri-* means "three."

USING THE PAGES

- Tell students they will use the prefixes *bi-* and *tri-* to identify objects on page 87 and to complete sentences on page 88. Have them read the directions and ask any questions they might have.
- **Critical Thinking** Read aloud the questions on page 88 and discuss answers with students.

Name _____

 Choose the word from the word bank that describes each picture, and write it on the line.

RULES
The prefixes **bi** and **tri** indicate number. The prefix **bi** means *two*. **Tri** means *three*.
bicycle = a vehicle with two wheels
tripod = a stand with three legs

| bifocals | biceps | triplets | biplane |
| triangle | trio | tripod | binoculars |

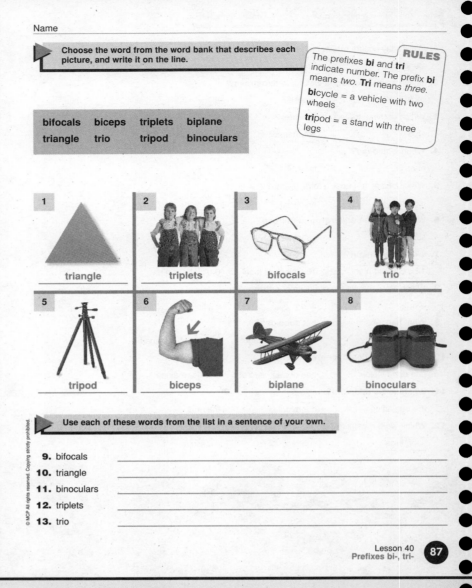

1. triangle
2. triplets
3. bifocals
4. trio
5. tripod
6. biceps
7. biplane
8. binoculars

 Use each of these words from the list in a sentence of your own.

9. bifocals _____
10. triangle _____
11. binoculars _____
12. triplets _____
13. trio _____

FOCUS ON ALL LEARNERS

ENGLISH LANGUAGE LEARNERS/ESL

Tell the ESL students that they are all bilingual and have them talk about what that means. Then ask if anyone is trilingual and have that person name the three languages.

VISUAL/KINESTHETIC LEARNERS

INDIVIDUAL

Write the following words on the board: *biplane, biped, bifocal, triplicate, tricolor, triangle.* Have students write their own definition of each word.

KINESTHETIC/AUDITORY LEARNERS

LARGE GROUP

Write *triple, triplets, bilingual,* and *biannually* on the board. Ask a question about each word such as *How often does something happen biannually?* As students answer, have them hold up two fingers if the question pertains to a *bi-* word, three fingers if it pertains to a *tri-* word.

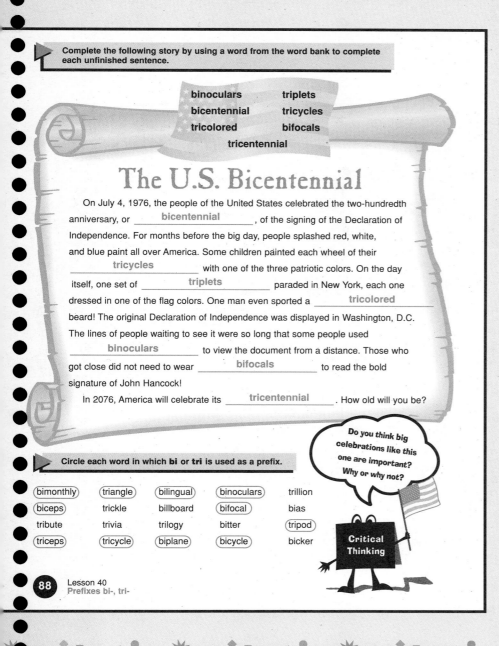

Complete the following story by using a word from the word bank to complete each unfinished sentence.

Word Bank:
binoculars triplets
bicentennial tricycles
tricolored bifocals
tricentennial

The U.S. Bicentennial

On July 4, 1976, the people of the United States celebrated the two-hundredth anniversary, or _____bicentennial_____ , of the signing of the Declaration of Independence. For months before the big day, people splashed red, white, and blue paint all over America. Some children painted each wheel of their _____tricycles_____ with one of the three patriotic colors. On the day itself, one set of _____triplets_____ paraded in New York, each one dressed in one of the flag colors. One man even sported a _____tricolored_____ beard! The original Declaration of Independence was displayed in Washington, D.C. The lines of people waiting to see it were so long that some people used _____binoculars_____ to view the document from a distance. Those who got close did not need to wear _____bifocals_____ to read the bold signature of John Hancock!

In 2076, America will celebrate its _____tricentennial_____ . How old will you be?

Do you think big celebrations like this one are important? Why or why not?

Critical Thinking

Circle each word in which **bi** or **tri** is used as a prefix.

(bimonthly) (triangle) (bilingual) (binoculars) trillion
(biceps) trickle billboard (bifocal) bias
tribute trivia trilogy bitter (tripod)
(triceps) (tricycle) (biplane) (bicycle) bicker

(88) Lesson 40
Prefixes bi-, tri-

CURRICULUM CONNECTIONS

SPELLING

Prepare slips of paper with one list word (*recite, export, return, overeager, coauthor, combine, conspire, midnight, subway,* and *tripod*) written on each. Place slips of paper in a box or bag. Invite students to draw a word from the box to act out as classmates try to guess the word. The student who guesses correctly spells the word aloud and writes it on the board.

WRITING

Portfolio Challenge students to project themselves into the future and write a newspaper story about a celebration for the United States Tricentennial in 2076. What is the world like? How do people celebrate?

SOCIAL STUDIES/SPORTS

Explain to students that most athletic competitions require participants to compete in only one area, but in one winter-sports event, the biathlon, participants cross-country ski and shoot a rifle. Ask students to research other multi-event competitions, such as the triathlon and decathlon, to find out what they include. Encourage students to share their information during special "Olympic" presentations.

MATH

Remind students that *bi-* means "two" and *tri-* means "three." Challenge students to find the names of the prefixes for the remaining numbers one through ten and a word that contains each prefix. Some students may want to illustrate the words as well.

Technology

AstroWord Prefixes. ©1998 Silver Burdett Ginn, Inc. Division of Simon & Schuster.

AUDITORY LEARNERS

LARGE GROUP Ask students who are bilingual or trilingual to demonstrate the words for the class by saying the same phrase in each language. Ask any students who know even a phrase in another language to share that as well.

GIFTED LEARNERS

Challenge students to travel in a time capsule back to July 4, 1776, and write a conversation they have with the signers of the Declaration of Independence. Encourage them to use words with the prefixes *bi-* and *tri-*.

LEARNERS WHO NEED EXTRA SUPPORT

Work with students to complete the top of page 87 together. Help them read the words in the box, then have students take turns identifying a picture. Point out that *bi-* has two letters, *tri-* has three. **See Daily Word Study Practice, pages 186–187.**

Lesson 41

 Reading  **Writing**

Reviewing Prefixes

re-, ex-, fore-, post-, over-, bi-, tri-, sub-, mid-, con-, co-, com-

INFORMAL ASSESSMENT OBJECTIVES

Can students

✔ read an article containing the prefixes *re-, ex-, fore-, post-, over-, bi-, tri-, sub-, mid-, con-, co-,* and *com-*?

✔ write a recruiting poster for an after-school sports club using these words?

Lesson Focus

READING

Write this exercise on the board. Have students draw lines to match.

Prefixes	Meanings
1. re	with, together
2. ex	under
3. fore	three
4. post	again, back
5. over	middle part of
6. sub	out of, from
7. mid	two
8. co	front, before
9. bi	too much
10. tri	after

WRITING

Review the list of positive aspects of a sports program on the page. Specify that students should use words from the word box when writing their stories.

 Reading ▶ Read this article about the young golf player Tiger Woods. Then write your answer to the question at the end.

He's a Tiger!

On April 13, 1997, an extraordinary young man put on his new green blazer—the symbol of the U.S. Masters Golf Champion. At age 21, golfer Tiger Woods became not only the youngest Masters champion, but the first person of color to win that prestigious title.

Setting new records isn't a new achievement for Tiger, though. As an amateur golfer, he was U.S. Amateur Golf Champion an unprecedented 3 times, breaking the record of golf great Jack Nicklaus. Tiger was also the youngest person to ever win that title.

Tiger's dedication, insight into the game, and his ability to predict where the ball is going before he swings the club are some of the keys to his success. The young golfer's concentration is legendary—nothing distracts him and he rarely miscalculates a shot. But that doesn't make him overconfident because Tiger comes prepared to play—and win!

Eldrick "Tiger" Woods knew how to swing a golf club before he could walk. By the time he was ten, Tiger was unbeatable on the golf course, and destined to be a champion. "Expect the best but prepare for the worst," his parents told him. It is commendable advice, and that's what Tiger has done.

What do you think "Expect the best but prepare for the worst" means? How would this advice help a young person?

FOCUS ON ALL LEARNERS

ENGLISH LANGUAGE LEARNERS/ESL

Before students begin page 89, generate a discussion about the game of golf. Display photographs from sports magazines and, if possible, have students experiment with a putter-type golf club and plastic golf balls.

VISUAL LEARNERS

PARTNER Have pairs of students use as many words with *fore-, ex-, re-, post-,* and *over-* as they can in one sentence, for example: *He was forewarned that those without team uniforms will be rejected.* Have students write their sentences on the board.

KINESTHETIC LEARNERS

INDIVIDUAL **Materials:** newspapers. 11" x 17" paper

Have students write *re-, ex-, fore-, post-, over-, bi-, tri-, sub-, mid-, con-, co-,* and *com-* as column headings; find and list words containing the prefixes in the appropriate column, then look up one unfamiliar word in a dictionary and use it in a sentence.

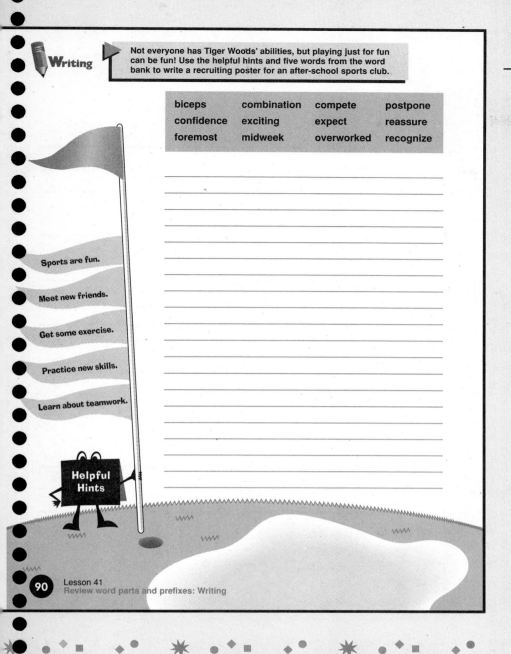

Writing

Not everyone has Tiger Woods' abilities, but playing just for fun can be fun! Use the helpful hints and five words from the word bank to write a recruiting poster for an after-school sports club.

biceps	combination	compete	postpone
confidence	exciting	expect	reassure
foremost	midweek	overworked	recognize

Sports are fun.

Meet new friends.

Get some exercise.

Practice new skills.

Learn about teamwork.

Helpful Hints

Lesson 41
Review word parts and prefixes: Writing

CURRICULUM CONNECTIONS

SPELLING

The following sentences can be used as a spelling posttest.

1. **recite**   Did you **recite** the poem?
2. **export**   Our country **exports** cars to Asia.
3. **return**   Please **return** my sweater.
4. **overeager** I was **overeager** to begin.
5. **coauthor** The **coauthor** is a girl.
6. **combine**   When you **combine** red and yellow, you make orange.
7. **conspire** Did they **conspire** to make some mischief?
8. **midnight** I am in bed at **midnight.**
9. **subway**   The **subway** is crowded.
10. **tripod**   She balanced the picture on a wooden **tripod.**

PHYSICAL EDUCATION

Sponsor a class putting contest! Have students use a rolled newspaper for a golf club and a crushed-paper ball. Create a putting green and hole with chalk on the floor.

MATH

Have a guest golfer. Using a score card from a local course, explain the scoring process in the official game of golf. Students unfamiliar with the game will be interested to learn that the lowest score wins. Have students figure out a number of golf scores by subtracting typical handicaps from imaginary scores.

AUDITORY/KINESTHETIC LEARNERS

LARGE GROUP

Materials: Word cards with words containing the prefixes *re-, ex-, fore-, post-, over-, bi-, tri-, sub-, mid-, con-, co-,* and *com-*.

Distribute a word card to each student. Have students take turns reading a word aloud. Then challenge students to find all the other players in the room who have a card with a word beginning with the same prefix as their word.

GIFTED LEARNERS

Challenge students to use *Bartlett's Familiar Quotations* or another source to locate quotations that give advice about life and that they feel are particularly relevant to them and their future.

LEARNERS WHO NEED EXTRA SUPPORT

Review the words in the word box before students begin writing their poster copy. Help them create a number of model sentences about the advantages of school sports that use the words. **See Daily Word Study Practice, on pages 186–187.**

Lesson 42

Pages 91–92

Unit Checkup

Reviewing Prefixes, Base Words, Suffixes

Can students

✔ identify prefixes, base words, and suffixes?

✔ read words that contain prefixes?

Lesson Focus

PREPARING FOR THE CHECKUP

● Read these words aloud and have students point out the prefix, base word, and suffix in each word: *relocated, unlawful, disappearance, unsuccessful, insightful.*

● On the board, write the heading *Prefixes.* Then write the following 22 prefixes as column headings: *un, dis, ir, in, im, en, mis, mal, pre, pro, re, ex, fore, post, over, co, com, con, sub, mid, bi,* and *tri.* Have volunteers write each of these words under the correct heading as you read them aloud: *forecast, proceed, mismatch, incredible, malformed, recite, triplets, subdue, encourage, costars, prejudge, disappoint, postpone, irregular, excuse, overdo, unhappy, conquer, impossible, compete, biceps,* and *midway.*

USING THE PAGES

Make sure students understand each set of directions on pages 91 and 92. Point out that although the directions repeat after item 5 on page 91, the categories of answer choices change.

91

UNIT 3 CHECKUP

Fill in the circle beside the answer that best completes each sentence.

1. In the word *uncovered, cover* is the _____ .
   - ○ suffix
   - ● base word
   - ○ prefix

2. In the word *discomfort, dis* is the _____ .
   - ○ suffix
   - ○ base word
   - ● prefix

3. In the word *unpolished, ed* is the _____ .
   - ● suffix
   - ○ base word
   - ○ prefix

4. In the word *misbehaved, mis* is the _____ .
   - ○ suffix
   - ○ base word
   - ● prefix

5. In the word *overworked, work* is the _____ .
   - ○ suffix
   - ● base word
   - ○ prefix

6. The _____ of a new comet thrilled the astronomers.
   - ○ mistake
   - ● discovery
   - ○ discard

7. The deer was so _____ it could barely walk.
   - ● malnourished
   - ○ misinformed
   - ○ disorganized

8. Our plan to make all our own costumes turned out to be _____ .
   - ○ entitled
   - ○ inedible
   - ● impractical

9. That _____ dance performance could never be repeated.
   - ● unforgettable
   - ○ irresponsible
   - ○ inscription

10. The members of the food _____ decided to serve soup and salads.
    - ○ combination
    - ● committee
    - ○ foremost

Lesson 42
Prefixes, word parts: Checkup **91**

FOCUS ON ALL LEARNERS

ENGLISH LANGUAGE LEARNERS/ESL

Before beginning page 91, ask students to bring in stamps from home, especially those sent from other countries. Display these and any other stamps or stamp collections and guide a discussion about the hobby of stamp collecting.

VISUAL LEARNERS

LARGE GROUP Have students fold a sheet of paper into thirds and label the sections *prefixes, base or root words, suffixes,* and then search in books for words that can be placed under each heading. Challenge students to find at least five words for each column.

KINESTHETIC LEARNERS

PARTNER **Materials:** index cards

Make word cards for *correct, comfort, happy, safe, locate, place, open, behave, un-, in-, dis-, re-,* and *mis-.* Have pairs of students use the word cards to make as many new words as they can. As one partner makes a word, the other writes it down.

UNIT 3 CHECKUP

Read the words in the box. Then read the story. Write the correct word from the box on the line to complete each unfinished sentence. Then answer the questions.

| biplane | discovers | displayed | inspired | posterity | unforgettable |
| irregular | midway | mistake | overpriced | prohibited | unusual |

Collecting Stamps

Stamp collecting is popular all over the world. A novice collector quickly _____discovers_____ that stamps from around the world can be purchased for a few cents each. A stamp collection can become an historical record for _____posterity_____ by showing examples of a country's art and important people.

Presidents and hundreds of Americans have _____inspired_____ the portraits on U.S. stamps. Pictures of living women and men, however, are _____prohibited_____ from being _____displayed_____ on stamps.

What makes certain stamps valuable? Their rarity! Such stamps usually have something _____irregular_____ about them. One of the most famous rare stamps, a 1918 United States 24-cent stamp, featured a _____biplane_____ _____midway_____ on the stamp. One hundred stamps were printed with the plane upside down before the _____mistake_____ was noticed! Four of these stamps sold for one million dollars in 1989. You might think that amount is _____overpriced_____ for postage stamps, but what if you found the next rare stamp? Then you would have the _____unforgettable_____ experience of adding a rare and _____unusual_____ stamp to your collection!

1. What are some of the reasons people collect stamps?

_____

_____

2. What irregularity appeared on the 1918 issue of a 24-cent-stamp?

A biplane placed midway on the stamp was printed upside down.

_____

92 Lesson 42
Prefixes, word parts: Checkup

AUDITORY/KINESTHETIC LEARNERS

SMALL GROUP

Have students stand in a circle. One group member announces a prefix. Then each student in the circle says one word that begins with that prefix. The last person to name a word calls out another prefix and the game continues.

GIFTED LEARNERS

Challenge students to write an imaginary story about the life and times of a postage stamp, using as many prefixes from this unit as they can.

LEARNERS WHO NEED EXTRA SUPPORT

Materials: index cards, markers

Help students make their own word cards for any words with prefixes that are giving them difficulty. Have them use one color for the prefix and another color for the base or root word for each word they choose. Partners can quiz each other on their words. **See Daily Word Study Practice, pages 185–187.**

ASSESSING UNDERSTANDING OF UNIT SKILLS

Student Progress Assessment Review the observational notes you made as students worked through the activities in the unit. Your notes will help you evaluate the progress students made with prefixes, base words, and suffixes.

Portfolio Assessment Review the materials students have collected in their portfolios. You may wish to have interviews with students to discuss their written work and the progress they have made since the beginning of the unit. As you review students' work, evaluate how well they use these word study skills.

Daily Word Study Practice For students who need additional practice with any of the topics in this unit, quick reviews are provided on pages 185–187 in Daily Word Study Practice.

Word Study Posttest To assess students' mastery of skills covered in this unit, use the posttest on pages 63g–63h.

SPELLING CUMULATIVE POSTTEST

Use the following words and dictation sentences.

1. **unhappy** He was **unhappy** with his grade.
2. **disapprove** We **disapprove** of the mayor's actions.
3. **irregular** Does this **irregular** shape have a name?
4. **impractical** Traveling with the dog would be **impractical.**
5. **indent** Why did you **indent** this sentence?
6. **misbehave** Visitors who **misbehave** are asked to leave.
7. **proceed** Turn left and **proceed** down the street.
8. **entangle** How did I manage to **entangle** this thread?
9. **recite** She can **recite** the names of everyone in the class.
10. **export** We **export** wheat to other countries.
11. **overeager** The fans were **overeager** to meet the actor.
12. **conspire** We will **conspire** together to plan the surprise party.
13. **midnight** The bells rang twelve times at **midnight.**
14. **tripod** She used a **tripod** to keep the camera steady.

Teacher Notes

Assessment Strategy Overview

In Unit 4, assess students' ability to recognize and understand roots and their meanings, compound words, the apostrophe in forming possessives and contractions, and the number of syllables in words. You may also want to encourage students to evaluate their work and participate in setting goals for their own learning.

FORMAL ASSESSMENT

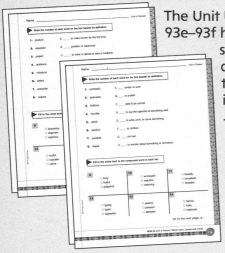

The Unit 4 Pretest on pages 93e–93f helps to assess a student's knowledge at the beginning of the unit and to plan instruction.

The Unit 4 Posttest on pages 93g–93h helps to assess mastery of unit objectives and to plan for reteaching, if necessary.

INFORMAL ASSESSMENT

The Reading & Writing pages and Unit Checkup in the student book are an effective means of evaluating students' performance.

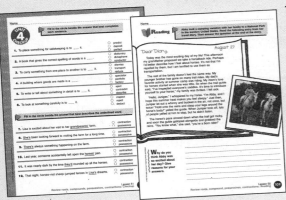

Skill	Reading & Writing Pages	Unit Checkup
Roots *pos, pel, pul*	109–110	111–112
Roots *port, ject*	109–110	111–112
Roots *aud, dict*	109–110	111–112
Roots *duct, duce, duc*	109–110	111–112
Roots *scribe, script*	109–110	111–112
Roots *spec, spect, mit, miss*	109–110	111–112
Roots *fac, fect, fic, feit*	109–110	111–112
Compound Words	109–110	111–112
Possessives	109–110	111–112
Contractions	109–110	111–112
Syllables	109–110	111–112

PORTFOLIO ASSESSMENT

Portfolio

This logo appears throughout the teaching plans. It signals opportunities for collecting students' work to place in individual portfolios. You may also want to collect the following pages.

❖ Unit 4 Pretest and Posttest, pages 93e–93h

❖ Unit 4 Reading & Writing, pages 109–110

❖ Unit 4 Checkup, pages 111–112

STUDENT PROGRESS CHECKLIST

Use the checklist on page 93i to record students' progress. You may want to cut the sections apart to place each student's checklist in his or her portfolio.

93c

Administering and Evaluating the
Pretest and Posttest

DIRECTIONS

To help you assess students' progress in learning Unit 4 skills, tests are available on pages 93e–93h. Administer the Pretest before students begin the unit. The results of the Pretest will help you identify each student's strengths and needs in advance, allowing you to structure lesson plans to meet individual needs. Administer the Posttest to assess students' overall mastery of skills taught in the unit and to identify specific areas that will require reteaching.

PERFORMANCE ASSESSMENT PROFILE

The following chart will help you identify specific skills as they appear on the tests and enable you to identify and record specific information about an individual's or the class's performance on the tests.

Depending on the results of the tests, refer to the Reteaching column for lesson-plan pages where you can find activities that will be useful for meeting individual needs or for daily word study practice.

PERFORMANCE ASSESSMENT PROFILE

Skill	Pretest Questions	Posttest Questions	Reteaching Focus on All Learners	Daily Word Study Practice
Roots *pos, pel, pul*	6, 8	1, 2	95–96, 109–110	187
Roots *port, ject*	7, 24	3	95–96, 109–110	187
Roots *aud, dict*	1	4	97–98, 109–110	187
Roots *duct, duce, duc*	23, 26	5, 23	97–98, 109–110	187
Roots *scribe, script*	4	7	97–98, 109–110	187
Roots *spec, spect, mit, miss*	2, 5	8	99–100, 109–110	187
Roots *fac, fect, fic, feit*	3, 25	6	99–100, 109–110	187
Compound Words	9–14	9–14, 24–26	101–102, 109–110	188
Possessives	19–22	19–22	103–104, 109–110	188
Contractions	15–18	15–18	105–106, 109–110	188
Syllables	23–26	23–26	107–108	193

> **Write the number of each word on the line beside its definition.**

1. contradict

A. _____ certain or sure

2. speculate

B. _____ to scatter

3. fictitious

C. _____ able to be carried

4. inscribe

D. _____ to say the opposite of something said

5. admit

E. _____ to write, print, or carve something

6. positive

F. _____ to confess

7. portable

G. _____ not real

8. dispel

H. _____ to wonder about something or someone

> **Fill in the circle next to the compound word in each set.**

9	10	11
○ fruity	○ wristwatch	○ broadly
○ fruitful	○ watchful	○ broadcast
○ grapefruit	○ watching	○ broaden

12	13	14
○ typing	○ peanut	○ harrow
○ typist	○ peasant	○ hairy
○ typewriter	○ appease	○ hairbrush

Go to the next page. →

> **Fill in the circle beside the two words that make up each contraction.**

15. that's   ○ it is   ○ that is   ○ that are

16. you've   ○ you have   ○ we have   ○ you are

17. can't   ○ can do   ○ did not   ○ can not

18. Paul's   ○ Paul says   ○ Paul is   ○ Paul has

> **Fill in the circle beside the possessive that matches each clue.**

19 the cat that belongs to Karen	○ Karens cat ○ Karens' cat ○ Karen's cat
20 the hills of the community	○ communitys' hills ○ community's hills ○ communities hills
21 the toys of the children	○ childrens' toys ○ children's toys ○ childrens toys
22 the people of the city	○ citys' people ○ cities' people ○ city's people

> **Fill in the circle beside the word that is correctly divided into syllables.**

23. conduct   ○ cond/uct   ○ con/duct   ○ co/nduct

24. reporter   ○ re/port/er   ○ repor/ter   ○ re/porter

25. counterfeit   ○ counter/feit   ○ count/er/feit   ○ coun/ter/feit

26. introduce   ○ intro/duce   ○ in/troduce   ○ in/tro/duce

Possible score on Unit 4 Pretest is 26. Number correct _____

▶ **Write the number of each word on the line beside its definition.**

1. posture   A. _____ to make known for the first time

2. expulsion   B. _____ problem or weakness

3. project   C. _____ to order or advise to take a medicine

4. audience   D. _____ to admire someone

5. introduce   E. _____ a group of people gathered to hear something

6. defect   F. _____ to throw foward or force out

7. prescribe   G. _____ act of forcing out

8. respect   H. _____ position of the body

▶ **Fill in the circle beside the word that is a compound word.**

9	**10**	**11**
○ spaceship	○ pines	○ boarder
○ shipment	○ apple	○ dashboard
○ spacious	○ pineapple	○ dashing
12	**13**	**14**
○ cupful	○ lightning	○ course
○ cupcake	○ sunny	○ courtesy
○ cakes	○ sunlight	○ courthouse

Go to the next page. →

> **Fill in the circle beside the two words that make up each contraction.**

15. couldn't   ○ could not   ○ could do   ○ would not

16. I've   ○ I am   ○ You are   ○ I have

17. we'll   ○ we are   ○ we will   ○ we should

18. Sheila's   ○ Sheila did   ○ Sheila was   ○ Sheila is

> **Fill in the circle beside the possessive that matches each clue.**

19	the coat belonging to Jamie	○ Jamies' coat ○ Jamie's coat ○ Jamies coat
20	the uniforms of the team	○ team's uniforms ○ teams' uniforms ○ team uniforms
21	the lounge for the teachers	○ teachers lounge ○ teacher's lounge ○ teachers' lounge
22	the park belonging to the county	○ countys' park ○ counties park ○ county's park

> **Fill in the circle beside the word that is correctly divided into syllables.**

23. induction   ○ in/duct/ion   ○ in/duction   ○ in/duc/tion

24. fingerprint   ○ fin/ger/print   ○ finger/print   ○ fing/er/print

25. newspaper   ○ news/paper   ○ new/spa/per   ○ news/pa/per

26. watermelon   ○ wa/ter/mel/on   ○ wat/er/me/lon   ○ water/mel/on

Possible score on Unit 4 Posttest is 26. Number correct _____

Student Progress Checklist

Make as many copies as needed to use for a class list. For individual portfolio use, cut apart each student's section. As indicated by the code, color in boxes next to skills satisfactorily assessed and mark an X by those requiring reteaching. Marked boxes can later be colored in to indicate mastery.

STUDENT PROGRESS CHECKLIST

Code: ■ Satisfactory   ☒ Needs Reteaching

Student: _____ _____ Pretest Score: _____ Posttest Score: _____	Skills ❑ Roots ❑ Compound Words ❑ Possessives ❑ Contractions ❑ Syllables	Comments / Learning Goals
Student: _____ _____ Pretest Score: _____ Posttest Score: _____	Skills ❑ Roots ❑ Compound Words ❑ Possessives ❑ Contractions ❑ Syllables	Comments / Learning Goals
Student: _____ _____ Pretest Score: _____ Posttest Score: _____	Skills ❑ Roots ❑ Compound Words ❑ Possessives ❑ Contractions ❑ Syllables	Comments / Learning Goals
Student: _____ _____ Pretest Score: _____ Posttest Score: _____	Skills ❑ Roots ❑ Compound Words ❑ Possessives ❑ Contractions ❑ Syllables	Comments / Learning Goals

Spelling Connections

INTRODUCTION

The Unit Word List is a comprehensive list of spelling words drawn from this unit. The words are grouped by roots, compound words, contractions, possessives, and syllables. To incorporate spelling into your word study program, use the activity in the Curriculum Connections section of each teaching plan.

The spelling lessons utilize the following approach for each set of words.

1. Administer a pretest of the words that have not yet been introduced. Dictation sentences are provided.

2. Provide practice.

3. Reassess. Dictation sentences are provided.

A final test is provided in Lesson 51 on page 112.

DIRECTIONS

Make a copy of Blackline Master 30 for each student. After administering the pretest, give each student a copy of the appropriate word list.

Students can work with a partner to practice spelling the words orally and identifying the root or other word study element in each word. They can also make and use letter cards to form the words on the list. You may want to challenge students to identify other words that have the same roots, word parts, or number of syllables, or similar forms of contractions or possessives. Students can write words of their own on *My Own Word List* (see Blackline Master 30).

Have students store their list words in an envelope or plastic zipper bag in the back of their books or notebooks. Alternatively, you may want to suggest that students keep a spelling notebook, listing words with similar patterns. You could also invite students to build word-wall displays in the classroom. Each section of the wall could focus on words with a single word study element. The walls will become a good spelling resource when students are writing.

UNIT WORD LIST

Roots *pos, pel, port, ject, aud, dict, duct, duce, scribe*

position
propel
portable
eject
audible
predict
conduct
introduce
inscribe

Roots *spect, miss, fac, fect, fic, feit*; Compound Words

inspected
dismiss
factual
infect
sufficient
forfeit
cupcake
doghouse

Contractions, Possessives, Syllables

it's
I'll
we're
boys'
children's
antidote
underground

Name _____

 Spelling # UNIT 4 WORD LIST

Roots pos, pel, port, ject, aud, dict, duct, duce, scribe

position
propel
portable
eject
audible
predict
conduct
introduce
inscribe

Roots spect, miss, fac, fect, fic, feit; Compound Words

inspected
dismiss
factual
infect
sufficient
forfeit
cupcake
doghouse

Contractions, Possessives, Syllables

it's
I'll
we're
boys'
children's
antidote
underground

My Own Word List

Word Study Games, Activities, and Technology

The following collection of ideas offers a variety of opportunities to reinforce word study skills while actively engaging students. The games, activities, and technology suggestions can easily be adapted to meet the needs of your group of learners. They vary in approach so as to consider students' different learning styles.

● SPACE MISSION

Distribute to students copies of the story at the right. Invite them to complete the story by writing words containing roots discussed in this unit in the spaces provided. (Possible answers: <u>mission</u>; trans<u>port</u>; in<u>spec</u>ting; <u>manu</u>facturer; pro<u>pell</u>ed; <u>object</u>; re<u>duc</u>ed; <u>capt</u>ured; trans<u>mitt</u>ed or <u>dict</u>ated; <u>aud</u>ible.)

Variation: Have partners work together to write a paragraph about another mission undertaken by astronauts Shannon and Luis. Challenge students to include as many words with roots as they can.

> Astronauts Shannon and Luis are on a _____. Their assignment is to retrieve a weather satellite that is not working properly and _____ it back to Earth. After _____ it, the _____ who made the satellite will repair it. Thruster rockets _____ the ship into orbit. As Luis and Shannon approached the _____, they _____ speed. Moving slowly closer, they _____ the satellite and brought it aboard. The astronauts _____ the message "Mission accomplished." Their words were _____; they came through loud and clear. The waiting scientists cheered.

▲ CLAPPING FOR SYLLABLES

Read any list of words to students and instruct them to listen carefully for the number of syllables in each word. Have them clap their hands to indicate the number of syllables. To vary this activity, you might have groups write the lyrics to a favorite song. After practicing, they might sing the song, substituting the appropriate number of rhythmic claps for certain words. When they finish, ask volunteers to identify the unsung words and the number of syllables in each word.

◆ SYNONYM SYLLABLE ADDITION

Invite partners to play a game of "synonym syllable addition." Each writes a familiar word (such as *happy* or *sad*) on a sheet of paper. Next, each lists as many synonyms as he or she can in 5 minutes. Then each divides those words into syllables, using vertical lines. Finally, partners add the total number of syllables in one another's words. The partner with the highest score wins.

■ CREATING A PLANT CATALOG

Have students work in small groups to brainstorm lists of flowers and trees whose names are compound words. Examples include *sunflower, goldenrod, snapdragon, crabapple, dogwood,* and *redwood.* After compiling their list, group members can work together to compile a catalog. Tell them to include illustrations, short descriptions, and planting information (springtime, summertime). Encourage groups to include as many compound words as possible. You might provide seed or garden catalogs to help students with ideas.

✳ BEFORE AND AFTER

Organize students in teams of three, and pair the teams. Tell the first team to write a compound word and pass its paper to the other. That team writes a compound word based on one of the two parts of the first word and passes the paper back. The first team writes a new compound word based on part of the second word, and so on. Examples: *doughnut* = *peanut* or *nutcracker*; *cupcake* = *teacup* or *pancake*. If one team cannot form a new compound from the word given, the other team gets the opportunity and play continues. If that team cannot write a new word, it passes the paper back and the other team writes an entirely new compound word. Play for a set period of time. Teams receive one point for each word they write; the team with the most points wins.

● PARAGRAPH BUILDING

Have partners work together to write a paragraph. One partner writes a sentence containing at least one word formed from a root and passes the paper to the other. The second partner adds a sentence that follows logically and returns the paper. The first adds a third sentence, and so on. Encourage partners to revise their finished paragraphs by checking sequence and combining sentences. An example follows.

"The <u>spect</u>ators were <u>c</u>aptivated. Felicia Washington was being in<u>duct</u>ed into the Engineering Hall of Fame. She thanked her family and friends in her ac<u>cept</u>ance speech, <u>o</u>mitting no one. Everyone could hear because her pro<u>ject</u>ion was good and her <u>dict</u>ion was perfect. The crowd app<u>laud</u>ed when Felicia finished."

▲ WRITING A MYSTERY

Have students work in groups of three or four to write a mystery using words formed from roots. You might suggest the following plot: A scientist who has made a startling medical discovery has vanished. Scott and Sandra, who write for the school newspaper, learn that he is locked in a deserted warehouse. They free the scientist, notify police, and help arrest those responsible. Remind students to explain how Scott and Sandra discovered where the scientist was. The end of the mystery should reveal who locked the scientist in the warehouse and why. Collect the finished works and bind them into a class anthology for all to read. Encourage students to write other mysteries in which they use compound words and include possessives and contractions in dialogue.

◆ MONTAGE MADNESS

Have students draw or trace on separate sheets of paper simple pictures of common objects whose names make up parts of compound words. You might allow them to consult old magazines, picture books, or reference works for ideas. Tell them that they should make 12 drawings that can be used as clues to form 6 compound words. Examples: a light bulb and a house *(lighthouse)*; a pine tree and an apple *(pineapple)*; a teacup and a cake *(cupcake)*. After displaying their completed pictures, students can arrange the pictures on their desks in a mismatched pattern (such as that of a teacup and a house) to create "montage madness." Have partners rearrange one another's projects to illustrate and write the names of six compound words.

■ **POSSESSIVES ABOUT A PLACE**

Tell pairs of students to write a group of possessives about a particular place, such as a farm, a supermarket, or an amusement park. Encourage them to include an example of each type of possessive studied. Call on students to share their completed work.

✴ **WORD RUMMY**

Use Blackline Master 31 to make a 24-card deck featuring prefixes and roots. Write 12 different roots of your choosing on the blank cards, and distribute copies to pairs of students. Suggest partners create a colorful design on the opposite side before they cut out each card. Partners take turns shuffling the deck and dealing 6 cards to each player. The remaining cards are placed face down in the center of the table. Each player examines his or her cards. If a person can form one or more words by combining a prefix card and a root card, the combination(s) should be placed face up on his or her side of the table. If neither partner can form a word, players take turns drawing a card from the pile until they can form a word. In addition, for each card played, players take turns drawing another card from the pile. Play continues until all cards are played or until there are no cards remaining in the pile. A player receives one point for each card played, but subtracts one point from the total for each card remaining in his or her hand. Play continues until someone scores 25 points.

Variations: Use other prefixes or create an expanded deck by adding 6 suffix cards, which players can add to their words for extra points. To extend the game, create a similar deck in which each card represents one part of a compound word.

Technology

The following software products are designed to develop students' knowledge of vocabulary.

Super Solvers: Midnight Rescue! Students ages 7–10 are challenged to catch the Master of Mischief by using thinking, reading, and reasoning skills in a timed video-game format. The program emphasizes reading for main ideas, recalling key facts, drawing inferences, and building vocabulary.
** The Learning Company
  1 Athenaeum Street
  Cambridge, MA 02142
  (800) 227-5609

Word Adventure Students ages 7–12 develop vocabulary skills as they zoom around in space. Two hundred core words are covered through games such as "Flash Cards" and "Laser Review." (Record-keeping

features and progress reports are available for teachers.)
** Smartek
  7908 Convoy Court
  San Diego, CA 92111
  (800) 858-9673

Alien Tales Classic children's literature is explored through this humorous quiz-show format, with an emphasis on comprehension and vocabulary development. Titles include *Charlotte's Web*, *The Wizard of Oz*, and *Mathilda*.
** Broderbund Software
  P.O. Box 6125
  Novato, CA 94948-6125
  (800) 521-6263

Word Rummy

in	in	re	re
pro	pro	sub	sub
de	de	con	con

Home Connection

HOME LETTER

A letter is available to be sent home at the beginning of Unit 4. This letter informs family members that students will be exploring the roots of words, compound words, possessives, and contractions and also continuing to learn about syllables. The suggested home activity revolves around science experiments and projects the student might have seen or done. This activity promotes interaction between child and family members while supporting the student's learning of reading and writing words with the targeted word study skills. A letter is also available in Spanish on page 93q.

Home Letter

Dear Family,

In the upcoming weeks your child will be exploring the roots of words, compound words, possessives, and contractions. We'll also continue to learn about syllables.

At-Home Activities

▶ Look at the poem on the other side of this letter with your child. See if he or she can find words containing the roots **mit, ject, duct, spec, spect** (sub**mit**ted, pro**ject**, pro**duct**, **spec**imens, in**spect**ed). See if your child can also find compound words, contractions, and possessives.

▶ Help your child make a list of science experiments and projects he or she has done or has seen somewhere (including on TV science shows). Which experiment interests your child most? Ask why.

▶ Encourage your child to research places to visit in your local area where science is a focus. Such places include museums, state, local, or national parks and nature preserves. Then plan a day there with your child to promote science!

Book Corner

You and your child might enjoy reading these books together. Look for them in your local library.

Insect Metamorphosis
by Ron and Nancy Goor

Learn about the developmental stages of many common insects.

A Young Person's Guide to Science
by Roy A. Gallant

Explore scientific theories and innovations in this authoritative text.

Sincerely,

Carta para la casa

Estimada familia,

En las semanas próximas, su hijo/a va a explorar las raíces de palabras, palabras compuestas, posesivos y contracciones en inglés. También seguiremos aprendiendo acerca de las sílabas.

Actividades para hacer en casa

▶ Miren el poema al dorso de esta carta con su hijo/a. Miren a ver si él o ella puede hallar palabras que contengan las raíces **mit**, **ject**, **duct**, **spec**, **[submitted (sometido), project (proyecto), products (productos), specimens (especímenes)]**. Miren a ver si su hijo/a también puede hallar palabras compuestas, contracciones y posesivos.

▶ Ayuden a su hijo/a a hacer una lista de experimentos y proyectos de ciencia que él o ella ha hecho o que haya visto en algún sitio (incluyendo programas de ciencia en la televisión). ¿Qué experimento le interesa más a su hijo/a? Pregúntenle la razón.

▶ Animen a su hijo/a a investigar los lugares que se puedan visitar en su localidad que se concentren en las ciencias. Estos lugares pueden incluir museos, parques estatales, locales o nacionales y reservas naturales. Luego, planeen pasarse un día con su hijo/a en este lugar para ¡explorar las ciencias!

Quizás a su hijo/a y a ustedes les guste leer estos libros juntos. Búsquenlos en la biblioteca de su localidad.

Insect Metamorphosis
por Ron and Nancy Goor

Aprendan sobre las etapas del desarrollo de muchos insectos comunes.

A Young Person's Guide to Science
por Roy A. Gallant

Exploren teorías e innovaciones científicas en este texto autorizado en la materia.

Atentamente, _____

Unit 4

Pages 93–94

Roots, Compounds, Possessives, Contractions, Syllables

Unit Focus

USING THE PAGE

- Read the poem aloud emphasizing the rhythm and then have volunteers reread each verse.

- Ask students to describe in their own words science fair images they enjoyed the most.

- **Critical Thinking** Read aloud and discuss the answer to the question the character asks at the bottom of page 93. Encourage recollections of pride at solving problems and completing a project whether or not one won a prize.

BUILDING A CONTEXT

- As you read the poem aloud again, have students identify the compound word, or a word that is made up of two smaller words they know (*earthquake*), and then words that show possession, or ownership (*Jones's friend's, Zack's*).

- Then challenge students to pick out the contractions, or two words written together with one or more letters left out (*couldn't, Mine's, I've*).

- Read the poem slowly. See if students can find words containing the roots *mit, ject, duct, spec, spect, pul,* and *pel.* Then ask volunteers to count the number of beats, or syllables, in a line.

UNIT 4 — Roots, Compounds, Possessives, Contractions, Syllables

At the Science Fair

We rushed into the science fair,
We couldn't wait at all,
To see the kinds of projects made
From stuff bought at the mall.

We looked about for projects
that each of us submitted,
After all the work we did
It was time to see who'd win it!

There was a tree with pointed leaves,
That I grew from a nut.
And Betty Jones's frog display,
I suspect will make first cut!

We inspected tiny specimens;
A volcano spouting steam.
But my friend's video on molds
Was the weirdest thing I've seen!

Then we saw Zack's earthquake,
Made from wire and clay,
A motor produced vibrations—
And it won first prize today!

What kinds of projects have you produced for the science fair?

Critical Thinking

UNIT OPENER ACTIVITIES

ANYBODY CAN DO IT!

Have students look through library books and science magazines to find and report on one really good and unusual science fair project many in the class might want to try.

ANOTHER PROJECT FOR THE FAIR

Invite students to write an additional verse for the poem that describes a project they might have submitted to the fair. Encourage students to have fun coming up with an idea. Invite students to read their verses aloud.

BIG BOARD WORD SEARCH

Challenge students to make a word-search puzzle of science fair words, such as *volcano, electricity, earthquakes,* and *experiment.* Have them create a large-scale version of the puzzle on the board so their classmates can search for the words.

Home Letter

Dear Family,

In the upcoming weeks your child will be exploring the roots of words, compound words, possessives, and contractions. We'll also continue to learn about syllables.

At-Home Activities

▶ Look at the poem on the other side of this letter with your child. See if he or she can find words containing the roots **mit, ject, duct, spec, spect** (sub**mit**ted, pro**ject**, pro**duct**, **spec**imens, in**spect**ed). See if your child can also find compound words, contractions, and possessives.

▶ Help your child make a list of science experiments and projects he or she has done or has seen somewhere (including on TV science shows). Which experiment interests your child most? Ask why.

▶ Encourage your child to research places to visit in your local area where science is a focus. Such places include museums, state, local, or national parks and nature preserves. Then plan a day there with your child to promote science!

Book Corner

You and your child might enjoy reading these books together. Look for them in your local library.

Insect Metamorphosis by Ron and Nancy Goor

Learn about the developmental stages of many common insects.

A Young Person's Guide to Science by Roy A. Gallant

Explore scientific theories and innovations in this authoritative text.

Sincerely,

_____

94 Unit 4 Introduction

BULLETIN BOARD

Invite students to create posters advertising a science fair at their school. Remind students to include illustrations of some of the projects at the fair, as well as the time, date, and place. Display the posters on a bulletin board entitled "Come to the Fair."

- The Home Letter on page 94 is intended to acquaint family members with the word study skills students will be studying in the unit. Students may tear out page 94 and take it home. Encourage students to complete the activities on the page with a family member and encourage them to look in the library for the books listed on page 94.

- The Home Letter can also be found on page 93q in Spanish.

CURRICULUM CONNECTIONS ✳ ● ◆ ■ ◆

WRITING

Invite students to make a list of animals, insects, or other science-fair topics. Then have students choose one topic and write alliterative pyramids about that topic, such as

trees

thorny trees

terribly thorny trees

terribly thorny trees tangle

FINE ARTS

Have students do their own experiments with animation by making a simple flip book. In the top corner of each page of a small notebook, or some sheets of paper folded up, have students draw a ball, changing its position a little each time. Explain that if they bend the corner of the book back and flick the pages, the ball will appear to bounce up and down on the page.

SCIENCE

Challenge students to research one of the science topics mentioned in the poem, such as miniature trees, called bonsai, or volcanoes. Encourage students to give an oral presentation, including a photograph, a picture, or a chart to illustrate the information.

Lesson 43

Pages 95–96

Roots
pos, pel, pul, port, ject

Lesson Focus

INTRODUCING THE SKILL

● Remind students that a root is a word part to which a prefix or suffix may be added to change its meaning.

● Write these roots on the board and discuss them.

  pos—to put or place

  pel, pul—to push, drive, or thrust

  port—to carry

  ject—to throw or force

● Write the following words on the board: *composer, repellent, repulsive, portable, injected.* Call on volunteers to circle the roots.

● Ask other volunteers to use each word in a sentence and to explain the meaning of the word.

USING THE PAGES

Be sure students understand how to complete pages 95 and 96. After they have completed the pages, encourage them to talk about the words they found in the word puzzle on page 95.

Name _____

▶ Read the sentences and underline the words that contain the roots **pos, pel,** or **pul.**

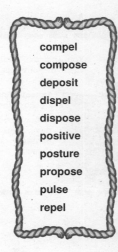

DEFINITIONS
A **root** is a word part to which a prefix or suffix may be added to change its meaning. **Pos** usually means *put* or *place.* **Pel** or **pul** usually means *push* or *drive.*

position = the way in which a person or thing is placed or arranged

pro**pel** = to push or drive forward

1. Our gym teacher <u>proposed</u> that our class complete a ropes course.

2. I was nervous, but I was <u>positively</u> sure I wanted to go.

3. My <u>pulse</u> raced when I first saw the ropes course.

4. I stared at the steel cables and ropes and tried to <u>dispel</u> my fear.

5. For safety we were <u>compelled</u> to wear helmets and harnesses.

6. The mosquitoes made me wish I'd remembered insect <u>repellent</u>.

7. I cheered my best friend as she got into <u>position</u> to start the course.

8. At the end of the day, we were happy to <u>repose</u> on the grass.

▶ Find and circle the words with the roots **pos, pel,** or **pul** in the puzzle. Some of the words go across, and some go down. Use the word bank to help you.

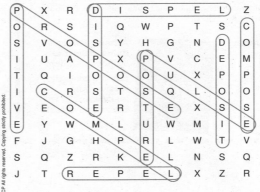

compel
compose
deposit
dispel
dispose
positive
posture
propose
pulse
repel

FOCUS ON ALL LEARNERS

ENGLISH LANGUAGE LEARNERS/ESL

Before students complete the second activity on page 95, help them try to visualize what a ropes course is. Invite volunteers to role-play the scene as you discuss the kinds of activities students would encounter at a ropes course.

LARGE GROUP

VISUAL/AUDITORY LEARNERS

Write the following roots and clues on the board. Ask the class to answer each clue orally with a word that contains the underlined root.

<u>port</u>: products brought into a country (*imports*)

<u>pel</u>: throw out (*expel*)

<u>pos</u>: to suggest (*propose*)

<u>ject</u>: refuse to use (*reject*)

<u>pul</u>: force out (*expulsion*)

PARTNER

KINESTHETIC LEARNERS

Materials: index cards

Have partners write the following roots on index cards: *pos, pel, pul, port, ject.* As partners draw from the pile of cards, they say a word with that root and use the word correctly in a sentence. Each correctly used word earns one point.

Fill in the blanks with the word from the word bank that fits the definition. Then write the circled letters on the last line to answer the riddle.

| subject | adjectives | portfolio | important |
| projector | reporter | transported | |

1. machine to show movies — p (r) o j e c t o r
2. describing words — (a) d j e c t i v e s
3. having great value — i m p o r (t) a n t
4. person who gathers news — r e p o r t (e) r
5. a case for carrying papers — p o r t f o l (i) o
6. carried — t r a n s p o r t (e) d
7. topic — (s) u b j e c t

Riddle

Why did the baby snakes cry? They lost their ___ rattles ___ !

Write the word from the word bank that correctly completes the sentence.

1. The _____ **subject** _____ of Sasha's science report was the migration of birds.
2. She used colorful _____ **adjectives** _____ to describe the birds.
3. A _____ **portfolio** _____ of famous bird prints was part of Sasha's report.
4. With a movie _____ **projector** _____, Sasha showed films of migrating birds.
5. Like an experienced news _____ **reporter** _____, she used a world map to explain bird migratory routes.
6. Sasha explained that bird migration is automatic, almost as if something _____ **transported** _____ them south for the winter.
7. Birds use different methods to find their way, including using _____ **important** _____ land forms as markers.

96 Lesson 43
Roots port, ject

SPELLING

The following sentences can be used as a pretest for spelling words with roots *pos, pel, port, ject, aud, dict, duct, duce, scribe, script*.

1. **position**	I sit in one **position** without moving.
2. **propel**	The force of the engines will **propel** the plane forward.
3. **portable**	I can carry a **portable** radio.
4. **eject**	Will the pilot **eject** out of the plane?
5. **audible**	The music is barely **audible.**
6. **predict**	I **predict** you will win the race.
7. **conduct**	Will you **conduct** the orchestra?
8. **inscribe**	Will you **inscribe** the book to me?
9. **introduce**	**Introduce** me to your friend.
10. **subscription**	I have a magazine **subscription.**

WRITING

Portfolio Invite students to imagine they have spent a day with their classmates at a ropes course. Have students write a description of what they did and how they felt. Challenge students to use words with the roots studied in this lesson in their descriptions.

SCIENCE

Encourage students to research their favorite bird, finding out where these birds live and what their migration patterns are like. Have students draw a map to show the bird's migration pattern.

ART

Invite students to create a portfolio of bird prints by drawing their favorite birds on separate sheets of chart paper and displaying them together in a class portfolio.

AUDITORY/VISUAL LEARNERS

LARGE GROUP

Write these words on the board, omitting the underlined parts: *pulse, object, support, propose, compelled, positive, position, subject, reject, important*. Have students copy the words and underline the roots. Then challenge them to use the words in a paragraph about an issue they support or oppose.

GIFTED LEARNERS

Challenge students to make a crossword puzzle with words from the lesson. Encourage students to complete each other's puzzles.

LEARNERS WHO NEED EXTRA SUPPORT

Have students take turns using one word from the lesson in a sentence. Another student can then use the same word in a different sentence. **See Daily Word Study Practice, page 187.**

Roots
aud, dict, duct, duce, duc, scribe, script

Lesson Focus

INTRODUCING THE SKILL

- Ask volunteers to write the following roots on the board: *aud, dict, duct, duce, duc, scribe, script.*

- Discuss the meaning of *aud* (hear). Write *audience* on the board and ask a volunteer to use the word in a sentence and to explain its meaning.

- Repeat this procedure, using these definitions and words: *dict* (tell or say), *dictate; duct* (lead), *inducted; duce* (lead), *produced; duc* (lead), *educate; scribe* (write or something written), *inscribed; script* (write or something written), *prescription.*

- Challenge students to name additional words with these roots and to use them in sentences.

USING THE PAGES

Be sure students understand how to complete pages 97 and 98 and provide help as needed as they work. After they have completed the pages, have students speculate about Kim's future and why Rick's sales techniques are good ones. Then ask them how knowing the meanings of word roots can help them figure out the meaning of unfamiliar words.

97

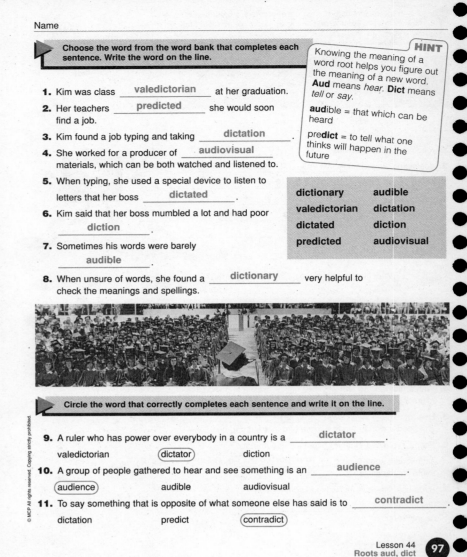

Name _____

▶ Choose the word from the word bank that completes each sentence. Write the word on the line.

HINT

Knowing the meaning of a word root helps you figure out the meaning of a new word. **Aud** means *hear.* **Dict** means *tell* or *say.*

audible = that which can be heard

pre**dict** = to tell what one thinks will happen in the future

1. Kim was class ____valedictorian____ at her graduation.

2. Her teachers ____predicted____ she would soon find a job.

3. Kim found a job typing and taking ____dictation____

4. She worked for a producer of ____audiovisual____ materials, which can be both watched and listened to.

5. When typing, she used a special device to listen to letters that her boss ____dictated____

6. Kim said that her boss mumbled a lot and had poor ____diction____.

7. Sometimes his words were barely ____audible____.

8. When unsure of words, she found a ____dictionary____ very helpful to check the meanings and spellings.

dictionary	audible
valedictorian	dictation
dictated	diction
predicted	audiovisual

▶ Circle the word that correctly completes each sentence and write it on the line.

9. A ruler who has power over everybody in a country is a ____dictator____.

valedictorian   (dictator)   diction

10. A group of people gathered to hear and see something is an ____audience____

(audience)   audible   audiovisual

11. To say something that is opposite of what someone else has said is to ____contradict____

dictation   predict   (contradict)

FOCUS ON ALL LEARNERS

ENGLISH LANGUAGE LEARNERS/ESL

Before beginning page 98, ask volunteers to role-play the scene in items 1–7 in which a boy sells magazine subscriptions door-to-door.

VISUAL LEARNERS

PARTNER Challenge pairs to collaborate on sentences using the following words: *audible, diction, conductor, subscribes, induced.* Suggest that they exchange sentences with another pair to compare each other's work.

KINESTHETIC/AUDITORY LEARNERS

LARGE GROUP Post the roots *aud, dict, duct, duce, duc, scribe,* and *script* in different parts of the room. Read each word below and have students stand next to its posted root. Ask them to use each word in a sentence. Try *diction, audience, conduct, describe, reduce,* and *educate.*

Read each word in the list. Underline the prefix and circle the root in each word.

HINT
Roots and prefixes can be combined in different ways to create many words. Knowing the meaning of both roots and prefixes can add many words to your vocabulary.

Root: Duct, duc, or **duce** usually means *lead*.

Scribe or **script** usually mean *write* or *something written*.

con**duct** = to lead or guide

in**scribe** = to write, print, carve, or engrave

Prefix: Intro usually means *in* or *into*. **E** usually means *from* or *away*. **Re** usually means *back* or *again*.

introduce = to add or put in

eject = to force out or from

recur = to happen or come again

de(scribe)   re(duce)d   intro(duce)
sub(scribe)   de(duc)e   e(duc)ate
con(script)   con(duct)   pro(duce)
(educ)ation   sub(scrip)tions   de(duct)

Use a word from the words above to complete each sentence. The roots and prefixes will help you find the correct word.

1. Rick decided to make money by selling magazine _____subscriptions_____ .

2. Rick learned to _____conduct_____ business in a very professional way.

3. He would knock on doors, _____introduce_____ himself by giving his name, and ask for orders.

4. Then he would _____describe_____ the various magazines on his list in great detail.

5. To promote sales, he offered to _____deduct_____ the cost of the first issue from the total bill.

6. He found that even though this _____reduced_____ his initial profits, it increased his total sales.

7. The experience added greatly to his math _____education_____

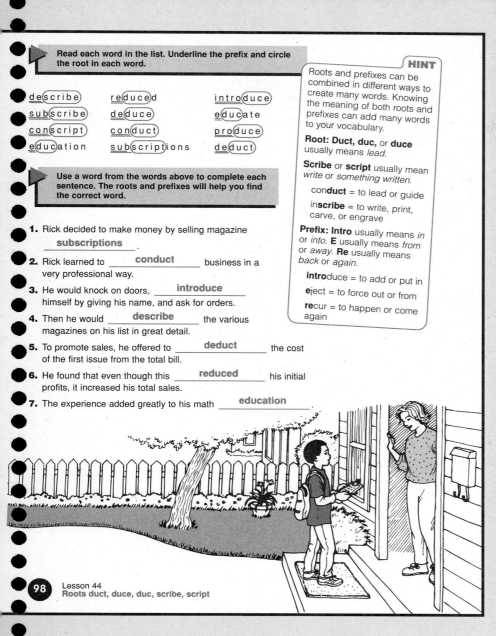

98 Lesson 44
Roots duct, duce, duc, scribe, script

SPELLING

The following sentences can be used as a posttest for spelling words with roots *pos, pel, port, ject, aud, dict, duct, duce, scribe, script*.

1. **position**   What **position** do you play?
2. **propel**   My legs **propel** the swing.
3. **portable**   They have a **portable** stove.
4. **eject**   The tape will **eject** from the player when it is finished.
5. **audible**   Your voice is not **audible** on the tape.
6. **predict**   Who can **predict** the future?
7. **conduct**   I will **conduct** the band.
8. **inscribe**   Please **inscribe** the book neatly.
9. **introduce**   Let me **introduce** my teacher.
10. **subscription** The **subscription** was ten dollars.

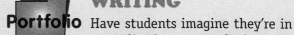

WRITING

Portfolio Have students imagine they're in an auditorium, part of a large audience, and something is happening on stage that is barely audible. What's going on? Ask students to describe the event and what's happened to produce this state of affairs. Encourage them to use words from the lesson in their stories.

SOCIAL STUDIES

Have students imagine a group of students are visiting your school from another country. Ask students to write an introduction to your school, including a general description of the school and a map of the inside of the building.

MUSIC

Play recordings of classical music—try Beethoven, Mozart, or Handel. Invite students to listen to several minutes (or more) of each composer, then write what they liked or didn't like about what they heard as they make comparisons. Ask them to use words with roots *aud, dict, duct, scribe,* and *script*.

AUDITORY LEARNERS

LARGE GROUP Write *scribe, script, duct, aud, duce,* and *dict* on the board. Say *prepares a manuscript, prescribes medicine, auditions for a play, introduces speakers, dictates letters, predicts an eclipse.* Have students identify which root was used and who is described.

GIFTED LEARNERS

Ask students to describe a job they have done to make money, such as baby-sitting, dog-walking, yardwork, or housework, using as many words with the roots *aud, dict, duct, duce, duc, scribe,* and *script* as possible.

LEARNERS WHO NEED EXTRA SUPPORT

Read the words in the box on page 97 and at the top of page 98 with students. Help them define each word before they begin the practice. **See Daily Word Study Practice, page 187.**

Lesson 45
Pages 99–100

Roots
spec, spect, mit, miss, fac, fect, fic, feit

INFORMAL ASSESSMENT OBJECTIVES

Can students

✔ associate the roots *spec, spect, mit, miss, fac, fect, fic,* and *feit* with their meanings?

✔ identify and write words with the roots *spec, spect, mit, miss, fac, fect, fic,* and *feit*?

Lesson Focus

INTRODUCING THE SKILL

- Write the following roots and their meanings on the board.

  spec, spect—see, look, examine

  mit, miss—send, or let go

  fac, fect, fic, feit—do, make, or cause

- Discuss the roots and their meanings. Then write these words on the board beside their roots: *speculate, spectator, permit, dismiss, factory, perfect, fiction, counterfeit.* Call on volunteers to circle the roots.

- Discuss the meanings of the words and encourage volunteers to use the words in sentences.

- Challenge the class to suggest additional words with the roots *spec, spect, mit, miss, fac, fect, fic,* and *feit.*

USING THE PAGES

Give students help as necessary to complete pages 99 and 100. After students have completed the pages, encourage them to talk about how they figured out the words in the puzzle.

Name _____

▶ **Read the sentences and underline the words that contain the roots spec, spect, mit, or miss.**

HINT
Knowing the meaning of a word root helps you figure out the meaning of a new word. **Spec** or **spect** can mean *see, look,* or *examine.* **Mit** or **miss** can mean *send* or *let go.*
in**spect**ed = to look at carefully
dis**miss** = to send away

1. I have to admit it, I love a good mystery novel or movie.

2. I always feel like a spectator at the scene of a crime!

3. My favorite detective is the great Sherlock Holmes, who inspected the smallest details at a crime site.

4. His acute sense of observation enabled him to solve mysteries by deductive speculation.

5. He never dismissed a single shred of evidence as unimportant.

6. Holmes' often permitted his assistant, Dr. Watson, to examine the evidence as well.

7. But Holmes rarely respected anyone's opinions other than his own.

8. Sherlock Holmes amazes me—and the prospect of reading another story about him fills me with . . . well, you read one, you'll see what I mean.

▶ **Write the number of each word beside its meaning.**

9. admit   _18_   to think of as probably guilty

10. dismiss   _9_   to acknowledge or confess

11. inspect   _14_   a future possibility one is looking for

12. intermission   _12_   a period between acts in a play

13. permit   _13_   to let or allow someone to do something

14. prospect   _10_   to send from one's mind

15. respect   _15_   to think of someone with admiration

16. spectator   _16_   a person who watches or looks at something

17. speculate   _11_   to examine or look at carefully

18. suspect   _17_   to think about or consider something

Lesson 45
Roots spec, spect, mit, miss   **99**

FOCUS ON ALL LEARNERS

ENGLISH LANGUAGE LEARNERS/ESL

To build background for page 99, explain that Sherlock Holmes is one of the most famous fictional detectives ever created. Have students describe their favorite detective or mystery characters.

VISUAL LEARNERS

PARTNER   Challenge students to create word-search puzzles using words with the roots *spec, spect, mit, miss, fac, fect, fic,* and *feit.* Before beginning, they may want to go on a word hunt. Students can exchange papers with a partner and solve each other's puzzle.

KINESTHETIC/VISUAL LEARNERS

LARGE GROUP   On the board, write *inspect, dismiss, spectator, defective,* and *forfeit.* Invite volunteers to choose one word and then draw a sketch or role-play its meaning for classmates to guess the word.

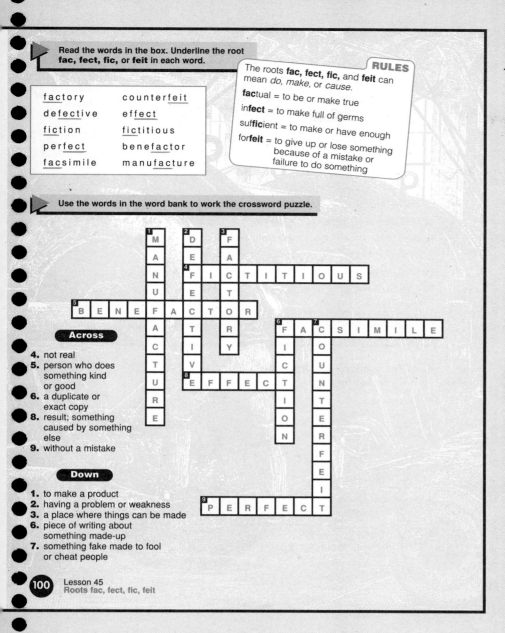

▶ Read the words in the box. Underline the root **fac, fect, fic,** or **feit** in each word.

RULES

The roots **fac, fect, fic,** and **feit** can mean *do, make,* or *cause.*

factual = to be or make true
in**fect** = to make full of germs
suf**fic**ient = to make or have enough
for**feit** = to give up or lose something because of a mistake or failure to do something

factory	counterfeit
defective	effect
fiction	fictitious
perfect	benefactor
facsimile	manufacture

▶ Use the words in the word bank to work the crossword puzzle.

Across

4. not real
5. person who does something kind or good
6. a duplicate or exact copy
8. result; something caused by something else
9. without a mistake

Down

1. to make a product
2. having a problem or weakness
3. a place where things can be made
6. piece of writing about something made-up
7. something fake made to fool or cheat people

100 Lesson 45
Roots fac, fect, fic, feit

SPELLING

The following sentences can be used as a pretest for this set of spelling words.

1. **inspected** Dad **inspected** our room.
2. **dismiss** Don't **dismiss** my plan so quickly.
3. **factual** The report is **factual.**
4. **infect** Dirt can **infect** a cut.
5. **sufficient** I have **sufficient** information for my report.
6. **forfeit** Let's not **forfeit** the game.
7. **cupcake** May I eat a **cupcake?**
8. **doghouse** My pet has a **doghouse.**

WRITING

Portfolio Challenge students to write a fiction and a nonfiction paragraph, making sure to show the difference between the two types of paragraphs. Invite volunteers to read their paragraphs aloud so their classmates can guess which is fiction and which is nonfiction.

MATH

Ask students to do a survey on the kinds of books their friends and family members read for enjoyment. Have students make a list of categories such as mysteries, romances, sports, and biographies and then conduct the survey and tally the results on a chart.

ART

Invite students to make a poster advertising one of their favorite books or short stories. Remind students to show in their illustrations and their words why readers should read this particular book or story.

AUDITORY LEARNERS

PARTNER Have pairs of students conduct conversations in which they use words with the roots *spec, spect, mit, miss, fac, fect, fic,* and *feit.* Suggest that they brainstorm a list of suitable words before they begin their conversations.

GIFTED LEARNERS

Challenge students to read a Sherlock Holmes story and give a presentation to the class about the case. Encourage students to be creative—for example, they might dramatize the story or create a type of news broadcast.

LEARNERS WHO NEED EXTRA SUPPORT

Work as a group to begin each page. Have students take turns reading an item aloud and suggesting an answer. Work together to figure out the necessary words to complete the crossword puzzle. **See Daily Word Study Practice, page 187.**

Lesson 46

Pages 101-102

Compound Words

Lesson Focus

INTRODUCING THE SKILL

- Write the following sentences on the board: *This <u>afternoon</u> we will rent a <u>speedy</u> <u>motorboat</u>; Mom was <u>careful</u> to put the <u>screwdriver</u> in the <u>toolbox</u>; Ron was <u>using</u> a <u>paintbrush</u> to create the <u>cloudy</u> look on the <u>backdrop</u>.*

- Ask students to explain what a compound word is. *(a word made up of two or more smaller words; each small word can stand on its own)*

- Then have students read each sentence on the board and identify the compound words in each. *(afternoon, motorboat, screwdriver, toolbox, paintbrush, backdrop)*

- Ask why the other underlined words are not compounds. *(They are single words with suffixes.)*

- Have students write other compound words on the board and use them in sentences.

USING THE PAGES

- Ask students to read and discuss both sets of directions on page 101.

- When students have completed the practices, have them review their answers.

Name _____

 Read each sentence and underline each compound word. Be sure the words you underline are made up of two words that can stand on their own.

> **DEFINITION**
> A **compound word** is made up of two or more smaller words. Each small word can stand alone and still have meaning.
>
> cup + cake = cupcake
> dog + house = doghouse

1. Captain Orr spun the dials on the <u>dashboard</u> of the <u>spaceship</u>.
2. She pointed the ship's nose toward the <u>sunrise</u>.
3. The <u>countdown</u> and the <u>blastoff</u> went smoothly.
4. The launch, canceled twice by bad weather, had been <u>overdue</u>.
5. Now came the <u>payoff</u> for the long training of the astronauts.
6. Word of the successful launch was being <u>broadcast</u> <u>nationwide</u>.
7. Dugan watched Captain Orr chew calmly on a <u>toothpick</u>.
8. It was his first <u>spaceflight</u>, and he felt like a boy on his <u>birthday</u>.
9. <u>Someday</u> he would tell his <u>grandchildren</u> of this great adventure.

 Find the correct compound word from those you underlined above to match each definition below. Write the word on the line.

10. the instrument panel on a vehicle
    dashboard

11. a vehicle used for travel in outer space
    spaceship

12. beginning of day
    sunrise

13. the launching of a rocket
    blastoff

14. a reward for hard work
    payoff

15. a radio or television program
    broadcast

FOCUS ON ALL LEARNERS

ENGLISH LANGUAGE LEARNERS/ESL

Before they begin page 102, discuss the categories listed on the page with students. Brainstorm lists of different kinds of foods, animals, and things to wear.

VISUAL/KINESTHETIC LEARNERS

LARGE GROUP

Make two columns on the board—one with the words *light, house, coast, land,* and *summer* and the other with the words *mark, time, house, line,* and *boat.* Have students form compound words by connecting one word in each column. Ask volunteers to write the completed words on the board.

KINESTHETIC LEARNERS

 PARTNER

Materials: index cards

Make word cards for *pea, nut, wrist, watch, lady, bug, paint, box, space, flight, grand, child, sun,* and *rise.* Partners place the cards face down in a stack and draw cards to make compound word matches.

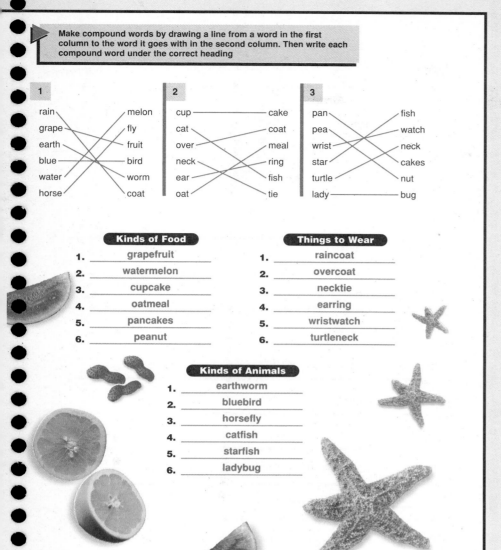

Make compound words by drawing a line from a word in the first column to the word it goes with in the second column. Then write each compound word under the correct heading

1

rain — melon
grape — fly
earth — fruit
blue — bird
water — worm
horse — coat

2

cup — cake
cat — coat
over — meal
neck — ring
ear — fish
oat — tie

3

pan — fish
pea — watch
wrist — neck
star — cakes
turtle — nut
lady — bug

Kinds of Food

1. grapefruit
2. watermelon
3. cupcake
4. oatmeal
5. pancakes
6. peanut

Things to Wear

1. raincoat
2. overcoat
3. necktie
4. earring
5. wristwatch
6. turtleneck

Kinds of Animals

1. earthworm
2. bluebird
3. horsefly
4. catfish
5. starfish
6. ladybug

CURRICULUM CONNECTIONS

SPELLING

The following sentences can be used as a posttest for this set of spelling words.

1. **inspected** The coach **inspected** our lockers.
2. **dismiss** The teacher will **dismiss** the class.
3. **factual** I have **factual** information.
4. **infect** Don't **infect** us with your illness.
5. **sufficient** Do we have a **sufficient** amount of food for the trip?
6. **forfeit** The team will **forfeit** three points.
7. **cupcake** Look at that delicious **cupcake**.
8. **doghouse** That's a huge **doghouse**.

WRITING

Portfolio Challenge students to imagine they are tour guides and write a short script about an attraction on their tour. Suggest they use the compound words in their script. Provide "tour time" so guides can show classmates the sights.

SCIENCE/MATH

Suggest students compare the times of sunrise and sunset at your latitude for today, at the solstices (June 21 and December 21), and at the equinoxes (March 21 and September 21). Have them make a graph showing how the amount of daylight changes throughout the year.

FINE ARTS

Portfolio Invite students to design a menu for a new restaurant serving only food whose names are compound words. Breakfast might include oatmeal and pancakes. Encourage them to decorate their menus and give the restaurant a catchy name.

AstroWord Compound Words ©1998 Silver Burdett Ginn Inc. Division of Simon & Schuster.

AUDITORY LEARNERS

SMALL GROUP Have group members take turns offering compound words for the others to define as well as identify the words that make up the compound.

GIFTED LEARNERS

Challenge students to create riddles for nonsense compound words such as: *What's an ultrasweet breakfast food? (pancandy)* Invite volunteers to dramatize their riddles for their classmates.

LEARNERS WHO NEED EXTRA SUPPORT

Visit each student as he or she works. Review work already completed, and help the student identify the words that form each compound word. **See Daily Word Study Practice, page 188.**

Lesson 47

Pages 103–104

Possessives

INFORMAL ASSESSMENT OBJECTIVE

Can students
✔ form possessives by using the apostrophe?

Lesson Focus

INTRODUCING THE SKILL

● Write these pairs of sentences on the board: *Bill has a dog named Spike. Bill's dog is named Spike. The students took interesting courses. The students' courses were interesting. The children have a special room in the library. The children's room in the library is special.*

● Use the first two pairs of sentences to help students recall that adding *'s* to singular nouns shows that someone owns, has, or possesses something (*Bill's dog*) and that only an apostrophe is added to plural nouns that end in *s* to show possession (*students' courses*).

● Have students read the third pair of sentences. Point out *children* in the first sentence and have students identify it as a plural noun. Ask how the possessive of these irregular plural nouns are formed. *(by adding 's)*

USING THE PAGES

Ask students to read the directions and the definition on page 103. Explain that not all sentences will be completed by a possessive, so they'll need to read the sentences carefully.

● **Critical Thinking** Read aloud the question on page 104 and discuss answers with students.

Name _____

▶ Read each sentence. Then fill in the circle beside the word that correctly completes the sentence.

Critical Thinking

How does Tom celebrate his special day? Read the story to find out.

DEFINITION
This mark (') is called an apostrophe. An **'s** can be added to a word to show ownership or possession.

Ella**'s** book = a book belonging to Ella

1. On Saturday night, Tom threw back the _____ on his bed.
   - ● covers
   - ○ cover's

2. His _____ noisy growling confirmed his hunger.
   - ○ stomach
   - ● stomach's

3. The _____ creaked as he crept down for a late-night snack.
   - ● stairs
   - ○ stair's

4. He heard his _____ voice in the living room.
   - ○ mothers
   - ● mother's

5. Sunday was the _____ tenth birthday.
   - ○ boys
   - ● boy's

6. His _____ were planning a surprise party.
   - ● parents
   - ○ parent's

7. On Sunday he obeyed his _____ call to come downstairs.
   - ○ sisters
   - ● sister's

8. Twenty _____ yelled "Happy Birthday!"
   - ● voices
   - ○ voice's

9. A _____ wheel peeked through the huge package.
   - ○ bikes
   - ● bike's

10. _____ surprise was real, but it had nothing to do with the party.
    - ○ Toms
    - ● Tom's

Lesson 47
Possessives **103**

FOCUS ON ALL LEARNERS

ENGLISH LANGUAGE LEARNERS/ESL

Before students work on page 103 independently, read the answer choice words on the page together and have them identify which is a plural and which is a possessive.

VISUAL LEARNERS

INDIVIDUAL Have students write three story titles that contain possessives—one singular, one a plural ending in *s*, one an irregular plural not ending in *s*, for example, *Molly's Magic Glasses; The Pilots' Secret Mission; The Geese's Golden Eggs.*

KINESTHETIC LEARNERS

LARGE GROUP Write these phrases on the board: *the award won by Gary; the painting that the men had; the backpacks of the hikers.* Ask students to write the possessive for each phrase. Then have students suggest other phrases.

Read each sentence below. Write the correct possessive form of the word you see below the line. Look back at the rules if you need to.

1. _____ **Maria's** _____ greatest wish was to

Maria

explore caves.

2. There are many caves to explore in her

_____ **community's** _____ hills.

community

3. She tried to get her _____ **parents'** _____

parents

permission to go exploring.

4. "It isn't a safe _____ **children's** _____

children

hobby," her mother said.

5. Her Dad belongs to a _____ **men's** _____

men

group for spelunkers, or cave explorers.

6. She finally got her _____ **father's** _____

father

promise to take her exploring.

7. They invited Ron, _____ **Maria's** _____ friend, to

Maria

go with them.

8. Ron's father belongs to the cave

_____ **explorers'** _____ group, too.

explorers

9. On the _____ **friends'** _____ first cave visit,

friends

they heard a strange noise.

10. It was the sound of hundreds of

_____ **bats'** _____ wings.

bats

11. Maria ran back to the _____ **cave's** _____ mouth.

cave

12. Neither Maria nor Ron have asked to explore a

_____ **bat's** _____ cave since!

bat

104 Lesson 47
Possessives

Do you think Maria and Ron will want to explore a cave again? Why or why not?

Critical Thinking

CURRICULUM CONNECTIONS

SPELLING

The following sentences can be used as a pretest for spelling words that are either possessives, contractions, or have two or more syllables.

1. **it's** — It's a great idea!
2. **I'll** — I'll clean my room now.
3. **we're** — We're going to the movies today.
4. **boys'** — That is the door to the boys' gym.
5. **children's** — I like the children's friends.
6. **antidote** — Sleep is an antidote for exhaustion.
7. **underground** — The water pipes are underground.

WRITING

Portfolio Challenge students to write alliterative sentences with possessives. Examples are *Bill's brother buys balloons* and *Heather's horse hurdles high hedges.*

SOCIAL STUDIES

Encourage students to research the natural features—caves, mountains, waterfalls, marshes—of their state. Have them choose one to report orally to the class during a "Touring [your state name] Naturally" period.

SCIENCE

Explain to students that a spelunker is a person who explores caves. Challenge them to find out how caves are formed, what kinds of animals live in them, where they are most frequently found in the United States, and why spelunking is a popular pastime. Ask them to use three possessives in their reports.

Lesson 48

Pages 105–106

Contractions

Lesson Focus

INTRODUCING THE SKILL

- Help students recall that a contraction is a short way of writing two words. In a contraction, two words are written together with one or more letters left out. An apostrophe stands for the missing letters.

- Write these contractions on the board: *couldn't, she's, you've, they're, they'll, he'd, I'm.* Ask students what two words are represented by each contraction and which letter or letters are missing.

- Point out that the contraction *can't* is a short way of writing the word *cannot.* Write both words on the board.

USING THE PAGES

Be sure students understand how to complete pages 105 and 106. Suggest they first read the story on page 106 before they underline the contractions. When they have finished, encourage them to review their work with a partner.

105

Name _____

On the first line, write the contraction from the word bank that stands for each pair of words. Then, on the second line, write the letter or letters that have been left out.

DEFINITION

A **contraction** is a short way of writing two words. The two words are written together with one or more letters left out. An apostrophe stands for the missing letters.

it is = it's (The letter **i** has been left out.)

I will = I'll (The letters **wi** have been left out.)

We are = we're (The letter **a** has been left out.)

wouldn't	you're	they'll
didn't	we're	I'm
it's	we'll	I've

	Contraction	Letters
1. we are	we're	a
2. did not	didn't	o
3. I am	I'm	a
4. would not	wouldn't	o
5. they will	they'll	wi
6. you are	you're	a
7. it is	it's	i
8. I have	I've	ha
9. we will	we'll	wi

can't	she'll	you've	that's
let's	don't	he's	isn't

	Contraction	Letters
10. she will	she'll	wi
11. you have	you've	ha
12. is not	isn't	o
13. let us	let's	u
14. he is	he's	i
15. can not	can't	no
16. that is	that's	i
17. do not	don't	o

Lesson 48
Contractions
105

FOCUS ON ALL LEARNERS

ENGLISH LANGUAGE LEARNERS/ESL

Before students begin page 105, have them make up sentences to show how they would use a contraction for *did not, is not, do not,* and *I am.*

VISUAL LEARNERS

SMALL GROUP Divide the class into three groups. Ask the first group to list contractions with *not;* the second group to list contractions with *will;* and the last group to list contractions with *is.* Invite each group to share its list with the rest of the class.

KINESTHETIC LEARNERS

INDIVIDUAL **Materials:** construction paper, felt-tip markers

Have each student design a thank-you note to send to someone who has done something nice for him or her. Ask students to include contractions in their notes so that the notes sound natural and informal.

Read the story and underline each contraction. Then write the two words that each contraction stands for.

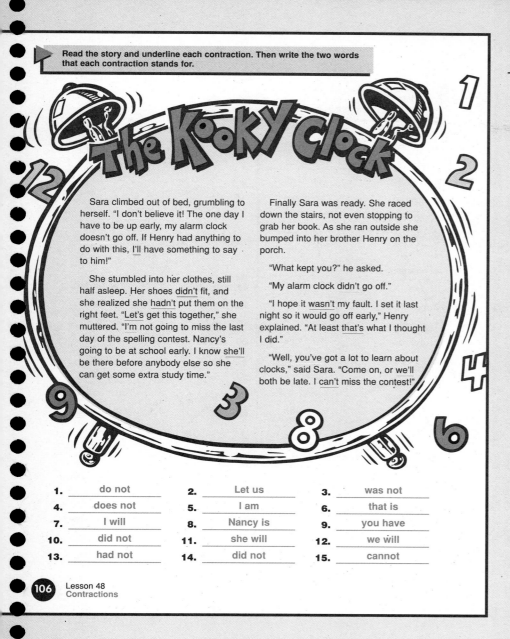

The Kooky Clock

Sara climbed out of bed, grumbling to herself. "I don't believe it! The one day I have to be up early, my alarm clock doesn't go off. If Henry had anything to do with this, I'll have something to say to him!"

She stumbled into her clothes, still half asleep. Her shoes didn't fit, and she realized she hadn't put them on the right feet. "Let's get this together," she muttered. "I'm not going to miss the last day of the spelling contest. Nancy's going to be at school early. I know she'll be there before anybody else so she can get some extra study time."

Finally Sara was ready. She raced down the stairs, not even stopping to grab her book. As she ran outside she bumped into her brother Henry on the porch.

"What kept you?" he asked.

"My alarm clock didn't go off."

"I hope it wasn't my fault. I set it last night so it would go off early," Henry explained. "At least that's what I thought I did."

"Well, you've got a lot to learn about clocks," said Sara. "Come on, or we'll both be late. I can't miss the contest!"

1.	do not	2.	Let us	3.	was not
4.	does not	5.	I am	6.	that is
7.	I will	8.	Nancy is	9.	you have
10.	did not	11.	she will	12.	we will
13.	had not	14.	did not	15.	cannot

Lesson 48
Contractions

106

CURRICULUM CONNECTIONS

SPELLING

Write the words *it's, I'll, we're, boys', children's, antidote, underground* on the chalkboard and ask students to write a sentence using each one.

WRITING

Portfolio Suggest students write both a formal and an informal report about a contest or a match. It can be one they attended, a spelling bee or race, or one they made up. Remind them to use contractions in the informal version.

MATH

Have students turn the contractions from the lesson into equations by writing them with symbols. For example: *they will – wi + ' = they'll.*

SOCIAL STUDIES

Plan a debate about a school issue, such as Should there be in-school contests? longer school hours? a school newspaper? Let students choose pro or con and write a persuasive speech explaining their views. Give them time to research their topic and to brainstorm with students who share their position. Encourage them to use possessives and contractions in their speeches. Set aside time for a debate.

LARGE GROUP

AUDITORY LEARNERS

Read the following idioms and have students identify the two words in each that could be combined to form a contraction: *He is* pulling my leg. *I am* in the doghouse. *It is* raining cats and dogs. *You are* barking up the wrong tree. *I have* had a change of heart.

GIFTED LEARNERS

Challenge students to work with a partner to have a conversation without using any contractions. A third person can keep track of how many times each partner accidentally uses a contraction. The student with the lowest score wins.

LEARNERS WHO NEED EXTRA SUPPORT

Let students work in pairs to complete the practice on page 105. Since contractions are mainly used when we speak, suggest that reading each item aloud may help them match the item with its contraction in the box. **See Daily Word Study Practice, page 188.**

Lesson 49

Pages 107–108

Syllables

Lesson Focus

INTRODUCING THE SKILL

- Remind students that a word has as many syllables as it has vowel sounds. Write these examples on the board: *tram/po/line, do/nate, plum.*

- Tell students that some prefixes have more than one syllable. Words that have a prefix are always divided between the prefix and the base word.

- Write these words on the board, omitting the slashes, and ask volunteers to divide the words into syllables: *au/to/bi/og/ra/phy, un/like/ly, pro/long, dis/o/bey, o/ver/come, pre/dict, in/crease, an/ti/slav/er/ly, mon/o/rail.*

- Write the following compound words on the board, omitting the slashes: *star/fish, bed/room, Thanks/giv/ing, waste/bas/ket.* Ask students to divide the words into syllables. Suggest that they first divide the two words that make up the compound word and then divide the smaller words.

USING THE PAGES

Help students if they need it as they complete pages 107 and 108. After they have completed the pages, ask them to summarize the rules for dividing a word with a prefix into syllables.

Name _____

Say each word. On the first line, write the number of syllables it has. Then write the word and divide it into syllables, using vertical lines.

HINT
A word has as many syllables as it has vowel sounds. A prefix is a syllable in itself if it contains a vowel sound. Divide the word between the prefix and the base word. Remember that some prefixes have more than one syllable.
re/turn   an/ti/dote

1. dispose	2	dis/pose	
2. subject	2	sub/ject	
3. predict	2	pre/dict	
4. audible	3	au/di/ble	
5. introduce	3	in/tro/duce	
6. reduce	2	re/duce	
7. permit	2	per/mit	
8. spectator	3	spec/ta/tor	
9. defect	2	de/fect	
10. posture	2	pos/ture	
11. subdivide	3	sub/di/vide	
12. biennial	4	bi/en/ni/al	
13. transport	2	trans/port	
14. dictation	3	dic/ta/tion	
15. subscribe	2	sub/scribe	
16. mission	2	mis/sion	

17. counterfeit	3	coun/ter/feit
18. perfect	2	per/fect
19. deceive	2	de/ceive
20. expect	2	ex/pect
21. conduct	2	con/duct
22. reporter	3	re/port/er
23. postscript	2	post/script
24. submerge	2	sub/merge

Read each sentence, find the missing word, and write it on the line.

25. Mom said I could __subscribe__ to the magazine for the summer.

subscribe
subject

26. A __reporter__ from a magazine interviewed the girl who saved the drowning child.

reporter
spectator

Lesson 49
Syllables **107**

FOCUS ON ALL LEARNERS

ENGLISH LANGUAGE LEARNERS/ESL

Before beginning page 108, ask students if they have ever seen the ocean. Have them describe what an outing to the seashore might be like. You may want to read the words at the top of page 107 aloud so students can hear them pronounced.

VISUAL/KINESTHETIC LEARNERS

LARGE GROUP

Materials: colored chalk

Write *expect, transport, prescribe, receive, report, produce, microscope, disappoint,* and *object* on the board. Have students use colored chalk to divide each word into syllables.

KINESTHETIC/AUDITORY LEARNERS

LARGE GROUP

With the class in teams, say each word below. A member from each team divides the word on the board into syllables. The fastest correct division earns a point for that team. Say *monogram, inside, reading, antifreeze, overcoat, fingerprints, kangaroo, curiosity.*

Write each compound word and divide it into two words, using vertical lines. If necessary, divide the smaller words into syllables.

> **RULE**
> Divide a compound word between the two words that make up the compound word. Then, divide the smaller words into syllables.
>
> pea/nut
>
> under/ground = un/der/ground

1. seashells	sea/shells	2. strawberry	straw/ber/ry	
3. everyone	ev/ery/one	4. skyscraper	sky/scrap/er	
5. seashore	sea/shore	6. footprints	foot/prints	
7. buttonhole	but/ton/hole	8. overcoat	o/ver/coat	
9. clothespin	clothes/pin	10. classmate	class/mate	
11. anthill	ant/hill	12. workbook	work/book	
13. wristwatch	wrist/watch	14. sailboat	sail/boat	
15. mailbox	mail/box	16. newspaper	news/pa/per	
17. fingerprint	fin/ger/print	18. watermelon	wa/ter/mel/on	

Write the word from above that completes each sentence.

19. This year the class outing was held at the _____seashore_____ .
20. One _____classmate_____ had never seen the ocean before.
21. Sarah saw a sand dune and thought it looked like a giant _____anthill_____ .
22. Carl enjoyed watching a _____sailboat_____ drift in the water.
23. Louis searched for pretty _____seashells_____ in the sand.
24. We saw a dog's _____footprints_____ on the beach.
25. Our teacher looked at her _____wristwatch_____ and said it was time to go.
26. At the end of the day, _____everyone_____ went home tired but happy.

(108) Lesson 49
Syllables

CURRICULUM CONNECTIONS

SPELLING

Ask students to select and spell aloud a spelling word that corresponds to each of the following words or phrases.

1. it is *(it's)*
2. we are *(we're)*
3. I will *(I'll)*
4. belonging to the children *(children's)*
5. a remedy *(antidote)*
6. beneath the ground *(underground)*
7. belonging to the boys *(boys')*

WRITING

Portfolio Tell students that writers get their story ideas from different places, even from word lists. Challenge them to choose four words from items 1–18 on page 107 to use as a base for a story. Stories can be realistic or imaginary. When they're finished, have them choose four other words with more than two syllables to divide into syllables at the bottom of the page.

SCIENCE

Footprints are often used to solve a mystery. Have students compare the footprints their shoes would leave. How similar or different are the tread patterns? How many different patterns are there in the class? What is the most distinctive feature of each tread?

SOCIAL STUDIES/FINE ARTS

Have students create a fleet of sailboats as sculpture or collage. Suggest they research the history of sailing craft and the design of recreational sailboats of all sizes. Then they should use what they have learned to design a sailboat of their own.

AstroWord Multisyllabic Words ©1998 Silver Burdett Ginn Inc. Division of Simon & Schuster.

AUDITORY LEARNERS

SMALL GROUP Introduce the prefixes *extra*, *ultra*, and *super* to students and have them identify the number of syllables in each. *(two)* Explain that they all mean "going beyond what is usual or ordinary." Ask groups to use the prefixes to describe a product to try to "sell" to the class.

GIFTED LEARNERS

Challenge students to write as many compound words with *back* as they can. *Back* can appear anywhere in the word.

LEARNERS WHO NEED EXTRA SUPPORT

Materials: index cards

Read each word on page 107 aloud slowly so students can distinctly hear each syllable. Have students repeat each word after you. **See Daily Word Study Practice, page 193.**

108

Lesson 50

 **Reading**  **Writing**

Reviewing Roots, Compounds, Possessives, Contractions

INFORMAL ASSESSMENT OBJECTIVES

Can students

✔ read an article containing words with familiar roots?

✔ read an article containing compound words, possessives, and contractions?

✔ write a description?

Lesson Focus

READING

● On the board, write the following paragraph and have students identify the compound words, possessives and contractions.

Our family's picnic was a weekend event we'd all been awaiting. My cheeseburgers and our aunt's blueberry pies weren't all we were anticipating. The softball game was really the highlight. Teamwork was the players' motto. By nightfall, we were still playing and talking together.

WRITING

Encourage students to use the questions on page 110 to help them organize their descriptions.

Name _____

 **Reading** Abby took a camping vacation with her family to a National Park in the western United States. Read the following entry from her travel diary. Then answer the question at the end of the story.

Dear Diary,   *August 27*

Today was the most exciting day of my life! This afternoon my grandfather proposed we take a horseback ride. Perhaps I'd better describe how I feel about horses. It's not that I'm repelled by them, but I am terrified to use them as transportation.

The rest of the family doesn't feel the same way. My younger brother has gone on many trail rides. My dad's favorite activity at summer camp was riding. My mom's love for horses started when she was little. So when the trail guide said, "I've inspected everyone's saddles. It's time to introduce yourself to your horse," my family was thrilled. I felt sick.

"Hello, Juniper," I whispered to my horse. "I'm Abby, and I hope this summer heat makes you feel sleepy." Just then, Juniper let out a whinny and bucked in the air, not once, but twice! "Hold onto the reins and clasp your legs around the horse's body!" yelled the guide. When Juniper took off, lots of people yelled at him to stop, but he didn't listen.

The horse's pace slowed down when the trail got rocky, and soon the guide galloped alongside and grabbed the reins. "You know what," she said, "you're a born rider!"

Why do you think Abby was so excited about her day? Give reasons for your answers.

_____
_____
_____
_____
_____

FOCUS ON ALL LEARNERS

ENGLISH LANGUAGE LEARNERS/ESL

To build background for page 109, invite students to talk about their own experiences with horses and horseback riding. Point out the journal entry format and ask students to talk about why people of all ages enjoy writing in journals.

VISUAL LEARNERS

SMALL GROUP   Ask students to look through any reading materials to find and list words with the roots being reviewed in the lesson, circle the roots, and define the words, using a dictionary if necessary. Encourage students to compare their lists with one another.

KINESTHETIC LEARNERS

LARGE GROUP   **Materials:** index cards, paper bag

Label each corner of the room with one of the following labels: *compound words, possessives,* or *contractions.* Make a set of word cards with examples on different cards. Place the cards in a bag and ask volunteers to draw a card, go to the appropriate corner, and use the word in a sentence.

Writing

Suppose you were the guide on Abby's trail ride. Write a letter to your parents, describing what happened on the trail ride. Use at least five words from the word bank. Below are some questions to help you.

audience	didn't	horses'
cowgirl	important	parents'
I'm	permitted	positive
perfect	predicted	she'd
		sunset

What happened?

Who was involved?

What contributed to the problem?

How did you solve it?

Helpful Hints

110 Lesson 50
Review roots, compounds, possessives, contractions: Writing

AUDITORY LEARNERS

SMALL GROUP

Challenge the group to tell a round-robin story about an imaginary adventure, such as a horseback ride on a trail in Yellowstone. Encourage students to use contractions, compounds, possessives, and words with the roots studied in this unit.

GIFTED LEARNERS

Challenge students to imagine they are members of Abby's family and to write about a family outing. Encourage students to use as many compound words, possessives, contractions, and words with the roots studied in this unit as possible.

LEARNERS WHO NEED EXTRA SUPPORT

Before students begin working, have them follow along as you read aloud the journal entry on page 109. Be sure students are familiar with the meaning of each compound word, possessive, and contraction. Help students pick out words with the roots studied in this unit. **See Daily Word Study Practice, pages 187-188.**

CURRICULUM CONNECTIONS

SPELLING

The following sentences can be used as a posttest for spelling words that are either possessives, contractions, or have several syllables.

1. **it's** — It's a gift for you.
2. **I'll** — I'll help my little brother with homework.
3. **we're** — We're planning a trip in school.
4. **boys'** — All the boys' clothes are over there.
5. **children's** — She is the children's doctor.
6. **antidote** — Is there an antidote for sadness?
7. **underground** — The sewers run underground.

SOCIAL STUDIES/FINE ARTS/MATH

Encourage students to make a map of Yellowstone National Park, highlighting a possible route for Abby's horseback adventure. Students might also create a map key and scale of miles and then calculate the distance along the trail route.

SCIENCE

Invite students to research different types of horses and then draw and cut out a portrait of one kind of horse. On a classroom mural, have students display their horses alongside a label with information about that type of horse.

110

Lesson 51

Pages 111–112

Unit Checkup

Reviewing Roots, Compound Words, Possessives, Contractions, Syllables

INFORMAL ASSESSMENT OBJECTIVES

Can students

✔ identify and read words with roots, compound words, possessives, and contractions?

✔ identify the number of syllables in words?

Lesson Focus

PREPARING FOR THE CHECKUP

- Write these roots across the top of the chalkboard: *pos, pel, pul, port, ject, aud, dict, duct, duce, duc, scribe, script, spec, spect, mit, miss, fac, fect, fic,* and *feit.* Ask volunteers to come to the board and write words to go beneath each root.

- On the board, write the following headings: *Compound Word, Possessive,* and *Contraction.* Have volunteers tell you whether each of the following is a compound word, a possessive, or a contraction and why: *baseball, doesn't, friend's, seashore, can't, Sally's.*

- Read the following words aloud and ask volunteers to divide each word into syllables: *mailbox, classmate, introduce, reporter, subscribe, fingerprint.*

USING THE PAGES

Make sure students understand the directions for pages 111 and 112. After students have completed the pages, talk about the questions on page 112.

Name _____

 UNIT 4 CHECKUP

▶ Fill in the circle beside the answer that best completes each sentence.

1. To place something for safekeeping is to ____ it.
- ○ predict
- ● deposit
- ○ perfect

2. A book that gives the correct spelling of words is a ____.
- ● dictionary
- ○ dictaphone
- ○ conductor

3. To carry something from one place to another is to ____ it.
- ○ dismiss
- ● transport
- ○ reduce

4. A building where goods are made is a ____.
- ○ spectator
- ○ portfolio
- ● factory

5. To write or tell about something in detail is to ____ it.
- ○ eject
- ○ contradict
- ● describe

6. To look at something carefully is to ____ it.
- ● inspect
- ○ reject
- ○ deduct

▶ Fill in the circle beside the answer that best describes the underlined word.

7. Lisa is excited about her visit to her <u>grandparents'</u> farm.
- ○ contraction
- ● possessive

8. <u>She's</u> been looking forward to visiting the farm for a long time.
- ● contraction
- ○ possessive

9. <u>There's</u> always something happening on the farm.
- ● contraction
- ○ possessive

10. Last year, someone accidentally left open the <u>horses'</u> pen.
- ○ contraction
- ● possessive

11. It was nearly dark by the time <u>they'd</u> rounded up all the horses.
- ● contraction
- ○ possessive

12. That night, horses—not sheep—jumped fences in <u>Lisa's</u> dreams.
- ○ contraction
- ● possessive

Lesson 51
Review roots, compounds, possessives, contractions: Checkup **111**

FOCUS ON ALL LEARNERS

ENGLISH LANGUAGE LEARNERS/ESL

Before students begin page 112, write the words *Salt Pond Preserve* on the board. Talk about what a salt pond is and what kinds of things students might expect to see at a salt pond (for example: *fish, seaweed, barnacles, snails, mussels, sea stars*).

VISUAL LEARNERS

PARTNER List the following categories on the board and challenge students to write an example of each: *Words With the Root pos, pel, pul, port, ject, aud, dict, duct, duce, duc, scribe, script, spec, spect, mit, miss, fac, fect, fic,* and *feit; Compound Words; Possessives; Contractions.*

KINESTHETIC LEARNERS/AUDITORY

LARGE GROUP **Materials:** bag, index cards, marker

Make word cards for several words from each lesson in the unit and place the cards in a bag. Have students take turns drawing out a word, using it in a sentence, and telling whether it is a compound, a possessive, a contraction, or a word with a root.

UNIT 4 CHECKUP

Read the words in the word bank. Then read the paragraphs. Write the correct word from the word bank on the line to complete each sentence. Then answer the questions.

educated	important	seashore	misuse
grandparents'	weekend	spectators	lawmakers
I'll	sailboats	subject	environmental

Honoring Rachel Carson

Last summer, a special anniversary was celebrated at the Rachel Carson Salt Pond Preserve, next to the _____seashore_____ near the town of Round Pond, Maine. That weekend, people came on foot, on bicycles, in canoes and kayaks, and even in _____sailboats_____, to celebrate the life and work of Rachel Carson. She was a prominent scientist and writer who _____educated_____ the public about protecting the environment. The _____subject_____ of her most famous book, *Silent Spring*, was the _____misuse_____ of pesticides. This _____important_____ book helped convince _____lawmakers_____ to pass legislation requiring _____environmental_____ protection measures.

Because my _____grandparents'_____ cottage is near the salt pond, my friend Rebecca and I were _____spectators_____ for all the activities. We learned a lot about an important woman. When she left, Rebecca said, "_____I'll_____ remember this _____weekend_____ forever!"

1. Why did people come to this specific salt pond in Maine?
They were there to attend the anniversary celebration of the life and work of Rachel Carson.

2. What effect did Rachel Carson's writings have on the environment?
Her book, *Silent Spring*, helped convince lawmakers to pass environmental protection measures.

112 Lesson 51
Review roots, compounds, possessives, contractions: Checkup

AUDITORY LEARNERS

LARGE GROUP

Invite students to create a round-robin story about an adventure at the seashore, using as many compound words, possessives, and contractions as possible. Before beginning the story, encourage students to brainstorm a list of words to use.

GIFTED LEARNERS

Challenge students to create advertisements for products with nonsense compound words in their names, such as *chocolatebanana* milk or *bookfilm* character.

LEARNERS WHO NEED EXTRA SUPPORT

On the board, write examples of words from each lesson in this unit, such as: *grandparent's, she's, baseball, wasn't, dictionary,* and *transport*. With students, summarize what they have learned about each word in this unit. **See Daily Word Study Practice, pages 187–188, 193.**

Student Progress Assessment You may wish to review the observational notes you made as students worked through the activities in the unit. Your notes will help you evaluate the progress students made with roots, compounds, possessives, contractions, and syllables.

Portfolio Assessment Review the materials students have collected in their portfolios. You may wish to have interviews with students to discuss their written work and the progress they have made since the beginning of the unit. As you review students' work, evaluate how well they use the unit skills.

Daily Word Study Practice For students who need additional practice with any of the topics in this unit, quick reviews are provided on pages 187–188, 193 in Daily Word Study Practice.

Word Study Posttest To assess students' mastery of the skills covered in this unit, use the posttest on pages 93g–93h.

Spelling Cumulative Posttest Use the following words and dictation sentences.
  1. **position** She's in a comfortable **position.**
  2. **propel** Can he **propel** the bike forward?
  3. **portable** Pass the **portable** telephone, please.
  4. **eject** Please **eject** the video tape.
  8. **inscribe** The author will **inscribe** the book to me.
  9. **introduce** Can you **introduce** me to your teacher?
 10. **recur** Special memories often **recur.**
 11. **inspected** The coach **inspected** the lockers.
 12. **dismiss** I will **dismiss** the idea first.
 13. **factual** The information is all **factual.**
 14. **infect** One case of mumps can **infect** the whole class.
 15. **sufficient** Are you bringing **sufficient** food for one week of camping?
 16. **forfeit** Must we **forfeit** the game because we were late?
 17. **cupcake** I prefer a cookie to a **cupcake.**
 18. **it's** **It's** a date!
 19. **I'll** **I'll** introduce you to my parents now.
 20. **we're** **We're** excited about the trip.
 21. **boys'** The **boys'** games are in the closet.
 22. **antidote** Work can be a great **antidote.**
 23. **underground** Moles see poorly because they live **underground.**

Teacher Notes

Assessment Strategy Overview

Throughout Unit 5, assess students' ability to recognize and understand suffixes and their meanings. There are various ways to assess students' progress. You may also want to encourage students to evaluate their own work and participate in setting goals for their own learning.

FORMAL ASSESSMENT

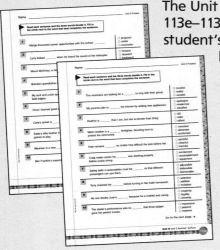

The Unit 5 Pretest on pages 113e–113f helps to assess a student's knowledge at the beginning of the unit and to plan instruction.

The Unit 5 Posttest on pages 113g–113h helps to assess mastery of unit objectives and to plan for reteaching, if necessary.

PORTFOLIO ASSESSMENT

This logo appears throughout the teaching plans. It signals opportunities for collecting students' work for individual portfolios. You may also want to collect the following pages.

❖ Unit 5 Pretest and Posttest, pages 113e–113h
❖ Unit 5 Reading & Writing, pages 131–132
❖ Unit 5 Checkup, pages 133–134

STUDENT PROGRESS CHECKLIST

Use the checklist on page 113i to record students' progress. You may want to cut the sections apart to place each student's checklist in his or her portfolio.

INFORMAL ASSESSMENT

The Reading & Writing pages and Unit Checkup in the student book are an effective means of evaluating students' performance.

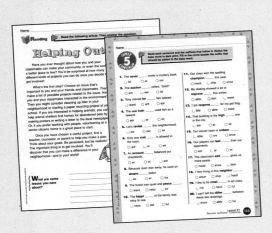

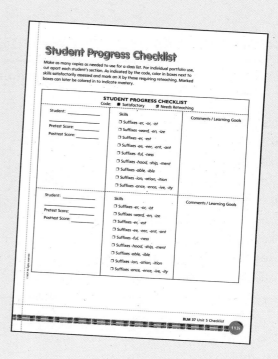

Skill	Reading & Writing Pages	Unit Checkup
Suffixes -er, -or, -ist	131–132	133–134
Suffixes -ward, -en, -ize	131–132	133–134
Suffixes -er, -est	131–132	133–134
Suffixes -ee, -eer, -ent, -ant	131–132	133–134
Suffixes -ful, -ness	131–132	133–134
Suffixes -hood, -ship, -ment	131–132	133–134
Suffixes -able, -ible	131–132	133–134
Suffixes -ion, -ation, -ition	131–132	133–134
Suffixes -ance, -ence, -ive, -ity	131–132	133–134

Administering and Evaluating the
Pretest and Posttest

DIRECTIONS

To help you assess students' progress in learning Unit 5 skills, tests are available on pages 113e–113h. Administer the Pretest before students begin the unit. The results of the Pretest will help you identify each student's strengths and needs in advance, allowing you to structure lesson plans to meet individual needs. Administer the Posttest to assess students' overall mastery of skills taught in the unit and to identify specific areas that will require reteaching.

PERFORMANCE ASSESSMENT PROFILE

The following chart will help you identify specific skills as they appear on the tests and enable you to identify and record specific information about an individual's or the class's performance on the tests.

Depending on the results of the tests, refer to the Reteaching column for lesson-plan pages where you can find activities that will be useful for meeting individual needs or for daily word study practice.

PERFORMANCE ASSESSMENT PROFILE

Skill	Pretest Questions	Posttest Questions	Reteaching Focus on All Learners	Daily Word Study Practice
Suffixes -er, -or, -ist	1, 11, 19	1, 11, 18	115–116, 131–132	188–189
Suffixes -ward, -en, -ize	2, 20, 23	2, 19, 20	115–116, 131–132	188–189
Suffixes -er, -est	3, 16	3, 16	117–118, 131–132	188–189
Suffixes -ee, -eer, -ent, -ant	4, 12, 21, 24	4, 13, 14, 24	119–120, 131–132	188–189
Suffixes -ful, -ness	5, 13	5, 21	121–122, 131–132	188–189
Suffixes -hood, -ship, -ment	6, 15, 22	6, 12, 15	123–124, 131–132	188–189
Suffixes -able, -ible	7, 25	7, 25	125–126, 131–132	189
Suffixes -ion, -ation, -ition	8, 17, 26	8, 17, 22	127–128, 131–132	189
Suffixes -ance, -ence, -ive, -ity	9, 10, 14, 18	9, 10, 23, 26	129–132	189

> **Read each sentence and the three words beside it. Fill in the circle next to the word that best completes the sentence.**

1 Marge discussed career opportunities with the school _____.

- ○ projector
- ○ visitor
- ○ counselor

2 Larry looked _____ when he heard the sound of the helicopter.

- ○ forward
- ○ skyward
- ○ backward

3 Mount McKinley, in Alaska, is the _____ peak in North America.

- ○ highest
- ○ higher
- ○ high

4 Brenda's grandfather is a lifelong _____ of our town.

- ○ dependent
- ○ resident
- ○ opponent

5 My aunt and uncle spent two weeks in the _____ photographing bald eagles.

- ○ sleepiness
- ○ quietness
- ○ wilderness

6 Once I learned good study habits, my grades showed _____.

- ○ amazement
- ○ improvement
- ○ argument

7 Carla's jacket is _____, red on one side and white on the other.

- ○ reversible
- ○ perishable
- ○ collapsible

8 Eddie's little brother has a vivid _____ and often makes up new games to play.

- ○ illustration
- ○ imagination
- ○ definition

9 Maureen is a new _____, but I think we will become good friends.

- ○ confidence
- ○ observance
- ○ acquaintance

10 Ben Franklin's experiments led to a greater understanding of _____.

- ○ electrical
- ○ electricity
- ○ electrician

Go to the next page. →

▶ **Fill in the circle beside the correct base word for each word with a suffix.**

11 teacher
- ○ teachers
- ○ teach
- ○ teaching

12 employee
- ○ employ
- ○ employment
- ○ employer

13 useful
- ○ use
- ○ amuse
- ○ using

14 difference
- ○ differ
- ○ different
- ○ differing

15 friendship
- ○ befriend
- ○ friendly
- ○ friend

16 smarter
- ○ smartly
- ○ smartest
- ○ smart

17 addition
- ○ adder
- ○ additional
- ○ add

18 attractive
- ○ attraction
- ○ attract
- ○ react

▶ **In each box, fill in the circle beside the word to which the suffix can best be added.**

19 ist
- ○ counsel
- ○ visit
- ○ novel

20 en
- ○ modern
- ○ wool
- ○ material

21 ant
- ○ war
- ○ assist
- ○ edit

22 hood
- ○ accept
- ○ act
- ○ child

23 ize
- ○ clock
- ○ brother
- ○ equal

24 eer
- ○ engine
- ○ teach
- ○ big

25 able
- ○ break
- ○ hungry
- ○ soon

26 ion
- ○ neighbor
- ○ select
- ○ present

Possible score on Unit 5 Pretest is 26. Number correct _____

> **Read each sentence and the three words beside it. Fill in the circle next to the word that best completes the sentence.**

1 The musicians are looking for a _____ to sing with their group.
- ○ novelist
- ○ realist
- ○ vocalist

2 My parents plan to _____ the kitchen by adding new appliances.
- ○ apologize
- ○ modernize
- ○ equalize

3 Heather is _____ than I am, but she is shorter than Greg.
- ○ tall
- ○ taller
- ○ tallest

4 Matt's brother is a _____ firefighter, devoting time to protect the community.
- ○ volunteer
- ○ absentee
- ○ auctioneer

5 Kate remains _____ no matter how difficult the task before her.
- ○ plentiful
- ○ cheerful
- ○ harmful

6 Craig made certain his _____ was working properly before scuba diving.
- ○ excitement
- ○ accomplishment
- ○ equipment

7 Safety belts in automobiles must be _____ so that different passengers can use them.
- ○ adjustable
- ○ defensible
- ○ fashionable

8 Terry checked her _____ before turning in her math homework.
- ○ selection
- ○ addition
- ○ invitation

9 No one doubts Juan's _____ because he is truthful and caring.
- ○ creativity
- ○ legality
- ○ sincerity

10 The skater's performance was so _____ that three judges gave her perfect scores.
- ○ impressive
- ○ passive
- ○ massive

Go to the next page. →

> ▶ **Fill in the circle beside the correct base word for each word with a suffix.**

11 trainer
- ○ retrain
- ○ train
- ○ trainable

12 likelihood
- ○ likely
- ○ likeli
- ○ like

13 servant
- ○ server
- ○ serve
- ○ serving

14 appointee
- ○ appoint
- ○ point
- ○ reappoint

15 township
- ○ tow
- ○ downtown
- ○ town

16 lowest
- ○ lowly
- ○ lower
- ○ low

17 composition
- ○ compose
- ○ compost
- ○ composing

18 visitor
- ○ visited
- ○ visiting
- ○ visit

> ▶ **In each box, fill in the circle beside the word to which the suffix can best be added.**

19 **ward**
- ○ conduct
- ○ for
- ○ wood

20 **en**
- ○ vital
- ○ pretty
- ○ sharp

21 **ness**
- ○ cool
- ○ mouth
- ○ delight

22 **ion**
- ○ tar
- ○ illustrate
- ○ break

23 **ance**
- ○ equal
- ○ accept
- ○ forgot

24 **ent**
- ○ appoint
- ○ repel
- ○ archaeology

25 **ible**
- ○ friend
- ○ dark
- ○ convert

26 **ence**
- ○ person
- ○ humid
- ○ confide

Possible score on Unit 5 Posttest is 26. Number correct _____

BLM 36 Unit 5 Posttest: Suffixes

Student Progress Checklist

Make as many copies as needed to use for a class list. For individual portfolio use, cut apart each student's section. As indicated by the code, color in boxes next to skills satisfactorily assessed and mark an X by those requiring reteaching. Marked boxes can later be colored in to indicate mastery.

STUDENT PROGRESS CHECKLIST
Code:　■ Satisfactory　　☒ Needs Reteaching

Student: _____ _____ Pretest Score: _____ Posttest Score: _____	Skills ❐ Suffixes -er, -or, -ist ❐ Suffixes -ward, -en, -ize ❐ Suffixes -er, -est ❐ Suffixes -ee, -eer, -ent, -ant ❐ Suffixes -ful, -ness ❐ Suffixes -hood, -ship, -ment ❐ Suffixes -able, -ible ❐ Suffixes -ion, -ation, -ition ❐ Suffixes -ance, -ence, -ive, -ity	Comments / Learning Goals
Student: _____ _____ Pretest Score: _____ Posttest Score: _____	Skills ❐ Suffixes -er, -or, -ist ❐ Suffixes -ward, -en, -ize ❐ Suffixes -er, -est ❐ Suffixes -ee, -eer, -ent, -ant ❐ Suffixes -ful, -ness ❐ Suffixes -hood, -ship, -ment ❐ Suffixes -able, -ible ❐ Suffixes -ion, -ation, -ition ❐ Suffixes -ance, -ence, -ive, -ity	Comments / Learning Goals

Spelling Connections

INTRODUCTION

The Unit Word List is a comprehensive list of spelling words drawn from this unit. The words are grouped by suffixes. To incorporate spelling into your word study program, use the activity in the Curriculum Connections section of each teaching plan.

The spelling lessons utilize the following approach for each set of words.

1. Administer a pretest of the words that have not yet been introduced. Dictation sentences are provided.

2. Provide practice.

3. Reassess. Dictation sentences are provided.

A final test is provided in Lesson 61 on page 134.

DIRECTIONS

Make a copy of Blackline Master 38 for each student. After administering the pretest for each set of suffixes, give each student a copy of the appropriate word list.

Students can work with a partner to practice spelling the words orally and identifying the suffix in each word. They can also make and use letter cards to form the words on the list. You may want to challenge students to identify other words that have the same suffixes. Students can write words of their own on *My Own Word List* (see Blackline Master 38).

Have students store their list words in an envelope or plastic zipper bag in the back of their books or notebooks. Alternatively, you may want to suggest that students keep a spelling notebook, listing words with similar patterns. You could also invite students to build word-wall displays in the classroom. Each section of the wall can focus on words with a single word study element. The walls will become a good spelling resource when students are writing.

UNIT WORD LIST

Suffixes -er, -or, -ist, -en, -ize, -er, -ee, -eer, -ent, -ant

leader
collector
novelist
loosen
equalize
hotter
payee
puppeteer
repellent
servant

Suffixes -ful, -ness, -ship, -ment, -ible, -ation, -ition, -ance, -ive, -ity

cheerful
newness
leadership
retirement
sensible
elation
composition
importance
impressive
reality

Name _____

 Spelling # UNIT 5 WORD LIST

Suffixes er, or, ist, en, ize, er, ee, eer, ent, ant

leader
collector
novelist
loosen
equalize
hotter
payee
puppeteer
repellent
servant

Suffixes ful, ness, ship, ment, ible, ation, ition, ance, ive, ity

cheerful
newness
leadership
retirement
sensible
elation
composition
importance
impressive
reality

My Own Word List

Word Study Games, Activities, and Technology

The following collection of ideas offers a variety of opportunities to reinforce word study skills while actively engaging students. The games, activities, and technology suggestions can easily be adapted to meet the needs of your group of learners. They vary in approach so as to consider students' different learning styles.

● ADD A TAIL TO THE WHALE

Have volunteers write the following suffixes on different index cards: *-er, -or, -ist, -ward, -en, -ize*. Place the cards face down side by side on your desk. Then write each of the following words on a card and tape the cards, one at a time, to a whale-body shape on the chalkboard or on a wall: *play, humor, project, west, character, sharp*. Call on students to select a suffix card from your desk, tape it to a tagboard "tail," and then add it to the whale to make a new word. Have each student define the word he or she has made. Return the suffix cards to your desk and encourage students to write new words on cards that can be used to play again. You might extend the activity by creating new cards, using suffixes from other lessons.

▲ ALIKE OR DIFFERENT

Discuss words that have similar and dissimilar meanings. Write the following words on the chalkboard: *exhaustion, happiness, plentiful, novelist, resident, knowledgeable, elation, sleepiness, author, permanent, visitor, abundant, ignorant, assistant, supervisor, perishable*. Call on volunteers to match the words with similar meanings and identify the suffix in each. Repeat the exercise with other volunteers, this time identifying words with dissimilar meanings and their suffixes. To extend the activity, have partners work together to find additional pairs of similar and dissimilar words with suffixes that can be added to the list. (Answers: *exhaustion, sleepiness*; *plentiful, abundant*; *elation, happiness*; *author, novelist*; *visitor, resident*; *permanent, perishable*; *assistant, supervisor*; *knowledgeable, ignorant*)

◆ FRIENDLY PERSUASION

Bring to class or ask students to bring examples of newspaper and magazine advertisements. Discuss ways that advertisers try to persuade readers to buy products or services or attend events. Ask students to find persuasive words and sentences in each advertisement. Encourage them to find words with suffixes, especially those with base words that had to change when a suffix was added. Then invite students to work in groups of three or four to write an advertisement for something such as an upcoming school event, a food product, or an exciting but safe new toy. Encourage them to illustrate their advertisements. Display the finished products for all to see and find words with suffixes.

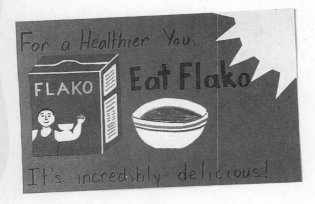

■ ANALYZING AN EDITORIAL

Give photocopies of a headline story and a newspaper editorial on the same topic to each student. Tell students to underline any words that include suffixes. Have students identify the topic and discuss differences in the approach. Guide them to understand that the purpose of the news article is to inform and that the purpose of the editorial is to persuade. Encourage small groups to work together to write an informative article and a persuasive editorial about a topic of school or community interest.

✳ SUFFIX OLYMPICS

Tell partners to create four columns on a sheet of paper and write the following headings at the top: *Olympic Event, Bronze Medalist, Silver Medalist, Gold Medalist.* Encourage them to think of adjectives that can be used to describe performance in different kinds of Olympic competitions. You might provide the following example: *The bronze medalist in weightlifting is strong. The silver medalist is stronger. The gold medalist is strongest.* Have partners work together to come up with adjectives to describe other competitions. On a separate sheet of paper, they can write sentences based on your model. In each of the columns, they can list the competition and the correct form of the descriptive adjective. Examples are *fast, quick, short* (as in time), *high, far,* and *long.*

● WHAT'S MY LINE?

Have groups of three or four students play "What's my line?" Each can take turns role-playing a "mystery guest" with a specific occupation. The others try to guess the line of work by asking questions. Explain that they cannot ask what the person does. They must ask questions such as "Do you work in education?" "Are you a scientist?" "Do you entertain people?" "Where do you work?" "What kinds of things do you make or do?" Examples of occupations featuring suffixes studied in this unit are counsel<u>or</u>, superintend<u>ent</u>, biolog<u>ist</u>, chem<u>ist</u>.

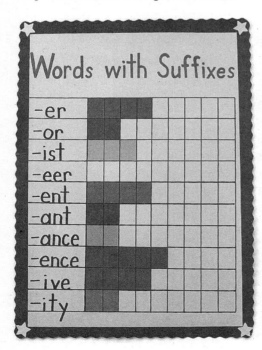

▲ FORMING AND GRAPHING WORDS WITH SUFFIXES

Write the following suffixes on the board: *-er, -or, -ist, -eer, -ent, -ant, -ance, -ence, -ive, -ity.* Divide the class into small groups. Have each group generate a list of words for each suffix. Tell them not to include any *-er* words that show comparison. Allow students to consult dictionaries, spelling books, and other reference works. Set a time limit. Help each group to make a bar graph to show the number of words with each suffix on their list. After students have finished, have groups share their work and discuss similarities and differences in their lists and the results of their graphs.

◆ WORD EQUATIONS

Divide the class into small groups to play "word equations." On the board, write *base word + suffix = new word*. Invite students to use the formula to write and illustrate lists of words containing the suffixes discussed in any one of the lessons in this unit. Challenge them to create equations for making new words by changing *f* or *y* and adding suffixes, for example, *base word – f + suffix = new word*.

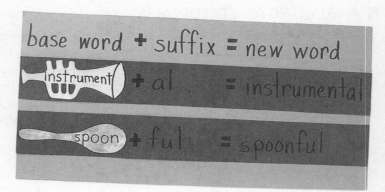

■ A PARADE OF SUFFIXES

Use Blackline Master 39 to make a game board featuring the 26 suffixes discussed in this unit. Note that the game board contains 26 blank spaces. Make a master copy by writing a suffix in each of the spaces. Make enough copies to distribute to teams of three or four players. Tell students to imagine that they are participants in a parade and that they are to follow the route shown on the game board. The parade starts at Celebration Way and ends in Championship Park. Suggest that each student make a paper marker in the shape of something seen in a parade, such as a float. Players take turns flipping a coin to see how many spaces they can move. If the coin comes up tails, the player moves one space; if the coin comes up heads, the player moves two spaces. When a player lands on a space, he or she must think of a base word that can be joined to the suffix to make a new word. If the player cannot create a word, he or she must return to the previously occupied space. Suggest that students consider people, places, and objects as well as descriptive words when trying to form new words. The first player whose token arrives at Championship Park is declared Grand Marshall.

Technology

The following software products are designed to reinforce students' logical thinking and language skills.

Mind Castle: The Spell of the Word Wizard By solving word puzzles and decoding passwords, students in grades 3 and up can escape from the dungeon tower the Word Wizard has locked them in.
** Lawrence Productions
  1800 South 35th Street
  Galesburg, MI 49053
  (616) 665-7075

Fleet Street Phantom Newspaper production offers students in grades 3–8 opportunities to match headlines and pictures to the correct stories, fix punctuation, correct crossword puzzles, put paragraphs in order, and take notes in a reporter's notepad.
** Terrapin
  10 Holworthy Street
  Cambridge, MA 02138
  (800) 972-8200

Word Hound Chester Cheesewich, a hungry mouse, devises strategies to work his way through mazes. Students in grades 4–8 match pictures accompanied by speech, words, or pictures with words to help Chester reach his goal—a hunk of cheese.
** Mindplay
  160 West Fort Lowell Street
  Tucson, AZ 85705
  (800) 221-7911

Name _____

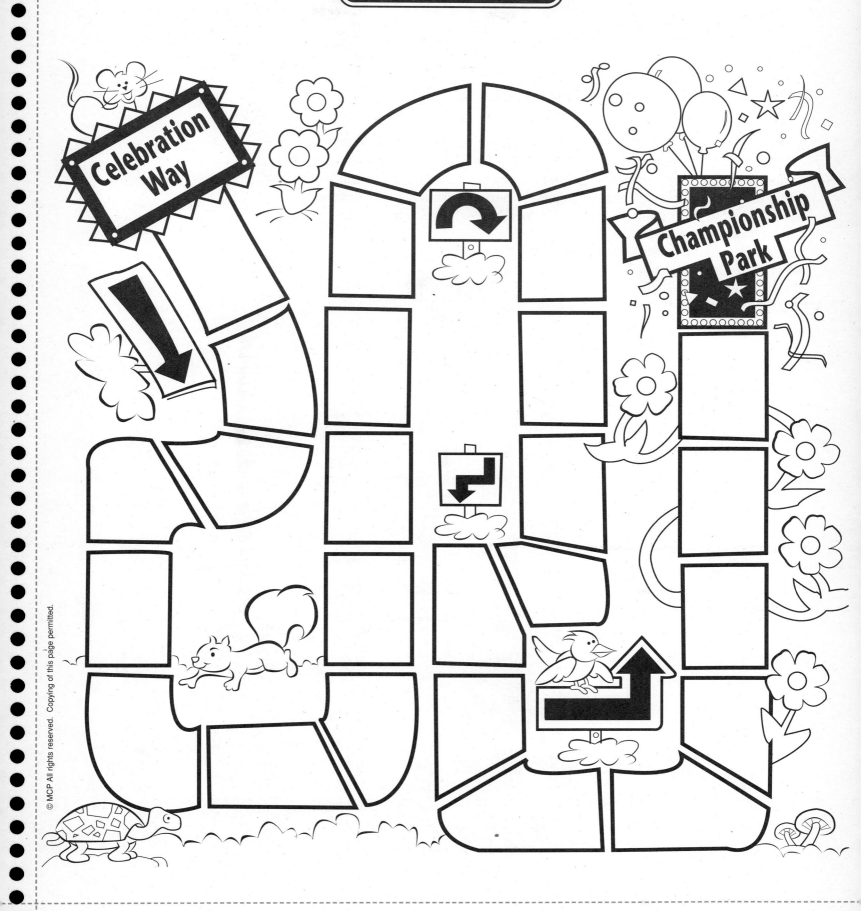

Home Connection

HOME LETTER

A letter is available to be sent home at the beginning of Unit 5. This letter informs family members that students will be studying suffixes. The suggested home activity revolves around discussing modern conveniences found in the home and the tasks that these help people perform. This activity promotes interaction between student and family members while supporting the student's learning of reading and writing words with the targeted word study skills. A letter is also available in Spanish on page 113q.

Dear Family,

In the next few weeks, your child will be learning about adding suffixes to words and how a suffix can change the meaning and the structure of a word. Suffixes are word parts that come at the end of base words. Some of the suffixes we'll be studying include or as in inventor, ful as in thoughtful, ness as in happiness, est as in safest, and able as in washable.

At-Home Activities

▶ Talk with your child about some of the conveniences in your home and the tasks they help you do. How would the family do the same tasks without those inventions?

▶ With your child, think of a new invention that would help make your life easier. Then draw up a plan of what your invention looks like. If you can, construct a model out of materials on hand, such as cardboard, construction paper, glue, and staples.

▶ Encourage your child to interview an older relative, friend, or neighbor about the conveniences available during that person's childhood. Invite your child to ask questions such as these: How was your childhood different from mine?; What did you do for fun?

Book Corner

You and your child might enjoy reading these books together. Look for them in your local library.

Winter Camp
by Kirkpatrick Hill

Two orphans learn the customs and traditions of their Athabascan roots when they spend the winter with their elderly neighbor.

If You Were There in 1776
by Barbara Brenner

Learn about the rigors and joys of everyday life during the time of the American Revolution.

Sincerely,

_____

114 Unit 5 Introduction

Estimada familia,

En las semanas próximas, su hijo/a va a aprender acerca de agregar sufijos a las palabras en inglés y acerca de cómo los sufijos pueden cambiar el significado y la estructura de una palabra. Los sufijos son partes de palabras que van al final de las palabras base. Algunos de los sufijos que vamos a estudiar incluyen **invent*or* (inventor)**, **thought*ful* (amable)**, **happi*ness* (felicidad)**, **saf*est* (lo más seguro)**, **wash*able* (lavable)**, **inspir*ation* (inspiración)** y **creat*ive* (imaginativo)**.

Actividades para hacer en casa

▶ Hablen con su hijo/a acerca de algunos de los efectos electrodomésticos que tienen en casa y de las tareas que les ayudan a realizar. ¿Cómo pudiera la familia hacer las mismas tareas sin estas invenciones?

▶ Con su hijo/a, piensen en una invención nueva que les haría la vida más fácil. Luego, hagan un plano de cuál sería la apariencia de su invención. Si pueden, hagan una maqueta con materiales tales como cartulina, papel grueso, pegamento y grapas.

Rincón del libro

Quizás a su hijo/a y a ustedes les guste leer estos libros juntos. Búsquenlos en la biblioteca de su localidad.

Winter Camp
por Kirkpatrick Hill

Dos huérfanos aprenden las costumbres y tradiciones de sus raíces atabascanas cuando pasan el invierno con su anciano vecino.

If You Were There in 1776
por Barbara Brenner

Conozcan los rigores y alegrías de la vida cotidiana en los años de la Revolución Norteamericana.

Atentamente, _____

Unit 5

Pages 113–114

Suffixes

Unit Focus

USING THE PAGE

- After students have had a chance to search for the inventions in the illustration, ask volunteers to point out some of the modern conveniences shown in the scene.

- **Critical Thinking** Invite a volunteer to read the question asked by the character. Encourage students to talk about how modern conveniences have made their lives different from the lives of people who lived during the time of George Washington.

BUILDING A CONTEXT

- Write the words *invention* and *inventor* on the board. Ask students to pick out the base word (*invent*) and tell the meanings of the two words. Explain that the endings *-ion* and *-or* change the meaning of the word *invent*.

- Tell students that *-ion* and *-or* are suffixes and ask a volunteer to recall the difference between a suffix and a prefix.

- Tell students that in this unit they will be learning about how a suffix can change the meaning and the structure of a word.

UNIT 5 Suffixes

Which conveniences could you live without? Why? What would you do instead?

Critical Thinking

Have you considered what your life would be like without the modern conveniences, or inventions, we use every day? Look at the picture carefully. Circle the conveniences you find.

Unit 5
Introduction

113

UNIT OPENER ACTIVITIES

BEING INVENTIVE

Challenge groups of students to role-play scenes in which inventions are being used and have their classmates figure out the invention. For example, students might role-play a person blow-drying his or her hair, driving a car, or using a computer.

MORE AND MORE INVENTIONS

Invite students to think of other modern conveniences they can't live without and to suggest where they would place them in the illustration on page 113.

BE AN INVENTOR!

Invite groups of students to invent something practical, such as eye glasses with built-in windshield wipers or an automatic bed maker. Have each group brainstorm a list of ideas for new inventions and then choose one idea to turn into an invention. Students might choose to create a scale model of the invention, draw a diagram of it, or write an advertisement for the product.

Dear Family,

In the next few weeks, your child will be learning about adding suffixes to words and how a suffix can change the meaning and the structure of a word. Suffixes are word parts that come at the end of base words. Some of the suffixes we'll be studying include *or* as in *inventor*, *ful* as in *thoughtful*, *ness* as in *happiness*, *est* as in *safest*, and *able* as in *washable*.

At-Home Activities

▶ Talk with your child about some of the conveniences in your home and the tasks they help you do. How would the family do the same tasks without those inventions?

▶ With your child, think of a new invention that would help make your life easier. Then draw up a plan of what your invention looks like. If you can, construct a model out of materials on hand, such as cardboard, construction paper, glue, and staples.

▶ Encourage your child to interview an older relative, friend, or neighbor about the conveniences available during that person's childhood. Invite your child to ask questions such as these: How was your childhood different from mine?; What did you do for fun?

Book Corner

You and your child might enjoy reading these books together. Look for them in your local library.

Winter Camp
by Kirkpatrick Hill

Two orphans learn the customs and traditions of their Athabascan roots when they spend the winter with their elderly neighbor.

If You Were There in 1776
by Barbara Brenner

Learn about the rigors and joys of everyday life during the time of the American Revolution.

Sincerely,

_____

BULLETIN BOARD

Invite students to create an "Inventions We Love" Wall by displaying the inventions they created in the preceding activity as well as photographs or pictures of real inventions. Each real or imaginary invention should have a caption with its name and factual or imaginative information about it.

● The Home Letter on page 114 is intended to acquaint family members with the word study skills students will be studying in the unit. Students may tear out page 114 and take it home. Encourage students to complete the activities on the page with a family member. If students draw up a plan for an invention with family members, encourage them to bring the plan to school to display on the inventions wall. Invite students to look in the local library for the books listed on page 114 and to read them with family members.

● The Home Letter can also be found on page 113q in Spanish.

CURRICULUM CONNECTIONS ✳

SCIENCE

Invite students to research the inventor of one of their favorite modern conveniences and give an oral presentation about that person's life.

SOCIAL STUDIES

Challenge students to choose one important invention and find out how people managed without it. For example, before refrigerators were invented, how did people keep their food cold? Encourage students to give oral presentations about what they learn.

WRITING

Have students write a newspaper article about the first public display of an important invention. For example, students might imagine they are interviewing the Wright brothers after one of their early flights.

.Lesson 52

Pages 115–116

Suffixes

-er, -or, -ist
-ward, -en, -ize

INFORMAL ASSESSMENT OBJECTIVES

Can students

- recognize the suffixes?.
- apply the rule to drop the final *e* or *y* before adding a suffix?
- use context clues to add the suffixes to base words?

Lesson Focus

INTRODUCING THE SKILL

- Write the following on the board. Ask students to tell how each base word was changed when a suffix was added. Help them notice that *e* or *y* was dropped in *admirer, operator,* and *apologize.*

| -er | -or | -ist | -ward | -en | -ize |

1. *admire* — *admirer*
2. *operate* — *operator*
3. *art* — *artist*
4. *on* — *onward*
5. *wood* — *wooden*
6. *apology* — *apologize*

USING THE PAGES

Remind students to read the rules as well as the directions before beginning each page. Point out that they will use words they wrote at the top of page 115 to complete the sentences at the bottom.

115

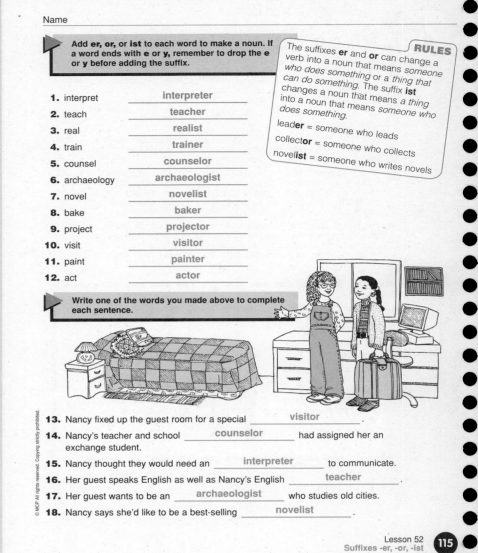

Name

Add **er, or,** or **ist** to each word to make a noun. If a word ends with **e** or **y,** remember to drop the **e** or **y** before adding the suffix.

RULES

The suffixes **er** and **or** can change a verb into a noun that means *someone who does something* or *a thing that can do something.* The suffix **ist** changes a noun that means *a thing* into a noun that means *someone who does something.*

lead**er** = someone who leads
collect**or** = someone who collects
novel**ist** = someone who writes novels

1. interpret — interpreter
2. teach — teacher
3. real — realist
4. train — trainer
5. counsel — counselor
6. archaeology — archaeologist
7. novel — novelist
8. bake — baker
9. project — projector
10. visit — visitor
11. paint — painter
12. act — actor

Write one of the words you made above to complete each sentence.

13. Nancy fixed up the guest room for a special _____ visitor _____.
14. Nancy's teacher and school _____ counselor _____ had assigned her an exchange student.
15. Nancy thought they would need an _____ interpreter _____ to communicate.
16. Her guest speaks English as well as Nancy's English _____ teacher _____.
17. Her guest wants to be an _____ archaeologist _____ who studies old cities.
18. Nancy says she'd like to be a best-selling _____ novelist _____.

Lesson 52
Suffixes -er, -or, -ist **115**

FOCUS ON ALL LEARNERS

ENGLISH LANGUAGE LEARNERS/ESL

Before students begin working, ask them to read the words at the top of page 115. Help them add the appropriate suffix and use each word in a sentence.

VISUAL/AUDITORY LEARNERS

INDIVIDUAL Have students write a paragraph about an occupation that interests them. Suggest that they use words containing the suffixes written on the board in the Lesson Focus. After they have finished, encourage students to share their paragraphs with one another.

KINESTHETIC LEARNERS

LARGE GROUP Write -er, -or, -ist, -ward, -en, and -ize on the board. Have teams of six line up several feet from the board. In turn, team members walk to the board and write a word with one of the suffixes. The team that finishes first with the most correctly spelled words wins.

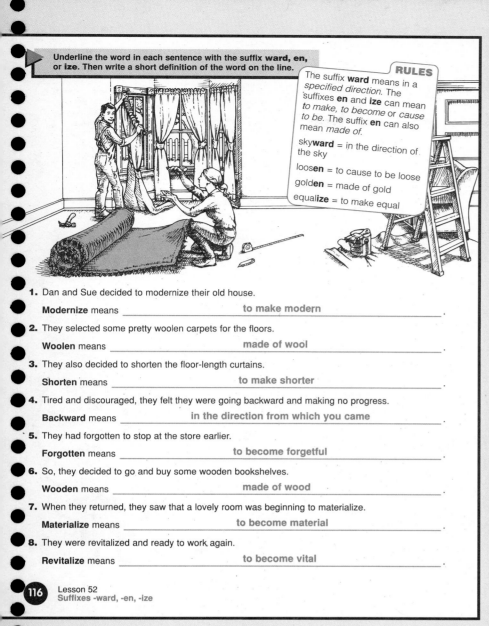

Underline the word in each sentence with the suffix **ward, en,** or **ize**. Then write a short definition of the word on the line.

RULES

The suffix **ward** means in a specified direction. The suffixes **en** and **ize** can mean *to make, to become* or *cause to be*. The suffix **en** can also mean *made of*.

sky**ward** = in the direction of the sky

loos**en** = to cause to be loose

gold**en** = made of gold

equal**ize** = to make equal

1. Dan and Sue decided to modernize their old house.

   Modernize means _____ to make modern _____ .

2. They selected some pretty woolen carpets for the floors.

   Woolen means _____ made of wool _____ .

3. They also decided to shorten the floor-length curtains.

   Shorten means _____ to make shorter _____ .

4. Tired and discouraged, they felt they were going backward and making no progress.

   Backward means _____ in the direction from which you came _____ .

5. They had forgotten to stop at the store earlier.

   Forgotten means _____ to become forgetful _____ .

6. So, they decided to go and buy some wooden bookshelves.

   Wooden means _____ made of wood _____ .

7. When they returned, they saw that a lovely room was beginning to materialize.

   Materialize means _____ to become material _____ .

8. They were revitalized and ready to work again.

   Revitalize means _____ to become vital _____ .

116 Lesson 52
Suffixes -ward, -en, -ize

SPELLING

The following is a pretest for spelling words with the suffixes *-er, -or, -ist, -ward, -en, -ize, -er, -est, -ee, -eer, -ent, -ant*.

1. **leader**   Will you be the **leader?**
2. **collector**   She is a coin **collector.**
3. **novelist**   I hope to be a **novelist.**
4. **loosen**   I'll **loosen** the dog's leash.
5. **equalize**   Let's **equalize** the weight.
6. **hotter**   Today is **hotter** than yesterday.
7. **puppeteer** I like that **puppeteer.**
8. **payee**   The **payee** took the coins.
9. **repellent** We need insect **repellent.**
10. **servant**   I'm my baby sister's **servant.**

WRITING

Portfolio Invite students to imagine they are archaeologists living in the year 3098. Have them write descriptions of your school that they have uncovered at an "ancient" site. Ask them to include words with the suffixes *-es, -er, -or, -ist, -ward, -en,* and *-ize.*

SOCIAL STUDIES

Invite students to find out about a country they might like to visit as an exchange student when they get older.

SCIENCE

Suggest that students "think skyward" and learn about one of the constellations. Have them each choose a constellation, draw a diagram of it, and write a caption that tells where in the sky it can be found.

AstroWord Suffixes © 1998 Silver Burdett Ginn Inc. Division of Simon & Schuster.

AUDITORY/VISUAL LEARNERS

PARTNER **Materials:** magazines, newspapers

Pairs can search in newspapers or magazines for words with the suffixes *-er, -or, -ist, -ward, -en,* and *-ize* and read them aloud for the partner to identify the suffix.

GIFTED LEARNERS

Challenge students to list directional words with *-ward* such as *forward, backward, upward,* and *downward.* Have them use the words to give humorous directions to each other.

LEARNERS WHO NEED EXTRA SUPPORT

Materials: word cards for *forgotten, novelist, teacher, counselor, apologize, baker, artist, materialize*

Display the cards and have the student read each word aloud, point out the suffix, and use the word in a sentence. **See Daily Word Study Practice, pages 188-189.**

Lesson 53

Pages 117–118

Suffixes -er, -est

INFORMAL ASSESSMENT OBJECTIVES

Can students

✓ recognize the use of the suffixes -er and -est in comparing?

✓ use context clues to complete a sentence using the proper degree of comparison?

Lesson Focus

INTRODUCING THE SKILL

- Write these sentences on the board.
  1. *The blue book is <u>heavy</u>.*
  2. *The red book is <u>heavier</u> than the blue book.*
  3. *The green book is the <u>heaviest</u> of the five books.*
- Have students identify the base word in *heavier* and *heaviest*. (*heavy*) Ask them how the spelling of *heavy* changed when the suffixes were added. (*The* y *was changed to* i.)
- Then help students understand that when two things are compared, *-er* is used. When more than two things are compared, *-est* is used.

USING THE PAGES

- On page 118, students will use each given word just once in each sentence.
- **Critical Thinking** Read aloud the question on page 117 and discuss answers with students.

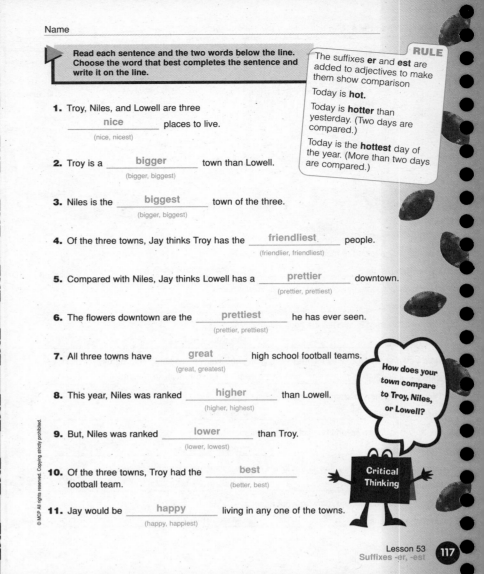

Name _____

> Read each sentence and the two words below the line. Choose the word that best completes the sentence and write it on the line.

RULE The suffixes **er** and **est** are added to adjectives to make them show comparison

Today is **hot**.

Today is **hotter** than yesterday. (Two days are compared.)

Today is the **hottest** day of the year. (More than two days are compared.)

1. Troy, Niles, and Lowell are three _____nice_____ places to live.
   (nice, nicest)

2. Troy is a _____bigger_____ town than Lowell.
   (bigger, biggest)

3. Niles is the _____biggest_____ town of the three.
   (bigger, biggest)

4. Of the three towns, Jay thinks Troy has the _____friendliest_____ people.
   (friendlier, friendliest)

5. Compared with Niles, Jay thinks Lowell has a _____prettier_____ downtown.
   (prettier, prettiest)

6. The flowers downtown are the _____prettiest_____ he has ever seen.
   (prettier, prettiest)

7. All three towns have _____great_____ high school football teams.
   (great, greatest)

8. This year, Niles was ranked _____higher_____ than Lowell.
   (higher, highest)

9. But, Niles was ranked _____lower_____ than Troy.
   (lower, lowest)

10. Of the three towns, Troy had the _____best_____ football team.
    (better, best)

11. Jay would be _____happy_____ living in any one of the towns.
    (happy, happiest)

How does your town compare to Troy, Niles, or Lowell?

Critical Thinking

Lesson 53
Suffixes -er, -est   **117**

FOCUS ON ALL LEARNERS

ENGLISH LANGUAGE LEARNERS/ESL

SMALL GROUP

Pair fluent English speakers with second-language learners to complete the pages. Encourage them to discuss each sentence and if, or how many, things are being compared before they choose the appropriate word.

VISUAL LEARNERS

INDIVIDUAL   **Materials:** newspapers

Arrange stacks of newspapers in several locations in the classroom. Encourage students to find and circle words of comparison used in the articles. Invite them to keep a list of the words they find and write how many things are being compared.

KINESTHETIC LEARNERS

LARGE GROUP   Write *drearier, busiest, brightest, wettest, greedier, wearier, sturdier,* and *cheapest* on the board. Read each word and have students raise two fingers or three fingers to show whether the word can be used to compare two things or three or more things.

117

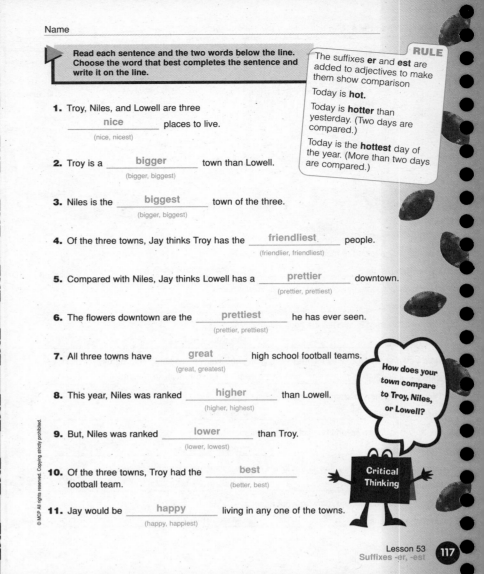

© MCP All rights reserved. Copying strictly prohibited.

weak   weaker   weakest

1. The radio signals grew _____**weaker**_____ as the evening storm wore on. They were _____**weak**_____ when the storm began. But they became the _____**weakest**_____ during the heavy thunder and lightning.

large   larger   largest

2. The sales clerk showed me some _____**large**_____ sweats. They were _____**larger**_____ than the ones I have at home. In fact they were the _____**largest**_____ sweats I'd ever seen!

hungry   hungrier   hungriest

3. Tad is the _____**hungriest**_____ boy I have ever known. He is usually _____**hungrier**_____ at dinner than he is at lunch. But then, he is _____**hungry**_____ most of the time.

dirty   dirtier   dirtiest

4. Last Saturday we washed our _____**dirty**_____ car. The inside windows were the _____**dirtiest**_____ parts on the whole car. The hubcaps were even _____**dirtier**_____ than they were the last time we washed them.

early   earlier   earliest

5. Ana gets up the _____**earliest**_____ of anyone in our class. Alex thinks he gets up _____**early**_____, but even I get up _____**earlier**_____ than he does!

118 Lesson 53
Suffixes -er, -est

CURRICULUM CONNECTIONS

SPELLING

Write the suffixes -er, -or, -ist, -ward, -en, -ize, -er, -est, -ee, -eer, -ent, -ant on separate cards and display them on the chalk ledge. Then say the spelling words *leader, collector,* and *novelist* one at a time. Call on volunteers to hold up the card with the suffix they hear and write the word on the board. Continue with the remaining spelling words *loosen, equalize, hotter, puppeteer, payee, repellent, servant.*

WRITING

Portfolio Invite students to write a description of three very different animals. Challenge them to use words of comparison in each sentence.

SOCIAL STUDIES

Have students work together to create an "Olympic" competition—athletic or academic—called Hard, Harder, Hardest.

MUSIC

Write *low, lower, lowest* on the board. Play music with a Latin beat as you describe the limbo, a dance of West Indian origin, in which the dancer bends backward and moves with a shuffling step under a horizontal bar that is lowered a little after each dancer passes. Invite students to try it and decide who bent the lowest under the bar without touching it.

AstroWord Suffixes © 1998 Silver Burdett Ginn Inc. Division of Simon & Schuster.

AUDITORY/VISUAL LEARNERS

PARTNER Invite pairs of students to write sentences that show comparisons, then read the sentences aloud for listeners to identify the comparative word with its suffix.

GIFTED LEARNERS

Challenge students to write a news story about their town or city. Challenge them to use as many words as possible that use the suffixes -er or -est to make comparisons about things found in the town or city.

LEARNERS WHO NEED EXTRA SUPPORT

Work with students as they begin page 117. Help them identify what things are compared. Point out that -er has two letters and compares two things, -est has three letters and compares three or more things. **See Daily Word Study Practice, pages 188-189.**

Lesson 54

Pages 119–120

Suffixes

-ee, -eer, -ent, -ant

✳ ◆ • ■ ■ ◆ ● ✳ ◆ ● ◆ ● ◆ ●

INFORMAL ASSESSMENT OBJECTIVES

Can students

✔ recognize the suffixes and identify their meanings?

✔ associate definitions with words with suffixes?

✔ use context clues to complete sentences using known base words and words with suffixes?

Lesson Focus

INTRODUCING THE SKILL

● Write the following suffixes, base words, and sentences on the board and have students complete the sentences.

-ee   -eer   -ent   -ant

observe   honor   preside   profit

1. An _____ person notices many things. *(observant)*
2. The _____ was pleased to accept the medal. *(honoree)*
3. The _____ made a large amount of money. *(profiteer)*
4. The _____ called the meeting to order. *(president)*

USING THE PAGES

● Discuss the information in the rule box.

● **Critical Thinking** Read aloud the question and discuss answers with students.

119

 **Read each sentence. Write a definition for the underlined word on the line below the sentence.**

RULES

The suffix **eer** usually means *someone who*. The suffixes **ee, ent,** and **ant** can also mean *someone who*. These suffixes can also mean *that which*.

puppet**eer** = someone who works puppets

pay**ee** = someone who is paid

repell**ent** = that which repels

serv**ant** = someone who serves

1. The current occupants are moving out of the apartment.

   Occupant means ___one who occupies___.

2. First they hired an auctioneer to sell some of their belongings.

   Auctioneer means ___one who auctions___.

3. Then they hired several assistants to help them move their other things.

   Assistant means ___one who assists___.

4. The assistants are employees of the local moving company.

   Employee means ___one who is employed___.

5. Even some of the dependents of the moving company employees came to help.

   Dependent means ___one who depends___.

6. The occupants voted in today's election by absentee ballot.

   Absentee means ___one who is absent___.

7. They wanted to be sure to get to vote for the new president.

   President means ___someone who presides___.

8. They were also anxious to elect a good school superintendent.

   Superintendent means ___someone who supervises___.

9. There will be a new city engineer this year, too.

   Engineer means ___someone who engineers___.

10. However, that person will be an appointee, not an elected official.

    Appointee means ___someone who is appointed___.

Lesson 54
Suffixes -ee, -eer, -ent, -ant **119**

FOCUS ON ALL LEARNERS ✳ • ◆ ■ ◆

ENGLISH LANGUAGE LEARNERS/ESL

SMALL GROUP

Pair fluent English speakers with second-language learners. Encourage them to talk about the meaning of the underlined words on page 119.

VISUAL LEARNERS

SMALL GROUP

Materials: magazines

Students can make lists of words that contain the suffixes *-ee, -eer, -ent,* and *-ant,* define them, then locate magazine photographs that illustrate what the words mean. Students can organize their information in scrapbooks.

KINESTHETIC LEARNERS

LARGE GROUP

Materials: cards for *-ee, -eer, -ent, -ant, trust, engine, occupy, reside*

Place the cards in random order on the chalkboard ledge. Call on volunteers to come to the board and combine a base word and a suffix to form a new word *(trustee, engineer, occupant, resident)* and use it in a sentence.

Read each sentence and the pair of words that follows it. Choose the word that best completes the sentence and write it on the line.

1. Ben is an _____engineer_____ and will be on a business trip on election day.

   puppeteer
   engineer

2. Since he will be away, he is voting by _____absentee_____ ballot.

   absentee
   payee

3. One of the issues on the ballot is especially _____important_____ to Ben.

   important
   accountant

4. It will affect where his _____dependents_____ go to school.

   repellents
   dependents

5. One _____appointee_____ to the school board has suggested some school boundary changes.

   appointee
   payee

6. Ben is a _____resident_____ of one of the areas that would be affected.

   precedent
   resident

7. Therefore, he is an _____opponent_____ of those who are proposing the change.

   assistant
   opponent

8. Another _____employee_____ who works with Ben is also opposed to the boundary changes.

   employee
   contestant

9. Some people have been very _____persistent_____ in campaigning about the boundary issue.

   persistent
   absorbent

10. Unfortunately, many others are _____ignorant_____ of the proposed changes.

    dependent
    ignorant

VOTE

Critical Thinking

Why is it important for all citizens to vote?

(120) Lesson 54
Suffixes -ee, -eer, -ent, -ant

CURRICULUM CONNECTIONS

SPELLING

The following sentences can be used as a posttest for spelling words with -er, -or, -ist, -ward, -en, -ize, -er, -est, -ee, -eer, -ent, -ant.

1. **leader**   She is a girl scout **leader.**
2. **collector**   Are you a stamp **collector?**
3. **novelist**   A **novelist** write fiction.
4. **loosen**   I need to **loosen** my belt.
5. **equalize**   I'll **equalize** the loads of supplies.
6. **hotter**   August is **hotter** than June.
7. **puppeteer**   I want to be a **puppeteer.**
8. **payee**   A **payee** is someone who is paid.
9. **repellent**   That fabric is water-**repellent.**
10. **servant**   Some days I'd like a **servant!**

WRITING

Portfolio Invite students to write an adventure about a puppeteer who is an employee of a traveling theater group. Have students use as many words as they can with the suffixes -ee, -eer, -ent, and -ant.

SOCIAL STUDIES

Have the class talk about what offices, such as president, secretary, and assistant, might be appropriate for the class and the duties involved in each. Challenge them to list three reasons they would like the job and would be good at it.

Technology

AstroWord Suffixes © 1998 Silver Burdett Ginn Inc. Division of Simon & Schuster.

AUDITORY LEARNERS

LARGE GROUP

Say the following words: *engineer, excellent, volunteer, abundant, honoree, resident, important, persistent, ignorant.* Have students identify the suffix and the base word in each word and explain what the word means.

GIFTED LEARNERS

Suggest students make a directory of jobs and the words used to refer to those people who perform them. Remind them that worker words are not limited to those with these lesson suffixes.

LEARNERS WHO NEED EXTRA SUPPORT

Materials: two sets of word cards for *employee, resident, important, engineer, volunteer, excellent, president, absentee*

Pairs can play concentration, matching words with the suffixes *-ee, -eer, -ent,* and *-ant.* **See Daily Word Study Practice, pages 188-189.**

Lesson 55

Pages 121–122

Suffixes -ful, -ness

INFORMAL ASSESSMENT OBJECTIVES

Can students

✔ recognize the suffixes *-ful* and *-ness* and identify their meanings?

✔ use context clues to complete sentences with words that contain the suffixes.

Lesson Focus

INTRODUCING THE SKILL

- Write these suffixes and clues on the board.

  -ful   -ness

  1. *full of <u>doubt</u>*
  2. *the quality of being <u>silky</u>*
  3. *enough to fill a <u>room</u>*

- Have students read the definitions aloud. Tell them to add a suffix to each underlined word to make a new word that matches the definition.

- Guide students to notice that the *y* in *silky* must be changed to *i* before a suffix is added.

USING THE PAGES

- Discuss the information in the rule box.

- **Critical Thinking** Read aloud the questions on pages 121 and 122 and discuss answers with students.

Name _____

Choose one word from the word bank to complete each of the following sentences. Write the word on the line.

| quietness | darkness | plentiful |
| spoonful | harmful | peaceful |

| successful | armful | mouthfuls |
| coolness | sleepiness | useful |

RULES

When added to a word to make an adjective, the suffix **ful** means *full of* or *having a tendency to*. When added to a word to make a noun, **ful** means *a certain amount*. The suffix **ness** means *the quality or condition of being*.

cheer**ful** = an adjective that means full of cheer

play**ful** = having a tendency to play

new**ness** = the condition of being new

1. Pat and Lynn chose a very relaxing and _____**peaceful**_____ campsite.
2. The _____**quietness**_____ was a pleasant relief from the noise of the city.
3. Lynn gathered an _____**armful**_____ of logs for the campfire.
4. Pat was _____**successful**_____ in building a roaring fire.
5. They were surprised at the _____**coolness**_____ of the air after the sun went down.
6. The fire not only kept them warm but made enough light so they could easily see in the _____**darkness**_____.
7. It also helped keep away _____**harmful**_____ animals.
8. Lynn cooked some stew and scooped a large _____**spoonful**_____ onto Pat's plate.
9. After several _____**mouthfuls**_____, Pat said, "That's delicious!"
10. The stew was _____**plentiful**_____, so Pat had a second helping.
11. The firelight was _____**useful**_____ as they washed their dishes.
12. They sat and talked until _____**sleepiness**_____ caused them to settle down for the night.

Do you think Pat and Lynn had been camping before? How do you know?

Critical Thinking

Lesson 55
Suffixes -ful, -ness

121

FOCUS ON ALL LEARNERS

ENGLISH LANGUAGE LEARNERS/ESL

Before students begin page 121, be sure they are familiar with the words in the box. To build background for the sentences, ask them about their experiences camping or cooking a meal outdoors.

VISUAL LEARNERS

INDIVIDUAL Encourage students to write a poem about a quiet evening, using at least four words with the suffix *-ful* or *-ness*. Students may enjoy holding a class poetry reading to share their work.

KINESTHETIC LEARNERS

LARGE GROUP **Materials:** index cards

Divide the class into two groups. One group writes *-ful* or *-ness* on cards, the other writes *harm, thought, quiet, care, kind, wonder, grace,* or *blind*. Each student finds a match with a member of the other group, then together the two make up a sentence for their word.

1. Lydia asked her mother to _____ plan her wedding.
   - ● help
   - ○ helped
   - ○ helpful

2. Lydia wanted the most _____ wedding she could afford.
   - ○ beauty
   - ○ beautify
   - ● beautiful

3. She wanted all her friends to share in her _____.
   - ● happiness
   - ○ happier
   - ○ happy

4. Much _____ planning was necessary.
   - ○ caring
   - ● careful
   - ○ carefully

5. Her fiancé, Steve, was very _____ with the wedding plans.
   - ○ help
   - ● helpful
   - ○ helper

6. He made some _____ suggestions for the wedding ceremony.
   - ○ use
   - ○ user
   - ● useful

7. Lydia's mother was impressed by Steve's _____.
   - ○ thoughtful
   - ● thoughtfulness
   - ○ thoughtless

8. She began to see what a _____ person Steve was.
   - ● kind
   - ○ kinder
   - ○ kindness

9. She was _____ her daughter was marrying such a fine man.
   - ● glad
   - ○ gladly
   - ○ gladness

10. All of the planning had a _____ result.
    - ○ success
    - ● successful
    - ○ succession

11. Everyone who came to the wedding had a _____ time.
    - ○ delight
    - ○ delighted
    - ● delightful

12. Steven and Lydia's _____ towards each other was obvious.
    - ○ tenderly
    - ● tenderness
    - ○ tender

13. Their wedding was the start of a _____ life together.
    - ● wonderful
    - ○ wondered
    - ○ wondering

Why is thoughtfulness important?

Critical Thinking

(122) Lesson 55
Suffixes -ful, -ness

CURRICULUM CONNECTIONS

SPELLING

The following sentences can be used as a pretest for spelling words with the suffixes *-ful, -ness, -hood, -ship, -ment, -able, -ible, -ion, -ation, -ition, -ance, -ence, -ive, -ity.*

1. **cheerful** — She is always **cheerful.**
2. **newness** — I can smell the **newness** of the car.
3. **leadership** — Her **leadership** helps the club.
4. **retirement** — The ball player is in **retirement.**
5. **sensible** — That's the **sensible** thing to do.
6. **elation** — I feel **elation** at your exciting news.
7. **composition** — Your **composition** is good.
8. **importance** — The **importance** of healthy food cannot be overlooked.
9. **reality** — Fantasy is the opposite of **reality.**
10. **impressive** — You are **impressive.**

WRITING

Portfolio Challenge students to write an essay about something wonderful that has happened to them or to someone they know. Encourage them to use words with the suffixes *-ful* and *-ness.*

SCIENCE

Brainstorm a list of healthful foods. Then have students plan menus for a camping trip.

SOCIAL STUDIES

Have students plan a two-week camping trip in some region they would like to explore, plotting the routes and distances between parks to create an itinerary.

Technology

AstroWord Suffixes © 1998 Silver Burdett Ginn Inc. Division of Simon & Schuster.

AUDITORY LEARNERS

LARGE GROUP Read each *What am I?* riddle for students to solve using a word with *-ful* or *-ness. I am silent and still. What am I? (quietness) I throw things away before they wear out. What am I? (wasteful)* Challenge students to make up riddles.

GIFTED LEARNERS

Invite students to write pairs of sentences using adjectives and nouns that end in *-ful*: For example, *We keep the* <u>harmful</u> *cleaners on a high shelf. Just a* <u>mouthful</u> *of detergent could make a child very sick.*

LEARNERS WHO NEED EXTRA SUPPORT

Visit students as they work to offer individual support. Review with them work on the pages they have already completed and help them correct any mistakes they have made. **See Daily Word Study Practice, pages 188-189.**

Lesson 56

Pages 123–124

Suffixes
-hood, -ship, -ment

INFORMAL ASSESSMENT OBJECTIVES

Can students

✔ recognize suffixes?

✔ use context clues and base words to form words with the suffixes -*hood*, -*ship*, and -*ment*?

Lesson Focus

INTRODUCING THE SKILL

● Write the following lists and sentences on the board, omitting the words in parentheses.

Base Word	Suffix
child	ment
amaze	ship
friend	hood

My grandfather loves to tell stories of his _____. (*childhood*)

To our _____ , Sam hit a home run. (*amazement*)

Your _____ is very important to me. (*friendship*)

● Explain that each suffix means "the state or condition of being." Then ask students to add the suffixes to the base words to complete the sentences. Have them define the new words.

USING THE PAGES

After they have finished working, encourage them to review what they have learned about the suffixes -*hood*, -*ship*, and -*ment*.

123

Name _____

▶ **Read the following paragraph. Circle each word that has the suffix hood, ship, or ment.**

> Our (neighborhood) track team won the (championship) this fall. There was a lot of (excitement) over this (accomplishment.) The (likelihood) of the (township) buying trophies for the members of the team was high. Matt Evans' (leadership) is one factor in the team's (improvement) this season. There is no (argument) about that! He has encouraged both trust and (friendship) among team members. We are still in (amazement) at the change in our team's attitude!

RULES

The suffixes **hood**, **ship**, and **ment** usually mean *the state* or *condition of being*.

child**hood** = the state or condition of being a child

leader**ship** = the state or condition of being a leader

retire**ment** = state or condition of being retired

▶ **Now write the correct circled word on the line next to its definition.**

1. something done well _____ accomplishment
2. place where people live _____ neighborhood
   or _____ township
3. probability _____ likelihood
4. something that has gotten better _____ improvement
5. quarrel _____ argument
6. state of being friends _____ friendship
7. first place position _____ championship
8. great thrill _____ excitement
9. guidance, direction _____ leadership
10. great surprise, astonishment _____ amazement

Lesson 56
Suffixes -hood, -ship, -ment **123**

FOCUS ON ALL LEARNERS

ENGLISH LANGUAGE LEARNERS/ESL

Before beginning page 124, ask students to describe an activity they enjoy sharing with an older person. Use words with the suffixes -*hood*, -*ship*, and -*ment*.

VISUAL LEARNERS

SMALL GROUP On the board, write *base word + suffix = new word*. Challenge students to use the formula, or a variation of it, to write word equations containing *hood*, *ship*, and *ment*; for example, *argue - e + ment = argument*.

KINESTHETIC/AUDITORY LEARNERS

INDIVIDUAL

Materials: tape; "blue ribbons" labeled *hood, ship, ment*; word cards for *champion, argue, friend, child, neighbor, move, leader, move, boy*

Tape the ribbons on the wall and display the word cards. Have students match the word cards with an appropriate suffix ribbon, tape the cards below the shape, and use the word in a sentence.

▶ Add the suffix **hood**, **ship**, or **ment** to each word below to form a new word. Write the new word on the line.

1. child   childhood
2. likely   likelihood
3. relation   relationship
4. equip   equipment
5. friend   friendship
6. enjoy   enjoyment
7. author   authorship
8. retire   retirement
9. neighbor   neighborhood
10. excite   excitement

▶ Write one of the words you made above to complete each of the following sentences. Use each word only once.

11. Since Grandpa's ____retirement____ from work, he and Juan do many things together.
12. Juan and Grandpa have always had a good ____relationship____ .
13. Grandpa enjoyed telling Juan stories of his early ____childhood____ days.
14. In those days, Grandpa lived on a farm, not in a close-knit ____neighborhood____ .
15. He told Juan how he learned to use heavy farm ____equipment____ as a child.
16. Grandpa told Juan about the ____excitement____ of harvesting crops on the farm.
17. Juan and Grandpa share the ____authorship____ of a story they wrote.
18. It is about the ____friendship____ between a young boy and his grandfather.
19. There is not much ____likelihood____ of the story ever being published.
20. What is important is the ____enjoyment____ they got from writing it!

CURRICULUM CONNECTIONS

SPELLING

Write spelling words on slips of paper: *cheerful, newness, leadership, retirement, sensible, elation, composition, importance, reality,* and *impressive.* Place the slips into a box or bag, and invite students to pick a word out of the box to act out for classmates. The student who guesses correctly, spells the word aloud and writes it on the board.

WRITING

Portfolio Challenge students to write a fantasy story about an unusual friendship in their neighborhood between a bird and a cat, for instance, or two people with very different personalities or interests.

LANGUAGE ARTS/FINE ARTS

Copy the diagram of the diver on the board. Ask students to identify the suffix in the caption. Explain that a diagram shows the important parts of something. Point out the lines drawn from the labels to the diver. Then challenge students to choose an activity or sport and draw and label a diagram of a participant and the equipment used.

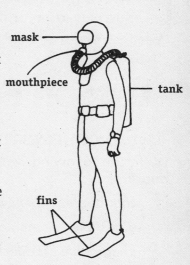

mask

mouthpiece

tank

fins

Equipment Used by Divers

AstroWord Suffixes © 1998 Silver Burdett Ginn Inc. Division of Simon & Schuster.

AUDITORY LEARNERS

SMALL GROUP Write the suffixes *-hood*, *-ship*, *-ment* and the words *boy, child, neighbor, girl, relation, owner, partner, hard, treat, equip, enjoy,* and *retire* on the board. Tell a group story about sailing, using words made by combining base words and suffixes.

GIFTED LEARNERS

Suggest students find out about the difference between the political divisions township, town, city, county, and district. They could also compare them to any local divisions specific to your area as well (such as *shire, hundred, territory*).

LEARNERS WHO NEED EXTRA SUPPORT

Materials: index cards, markers

Ask students to each make a card with a picture of a ship and a card with a picture of Red Riding Hood's hood. On the back of the cards, ask them to write as many words as they can that end in those suffixes. **See Daily Word Study Practice, pages 188-189.**

Lesson 57

Pages 125–126

Suffixes -able, -ible

Lesson Focus

INTRODUCING THE SKILL

- Write the following words on the board.

  collapsible   believable

  digestible   memorable

  imaginable   collectible

- Use colored chalk to circle the suffixes *-able* and *-ible*. Explain that both suffixes mean "*able to be.*"

- For each word, ask students to identify and give the meaning of the base word. Challenge them to formulate a definition of the entire word.

- Ask students to give additional words with *-able* and *-ible* and to use the words in sentences.

USING THE PAGES

Be sure students understand how to complete pages 125 and 126. After they have completed the pages, encourage them to review their work with a partner. Have them discuss how they figured out the answers to the crossword puzzle on page 126.

125

Name _____

▶ Circle the word that completes the sentence and write it on the line.

1. When clothing can be cleaned in water, it is called _____**washable**_____ .
   - (washable)   reversible

2. Something that can be made smaller is _____**reducible**_____ .
   - (reducible)   defensible

3. An activity that makes lots of money is _____**profitable**_____
   - collapsible   (profitable)

4. Something that can be damaged if it is dropped is _____**breakable**_____
   - (breakable)   adorable

5. A jacket that can be worn with either side out is _____**reversible**_____
   - (reversible)   reducible

6. Food that is not spoiled is _____**eatable**_____ .
   - (eatable)   excitable

7. Something that can be changed or moved to make it fit is _____**adjustable**_____
   - (adjustable)   dependable

8. Something that can spoil easily is _____**perishable**_____ .
   - (perishable)   reducible

9. Something that can be defended is _____**defensible**_____ .
   - dependable   (defensible)

10. Someone who can be trusted or depended upon is _____**responsible**_____
    - reducible   (responsible)

11. An object that can be folded together and put in a smaller package is _____**collapsible**_____ .
    - reversible   (collapsible)

12. A book is something that is _____**readable**_____
    - eatable   (readable)

13. When someone is intelligent, we say that he or she is _____**knowledgeable**_____
    - (knowledgeable)   fashionable

FOCUS ON ALL LEARNERS

ENGLISH LANGUAGE LEARNERS/ESL

Before students begin the crossword puzzle, have them work together to find the base words for the words in the box. Review the meanings of those words so that students are better able to complete the puzzle independently.

VISUAL LEARNERS

PARTNER   Ask pairs of students to choose the suffix *-able* or the suffix *-ible*. Have students use dictionaries and other resource books to compile a list of words containing their suffix. Suggest that they share their list with a pair of students who chose the other suffix.

KINESTHETIC LEARNERS

LARGE GROUP   Write these base words on the board: *wash, break, sense, read, reverse, enjoy, adore, use,* and *depend*. Invite teams to have a chalk relay race. At a signal, the first team member goes to the board, chooses one word, adds either *-able* or *-ible* to make a new word (making sure to drop the final *e* if necessary), then takes the chalk to the next player. The first team to write five new words wins.

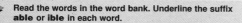

Read the words in the word bank. Underline the suffix **able** or **ible** in each word.

memorable	comfortable	accessible	movable
collapsible	adjustable	dependable	responsible
usable	sensible	enjoyable	reducible

Use the base words to complete the crossword puzzle.

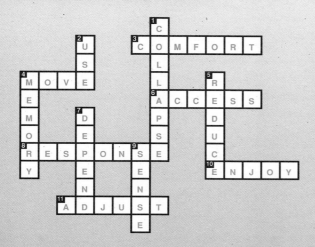

Across

3. to soothe someone who is sad
4. to change position
6. a way to get into or reach some place
8. an answer
10. to do something that makes you happy
11. to move to a different position

Down

1. to fall down; to fold together
2. to put into service for a particular purpose
4. something that is remembered
5. to make smaller
7. to trust; to be certain about
9. good judgment

SPELLING

Write the list words *cheerful, newness, leadership, retirement, sensible, elation, composition, importance, reality,* and *impressive* on the board. Then say riddles such as these and have students spell a spelling word to answer each one.

1. What word is full of good feelings? *(cheerful)*
2. What word has the words *spoon, on, not,* and *cost* in it? *(composition)*
3. What's the opposite of the condition of being old? *(newness)*

WRITING

Portfolio Invite students to write a description of their favorite piece of clothing. Challenge students to use words that contain the suffixes *-able* or *-ible.*

SOCIAL STUDIES

Invite groups of students to role-play a memorable experience they have had at school, such as acting in a play, playing on a sports team, or winning a contest.

ART

Have students draw a humorous advertisement for a real or imaginary product. They should use as many words as possible that contain the suffixes.

AstroWord Suffixes © 1998 Silver Burdett Ginn Inc. Division of Simon & Schuster.

AUDITORY LEARNERS

LARGE GROUP Play "guesswork" with the class by thinking of an object and having students guess what it is by asking questions that contain words with *-able* or *-ible.* For example, students might ask: *Is it breakable? Is it washable? Is it collapsible?* Whoever guesses the answer chooses another object to guess.

GIFTED LEARNERS

Challenge students to make a word game, such as the crossword puzzle on page 126 or a hidden-word search, for words that contain the suffixes *-able* or *-ible.* Have students exchange their puzzles for completion by their classmates.

LEARNERS WHO NEED EXTRA SUPPORT

Materials: two sets of word cards

Ask students to work with partners to play a memory game using word cards with words containing the suffixes *-able* or *-ible.* Possible words to be used may include *breakable, fashionable, enjoyable, reversible, convertible, adjustable, likable, readable,* and *responsible.*
See Daily Word Study Practice, page 189.

Lesson 58

Pages 127–128

Suffixes
-ion, -ation, -ition

Lesson Focus

INTRODUCING THE SKILL

Materials: Teacher-made word cards for *correct, invite, define, decorate, consider, add*

● On the board, write the following suffixes preceded by blank lines:

__ation, __ion, __ition

Place the word cards on the chalkboard ledge. Have volunteers choose a card and hold it in front of a suffix to form a new word.

● Ask volunteers to say the new words and explain any spelling changes that occur when suffixes are added. Challenge students to use the new words in sentences.

USING THE PAGES

Offer assistance as needed as students complete pages 127 and 128. After they have completed the pages, you might wish to discuss the meanings of some difficult words on page 127, such as *inspiration* in item 4 and *depiction* in item 7. Encourage students to discuss what they have learned about the suffixes *-able* and *-ible*.

Name _____

> Read each sentence and the two words below the line. Choose the word that best completes the sentence and write it on the line.

RULES

The suffixes **ion, ation,** and **ition** usually mean *the act of* or *the condition of being.*

exhaus**tion** = the condition of being exhausted

invi**tation** = the act of inviting

ad**dition** = the act of adding

1. The lives of ordinary Americans have been the subjects of many different forms of artistic ___**expression**___.
   (expressed, expression)

2. Photographer Dorothea Lange, for example, depicted the plight of migrant workers during the Depression (1929–1938) in her photographic ___**compositions**___.
   (compositions, composed)

3. As she traveled throughout the country during this time, she was ___**fascinated**___ by the people she met.
   (fascination, fascinated)

4. The ___**inspiration**___ for many of her photographs was the courage she saw in the lives of many struggling Americans.
   (inspiration, inspired)

5. Walker Evans was another photographer whose work ___**illustrated**___ the widespread poverty of the Depression years.
   (illustrations, illustrated)

6. In ___**addition**___ to their stark lines, his photographs showed a remarkable understanding of his subjects.
   (addition, add)

7. The ___**depiction**___ of the lives of ordinary Americans has also been the focus of many American painters.
   (depicted, depiction)

8. If you ever have the chance to see a ___**presentation**___ of the paintings of Andrew Wyeth, be sure to go!
   (presented, presentation)

9. A ___**selection**___ of his work illustrates his understanding of the beauty and grace of nature.
   (selected, selection)

FOCUS ON ALL LEARNERS

ENGLISH LANGUAGE LEARNERS/ESL

Before students complete page 127, be sure they understand the meaning of the phrase *the plight of migrant workers.*

VISUAL LEARNERS

Materials: magazines

Have students fold a sheet of paper in thirds and label each section *-ion, -ation,* or *-ition.* Then challenge students to search in magazines for words that contain each of the suffixes and write each word beneath the correct label.

KINESTHETIC/VISUAL LEARNERS

LARGE GROUP

Materials: index cards

Have partners write base words and the suffixes *-ion, -ation,* and *-ition* on cards and place the base words and suffix cards in separate piles. In turn, players draw from each pile. If the player forms a word correctly, including dropping *e* if necessary, award a point.

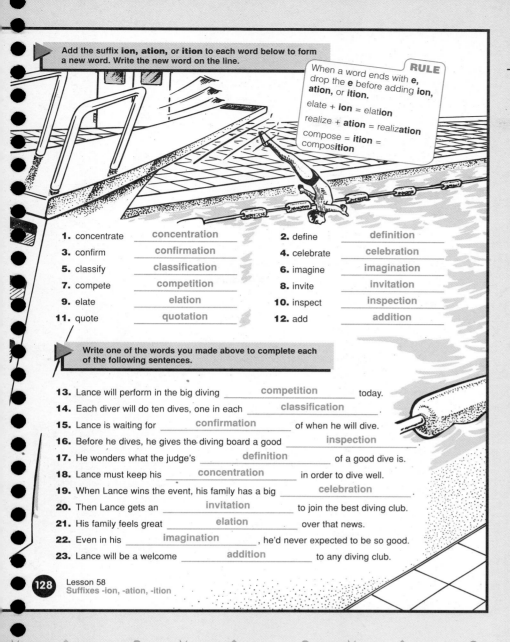

Add the suffix **ion**, **ation**, or **ition** to each word below to form a new word. Write the new word on the line.

RULE

When a word ends with **e**, drop the **e** before adding **ion**, **ation**, or **ition**.

elate + **ion** = elat**ion**

realize + **ation** = realiz**ation**

compose = **ition** = compos**ition**

1. concentrate	concentration		2. define	definition	
3. confirm	confirmation		4. celebrate	celebration	
5. classify	classification		6. imagine	imagination	
7. compete	competition		8. invite	invitation	
9. elate	elation		10. inspect	inspection	
11. quote	quotation		12. add	addition	

Write one of the words you made above to complete each of the following sentences.

13. Lance will perform in the big diving _____competition_____ today.

14. Each diver will do ten dives, one in each _____classification_____ .

15. Lance is waiting for _____confirmation_____ of when he will dive.

16. Before he dives, he gives the diving board a good _____inspection_____

17. He wonders what the judge's _____definition_____ of a good dive is.

18. Lance must keep his _____concentration_____ in order to dive well.

19. When Lance wins the event, his family has a big _____celebration_____

20. Then Lance gets an _____invitation_____ to join the best diving club.

21. His family feels great _____elation_____ over that news.

22. Even in his _____imagination_____ , he'd never expected to be so good.

23. Lance will be a welcome _____addition_____ to any diving club.

(128) Lesson 58
Suffixes -ion, -ation, -ition

Lesson 59

Pages 129–130

Suffixes

-ance, -ence, -ive, -ity

INFORMAL ASSESSMENT OBJECTIVES

Can students

✔ recognize the suffixes *-ance*, *-ence*, *-ive*, and *-ity*?

✔ complete analogies?

Lesson Focus

INTRODUCING THE SKILL

- Write the following on the board, omitting the words in parentheses.

  acquaint + ance = (*acquaintance*)

  serene + ity = (*serenity*)

  correspond + ence = (*correspondence*)

  appreciate + ive = (*appreciative*)

- Call on volunteers to combine the base words and the suffixes and to write the new words on the board.

- Help students conclude that the suffixes *-ance*, *-ence*, and *-ity* can mean "the quality or state of being" and that the suffix *-ive* can mean "likely to" or "having to do with."

- Encourage students to use the new words on the board in sentences.

USING THE PAGES

Be sure students understand how to complete pages 129 and 130. You may want to read the definition of an analogy on page 130 aloud and work several items along with the class before they work independently.

Name _____

▶ Write the base word and the suffix that were combined to make each of the following words.

1. publicity = ___public___ + ___ity___
2. confidence = ___confide___ + ___ence___
3. impressive = ___impress___ + ___ive___
4. acceptance = ___accept___ + ___ance___
5. active = ___act___ + ___ive___
6. sincerity = ___sincere___ + ___ity___
7. creative = ___create___ + ___ive___

> **RULES**
>
> The suffixes **ance, ence,** and **ity** usually mean *the quality or state of being.* The suffix **ive** usually means *likely to or having to do with.*
>
> import**ance** = the quality of being important
>
> depend**ence** = the quality of being dependent
>
> real**ity** = the quality of being real
>
> impress**ive** = likely to impress

▶ Use the words above in the sentences. Use each word only once.

8. Tara is always busy because she is ___active___ in so many groups.

9. She creates ___publicity___ for the groups so that new members will join.

10. She is a very caring person and shows it by her ___sincerity___.

11. She always has unique ideas because she is so ___creative___.

12. Other group members have great ___confidence___ in Tara's skills.

13. Whatever Tara is in charge of always ends up being done in a very ___impressive___ way.

14. This year, Tara won an award and gave a fine ___acceptance___ speech.

Lesson 59
Suffixes -ance, -ence, -ive, -ity **129**

FOCUS ON ALL LEARNERS ✳ ● ◆ ■ ◆ ●

ENGLISH LANGUAGE LEARNERS/ESL

Before beginning page 129, ask students to talk about the personality traits they most admire in other people.

VISUAL LEARNERS

SMALL GROUP

Materials: blank fish shapes

Give four blank fish shapes to each group and have students label each one *-ance*, *-ence*, *-ity*, or *-ive*. Invite students to "go fish" for a suffix by selecting a suffix, naming a word that contains the suffix, and using the word in a sentence.

KINESTHETIC/AUDITORY LEARNERS

LARGE GROUP

Materials: index cards

Have each student label cards with *-ance*, *-ence*, *-ity*, or *-ive*. Ask them to hold up the appropriate card every time they hear a word that ends with that suffix. Try *insurance, violence, active, dependence, humanity, allowance, personality,* and *creativity.*

**Circle the correct word to complete each analogy.
Then write the word.**

DEFINITION
An **analogy** tells the relationship that one thing has to another thing.
Car is to **garage** as **airplane** is to **hangar**.
Kitten is to **cat** as **puppy** is to **dog**.
Huge is to **massive** as **honesty** is to **sincerity**.

1. **Dynamite** is to **explosive** as **tape** is to _____adhesive_____
   (adhesive)   impressive   selective

2. **Helping** is to **assistance** as **watching** is to _____observance_____
   hindrance   (observance)   coincidence

3. **Negativity** is to **positivity** as **criminality** is to _____legality_____
   simplicity   complexity   (legality)

4. **Dance** is to **activity** as **uproar** is to _____disturbance_____
   (disturbance)   attendance   guidance

5. **Insecurity** is to **confidence** as **sameness** is to _____difference_____
   residence   conference   (difference)

6. **Leading** is to **guidance** as **forgiving** is to _____tolerance_____
   insurance   (tolerance)   observance

7. **Offense** is to **defense** as **superiority** is to _____inferiority_____
   (inferiority)   security   popularity

8. **Unusual** is to **distinctive** as **pretty** is to _____attractive_____
   (attractive)   selective   executive

9. **Advertisement** is to **publicity** as **generator** is to _____electricity_____
   mortality   (electricity)   legality

10. **Hot** is to **cold** as **active** is to _____passive_____
    (passive)   negative   disruptive

11. **Modesty** is to **arrogance** as **gentleness** is to _____violence_____
    reference   (violence)   absence

12. **Try** is to **attempt** as **escape** is to _____avoidance_____
    (avoidance)   annoyance   resistance

CURRICULUM CONNECTIONS

SPELLING

Materials: tagboard strips, envelopes

Write the spelling words *cheerful, newness, leadership, retirement, sensible, elation, composition, importance, reality,* and *impressive* on tagboard strips and cut the words into base words and suffixes. Put the pieces in an envelope. Prepare a set for each group of students. Ask groups to put the pieces together to spell words and then write their words on the board.

WRITING

Portfolio Discuss with students what award Tara might have won, then challenge them to imagine they are Tara and write the acceptance speech she gave.

SOCIAL STUDIES

Encourage students to research the kinds of activities that are available to students their age in their community. They can begin by polling their classmates about any groups they are active in.

FINE ARTS

Encourage students to think of a club, organization, or team they belong to or admire. Then ask them to design an award for an imaginary individual who has contributed his or her talent and energy to the group.

AstroWord Suffixes © 1998 Silver Burdett Ginn Inc. Division of Simon & Schuster.

AUDITORY/KINESTHETIC LEARNERS

LARGE GROUP

Write *-ance, -ence, -ive,* and *-ity* on the board. Say a word with one of the suffixes, then have students, in turn, say a word with that suffix. If a student can't think of one, he or she uses another lesson suffix for followers to copy. Keep the movement going quickly.

GIFTED LEARNERS

Challenge students to write and illustrate their own analogies using words with *-ance, -ence, -ity,* or *-ive.*

LEARNERS WHO NEED EXTRA SUPPORT

Before beginning the analogy activity, some students might need a review of synonyms and antonyms to help them determine what relationship to look for in each statement. **See Daily Word Study Practice, page 189.**

Lesson 60

Pages 131–132

Reviewing Suffixes

Lesson Focus

READING

● On the board, write the suffix *-er* in the middle of a circle. Invite students to suggest words that have the suffix *-er* and write the words in smaller circles placed around the suffix *-er*. They may suggest words such as *teacher, baker, trainer, longer, happier,* and *friendlier*. Ask students to use each of the words in a sentence.

● Repeat the procedure with the other suffixes studied in this unit.

● Explain to students that they will notice words that contain suffixes as they read an article about how to get involved in community service.

WRITING

Brainstorm ideas for writing by discussing the directives and questions at the top of page 132. Encourage students to use words from the word box in their descriptions.

131

Name

📖 Reading ▶ **Read the following article. Then answer the question.**

Helping Out

Have you ever thought about how you and your classmates can make your community, or even the world, a better place to live? You'd be surprised at how many different kinds of projects you can do once you decide to get involved!

What's the first step? Choose an issue that's important to you and your friends and classmates. Then make a list of possible projects related to the issue. Are you and your classmates interested in the environment? Then you might consider cleaning up litter in your neighborhood or starting a paper recycling project at your school. If you are interested in helping animals, you can help animal shelters find homes for abandoned pets by making posters or writing a letter to the local newspaper. Or, if you prefer working with people, volunteering at a senior citizens home is a great place to start.

Once you have chosen a useful project, find a teacher, counselor, or parent to help you make a plan. Think about your goals. Be persistent, but be realistic! The important thing is to get involved. You'll discover that you *can* make a difference in your neighborhood—and in your world!

What are some issues you care about?

_____

_____

_____

_____

_____

FOCUS ON ALL LEARNERS

ENGLISH LANGUAGE LEARNERS/ESL

To build background for page 131, discuss different kinds of local community projects students have heard or read about, such as soup kitchens, food shelves, and community theater groups. To build background for the questions at the bottom of the page, introduce the term *issue* and encourage students to talk about some issues that are important to them.

 ### VISUAL LEARNERS

PARTNER **Materials:** word cards for the suffixes in this unit and these base words: *woman, friend, argue, populate, accuse, compose, prefer, inherit, create, excuse, response*

Have pairs of students match appropriate suffixes and base words, compile a list of new words, and then compare lists.

KINESTHETIC LEARNERS

LARGE GROUP Draw a baseball diamond on the chalkboard and write a suffix studied in this unit in the middle of it. The first player writes a word containing that suffix. If that word is spelled correctly, the next player comes up to bat. Repeat the game with different suffixes.

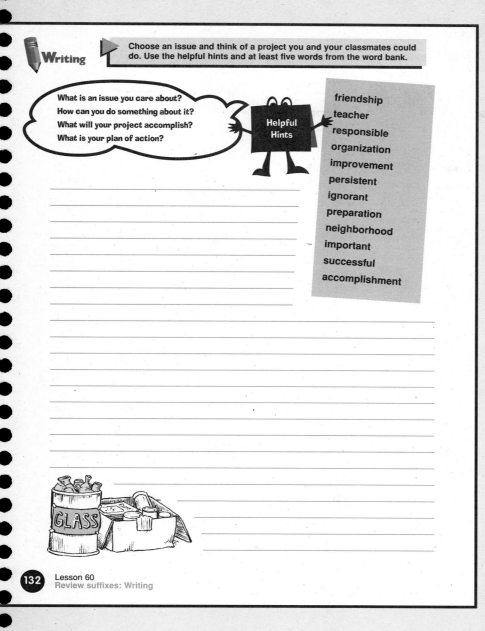

Writing ▶ Choose an issue and think of a project you and your classmates could do. Use the helpful hints and at least five words from the word bank.

What is an issue you care about?
How can you do something about it?
What will your project accomplish?
What is your plan of action?

Helpful Hints

friendship
teacher
responsible
organization
improvement
persistent
ignorant
preparation
neighborhood
important
successful
accomplishment

GLASS

132 Lesson 60
Review suffixes: Writing

SPELLING

The following sentences can be used as a posttest for spelling words with the suffixes *-ful, -ness, -hood, -ship, -ment, -able, -ible, -ion, -ation, -ition, -ance, -ence, -ive, -ity*.

1.	**cheerful**	My teacher is always **cheerful.**
2.	**newness**	The **newness** of a puppy is irresistible.
3.	**leadership**	Our class has **leadership.**
4.	**retirement**	My uncle is in **retirement.**
5.	**sensible**	My mom is always **sensible.**
6.	**elation**	I feel **elation** when I play ball.
7.	**composition**	My sister wrote an award-winning **composition.**
8.	**importance**	Rain is of great **importance** to farming.
9.	**reality**	Do you doubt the **reality** of her story?
10.	**impressive**	That's quite an **impressive** oak tree!

SOCIAL STUDIES

Encourage groups of students to research different community-service projects that kids in their town or city can do.

FINE ARTS

Ask students to draw a poster in support of an issue they care about, such as protecting the environment or helping abandoned pets. Display the posters on a classroom or hallway bulletin board.

AUDITORY/KINESTHETIC LEARNERS

LARGE GROUP

On the board, list the suffixes studied in the unit. Read a base word from the unit and ask students to pick out a suffix to make a new word. Have those who form a word walk over to a space designated as the winner's circle.

GIFTED LEARNERS

Challenge students to compare several of the words with suffixes studied in this unit with words with the same meanings in Spanish, French, or another language.

LEARNERS WHO NEED EXTRA SUPPORT

On the board, write words with suffixes studied in this unit. Ask volunteers to read each word aloud, underline the base word, circle the suffix, and tell the meaning of the word. Challenge students to use the words in oral sentences. **See Daily Word Study Practice, pages 188-189.**

Lesson 61

Pages 133–134

Unit Checkup
Reviewing Suffixes

Lesson Focus

PREPARING FOR THE CHECKUP

- On the chalkboard, write these suffixes: *er, or, ist, ward, en, ize, est, eer, ent, ant, ful, ness, hood, ship, ment, able, ible, ion, ation, ition, ance, ence,* and *ity*. Ask volunteers to come to the board and write words to go with each suffix.

- As each word is written, the group should confirm whether the word is valid. If someone suggests a word that cannot be turned into a new word using a given suffix, ask others to explain why that word doesn't fit.

USING THE PAGES

Make sure students understand the directions for pages 133 and 134. After students have completed the pages, discuss the questions on page 134. Encourage students to talk about the purpose of advertising and how students like themselves can be knowledgeable consumers. Then have students discuss what they have learned about suffixes during this unit.

Name _____

UNIT 5 CHECKUP

Read each sentence and the suffixes that follow it. Notice the base word in dark print. Fill in the circle beside the suffix that should be added to the base word.

1. The **novel**_____ wrote a mystery book.
   ● ist ○ or ○ eer

2. The **auction**_____ yelled, "Sold!"
   ○ ent ● eer ○ ist

3. Tony moved **for**_____ two spaces.
   ● ward ○ ant ○ est

4. The seal **train**_____ used fish as a reward.
   ○ eer ● er ○ ist

5. Let's **revital**_____ the neighborhood.
   ● ize ○ eer ○ ist

6. Only one **visit**_____ is allowed in the room.
   ○ ant ● or ○ ee

7. An **account**_____ balanced our checkbook.
   ○ er ○ or ● ant

8. Because Juan was away, he used an **absent**_____ ballot.
   ● ee ○ er ○ ize

9. The forest was quiet and **peace**_____.
   ○ ward ○ ness ● ful

10. The **happi**_____ of the family was easy to see.
    ● ness ○ est ○ ful

11. Our class won the spelling **champion**_____ this year.
    ○ ment ● ship ○ ence

12. My skating showed a lot of **improve**_____ this winter.
    ○ able ○ tion ● ment

13. I am **respons**_____ for my pet frog.
    ● ible ○ able ○ ment

14. That building is the **high**_____ one in the city.
    ● est ○ er ○ ist

15. Our soccer team is **unbeat**_____.
    ● able ○ ive ○ ence

16. Our players run **fast**_____ than our opponents.
    ○ est ● er ○ or

17. The classroom **add**_____ gives us more space.
    ○ hood ○ ence ● ition

18. I love living in this **neighbor**_____.
    ○ ence ○ ship ● hood

19. I like to be **creat**_____ in art class.
    ● ive ○ ness ○ ful

20. I can't tell the **differ**_____ between these two drawings.
    ● ence ○ able ○ ful

FOCUS ON ALL LEARNERS

ENGLISH LANGUAGE LEARNERS/ESL

To build background for the article on page 134, write the words *advertising* and *consumer* on the board. Define both terms with students and encourage a discussion about advertisements that students like or dislike and why.

VISUAL LEARNERS

List the suffixes for the unit on the board. Have students take turns coming up and writing a word for one of them.

KINESTHETIC LEARNERS

SMALL GROUP

Form five teams and assign each team one of the suffixes studied in the unit. Give teams five minutes to write as many words as they can with that suffix. Ask volunteers to read their lists aloud. Rotate suffixes and repeat.

Read the words in the word bank. Then read the article. Write the correct word from the word bank on the line to complete each sentence. Then answer the questions.

advertisements	competition	creative	durability
imaginations	impressive	knowledgeable	likelihood
passive	responsible	selection	sincerity

Consumer Alert

Have you ever considered how many times a day you are bombarded by all types of ___advertisements___ ? Advertising is a multi-billion dollar industry. Advertisers try to persuade consumers to buy a particular product or service. Since the ___competition___ among products is fierce, thousands of ___creative___ people use their ___imaginations___ every day to develop clever ads they hope will capture your attention. What is the ___likelihood___ that an intelligent, ___responsible (or knowledgeable)___ consumer will be affected by ads? It's very high! But you can be a ___knowledgeable (or responsible)___ consumer by researching a product before you buy it. For example, if you plan to buy a pair of athletic shoes, compare a wide ___selection___ of shoes. Look at the features, price, and ___durability___ of the shoes. Ask yourself whether this is the best pair of shoes for the price I can afford, or am I being swayed by a clever ad or the seeming ___sincerity___ of a celebrity spokesperson?

Remember that no matter how clever or ___impressive___ an ad might be, you should make an active decision, not a ___passive___ one about what to buy and when to buy it.

1. What is the purpose of advertising?
   The purpose of advertising is to persuade consumers to buy a product or service.

2. What are some ways you can be a knowledgeable consumer?
   (A knowledgeable consumer can research a product's features and price.)

134 Lesson 61
Review suffixes: Checkup

AUDITORY LEARNERS

PARTNER Invite students to play "guess the word" with the review answers. One player picks a word and says a clue about it, such as *I am thinking of a word that has four syllables, ends with* able, *and means* "can't be beat." The other player searches the review answers and finds the word *unbeatable*.

GIFTED LEARNERS

Challenge students to write a humorous story that includes words containing each suffix studied in the unit.

LEARNERS WHO NEED EXTRA SUPPORT

Work with students to review the unit by completing the pages with them orally, letting them read the items and answer choices aloud to you. **See Daily Word Study Practice, pages 188–189.**

ASSESSING UNDERSTANDING OF UNIT SKILLS

Student Progress Assessment You may wish to review the observational notes you made as students worked through the activities in the unit. Your notes will help you evaluate the progress students made with suffixes.

Portfolio Assessment Review the materials students have collected in their portfolios. You may wish to have interviews with students to discuss their written work and the progress they have made since the beginning of the unit. As you review students' work, evaluate how well they use the unit skills.

Daily Word Study Practice For students who need additional practice with any of the topics in this unit, quick reviews are provided on pages 188–189 in Daily Word Study Practice.

Word Study Posttest To assess students' mastery of the skills covered in this unit, use the posttest on pages 113g–113h.

SPELLING CUMULATIVE POSTTEST

Use the following words and dictation sentences.

1. **leader** May I be the next **leader?**
2. **collector** My aunt is a **collector** of glass cats.
3. **novelist** Is your goal to be a **novelist?**
4. **loosen** Nick will **loosen** his tie.
5. **equalize** Mom will **equalize** their chances of winning the game.
6. **hotter** Do you like soup **hotter** than this?
7. **puppeteer** Children love to watch a **puppeteer** at work.
8. **repellent** Will you pass the bug **repellent?**
9. **servant** The mayor of the town is a public **servant.**
10. **cheerful** I try to be **cheerful** most of the time.
11. **leadership** The **leadership** of the school band is important.
12. **retirement** When does your **retirement** begin?
13. **sensible** I'm not always **sensible.**
14. **composition** Please read me your **composition.**
15. **importance** Don't overlook the **importance** of a good night's sleep.
16. **reality** Will my dream ever become a **reality?**
17. **impressive** Your skating is very **impressive!**

Teacher Notes

Assessment Strategy Overview

Throughout Unit 6, assess students' ability to understand the rules for adding suffixes to words, forming irregular plurals of words, and dividing words into syllables. There are various ways to assess students' progress. You may also want to encourage students to evaluate their own work and participate in setting goals for their own learning.

FORMAL ASSESSMENT

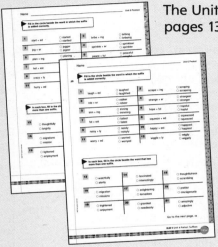

The Unit 6 Pretest on pages 135e–135f helps to assess a student's knowledge at the beginning of the unit and to plan instruction.

The Unit 6 Posttest on pages 135g–135h helps to assess mastery of unit objectives and to plan for reteaching, if necessary.

INFORMAL ASSESSMENT

The Reading & Writing pages and Unit Checkup in the student book are an effective means of evaluating students' performance.

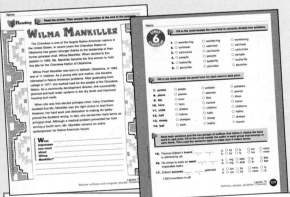

Skill	Reading & Writing Pages	Unit Checkup
Add Suffixes to Words that Double the Final Consonant	157–158	159–160
Add Suffixes to Words that End in *e*	157–158	159–160
Add Suffixes to Words that End in *y*	157–158	159–160
Words with Multiple Suffixes	157–158	159–160
Add Suffix *-ly* to Words Ending in *y* or *le*	157–158	159–160
Plurals of Words Ending in *f* and *fe*	157–158	159–160
Plurals of Words Ending in *o*	157–158	159–160
Irregular Plural Forms	157–158	159–160
Syllables	157–158	159–160

PORTFOLIO ASSESSMENT

This logo appears throughout the teaching plans. It signals opportunities for collecting students' work for individual portfolios. You may also want to collect the following pages.

❖ Unit 6 Pretest and Posttest, pages 135e–135h

❖ Unit 6 Reading & Writing, pages 157–158

❖ Unit 6 Checkup, pages 159–160

STUDENT PROGRESS CHECKLIST

Use the checklist on page 135i to record students' progress. You may want to cut the sections apart to place each student's checklist in his or her portfolio.

Administering and Evaluating the
Pretest and Posttest

DIRECTIONS

To help you assess students' progress in learning Unit 6 skills, tests are available on pages 135e–135h. Administer the Pretest before students begin the unit. The results of the Pretest will help you identify each student's strengths and needs in advance, allowing you to structure lesson plans to meet individual needs. Administer the Posttest to assess students' overall mastery of skills taught in the unit and to identify specific areas that will require reteaching.

PERFORMANCE ASSESSMENT PROFILE

The following chart will help you identify specific skills as they appear on the tests and enable you to identify and record specific information about an individual's or the class's performance on the tests.

Depending on the results of the tests, refer to the Reteaching column for lesson-plan pages where you can find activities that will be useful for meeting individual needs or for daily word study practice.

PERFORMANCE ASSESSMENT PROFILE

Skill	Pretest Questions	Posttest Questions	Reteaching — Focus on All Learners	Reteaching — Daily Word Study Practice
Add Suffixes to Words that Double the Final Consonant	3, 5, 7	3, 5, 7	137–138, 157–158	190
Add Suffixes to Words that End in e	2, 4, 6, 8, 12	2, 4, 6, 8, 12	139–140, 157–158	190
Words with Multiple Suffixes	13–21	13–21	141–142, 157–158	190–191
Add Suffixes to Words that End in y	9, 10, 11	9, 10, 11	143–144, 157–158	190–191
Add Suffix -ly to Words Ending in y or le	9, 12	9, 12	145–146, 157–158	190–191
Plurals of Words Ending in f and fe	23, 26, 27	23, 26, 27	147–148, 157–158	191–192
Plurals of Words Ending in o	24, 25	24, 25	149–150, 157–158	191–192
Irregular Plural Forms	22, 28	22, 28	151–152, 157–158	191–192
Syllables	29–38	29–38	153–156	193

> **Fill in the circle beside the word in which the suffix is added correctly.**

1 laugh + ed
- ○ laughed
- ○ laughhed

2 scrape + ing
- ○ scraping
- ○ scrapeing

3 rob + er
- ○ robber
- ○ robeer

4 strange + er
- ○ strangeer
- ○ stranger

5 trim + ing
- ○ triming
- ○ trimming

6 hope + ful
- ○ hopeful
- ○ hopful

7 fat + est
- ○ fattest
- ○ fatest

8 squeeze + ed
- ○ squeezeed
- ○ squeezed

9 noisy + ly
- ○ noisily
- ○ noisyly

10 happy + est
- ○ happyest
- ○ happiest

11 worry + ed
- ○ worried
- ○ worryed

12 wiggle + ly
- ○ wiggly
- ○ wiggely

> **In each box, fill in the circle beside the word that has more than one suffix.**

13
- ○ watchfully
- ○ alertly

14
- ○ fascinated
- ○ interestingly

15
- ○ thoughtfulness
- ○ scrambling

16
- ○ migrations
- ○ mission

17
- ○ enlightening
- ○ tornadoes

18
- ○ prettier
- ○ courageously

19
- ○ frightened
- ○ enjoyment

20
- ○ grandest
- ○ needlessly

21
- ○ amazingly
- ○ adjective

Go to the next page. →

> ► **Fill in the circle next to the correct plural that best completes each sentence.**

22. She caught three _____.   ○ trout   ○ trouts   ○ troutes

23. Look at the pack of _____.   ○ wolfs   ○ wolves   ○ wolfes

24. I own two transistor _____.   ○ radio   ○ radioes   ○ radios

25. Buy four ripe _____.   ○ tomato   ○ tomatos   ○ tomatoes

26. Be careful using _____.   ○ knifes   ○ knives   ○ knifies

27. Wind swept over the _____.   ○ bluffs   ○ bluffes   ○ bluves

28. Two _____ scurried away.   ○ mouses   ○ mousies   ○ mice

> ► **Fill in the circle beside the number that tells how many syllables are in the word in boldface.**

29. sheep
○ 1   ○ 2   ○ 3

30. oatmeal
○ 1   ○ 2   ○ 3

31. bees
○ 1   ○ 2   ○ 3

32. heroes
○ 2   ○ 3   ○ 4

33. cattle
○ 2   ○ 3   ○ 4

34. sleepily
○ 2   ○ 3   ○ 4

35. kangaroos
○ 3   ○ 4   ○ 5

36. excitably
○ 3   ○ 4   ○ 5

37. organization
○ 3   ○ 4   ○ 5

38. industrious
○ 3   ○ 4   ○ 5

Possible score on Unit 6 Pretest is 38. Number correct _____

BLM 42 Unit 6 Pretest: Plurals, syllables

> **Fill in the circle beside the word in which the suffix is added correctly.**

1 start + ed
- ○ started
- ○ startted

2 bribe + ing
- ○ bribing
- ○ bribeing

3 jog + er
- ○ jogger
- ○ jogeer

4 sprinkle + er
- ○ sprinkleer
- ○ sprinkler

5 plan + ing
- ○ planing
- ○ planning

6 peace + ful
- ○ peaceful
- ○ peacful

7 hot + est
- ○ hottest
- ○ hotest

8 humble + ed
- ○ humblled
- ○ humbled

9 crazy + ly
- ○ crazily
- ○ crazyly

10 rusty + est
- ○ rustyest
- ○ rustiest

11 hurry + ed
- ○ hurried
- ○ hurryed

12 probable + ly
- ○ probably
- ○ probabely

> **In each box, fill in the circle beside the word that has more than one suffix.**

13
- ○ thoughtfully
- ○ brightly

14
- ○ squeezed
- ○ disapprovingly

15
- ○ cheerfulness
- ○ observer

16
- ○ carelessness
- ○ careful

17
- ○ increasingly
- ○ buffaloes

18
- ○ peppier
- ○ gloriously

19
- ○ lightened
- ○ employment

20
- ○ mysterious
- ○ widening

21
- ○ uselessly
- ○ manufacture

Go to the next page. →

> **Fill in the circle next to the correct plural that best completes each sentence.**

22. Add two _____ to the salad.   ○ zucchinis   ○ zucchini   ○ zucchinum

23. The farmer owns two _____.   ○ calfs   ○ calfes   ○ calves

24. She took several _____.   ○ photos   ○ photoes   ○ phottos

25. _____ bounced off the cave's walls.   ○ Echos   ○ Echoes   ○ Echoos

26. Tropical fish live in coral _____.   ○ reeves   ○ reefes   ○ reefs

27. Ocean waves sprayed the _____.   ○ cliffs   ○ clives   ○ clifes

28. A flock of _____ flew overhead.   ○ gooses   ○ goose   ○ geese

> **Fill in the circle beside the number that tells how many syllables are in the word in boldface.**

29. weighed
   ○ 1   ○ 2   ○ 3

30. insight
   ○ 1   ○ 2   ○ 3

31. spaghetti
   ○ 1   ○ 2   ○ 3

32. wintertime
   ○ 2   ○ 3   ○ 4

33. scrubber
   ○ 2   ○ 3   ○ 4

34. handkerchiefs
   ○ 2   ○ 3   ○ 4

35. resolution
   ○ 3   ○ 4   ○ 5

36. indirectly
   ○ 3   ○ 4   ○ 5

37. imagination
   ○ 3   ○ 4   ○ 5

38. fingerprints
   ○ 3   ○ 4   ○ 5

Possible score on Unit 6 Posttest is 38. Number correct _____

Student Progress Checklist

Make as many copies as needed to use for a class list. For individual portfolio use, cut apart each student's section. As indicated by the code, color in boxes next to skills satisfactorily assessed and mark an X by those requiring reteaching. Marked boxes can later be colored in to indicate mastery.

STUDENT PROGRESS CHECKLIST

Code: ■ Satisfactory   ☒ Needs Reteaching

Student: _____ _____ Pretest Score: _____ Posttest Score: _____	Skills ❏ Suffixes ❏ Plurals ❏ Syllables	Comments / Learning Goals
Student: _____ _____ Pretest Score: _____ Posttest Score: _____	Skills ❏ Suffixes ❏ Plurals ❏ Syllables	Comments / Learning Goals
Student: _____ _____ Pretest Score: _____ Posttest Score: _____	Skills ❏ Suffixes ❏ Plurals ❏ Syllables	Comments / Learning Goals
Student: _____ _____ Pretest Score: _____ Posttest Score: _____	Skills ❏ Suffixes ❏ Plurals ❏ Syllables	Comments / Learning Goals
Student: _____ _____ Pretest Score: _____ Posttest Score: _____	Skills ❏ Suffixes ❏ Plurals ❏ Syllables	Comments / Learning Goals

Spelling Connections

INTRODUCTION

The Unit Word List is a comprehensive list of spelling words drawn from this unit. The words are grouped according to the rules of forming plurals and adding suffixes. To incorporate spelling into your word study program, use the activity in the Curriculum Connections section of each teaching plan.

The spelling lessons utilize the following approach for each set of words.

1. Administer a pretest of the words that have not yet been introduced. Dictation sentences are provided.

2. Provide practice.

3. Reassess. Dictation sentences are provided.

A final test is provided in Lesson 73 on page 160.

DIRECTIONS

Make a copy of Blackline Master 46 for each student. After administering the pretest for each word study element, give each student a copy of the appropriate word list.

Students can work with a partner to practice spelling the words orally and identifying the appropriate phonetic spelling rule for each word. They can also make and use letter cards to form the words on the list. You may want to challenge students to identify other words that have the same phonetic elements. Students can write words of their own on *My Own Word List* (see Blackline Master 46).

Have students store their list words in an envelope or plastic zipper bag in the back of their books or notebooks. You may want to suggest that students keep a spelling notebook, listing words with similar patterns. You could also invite students to build word-wall displays in the classroom. Each section of the wall can focus on words with a single word study element. The walls will become a good spelling resource when students are writing.

UNIT WORD LIST

Double Final Consonant to Add Suffix; Drop Final *e* to Add Suffix; More Than One Suffix; Add Suffix *-ly* to Words Ending in *y* or *le*

cutting

liking

activities

chimneys

painlessly

heavily

coyly

wobbly

Plurals of Words Ending in *f* or *fe*; Words Ending in *o*; Other Plural Forms

wolves

chiefs

cliffs

radios

potatoes

crises

oases

olden

mice

fungi

Spelling Connections

Spelling   # UNIT 6 WORD LIST

Double Final Consonant to Add Suffix; Drop Final e to Add Suffix; More Than One Suffix; Add Suffix ly to Words Ending in y or le

cutting
liking
activities
chimneys
painlessly
heavily
coyly
wobbly

Plurals of Words Ending in f, fe, or o; Other Plural Forms

wolves
chiefs
cliffs
radios
potatoes
crises
oases
olden
mice
fungi

My Own Word List

Word Study Games, Activities, and Technology

The following collection of ideas offers a variety of opportunities to reinforce word study skills while actively engaging students. The games, activities, and technology suggestions can easily be adapted to meet the needs of your group of learners. They vary in approach so as to consider students' different learning styles.

● **CLASSIFYING WORDS WITH SUFFIXES**

Tell each student to divide a sheet of paper into three columns with these headings: *Change, Double Consonants, Dropped* -e. Challenge students to think of five words containing suffixes for each category and to write each one in the appropriate column. Have students work in small groups to combine individual lists into one "superlist." You might collect the finished projects and display them on a word wall or in a class booklet.

Change	Double Consonants	Dropped -e
happiness	skidded	imagination
likelihood	stunned	sensitivity
		reversible

▲ **SUFFIX TRIVIA GAME**

Invite partners to create questions and answers for a *Trivial Pursuit©* type of game. Have them add the suffixes *-er* and *-est* to words that double the consonant before adding a suffix and create interesting factual questions that include those words. You might start them off by writing the following words on the board: *big, hot, tall, cold, fast, swim, run*. Encourage them to add other words that drop the final e before adding a suffix (such as *migrate, compute,* and *dance*) to their list and write questions that include those words. Allow them to use reference books to check the accuracy of their facts. When they have finished, sets of partners can create a game board and play a game of "suffix trivia" by asking each other questions.

◆ **CHANGING PARTNERS**

Pair students and tell partners to make a list of six words. The first two and last two words should form the plural by adding *-s*. The third and sixth words should form the plural by changing *y* to *i* and adding *-es*. Ask students to come to the board two pairs at a time. Tell partners to take turns listing their words on the board in separate columns. Each time they come to a word that changes to form the plural, the students writing should change partners and add that word to the other pair's list. You might extend this activity by substituting *f* and *ff*, adding *-s* or *-es* to words ending in *o,* or adapting the rules to words that add the suffix *-ly*.

holidays   mutinies

decoys   victories

■ A WRITER'S NOTEBOOK

Have students look through fiction books or textbooks in the classroom to find words that fit the rules in any one lesson in this unit. Tell them to list the words in a journal or notebook. Have students work individually or with a partner to write a descriptive paragraph using as many of these words as they can. Challenge students to add a paragraph that relates to the description and that outlines the plot of a mystery.

✳ SUFFIX CARDS

Suggest that students look for words that fit the rules for adding suffixes or forming irregular plurals as they read in and out of school. Ask them to write each word they find on an index card. At the end of each week, collect all the cards. Have each student choose a card and explain the rule for adding the suffix or forming the suffix. You might create a word wall to which each week students can add new words relevant to the lessons in this unit.

● WORD-SEARCH PUZZLE

Distribute an example of a word-search puzzle and allow students time to solve it. Challenge pairs of students to design a word-search puzzle using plurals. Explain that the words may be horizontal, vertical, or diagonal and that they should write a clue for each word. Encourage pairs to exchange their work with another set of partners and solve one another's puzzles.

▲ CHANGING FEELINGS

Have students work in groups of three or four to list at least six familiar words that describe feelings. Next, tell them to make new words by adding suffixes to each word on their list. Then, they should decide which rule for adding suffixes applied in each case. Challenge them to find a synonym for each of the original words that follows a different rule for adding suffixes. Allow them to use a thesaurus or other reference books to search for synonyms. Some examples are shown here.

| glad, gladly (no change) | merry, merrily (change the *y* to *i* and add *-ly*) |
| sad, sadly (no change) | gloomy, gloomily (change the *y* to *i* and add *-ly*) |

◆ ANIMAL CAFE

Provide students with printed copies of the paragraph shown at the right. Tell them to rewrite the paragraph, substituting the correct plural form for each of the words in parentheses. Discuss the use of words with only one form to describe groups of animals. Ask volunteers to identify three such words in the paragraph and mention other such words they have heard. Invite students to write another paragraph describing the experience of other patrons in the restaurant.

> Two (moose) and two (mouse) went to dinner with their (wife) and (child) at the Animal Cafe. A pack of (wolf) and a gaggle of (goose) were seated near them. The band, a yoke of (ox), played (piano). The (moose) had (loaf) of bread, which they cut with (knife). The (mouse) ate (oatmeal) and (potato). They all ordered (milk) with their meals.

■ WRITING RIDDLES

Invite students to work with a partner to create humorous riddles using words that form irregular plurals. Display the riddles on a bulletin board and challenge other students to solve them.

✳ HOT POTATO

Make a list of words from those discussed in this unit. Alternate words that do not change when forming suffixes with words that do change. Tell students that hot potato is a game in which a ball representing a hot potato is quickly tossed from player to player. Organize students in teams of six and have the members of each team arrange themselves in a circle. Give a ball to one player on each team. Begin by saying the first word on the list. The students holding the balls can add a suffix to make a new word. If no change to the original word ending was required, the player keeps the ball. If change was required, the player tosses the ball to the player on his or her right, who responds to the next two words, and so on.

● SYLLABLE HOPSCOTCH

Blackline Master 47 shows a game board featuring a hopscotch pattern. Make a master copy by printing a different number from 1 to 5 in each space on the board. Numbers furthest from the start base should be highest and vice versa. Make enough copies to distribute to teams of three or four players. Players take turns moving a small coin or paper marker from Start to Home. Explain that each student must touch every space as they move along the board. At each space, a player must say a word with the same number of syllables as the number indicates in order to move on. If a player cannot form a matching word, he or she stays in place until the next turn. The first player to reach Home wins. Challenge students to turn and repeat the game, moving back to Start. You might allow students to check a dictionary if there is a question about the number of syllables in a given word.

Technology

The following software products are designed to develop students' vocabulary skills.

Word Attack 3 A "vocabulary builder" for students ages 10 and up, this product offers crossword puzzles and arcade games involving definitions, spellings, and pronunciations of thousands of words, each categorized by subject and level of difficulty.
** Davidson & Associates, Inc.
   19840 Pioneer Avenue
   Torrance, CA 90503
   (800) 545-7677

Word City Students in grades 3–9 can develop their skills in vocabulary, spelling, and reading comprehension while exploring themes such as sports, science, and favorite tales.
** Sanctuary Woods
   1825 South Grant Street
   San Mateo, CA 94402
   (800) 943-3664

Name _____

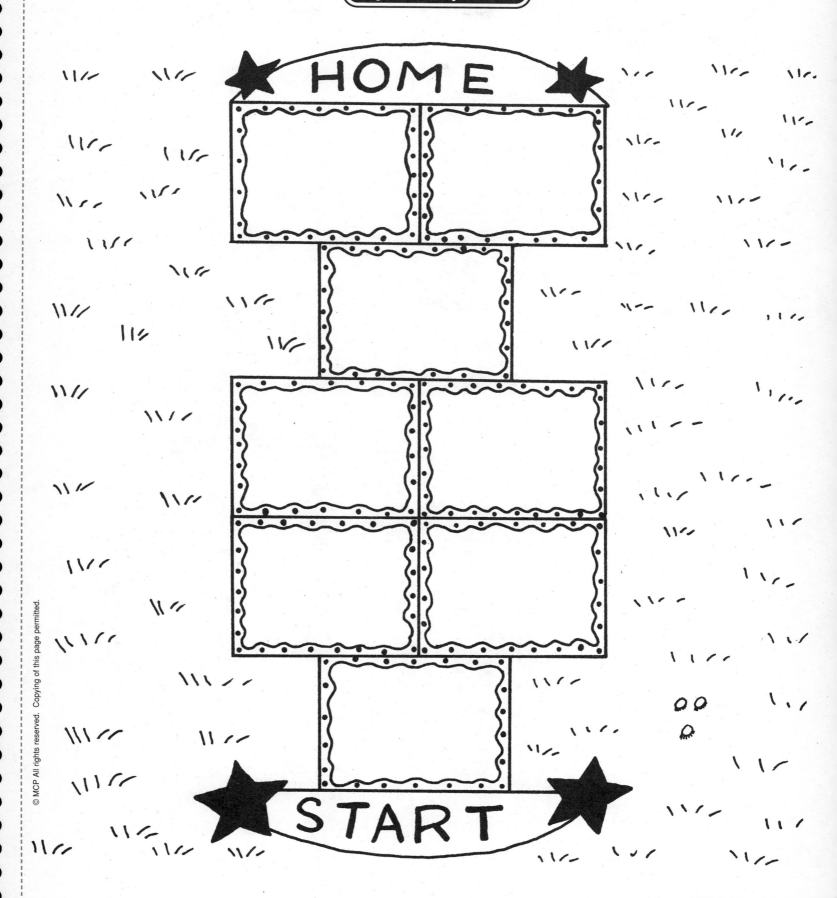

Syllable Hopscotch

HOME

START

Home Connection

HOME LETTER

A letter is available to be sent home at the beginning of Unit 6. This letter informs family members that students will be learning about words with irregular plurals and more about suffixes, including how the spelling of certain base words changes when a suffix is added. The suggested home activity revolves around "Fun With More Than One" and an accompanying illustration. After reading the poem, the family finds the singular and plural items rendered in the artwork. This activity promotes interaction between child and family members while supporting the student's learning of reading and writing words with the targeted word study skills. A letter is also available in Spanish on page 135q.

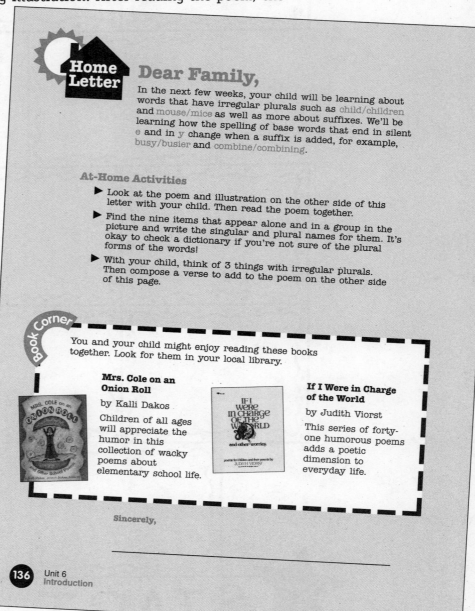

Home Letter

Dear Family,

In the next few weeks, your child will be learning about words that have irregular plurals such as child/children and mouse/mice as well as more about suffixes. We'll be learning how the spelling of base words that end in silent e and in y change when a suffix is added, for example, busy/busier and combine/combining.

At-Home Activities

▶ Look at the poem and illustration on the other side of this letter with your child. Then read the poem together.

▶ Find the nine items that appear alone and in a group in the picture and write the singular and plural names for them. It's okay to check a dictionary if you're not sure of the plural forms of the words!

▶ With your child, think of 3 things with irregular plurals. Then compose a verse to add to the poem on the other side of this page.

Book Corner

You and your child might enjoy reading these books together. Look for them in your local library.

Mrs. Cole on an Onion Roll

by Kalli Dakos

Children of all ages will appreciate the humor in this collection of wacky poems about elementary school life.

If I Were in Charge of the World

by Judith Viorst

This series of forty-one humorous poems adds a poetic dimension to everyday life.

Sincerely,

_____

136 Unit 6 Introduction

135p

Carta para la casa

Estimada familia,

En las semanas próximas, su hijo/a va a aprender acerca de palabras en inglés que tienen plurales irregulares tales como **child/children** (**niño/niños**) y **mouse/mice** (**ratón/ratones**) y también más acerca de los sufijos. Vamos a aprender cómo cambia la ortografía de las palabras base que terminan en **e** silente y en **y** cuando se les añade un sufijo, **busy/busier** (**ocupado/más ocupado**) y **combine/combining** (**combinado/combinando**).

Actividades para hacer en casa

▶ Miren con su hijo/a el poema y la ilustración al dorso de esta carta. Luego lean el poema juntos.

▶ Hallen los nueve artículos que aparecen solos y en un grupo en la ilustración, y escriban el singular y el plural de sus nombres en inglés. ¡Pueden consultar un diccionario si no están seguros de los plurales!

▶ Con su hijo/a, piensen en tres cosas con plurales irregulares en inglés. Luego, compongan un verso adicional para el poema.

Rincón del libro

Quizás a su hijo/a y a ustedes les guste leer estos libros juntos. Búsquenlos en la biblioteca de su localidad.

Mrs. Cole on an Onion Roll
por Kalli Dakos

Los niños de todas las edades podrán apreciar el humor en esta colección de poemas alocados acerca de la vida en una escuela primaria.

If I Were in Charge of the World and other Worries
por Judith Viorst

Esta serie de cuarenta y un poemas le añade una dimensión poética a la vida cotidiana.

Atentamente, _____

Unit 6

Pages 135–136

Suffixes, Plurals, and Syllables

ASSESSING PRIOR KNOWLEDGE

To assess students' prior knowledge of suffixes, plurals, and syllables, use the pretest on pages 135e–135f.

Unit Focus

USING THE PAGE

- Read "Fun With More Than One!" aloud. Invite students to read along as you read the poem again. Emphasize the singular and plural of each noun.

- Discuss the humor in the poem. Help students identify the word play in each stanza.

- Ask students what they enjoyed about the poem. Did the poem make them think about plurals in a different way?

- Read the poem again, asking students to pay special attention to the plurals. Ask them to stress the plurals, especially the nonsense words, as they take turns reading the poem aloud.

- **Critical Thinking** Read aloud the question the character asks at the bottom of page 135. Encourage students to share their ideas for finding correct plurals.

BUILDING A CONTEXT

- Have students identify each set of singular and plural words as you read the poem again. Make a two-column list of their words on the board.

UNIT 6 Suffixes, Plurals, Syllables

FUN WITH MORE THAN ONE!

When you walk by the lake,
You might see a goose,
Who will probably lead you to geese.
But if you happen upon a moose
Don't look for a number of meese!

More than one moose
Is two or three moose,
But more than one mouse
Is two mice!

So if you live in one house in the city,
And another small house by the lake,
Then you live in two houses,
Not in two hice,
So please, don't make that mistake!

Do you ever get confused when you're talking about more than one of something? Read the poem to help you remember!

If you're unsure of the plural form of a word, how can you find out what it is?

Critical Thinking

UNIT OPENER ACTIVITIES

MORE SILLY PLURALS!

Challenge students to brainstorm a list of irregular plurals. Then have them work together in small groups to write a new stanza for "Fun With More Than One!"

ONE MOOSE PLUS ONE MOOSE

Invite students to use a computer, if one (or more) is available, to write and illustrate equations for the plurals in the poem. For example, *one moose plus one moose equals two moose* and *one mouse plus one mouse equals two mice.*

A WALK BY THE LAKE

Challenge students to imagine they are walking by the lake mentioned in the poem. Have them tape-record their observations or write a journal entry. Remind them to mention any plants or animals they think they might see in such a setting.

Home Letter

Dear Family,

In the next few weeks, your child will be learning about words that have irregular plurals such as child/children and mouse/mice as well as more about suffixes. We'll be learning how the spelling of base words that end in silent e and in y change when a suffix is added, for example, busy/busier and combine/combining.

At-Home Activities

► Look at the poem and illustration on the other side of this letter with your child. Then read the poem together.

► Find the nine items that appear alone and in a group in the picture and write the singular and plural names for them. It's okay to check a dictionary if you're not sure of the plural forms of the words!

► With your child, think of 3 things with irregular plurals. Then compose a verse to add to the poem on the other side of this page.

Book Corner

You and your child might enjoy reading these books together. Look for them in your local library.

Mrs. Cole on an Onion Roll

by Kalli Dakos

Children of all ages will appreciate the humor in this collection of wacky poems about elementary school life.

If I Were in Charge of the World

by Judith Viorst

This series of forty-one humorous poems adds a poetic dimension to everyday life.

Sincerely,

_____

BULLETIN BOARD

Challenge students to illustrate and label the singular and plural forms of nouns for a "Plural Power" display. They can draw (or create with computer graphics) a single version of their nouns. To represent the plural of the word, they can use a photocopier to duplicate the illustration as many times as they choose.

● The Home Letter on page 136 is intended to acquaint family members with the word study skills students will be studying in the unit. Students can tear out page 136 and take it home. Suggest that they complete the activities on the page with a family member. Encourage students to look in the library for some of the books pictured on page 136 and then to read them with family members.

● The Home Letter can also be found on pages 135q in Spanish.

CURRICULUM CONNECTIONS ✳ ● ◆ ■ ◆ ●

WRITING

Have students write a humorous description of one class's visit to a zoo. Suggest that they use the plurals of at least ten animal names.

SOCIAL STUDIES

Students can research the number of people living in their town, their state, their country, and the world. Encourage them to find ways to show this information on a graph or a chart.

MATH

Challenge students to choose a category of items in the classroom and count them; for example, pencils, chairs, or windows. Have students pool their information to compile an inventory of classroom objects.

Lesson 62
Pages 137–138

Words That Double the Final Consonant to Add a Suffix

Lesson Focus

INTRODUCING THE SKILL

- Write the following suffixes and words on the board:

  -ing   -ed   -er   -est

  <u>hug</u> hugging   <u>sit</u> sitter

  <u>drop</u> dropped   <u>big</u> biggest

- Point out that each suffix begins with a vowel and that each underlined base word contains a short vowel sound followed by a single consonant.

- Have students study *hugging, sitter, dropped*, and *biggest* to determine what happens to each base word when a suffix beginning with a vowel is added.

- Help students conclude that when a word with a short vowel sound ends in a single consonant, the final consonant is usually doubled before a suffix that begins with a vowel is added.

USING THE PAGES

Have students scan the directions on pages 137 and 138 to be sure they understand how to complete the practices.

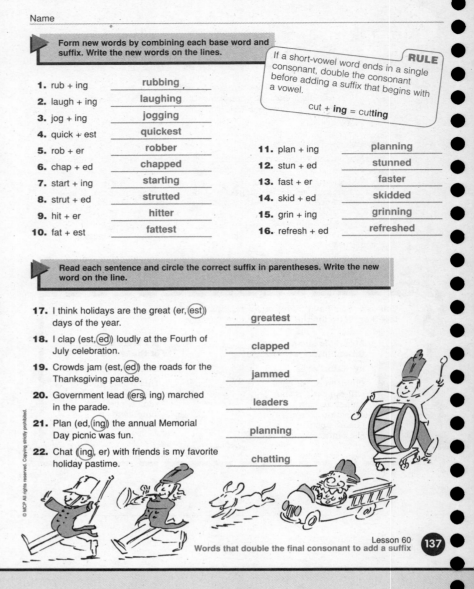

Name _____

Form new words by combining each base word and suffix. Write the new words on the lines.

RULE If a short-vowel word ends in a single consonant, double the consonant before adding a suffix that begins with a vowel.

cut + **ing** = cut**t**ing

1. rub + ing   rubbing
2. laugh + ing   laughing
3. jog + ing   jogging
4. quick + est   quickest
5. rob + er   robber
6. chap + ed   chapped
7. start + ing   starting
8. strut + ed   strutted
9. hit + er   hitter
10. fat + est   fattest

11. plan + ing   planning
12. stun + ed   stunned
13. fast + er   faster
14. skid + ed   skidded
15. grin + ing   grinning
16. refresh + ed   refreshed

Read each sentence and circle the correct suffix in parentheses. Write the new word on the line.

17. I think holidays are the great (er, (est)) days of the year.   greatest
18. I clap (est, (ed)) loudly at the Fourth of July celebration.   clapped
19. Crowds jam (est, (ed)) the roads for the Thanksgiving parade.   jammed
20. Government lead ((ers), ing) marched in the parade.   leaders
21. Plan (ed, (ing)) the annual Memorial Day picnic was fun.   planning
22. Chat ((ing), er) with friends is my favorite holiday pastime.   chatting

Lesson 60   **137**
Words that double the final consonant to add a suffix

FOCUS ON ALL LEARNERS

ENGLISH LANGUAGE LEARNERS/ESL

Before beginning page 137, encourage a discussion about the activities that take place during celebrations for the Fourth of July, Thanksgiving, and Memorial Day. Work several items on page 137 together to be sure students understand the doubling rule.

VISUAL LEARNERS

LARGE GROUP

Have students add the suffixes *-er* and *-est* to the adjectives *big, hot, tall, slow, wet, cold*, and *fast* and use the words in factual sentences to describe holidays.

KINESTHETIC LEARNERS

LARGE GROUP

Materials: index cards with *m, p, t, -er, -est*

Write *hot, wet, fast, swim, grim, clap*, and *drop* on the board. Display the cards on the chalkboard ledge. Students match a suffix and an additional letter as needed to each base word and write the word formed next to the base word.

▶ **Circle each suffix below that begins with a vowel. Form new words by putting each base word and suffix together. Write the new words on the lines.**

1. scan +(ing)   scanning
2. fast +(est)   fastest
3. hot +(est)   hottest
4. sad + ness   sadness
5. steep +(er)   steeper
6. plot +(ed)   plotted
7. equip + ment   equipment
8. hard + ness   hardness

9. drip +(ed)   dripped
10. snap +(ing)   snapping
11. heart + less   heartless
12. wet +(est)   wettest
13. cram +(ed)   crammed
14. cheer + ful   cheerful
15. rapid + ly   rapidly
16. strap +(ed)   strapped

▶ **Circle the base word in each word in the word bank. Then complete each sentence with a word from the word bank.**

throbbing   quitters   slipped   plugged
swimming   flippers   squatted   swimmer
raining   trapper   hottest   dimmest

17. We swam in the pool on the _____ hottest _____ day of the summer.
18. While I swam, I wore a face mask and _____ flippers _____.
19. Yesterday I _____ plugged _____ my ears, too.
20. I almost _____ slipped _____ when I walked onto the diving board.
21. We held a race to determine the fastest _____ swimmer _____.
22. Our muscles were _____ throbbing _____ from so much swimming.
23. If it isn't _____ raining _____ tomorrow, we'll go back to the pool.
24. I sure hope we can go _____ swimming _____ again!

138 Lesson 62
Words that double the final consonant to add a suffix

AUDITORY/VISUAL LEARNERS

LARGE GROUP

Read each sentence. Have students write the word with a suffix, identify the base word and the suffix, and explain any spelling change. Try the following: *My computer is slower than Rosa's. Chopping wood is hard work. The baby napped all afternoon. This is the dimmest lamp.*

GIFTED LEARNERS

Challenge students to role-play scenes that depict the following words and have their classmates guess what word is being demonstrated: *saddest, wettest, happiest, silliest, spinning, swimming, robbing, jogging, scrubbed.*

LEARNERS WHO NEED EXTRA SUPPORT

Write *wash, cut, plan, fill, grab, pet, nod, rest, big,* and *thin* on the board. Ask volunteers to add the suffix *-ing, -ed, -er,* or *-est* to each and use the word in an oral sentence. **See Daily Word Study Practice, page 190.**

CURRICULUM CONNECTIONS ✳ • ◆ ■ ◆

SPELLING

The following can be used as a pretest for this set of spelling words.

1. **cutting**   She keeps **cutting** her hair.
2. **liking**   How is he **liking** the book?
3. **activities**   I like music **activities.**
4. **chimneys**   Both **chimneys** have smoke.
5. **painlessly**   The dentist removed my tooth **painlessly.**
6. **heavily**   He sighed **heavily.**
7. **coyly**   The dancers **coyly** bent their head.
8. **wobbly**   The doll's **wobbly** head needs fixing.

WRITING

Portfolio Challenge students to write a narrative about what they like to do in the summer when it is very, very hot. Ask them to list the words they used that follow the doubling rule. Compile the narratives to make *A Hottest Daze* class book.

SOCIAL STUDIES

Encourage students to talk about ways in which they celebrate holidays. Then have them choose a holiday, imagine they are there, and write phrases that describe what they see, hear, smell, taste, and feel.

HEALTH/MATH

Invite students to make a list of activities such as swimming, running, and others that are good for their health, then survey the class to see which activities are most popular among students their age.

AstroWord Suffixes © 1998 Silver Burdett Ginn Inc. Division of Simon & Schuster.

Lesson 63

Pages 139–140

Words That Drop the Final e to Add a Suffix

Lesson Focus

INTRODUCING THE SKILL

- Write these words on the board: *decided, dancer, practicing, nicest.* Have volunteers underline the suffix in each word and write the base word. Ask what letter was dropped from each base word when a suffix beginning with a vowel was added. (e)

- Guide students to conclude that when a word ends in e, the e is dropped before a suffix that begins with a vowel is added.

- Have students suggest other suffixed words in which the final e was dropped before adding a suffix.

USING THE PAGES

Give students help as needed as they complete pages 139 and 140. After they have finished, encourage students to talk about how they figured out the correct words to complete the crossword puzzle.

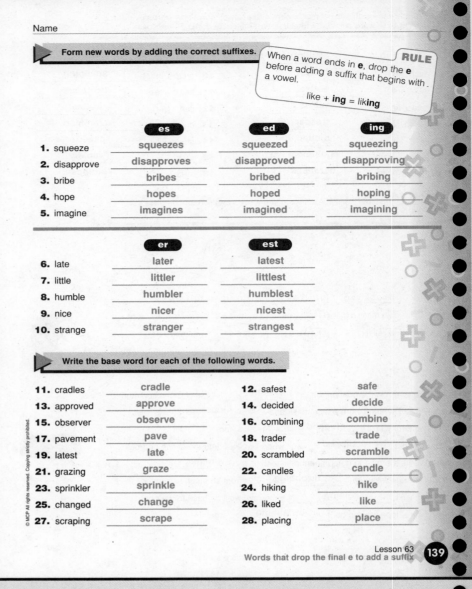

Name _____

Form new words by adding the correct suffixes.

> **RULE**
> When a word ends in **e**, drop the **e** before adding a suffix that begins with a vowel.
>
> like + **ing** = lik**ing**

		es	**ed**	**ing**
1.	squeeze	squeezes	squeezed	squeezing
2.	disapprove	disapproves	disapproved	disapproving
3.	bribe	bribes	bribed	bribing
4.	hope	hopes	hoped	hoping
5.	imagine	imagines	imagined	imagining

		er	**est**
6.	late	later	latest
7.	little	littler	littlest
8.	humble	humbler	humblest
9.	nice	nicer	nicest
10.	strange	stranger	strangest

Write the base word for each of the following words.

11.	cradles	cradle	12.	safest	safe
13.	approved	approve	14.	decided	decide
15.	observer	observe	16.	combining	combine
17.	pavement	pave	18.	trader	trade
19.	latest	late	20.	scrambled	scramble
21.	grazing	graze	22.	candles	candle
23.	sprinkler	sprinkle	24.	hiking	hike
25.	changed	change	26.	liked	like
27.	scraping	scrape	28.	placing	place

Lesson 63
Words that drop the final e to add a suffix **139**

FOCUS ON ALL LEARNERS

ENGLISH LANGUAGE LEARNERS/ESL

Work with students as they start page 139 to be sure they begin the practices successfully. Review the words needed to complete the crossword puzzle and then encourage students to work with a partner to complete the puzzle.

VISUAL LEARNERS

INDIVIDUAL Write these words and suffixes on the board *race + ed; sneeze + ing; bake + er; pure + er.* Have students make up a sentence for each word with the suffix added.

KINESTHETIC LEARNERS

 PARTNER Partners can give each other base words from the lesson to write on the board and then a suffix to add correctly. The base word should be written before the suffix is given.

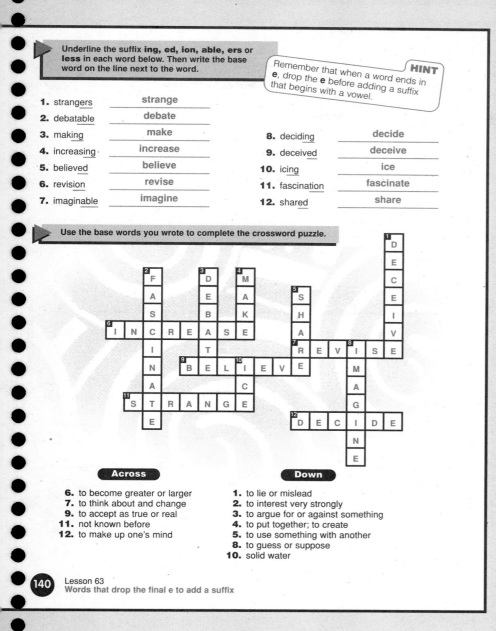

Underline the suffix **ing, ed, ion, able, ers** or **less** in each word below. Then write the base word on the line next to the word.

HINT
Remember that when a word ends in **e**, drop the **e** before adding a suffix that begins with a vowel.

1. strangers — strange
2. debatable — debate
3. making — make
4. increasing — increase
5. believed — believe
6. revision — revise
7. imaginable — imagine
8. deciding — decide
9. deceived — deceive
10. icing — ice
11. fascination — fascinate
12. shared — share

Use the base words you wrote to complete the crossword puzzle.

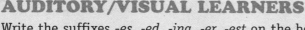

Across

6. to become greater or larger
7. to think about and change
9. to accept as true or real
11. not known before
12. to make up one's mind

Down

1. to lie or mislead
2. to interest very strongly
3. to argue for or against something
4. to put together; to create
5. to use something with another
8. to guess or suppose
10. solid water

SPELLING

Write the list words *cutting, liking, activities, chimneys, painlessly, heavily, coyly, wobbly* on a Word Wall. Have students line up in two teams. As you say each definition, challenge the first person in line on each team to go up to the Word Wall and choose and spell aloud the word that matches the definition.

WRITING

Portfolio Ask students to write a poem or story, accompanied by an illustration, about something that fascinates or strongly interests them. Tell students to use at least one word in the poem that drops the final *e* to add a suffix.

SOCIAL STUDIES

Challenge students to dramatize the word *debatable*. Have groups of students brainstorm a list of issues that group members consider debatable and then choose one issue to "debate," such as an argument between siblings over the contested ownership of an item of clothing.

Technology

AstroWord Suffixes © 1998 Silver Burdett Ginn Inc. Division of Simon & Schuster.

AUDITORY/VISUAL LEARNERS

LARGE GROUP Write the suffixes *-es, -ed, -ing, -er, -est* on the board. As you say each of the following words, point to a suffix: *little, strange, great, sneeze, fake, dance, hope, walk*. Together, the group spells the word with the suffix added.

GIFTED LEARNERS

Challenge students to create another word game, such as a hidden word search, using words that drop the final *e* to add a suffix. After students have completed their puzzles, invite them to exchange their puzzles with a partner and solve each other's puzzle.

LEARNERS WHO NEED EXTRA SUPPORT

Write *walking, riding, sneezes, nicest, stranger, dancing, traded, bravest, smaller,* and *believed* on the board. Have pairs work together to identify and write the base word of each. **See Daily Word Study Practice, page 190.**

Lesson 64

Pages 141–142

Words With More Than One Suffix

INFORMAL ASSESSMENT OBJECTIVES

Can students

✓ recognize and identify the base word in words with more than one suffix?

✓ recognize and identify the suffixes in words with more than one suffix?

Lesson Focus

INTRODUCING THE SKILL

- Write the following sentence on the board. *The editors carefully proofread the meaningful report on lawlessness.*

- Point out to students that some words have more than one suffix. Then call on volunteers to identify the base word and suffixes in each underlined word. Remind students that *s* can be a suffix.

- Give students an opportunity to suggest additional words with more than one suffix. Write the words on the board and have the class identify the base word and suffixes in each word.

- Allow time for the students to use the words in sentences.

USING THE PAGES

- If students need help completing pages 141 and 142, have them first read the page aloud.

- **Critical Thinking** Read aloud the question on page 141 and discuss answers with students.

Name _____

▶ Many words have more than one suffix. Read each word below. Underline the first suffix and circle the second suffix.

HINT
Remember that **s** can be a suffix.

watchful**ly**   amaz**ing**ly   painless**ly**
migrat**ion**s   careless**ness**   widen**ing**
publicat**ion**s   frightful**ness**   enlighten**ing**
attract**ion**s   thoughtful**ness**   powerless**ness**
increas**ing**ly   cheerful**ness**   successful**ly**
hopeful**ly**

▶ Use a word from above to complete each sentence. Write the word on the line. Use each word only once.

1. Tracking migrating birds is becoming _____**increasingly**_____ popular.
2. The _____**migrations**_____ of many birds take place in the spring and fall.
3. Some birds _____**successfully**_____ fly over 5,000 miles yearly.
4. _____**Amazingly**_____, some birds return to the same fields every year.
5. Studying migrating birds can be an _____**enlightening**_____ experience.
6. There are many _____**publications**_____ about birds.
7. Human _____**carelessness**_____ has blocked some migration paths.
8. The _____**thoughtfulness**_____ of some groups has helped to protect birds.
9. Bird lovers watch the sky _____**hopefully**_____ every year.

Why do you think tracking migrating birds might be popular?

Critical Thinking

Lesson 64
Words with more than one suffix
141

FOCUS ON ALL LEARNERS

ENGLISH LANGUAGE LEARNERS/ESL

Before beginning page 142, invite students to discuss any volunteer experiences they or members of their families have had. Point out that people of all ages can find ways to help others.

VISUAL LEARNERS

PARTNER   Write *loveableness, hopefully, fearlessness*, and *cheerfulness* on the board. Ask students to read each word and write the base word. Then have them form new words by adding two different suffixes to each base word. Encourage students to share their new words with a partner.

KINESTHETIC LEARNERS

LARGE GROUP   Write these sentences on the board. *The winds were blowing in an easterly direction. Donna chose the checkered cloth. The team played defensively. Greg sat motionlessly as the squirrel crept closer.* Challenge volunteers to find the words that contain two suffixes in the sentences.

> In each sentence, underline the two words with more than one suffix. Write each base word on a line next to the sentence.

1. When my mother <u>awakened</u> me today, I got out of bed <u>cheerfully</u>.

    awake   cheer

2. Mom was <u>heartened</u> to see my <u>fearlessness</u>.

    heart   fear

3. I felt <u>remarkably</u> ready to <u>thoughtfully</u> begin my first volunteer job.

    remark   thought

4. <u>Interestingly</u>, my school project was to help the <u>assistants</u> at a senior center.

    interest   assist

5. My heartbeat <u>quickened</u> as I <u>hesitatingly</u> approached the center.

    quick   hesitate

6. I felt <u>increasingly</u> nervous as I opened the door <u>carefully</u>.

    increase   care

7. My day passed <u>painlessly</u> and I enjoyed the <u>loveableness</u> of the people I met.

    pain   love

8. <u>Thankfully</u>, my project is continuing <u>successfully</u>.

    thank   success

9. The volunteer work I do is <u>meaningful</u> and <u>enlightening</u>—I love it!

    mean   light

> Circle each base word from the sentences above in the word search. The words may be horizontal, vertical or on the diagonal.

```
G L I G H T Q U I C K I
U Y I N T E R E S T Q N
A W A K E Z S L P H H C
F M K S V S X I C J E R
K E T H O U G H T Q A E
R I A X B C J M L A R A
E N G R W C V H E O T S
M C P F G E A Q C A V E
A R Q A I S J R H K N E
R A S S I S T S E R S Y
K S T H A N K C H E E R
```

CURRICULUM CONNECTIONS

SPELLING

Prepare slips of paper, one for each of the spelling words *cutting, liking, activities, chimneys, painlessly, heavily, coyly,* and *wobbly*. Place the slips of paper in a bag. Invite students to draw a word from the bag to act out as classmates try to guess the word. The student who guesses correctly, writes the word on the board.

WRITING

Portfolio Invite students to write and illustrate a recruiting poster for an organization looking for volunteers their age. Ask them to include words with more than one suffix in their text.

SOCIAL STUDIES

Ask students to compile a list of volunteer agencies and organizations in their area. Help them sort the information into volunteer opportunities for students and adults. If possible, invite a representative from one of the groups to speak to the class.

SCIENCE

Challenge students to research and write an article about different types of migrations or about the migrations of various animals. Have them proofread and edit their articles and circle any words that have more than one suffix. Call on volunteers to read their articles to the class.

Technology

AstroWord Suffixes © 1998 Silver Burdett Ginn Inc. Division of Simon & Schuster.

AUDITORY/KINESTHETIC LEARNERS

INDIVIDUAL

Materials: four index cards for each student

Have students write *-ly, -ful, -less,* or *-ness* on separate cards. As you name the following words, have students hold up the cards that represent the suffixes they hear: *cheerfully, meaningfulness, lawlessness, motionlessly, fearlessly,* and *thoughtfulness*.

GIFTED LEARNERS

Challenge students to write tongue twisters using words with more than one suffix. An example is *The successful success-story writer successfully succeeded.*

LEARNERS WHO NEED EXTRA SUPPORT

Materials: word cards, scissors

Make and distribute word cards for: *interestingly, meaningful, effortlessly, hopelessly, thoughtfulness, carelessness.* Have students cut apart each word so that the base word and each suffix are separate. Then have them work with partners to put the words back together. **See Daily Word Study Practice, pages 190–191.**

Lesson 65

Pages 143–144

Adding Suffixes to Words Ending in y

Lesson Focus

INTRODUCING THE SKILL

- Write these words on the board.

  <u>tiny</u> + er   tinier

  <u>duty</u> + ful   dutiful

  <u>delay</u> + ed   delayed

  <u>fly</u> + ing   flying

- Point to the y in each underlined base word and ask students whether or not y changed when a suffix was added.

- Lead students to see that if a word ends in y that is preceded by a consonant, the y changes to i before a suffix is added. If a word ends in y preceded by a vowel, the suffix is added without changing y.

- Point to the word *flying*. Explain that when the suffix -ing is added to a word that ends in y preceded by a consonant, the y does not change.

- Have students suggest words that end in y and have a suffix. Ask them to explain any spelling changes that occur in the base words.

USING THE PAGES

Be sure students understand how to complete pages 143 and 144 before they begin. Together, read the Rule on page 143.

Name _____

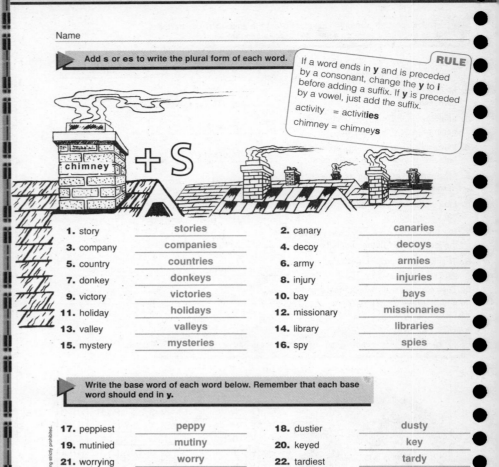

▶ Add **s** or **es** to write the plural form of each word.

> **RULE**
> If a word ends in **y** and is preceded by a consonant, change the **y** to **i** before adding a suffix. If **y** is preceded by a vowel, just add the suffix.
>
> activity = activit**ies**
>
> chimney = chimney**s**

1. story	stories	2. canary	canaries
3. company	companies	4. decoy	decoys
5. country	countries	6. army	armies
7. donkey	donkeys	8. injury	injuries
9. victory	victories	10. bay	bays
11. holiday	holidays	12. missionary	missionaries
13. valley	valleys	14. library	libraries
15. mystery	mysteries	16. spy	spies

▶ Write the base word of each word below. Remember that each base word should end in **y**.

17. peppiest	peppy	18. dustier	dusty
19. mutinied	mutiny	20. keyed	key
21. worrying	worry	22. tardiest	tardy
23. rustier	rusty	24. flies	fly
25. obeys	obey	26. luckiest	lucky
27. fancier	fancy	28. multiplying	multiply
29. relayed	relay	30. carried	carry

FOCUS ON ALL LEARNERS ✳ ● ◆ ■ ◆

ENGLISH LANGUAGE LEARNERS/ESL

Before begining the riddles on page 144, review each of the famous tales with students so they are able to identify all the fictional characters mentioned on the page.

VISUAL LEARNERS

SMALL GROUP

Write these base words and suffixes on the board: *happy + er, beauty + ful, carry + ed, healthy + est.* Have students combine each base word and suffix, write the new word, then use the word in a sentence.

KINESTHETIC LEARNERS

LARGE GROUP

Materials: colored chalk

Ask volunteers to write *lucky + er; puppy + s; busy + est; hungry + er; fly + ing* on the board. Have different students use colored chalk to write the new word, explaining the rule for using the suffix. Ask others to use the words in sentences.

Form a new word by combining each base word and suffix. Write the new word on the line.

HINT
Remember the rules for adding suffixes to words ending in **y**.

1. lucky + er _luckier_
2. greasy + est _greasiest_
3. worry + ed _worried_
4. busy + er _busier_
5. easy + er _easier_
6. salty + er _saltier_
7. obey + s _obeys_
8. toy + ed _toyed_
9. occupy + ed _occupied_
10. fancy + est _fanciest_
11. sleepy + est _sleepiest_
12. heavy + er _heavier_

Use the words you formed to complete the sentences. Then write the circled letters from the answers in order to answer the riddle.

13. Cinderella had the Ⓕ a n c i e s t gown at the ball.

14. One little pig was Ⓛ u c k i e r than the other two.

15. Jack shouldn't have t o Ⓨ e d with the magic beans.

16. Hansel and Gretel visited a house o c c u Ⓟ i e d by a witch.

17. Babe, the blue ox, made Paul Bunyan's work e Ⓐ s i e r .

18. Rip Van Winkle is the s l e e Ⓟ i e s t character in any book.

19. The Brothers Grimm were b u s i Ⓔ r than other authors.

20. The seven dwarfs w o Ⓡ r i e d about Snow White.

What is the best material for kites?

Riddle answer: f l y p a p e r

144   Lesson 65
Adding suffixes to words ending in y

Lesson 66

Pages 145–146

Adding Suffix -ly to Words Ending in y or le

✦ • ◆ • ' ◆ ■ ● ◆ ✦ ◆ • ◆ ■ ◆ • ●

INFORMAL ASSESSMENT OBJECTIVES

Can students

✔ add the suffix *-ly* to words ending in *-y* or *-le*?

✔ use words containing the suffix *-ly* in context?

Lesson Focus

INTRODUCING THE SKILL

● Write these rules on the board and discuss them.

If a word ends in y preceded by a consonant, change the *y* to *i* when adding the suffix *-ly*. Some exceptions are *dryly*, *shyly*, and *slyly*.

If a word ends in *-y* preceded by a vowel, just add the suffix *-ly*.

When *-ly* is added to a word ending in *-le*, the *-le* is dropped. Otherwise the word would be difficult to pronounce.

● Write *coy*, *hungry*, *single* and other words on the board and change them by adding *ly*. Have students suggest more examples.

USING THE PAGES

● Point out that they will use the words they wrote at the top of page 145 to complete the sentences at the bottom.

● **Critical Thinking** Read aloud the question on page 146 and discuss the answers with students.

Name _____

 Add **ly** to each word. Write the new word on the line.

> **RULES**
> If a word ends in **y** and is preceded by a consonant, change the **y** to **i** when adding **ly**. If the **y** is preceded by a vowel, add **ly**. if a word ends in **le**, the **le** is dropped.
> heavy + **ly** = heavi**ly**
> coy + **ly** = coy**ly**
> wobble + **ly** = wobb**ly**

1. noisy   noisily
2. coy   coyly
3. drizzle   drizzly
4. greedy   greedily
5. bubble   bubbly
6. dizzy   dizzily
7. hasty   hastily   10. wiggle   wiggly
8. merry   merrily   11. pebble   pebbly
9. probable   probably   12. lucky   luckily

 Complete each sentence with a word from above.

13. It was a _____drizzly_____ wet day, perfect for a trip to the indoor aquarium.

14. We could hear the sea lions barking ____merrily____ while we waited for tickets.

15. The aquarium was enormous, so we had to ____hastily____ view each exhibit.

16. The bottom of the largest aquarium tank was ____pebbly____, and not covered with sand.

17. The diver's air tanks made the water ____bubbly____.

18. The ____wiggly____ arms of the squid grabbed everything in sight.

19. ____Luckily____, the glass walls stopped it from grabbing us.

20. We watched the dolphins swim ____dizzily____ round and round.

21. I'll ____probably____ go back to the aquarium at least twice a year.

Lesson 66
Adding suffix -ly to words ending in y or le   **145**

FOCUS ON ALL LEARNERS ✦ • ◆ ■ • ✦

ENGLISH LANGUAGE LEARNERS/ESL

Before students begin page 145, read the words at the top of the page together. Since they will use forms of these words to complete the sentences that follow, be sure they understand what each word means.

VISUAL/KINESTHETIC LEARNERS

PARTNER

Introduce the class to Tom Swift jokes. These are statements modified by humorous and related adverbs; for example, *"Happy Valentine's Day!" Tom said heartily* or *"I've got to run!" Tom said hastily*. Invite student to work in pairs to write their own Tom Swifties.

KINESTHETIC LEARNERS

SMALL GROUP

Write words such as *luckily*, *daily*, and *wiggly* on the board. Offer clues such as *A worm's body moves like this*. As each word is identified, ask a volunteer to come to the board, point to the word, circle the suffix *-ly*, and write the base word without the suffix *-ly*.

Complete each sentence by adding **ly** to each word under the line. Write the new word on the line.

1. Eating _____ healthily _____ every day helps an athlete keep fit.
   (healthy)

2. A trainer should _____ reliably _____ supervise every workout.
   (reliable)

3. Proper training techniques can prevent _____ bodily _____ injury.
   (body)

4. Training _____ lazily _____ will not help an athlete.
   (lazy)

5. Jogging can strengthen _____ wobbly _____ legs.
   (wobble)

6. If athletes practice _____ sloppily _____, they will perform poorly.
   (sloppy)

7. Athletes should not begin weight training _____ hastily _____.
   (hasty)

8. They must always warm up _____ sensibly _____.
   (sensible)

9. _____ Luckily _____, many athletes are born with coordination.
   (Lucky)

10. People with good coordination can usually exercise more _____ readily _____.
    (ready)

11. Athletes in good shape can do exercises _____ easily _____.
    (easy)

12. Sometimes athletes should _____ happily _____ take time off from training.
    (happy)

13. It is not necessary to exercise _____ daily _____.
    (day)

14. Gymnasts can move _____ nimbly _____ on the parallel bars.
    (nimble)

15. Athletes should accept both victory and defeat _____ nobly _____.
    (noble)

What do you think accepting both victory and defeat nobly means?

Critical Thinking

146

Lesson 66
Adding suffix -ly to words ending in y or le

Lesson 67

Pages 147–148

Plural Form for Words Ending in _f_ or _fe_

INFORMAL ASSESSMENT OBJECTIVES

Can students

✔ change singular words that end in _f_ or _fe_ to plural form?

✔ use in context plural words ending in _f_ and _fe_?

Lesson Focus

INTRODUCING THE SKILL

- Write the following rule on the board and discuss it with the class.

  If a word ends in _f_ or _fe_, usually change the _f_ or _fe_ to _v_ and add _es_ to make the word plural. (_elf, elves_) Some exceptions are _chief, belief, reef, roof_.

- Have students suggest other words that fit the rule.

- Tell students that to make a word plural that ends in double _f_, they should just add _s_, as in _sniffs_. Encourage them to suggest other words that end in double _f_ and to form the plurals. (_cliffs, puffs_)

USING THE PAGES

- Give students help as necessary to complete pages 147 and 148. Point out that on page 147 they need only fill in the circle below the correct answer.

- **Critical Thinking** Read aloud the question on page 147 and discuss answers with students.

147

Name _____

▶ Fill in the circle under the word that completes each sentence.

1. Ranchers spent much of their ____ moving cattle.
   ● lives   ○ lifes   ○ lifves

2. Their ____ sometimes helped with the daily roundup.
   ○ wifes   ● wives   ○ wiffes

3. The cowboys often carried buck ____ .
   ● knives   ○ knifes   ○ kniffs

4. They wore scarves to protect ____ in dust storms.
   ○ themselfs   ● themselves   ○ themselfes

5. The cowboys used dried ____ as fuel for campfires.
   ○ leafes   ○ leafs   ● leaves

6. The cook brought ____ of bread.
   ○ loafs   ● loaves   ○ loafes

7. Mountain ____ stopped the herds from stampeding.
   ○ cliffes   ● cliffs   ○ clives

8. Sometimes the ____ were very steep.
   ● bluffs   ○ bluffes   ○ bluves

9. The young ____ often fell behind the herd.
   ○ calfs   ● calves   ○ calfes

10. The ranchers all shared similar ____ concerning cattle rustlers.
    ● beliefs   ○ believes   ○ beliefes

11. Tribal leaders, or ____, usually allowed the herds to pass.
    ○ chiefes   ○ chieves   ● chiefs

12. Packs of ____ sometimes attacked the herds.
    ○ wolfes   ● wolves   ○ wolfs

13. Cattle ____, or rustlers, were also a problem.
    ○ thiefes   ● thieves   ○ thiefs

> **RULE**
> If a word ends in **f** or **fe**, the **f** or **fe** is changed to **v** and **es** is added to form the plural. Exceptions are _chief, belief, reef,_ and _roof_. Plurals for these words are formed by just adding **s**. A word that ends in **ff** is made plural by adding **s**.
>
> wolf — wol**ves**
> chief — chief**s**
> cliff — cliff**s**

What would you like about being a cowboy?

Critical Thinking

FOCUS ON ALL LEARNERS

ENGLISH LANGUAGE LEARNERS/ESL

Before beginning page 147, encourage a discussion about the role of cowboys in the life and economy of the Wild West. Invite students to imagine what life was like for ranchers who spent much of their lives moving herds of cattle from one place to another.

VISUAL LEARNERS

INDIVIDUAL   Write _gulf_, _fife_, and _safe_ on the board. Explain that these words are exceptions to the rule presented in the lesson. Ask students to use a dictionary to define each word and to write a sentence that contains its plural form. (_gulfs, fifes, safes_)

KINESTHETIC LEARNERS

PARTNER   **Materials:** colored chalk

Have partners take turns writing the singular and plural forms of words from the lesson on the board, sometimes deliberately writing the plural incorrectly. The partner uses colored chalk to make the needed correction.

Write the plural form of each word.

1.	loaf	loaves	2.	calf	calves
3.	shelf	shelves	4.	half	halves
5.	knife	knives	6.	whiff	whiffs
7.	cuff	cuffs	8.	wife	wives
9.	chief	chiefs	10.	life	lives
11.	staff	staffs	12.	belief	beliefs
13.	scarf	scarves	14.	bluff	bluffs
15.	thief	thieves	16.	leaf	leaves
17.	safe	safes	18.	self	selves

Use the plural words you wrote to answer the questions below.

19. What do you call ideas you think are true or real?
beliefs

20. Who are the partners of husbands? _wives_

21. What can people wear on their head and tie under their chin?
scarves

22. What are places where you keep your valuables called?
safes

23. What are the flat, green parts that grow from the stem of a plant or tree? _leaves_

24. What do you call people who steal? _thieves_

25. What are the ends of a shirt sleeve called? _cuffs_

26. Which are kitchen tools used to cut and slice? _knives_

27. What are the shapes that breads come in? _loaves_

28. On what can you place books? _shelves_

29. Which two of these make one whole? _halves_

30. What does a cat supposedly have nine of? _lives_

31. What do you call young cattle? _calves_

148

Lesson 67
Plural form for words ending in f and fe

SPELLING

The following sentences can be used as a pretest for this set of spelling words.

1. **wolves** — The **wolves** howled in the night.
2. **chiefs** — Native American **chiefs** are heroes to their people.
3. **cliffs** — We climbed the **cliffs** to see the lake.
4. **radios** — I fixed the **radios** before the game.
5. **potatoes** — We used ten pounds of **potatoes.**
6. **crises** — The government has **crises.**
7. **oases** — The trip through the desert included visits to two **oases.**
8. **olden** — He lived in the **olden** days.
9. **mice** — The twelve **mice** were class pets.
10. **fungi** — Some **fungi** are delicious to eat.

WRITING

Portfolio Challenge students to write a story about a place where everything comes in pairs. Challenge students to use as many plural forms for words ending in *f* and *fe* as possible.

SCIENCE

Explain to students that some baby animals have special names: *Calves* refers both to young cattle and baby whales. Provide the following list and ask students to use reference books to find out what species each refers to. Write *bunny, calf, cub, eaglet, fawn, gosling, joey, kid, kitten,* and *owlet.*

MUSIC

Songs such as *Home on the Range* and *Sweet Betsy From Pike* represent the Old West. Cowboys sang these songs to quiet the cattle or to help fill the dark evening hours. Ask students to imagine they are sitting around a campfire as you play a recording of western songs. Then invite them to make up western titles, using words ending in *f* or *fe* and their plurals.

AUDITORY/VISUAL LEARNERS

SMALL GROUP Write *staff, reef, huff, half, cuff, sheaf, calf, chief, thief, roof, scarf,* and *life* on the board. Have pairs come to the board. One student writes the plural form of a word. If correct, the other explains the rule for the spelling. If not, the second student corrects it.

GIFTED LEARNERS

Challenge students to write riddles whose answers include plural forms of words that end in *f* or *fe,* for example, *What might be the title of a best-selling book written by a tailor? (Fitting Cuffs)*

LEARNERS WHO NEED EXTRA SUPPORT

Materials: index cards

Suggest that each student choose one *f* or *fe* word as a personal key word, write both its singular and plural form on a card, and refer to it as they complete the practices. **See Daily Word Study Practice, pages 191-192.**

148

Lesson 68

Pages 149–150

Plural Form for Words Ending in o

✦ • ◆ • ● ◆ • ● ✦ ✦ • ◆ • ■ • ◆ •

INFORMAL ASSESSMENT OBJECTIVES

Can students

✔ change singular words that end in *o* to plural form?

✔ recognize words that are exceptions to the rule?

Lesson Focus

INTRODUCING THE SKILL

- Write the following rule on a tagboard strip and ask students to read it silently.

  If a word ends in *o*, usually add *s* to make the word plural. Some exceptions are *potato, hero, tomato, buffalo*, and *tornado*, to which *es* is added.

- Write these words on the board, omitting the words in parentheses: *hello* (hellos), *tornado* (tornadoes), *silo* (silos), *potato* (potatoes).

- Ask students to tell how to make each word plural. Have them suggest additional words that end in *o* and challenge them to form the plurals.

USING THE PAGES

Offer assistance as needed as students complete pages 149 and 150. When they have completed the pages, review the lesson as you correct the pages together.

Name _____

▶ Write the plural of each word. You may use your dictionary if necessary.

1. banjo — banjos or banjoes
2. poncho — ponchos
3. piccolo — piccolos
4. patio — patios
5. echo — echoes
6. hero — heroes
7. radio — radios
8. rodeo — rodeos
9. tempo — tempos
10. studio — studios
11. solo — solos
12. cello — cellos
13. piano — pianos
14. alto — altos
15. photo — photos

▶ Choose the correct word to complete each sentence. Write the word on the line.

16. Our music teacher told us to bring our ___**radios**___ to class.
    (radios, rodeos)

17. We were studying elements of music, such as rhythms and ___**tempos**___
    (patios, tempos)

18. The sound of twenty radios sent ___**echoes**___ through the classroom.
    (solos, echoes)

19. We learned that ___**banjos**___ are not used in symphony orchestras.
    (ponchos, banjos)

20. ___**Cellos**___ look like violins, but are much bigger.
    (Cellos, Heroes)

21. There are eighty-eight keys on grand ___**pianos**___.
    (pianos, heroes)

22. We listened to ___**solos**___ and guessed which instrument was playing.
    (solos, patios)

23. We could easily hear the shrill notes of the small ___**piccolos**___.
    (photos, piccolos)

Lesson 68
Plural form for words ending in o   **149**

FOCUS ON ALL LEARNERS   ✦ • ◆ ■ • ◆

ENGLISH LANGUAGE LEARNERS/ESL

Before students begin page 149, talk about music and musical instruments. Invite them to share their favorite music on tape or to play an instrument they have been studying.

VISUAL LEARNERS

INDIVIDUAL   Write these words on the board: *torpedo, lasso, echo, dodo, domino, potato, tomato.* Invite pairs to form the plural of each word, then use the word in a book title; for example, *Echoes Through the Night.* Students could use a title to write an original story.

KINESTHETIC LEARNERS

PARTNER   Have students copy this story from the board and write plurals of the underlined words. *A <u>soprano</u> sang a <u>solo</u> on the <u>radio</u>. It was opera, but I didn't change to another station. The tune and <u>tempo</u> were catchy. I liked the <u>piano</u>, the <u>piccolo</u> and the <u>cello</u>.*

Write the plural form of each word. You may use your dictionary.

1. piano — pianos
2. alto — altos
3. photo — photos
4. igloo — igloos
5. piccolo — piccolos
6. tornado — tornados or tornadoes
7. poncho — ponchos
8. avocado — avocados
9. tomato — tomatoes
10. hero — heroes
11. banjo — banjos or banjoes
12. cello — cellos
13. patio — patios
14. rodeo — rodeos
15. potato — potatoes
16. kangaroo — kangaroos
17. studio — studios
18. solo — solos

Use the plural words you wrote to answer the questions below.

19. Which words name musical instruments? pianos
    piccolos   banjos   cellos
20. What are outdoor courtyards? patios
21. What are competitions in which contestants ride horses and rope cattle called?
    rodeos
22. What are terrible wind storms called? tornados
23. What are people called who do brave and wonderful deeds?
    heroes
24. Which vegetable is used to make spaghetti sauce and ketchup?
    tomatoes
25. What are pictures taken with a camera called? photos
26. What are large, waterproof cloaks often worn by campers?
    ponchos
27. What are dome-shaped huts made of snow? igloos
28. Which vegetable can taste good in all these forms: mashed, french fried, baked, and scalloped? potatoes
29. What are small rooms or buildings where artists work? studios

150 Lesson 68
Plural form for words ending in o

SPELLING

Write the list words *wolves, chiefs, cliffs, radios, potatoes, crises, oases, olden, mice, fungi* on the chalkboard. Give clues and ask students to choose a spelling word.

WRITING

Portfolio Challenge students to write a review of a radio program they enjoy listening to.

LANGUAGE ARTS

Write the following riddle and respellings on the board, omitting the boldfaced answers. Have students write the word for each dictionary respelling and use the letters in the boxes to answer the riddle. Riddle: *What have eyes but cannot see?*

P	O	T	A	T	O	E	S
1	2	3	4	5	6	7	8

1. (pē an' ōz) — p i a n o s
2. (rō' dē ōz) — r o d e o s
3. (al' tōz) — a l t o s
4. (ban' jōz) — b a n j o s
5. (fō' tōz) — p h o t o s
6. (ig' looz) — i g l o o s
7. (hir' ōz) — h e r o e s
8. (chel' ōz) — c e l l o s

MUSIC

Have students make their own kazoos by first fastening a piece of aluminum foil or wax paper around one end of a cardboard tube with a rubber band, then punching a hole in the tube one inch from the covered end with a pencil. If students hold the open end of their kazoos around their mouths and hum or sing, they will be able to "play" any song.

AUDITORY LEARNERS

LARGE GROUP Say the following sentences aloud. Have students identify and spell the plurals of words that end in -o. *We heard banjo music at the rodeo. The piccolo and the piano each had a solo during the concert. The photo showed an amazing view of a tornado.*

GIFTED LEARNERS

Challenge students to write an imaginary concert review. Invite them to use plurals for the words *soprano, alto, banjo, cello, piano, piccolo, solo, studio,* and *echo* in their review.

LEARNERS WHO NEED EXTRA SUPPORT

Materials: index cards

Partners can make word cards with the singular and plural forms on opposite sides of cards, then use the cards to practice spelling the plurals. Use *hero, igloo, banjo, tomato, piano, photo, rodeo, patio, studio,* and *buffalo.* **See Daily Word Study Practice, pages 191-192.**

150

Lesson 69

Pages 151–152

Other Plural Forms

Lesson Focus

INTRODUCING THE SKILL

- Write *foot, ox, woman, mouse,* and *crisis* on the board. Read each word aloud and have students name the plural form. Write the plurals on the board. (*feet, oxen, women, mice, crises*)

- Help students conclude that some words change completely in their plural form. Point out that these words do not follow any rules.

- Explain that some words, like *deer, sheep,* and *moose,* remain the same in their plural form. Write these sentences on the board: *The catfish were in the pond. The catfish was very old.*

- Ask students how they can figure out whether the word *catfish* is singular or plural. (*Use the context.*)

- Have students use *deer, sheep,* and *moose*—singular and plural—in sentences.

USING THE PAGES

Be sure students understand how to complete pages 151 and 152 before they begin.

151

Name _____

These words are the same in their singular and plural forms. If the word names a plant or a food that comes from a plant, write P. If it names an animal or a food that comes from an animal, write A.

> **HINT** Some words do not change at all in their plural form.

1. **P** spinach	2. **A** milk	3. **A** salmon	4. **P** zucchini
5. **A** moose	6. **A** sheep	7. **P** spaghetti	8. **A** shrimp
9. **A** cattle	10. **P** broccoli	11. **A** trout	12. **A** haddock
13. **A** deer	14. **P** popcorn	15. **A** honey	16. **P** bread
17. **P** rye	18. **A** bacon	19. **A** cod	20. **P** wheat
21. **A** butter	22. **P** sauerkraut		
23. **A** fish	24. **P** oatmeal		

Read each word, find its plural form in the word bank, and write the plural on the line beside the word. Then choose a word from the word bank to match each definition. Each singular form is given in parentheses.

> **HINT** Some words change completely in their plural form. Some other plural forms may not be familiar to you. They do not follow any of the rules.

fungi	geese	alumni	feet
women	oases	children	mice
teeth	men	oxen	crises

25. foot	feet	26. man	men
27. child	children	28. woman	women
29. goose	geese	30. mouse	mice
31. ox	oxen	32. tooth	teeth

33. **crises** times of danger or anxious waiting (crisis)
34. **alumni** people who have attended a school (alumnus)
35. **fungi** plants such as mushrooms and toadstools (fungus)
36. **oases** places in the desert where there is water (oasis)

Lesson 69
Other plural forms
151

FOCUS ON ALL LEARNERS

ENGLISH LANGUAGE LEARNERS/ESL

Before beginning page 151, encourage a discussion about agreement in a sentence. Have students think of a sentence about a singular subject and then help them change the subject to a plural and rearrange the sentence.

VISUAL LEARNERS

INDIVIDUAL Tell students to write a recipe for a nutritious salad using the plural form of *macaroni, cauliflower, broccoli,* and *asparagus.* Encourage them to be creative and add other ingredients.

KINESTHETIC LEARNERS

LARGE GROUP **Materials:** word cards shaped like fish and like mice

Give a fish card and a mouse card to each student. Say *ox, shrimp, goose, trout, woman, sheep, moose, foot, deer, milk, tooth, man,* and *child.* Students hold up a fish for words that have the same singular and plural forms, a mouse for a word that changes form.

Use the words in the word bank to work through the crossword puzzle.

Word Bank

sheep
sauerkraut
salmon
cactuses
women
mice
teeth
oatmeal
cattle
wheat
deer
moose
bacon
men
popcorn
spaghetti
milk
crises
geese

Across

4. farm animals sheared for their wool
5. salted, smoked meat often served with eggs
6. swift animals living in the woods
7. large ocean fish that swim up rivers to lay their eggs
8. cereal grasses used for making flour
9. cooked cereal made from ground, boiled oats
10. what you use to bite and chew food
11. more than one male
12. small rodents found in houses and fields
14. something to drink
15. stressful, anxious times

Down

1. animals of the cow family
2. large birds that honk and fly in V formations to migrate
3. corn that turns into white puffs when heated
4. cabbage that's spiced and tastes sour
7. noodles from Italy
8. more than one female
12. large woodland animals with wide antlers
13. prickly plants you wouldn't want to sit on

152 Lesson 69
Other plural forms

SPELLING

Prepare slips of paper to place in a box, with one for each of the spelling words *wolves, chiefs, cliffs, radios, potatoes, crises, oases, olden, mice,* and *fungi.* Distribute a sheet of drawing paper to each student. Invite students to pick a word from the box and draw a picture representing the word. Then have classmates study each picture to try to guess the word. The student who guesses correctly, spells the word aloud and writes it on the board.

WRITING

Portfolio Challenge students to write a short story about a group of people who have gone together on a fishing trip. Challenge them to use as many irregular plurals as they can.

LANGUAGE ARTS

Copy *meal, meat, meet,* and *feet* from the following columns of words. Show students how *meal* was changed one letter at a time to become *feet.* Challenge students to show the steps involved to change the top word into the bottom word in each list.

meal	honk	rake	peak
meat	monk	race	pear
meet	mink	rice	dear
feet	milk	mice	deer

AUDITORY/KINESTHETIC LEARNERS

LARGE GROUP Start a clapping rhythm and say a word. Students repeat the rhythm and say the plural form of the word (for example: *Mouse*-clap-clap-clap-clap. *Mice*-clap-clap-clap-clap). Try *foot, oasis, men, trout, tooth, goose, moose, sheep, deer,* and *cactus.*

GIFTED LEARNERS

Challenge students to write a singular and plural version of a nursery rhyme about farmyard animals like sheep, cattle, geese, and mice.

LEARNERS WHO NEED EXTRA SUPPORT

Materials: dictionary

Help students look up regular and irregular singular words in the dictionary to see how they can find out the plural of any word that is giving them difficulty. **See Daily Word Study Practice, pages 191-192.**

Lesson 70
Pages 153–154

Syllables

Lesson Focus

INTRODUCING THE SKILL

- Have students explain how they would determine the number of syllables in a word. (*the same as the number of vowel sounds*)

- Write *oatmeal* and *instead* on the board. Help students conclude that double vowels stand for only one vowel sound.

- Use *prewash* and *joyful* to help students recall that a prefix or a suffix is a syllable in itself if it contains a vowel.

- Point out that some prefixes and suffixes have more than one vowel sound and therefore have more than one syllable. (*superstar, ultraclean*)

USING THE PAGES

Be sure students understand how to complete pages 153 and 154. Point out that on page 154 they find plural forms in the hidden-word puzzle first. They then write the words divided into syllables on the lines. When students have finished, suggest that small groups review the pages together, with students correcting their own papers.

Name

Study the rules. Then write the number of vowels you see, the number of vowel sounds you hear, and the number of syllables in each word. Remember that **y** is sometimes a vowel.

RULES

1. Double vowels stand for only one vowel sound.

    inst**ea**d   sp**oo**nful

2. A prefix or suffix is a syllable in itself if it has a vowel sound.

    prewash   old**en**

3. Some prefixes and suffixes have more than one vowel sound and therefore have more than one syllable.

    ultrafine   **super**human

	Vowels Seen	Vowel Sounds	Syllables		Vowels Seen	Vowel Sounds	Syllables
1. congratulations	6	5	5	19. insight	2	2	2
2. encountered	5	3	3	20. exclamation	5	4	4
3. exaggerating	5	5	5	21. kangaroos	4	3	3
4. irresponsible	5	5	5	22. excitably	4	4	4
5. determination	6	5	5	23. handkerchiefs	4	3	3
6. indirectly	4	4	4	24. irritability	6	6	6
7. invisible	4	4	4	25. resolution	5	4	4
8. foreshadows	4	3	3	26. pavement	3	2	2
9. imprisoned	4	3	3	27. organizations	6	5	5
10. illogical	4	4	4	28. squeezing	4	2	2
11. torpedoes	4	3	3	29. scrubber	2	2	2
12. motionless	4	3	3	30. noisiest	4	3	3
13. quickened	4	2	2	31. sleepily	4	3	3
14. observer	3	3	3	32. entrusting	3	3	3
15. combinations	5	4	4	33. feebly	3	2	2
16. neighborhood	5	3	3	34. audible	4	3	3
17. imagination	6	5	5	35. overcook	4	3	3
18. peaceful	4	2	2	36. weighed	3	1	1

FOCUS ON ALL LEARNERS

ENGLISH LANGUAGE LEARNERS/ESL

Before beginning page 153, have students work with a partner to summarize, in their own words, the rules about vowel sounds and syllabication. Encourage students to work independently but to ask for help pronouncing a word if needed.

VISUAL LEARNERS

INDIVIDUAL Have students look through reading materials in the classroom to find words with double vowels and with prefixes and suffixes of more than one vowel sound. Have them copy the words on a sheet of paper and divide them into syllables.

KINESTHETIC LEARNERS

SMALL GROUP **Materials:** index cards

Give three index cards to each student. Ask them to write a one-syllable word on one card, a two-syllable word on the second, and a three-syllable word on the third. Say *one, two,* or *three* and have students stand in turn and read their word with that many syllables.

Find the plural forms of twenty words in the puzzle. They appear horizontally or vertically, from left to right, or from top to bottom. Circle the words as you find them. Then list them below, dividing them into syllables using vertical lines.

```
P  C  F  C  A  C  T  U  S  E  S  Z
O  A  T  M  E  A  L  J  M  N  P  R
P  B  C  S  W  V  E  H  O  N  E  Y
C  U  E  P  A  I  R  S  A  U  P  E
O  T  D  A  B  C  H  E  R  O  E  S
R  T  F  G  P  I  C  C  O  L  O  S
N  E  H  H  M  I  Y  D  A  S  A  C
G  R  D  E  E  R  A  P  U  H  V  E
L  G  K  T  R  R  Y  O  C  E  E  L
C  O  D  T  O  M  A  T  O  E  S  L
C  Z  A  I  D  Z  O  A  L  P  E  O
M  A  P  B  C  A  T  T  L  E  O  S
S  H  R  I  M  P  E  O  B  T  K  N
G  U  O  Z  O  B  E  E  S  R  S  I
M  Z  R  O  D  E  O  S  B  M  N  O
```

cac/tus/es	shrimp
oat/meal	bees
hon/ey	ro/de/os
pairs	pop/corn
he/roes	rye
pic/co/los	but/ter
deer	spa/ghet/ti
cod	sheep
to/ma/toes	cel/los
cat/tle	po/ta/toes

154 Lesson 70
Syllables

SPELLING

Practice the words *fungi, mice, olden, oases, crises, potatoes, radios, cliffs, chiefs,* and *wolves.* Have students take turns giving a definition while other students spell the word for it.

WRITING

Portfolio Challenge students to create a crossword puzzle using only two-or-more-syllable words with double vowels. After the puzzles are complete, distribute them to other students to solve.

LANGUAGE ARTS

Explain that a couplet is a two-line poem that rhymes and that each line has the same number of syllables. Then read the following.

Make a salad, but do not scrimp.

Add lots of lettuce, eggs, and shrimp.

Ask students to count the number of syllables in each line. Then suggest they write couplets of their own about one of the following: mice, popcorn, toes, fish, heroes, bees, or spaghetti.

PHYSICAL EDUCATION

Use page 153 of the pupil's book as a word source for a game of Hot Potato. Begin the game by pronouncing a word as you toss the ball to a student who must catch the ball, name the number of syllables in the word, and toss the ball across to another student as you say another word.

 AstroWord Multisyllabic Words © 1998 Silver Burdett Ginn Inc. Division of Simon & Schuster.

AUDITORY/KINESTHETIC LEARNERS

LARGE GROUP

Form teams. As you say a word, a member of each team writes the word on the board and divides it into syllables as fast as possible. Give everyone a turn. Try *midweek, overcook, extrasensory, dreadful, reread, superhuman, visitor, noodle, ultramodern,* and *neighborhood.*

GIFTED LEARNERS

Challenge students to recall or research some of the longer words in the English language and to write them, divide them into syllables, use them in a sentence, and share them with the class.

LEARNERS WHO NEED EXTRA SUPPORT

Since syllables are more easily heard when a word is spoken, suggest students say each word aloud quietly to help them hear the vowel sounds. **See Daily Word Study Practice, page 193.**

Lesson 71

Pages 155–156

Syllables

Lesson Focus

INTRODUCING THE SKILL

- Write these words on the board and divide them into syllables.

  ap/ple/sauce, flash/light, note/book, birth/day, wa/ter/mel/on

- Use the words to review this rule: Divide a compound word between the two words that make up the compound word. Then divide the smaller words into syllables.

- Write the words *trem/ble, sam/ple, whis/tle,* and *han/dle* on the board. Ask students what the words have in common. (*end in* le)

- Use the words to help students review this rule: When a word ends in a consonant followed by *le*, the word is usually divided before the consonant.

USING THE PAGES

Be sure students understand how to complete pages 155 and 156. After they have completed the pages, discuss with them what they learned about syllabicating compound words and words that end in *le*.

155

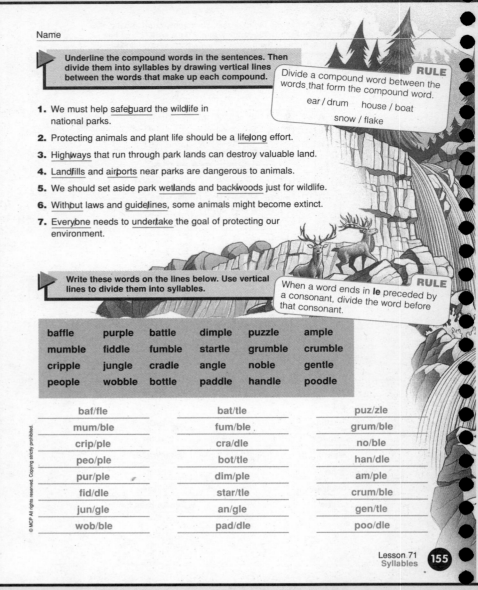

Name _____

> Underline the compound words in the sentences. Then divide them into syllables by drawing vertical lines between the words that make up each compound.

> **RULE** Divide a compound word between the words that form the compound word.
> ear / drum   house / boat
> snow / flake

1. We must help safeguard the wildlife in national parks.
2. Protecting animals and plant life should be a lifelong effort.
3. Highways that run through park lands can destroy valuable land.
4. Landfills and airports near parks are dangerous to animals.
5. We should set aside park wetlands and backwoods just for wildlife.
6. Without laws and guidelines, some animals might become extinct.
7. Everyone needs to undertake the goal of protecting our environment.

> Write these words on the lines below. Use vertical lines to divide them into syllables.

> **RULE** When a word ends in **le** preceded by a consonant, divide the word before that consonant.

baffle	purple	battle	dimple	puzzle	ample
mumble	fiddle	fumble	startle	grumble	crumble
cripple	jungle	cradle	angle	noble	gentle
people	wobble	bottle	paddle	handle	poodle

baf/fle	bat/tle	puz/zle
mum/ble	fum/ble	grum/ble
crip/ple	cra/dle	no/ble
peo/ple	bot/tle	han/dle
pur/ple	dim/ple	am/ple
fid/dle	star/tle	crum/ble
jun/gle	an/gle	gen/tle
wob/ble	pad/dle	poo/dle

Lesson 71
Syllables
155

FOCUS ON ALL LEARNERS

ENGLISH LANGUAGE LEARNERS/ESL

Before students begin page 155, talk about how huge and filled with animals the national parks are. Have students tell why they would like to visit one.

VISUAL LEARNERS

INDIVIDUAL Explain that compound words do not always combine the meanings of the two words. Write *anchorperson, copperhead, peppermint, blueprint, strawberry,* and *brainstorm* on the board, for students to divide into syllables and define.

KINESTHETIC LEARNERS

 LARGE GROUP Read each clue. Students write the answer, divide it into syllables, and explain the syllabication rule. Say *where lions live (jun/gle); a poisonous reptile (rat/tle/snake); big trees in California (red/woods); utensils (sil/ver/ware); easy to understand (sim/ple).*

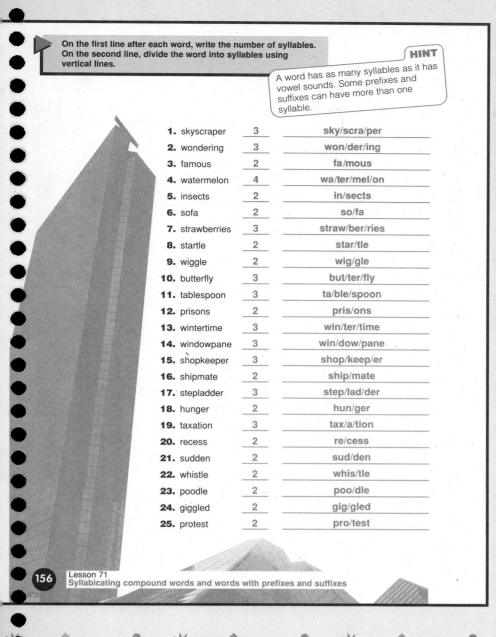

On the first line after each word, write the number of syllables. On the second line, divide the word into syllables using vertical lines.

HINT
A word has as many syllables as it has vowel sounds. Some prefixes and suffixes can have more than one syllable.

1.	skyscraper	3	sky/scra/per
2.	wondering	3	won/der/ing
3.	famous	2	fa/mous
4.	watermelon	4	wa/ter/mel/on
5.	insects	2	in/sects
6.	sofa	2	so/fa
7.	strawberries	3	straw/ber/ries
8.	startle	2	star/tle
9.	wiggle	2	wig/gle
10.	butterfly	3	but/ter/fly
11.	tablespoon	3	ta/ble/spoon
12.	prisons	2	pris/ons
13.	wintertime	3	win/ter/time
14.	windowpane	3	win/dow/pane
15.	shopkeeper	3	shop/keep/er
16.	shipmate	2	ship/mate
17.	stepladder	3	step/lad/der
18.	hunger	2	hun/ger
19.	taxation	3	tax/a/tion
20.	recess	2	re/cess
21.	sudden	2	sud/den
22.	whistle	2	whis/tle
23.	poodle	2	poo/dle
24.	giggled	2	gig/gled
25.	protest	2	pro/test

Lesson 71
Syllabicating compound words and words with prefixes and suffixes

AUDITORY/KINESTHETIC LEARNERS

SMALL GROUP

Materials: index cards

On 24 index cards, write ten compound words with two syllables, ten with three syllables, and four with four syllables. Display the cards, facing inward, and have students turn them around, matching words with the same number of syllables.

GIFTED LEARNERS

Challenge students to write silly phrases using as many compound words as possible. An example is *The shopkeeper stood on tiptoe on the stepladder to place the cupcakes near the windowpane, when she tripped on her shoelace and fell.*

LEARNERS WHO NEED EXTRA SUPPORT

Materials: slips of paper

Have students show how words that end in *-le* are divided into syllables by writing *gentle, fiddle, puzzle, poodle, jungle, people,* and *purple* on individual slips, then folding where the two syllables are divided. **See Daily Word Study Practice, page 193.**

CURRICULUM CONNECTIONS

SPELLING

Materials: small cards or tiles with letters of the alphabet in a paper bag

Draw a square on the board for each letter in one of the list words: *wolves, chiefs, cliffs, radios, potatoes, crises, oases, olden, mice,* and *fungi.* Have a student choose a card from the bag and ask, for example, "Is there an *f*?" If that letter is in the word, write it in place, and ask the player to guess the word. If the letter is not in th word, or the player cannot guess the word, let the next player pick another letter. Continue until all the words have been spelled.

WRITING

Portfolio Challenge students to write an essay about why it is important to protect the wildlife in our national parks. Ask them to list the words they used that end in *-le* and to divide them into syllables.

SOCIAL STUDIES

Challenge students to research in magazines and travel books the summertime and wintertime activities at one of America's national parks. Invite them to share their information with their classmates.

SCIENCE/MATH

Help students to research the Endangered Species Act. Ask them to find out how many plants and animals are protected now and how many were protected when the act first went into law. Challenge them to create a graph to show how some species have prospered because of the protective status.

Technology

AstroWord Multisyllabic Words © 1998 Silver Burdett Ginn Inc. Division of Simon & Schuster.

Lesson 72

Pages 157-158

Reviewing Suffixes and Irregular Plurals

INFORMAL ASSESSMENT OBJECTIVES

Can students

✔ read words with suffixes in context?

✔ write a speech using such words?

Lesson Focus

READING

- Write the following on the board and have students suggest words with suffixes for each one.

  1. Double the final consonant.
  2. Drop the final e.
  3. Words that end in y.
  4. Words that end in y or le.
  5. Change the *f* or *fe* to *v* and add *es*.
  6. Keep the *ff* and add *s*.
  7. If a word ends in *o*, usually add *s*.
  8. Some words do not change.

WRITING

Explain that on page 158, students will plan a speech to convince other students to join the student government. Before writing, have students discuss Helpful Hints.

157

📖 **Reading** ▶ Read the article. Then answer the question at the end of the passage.

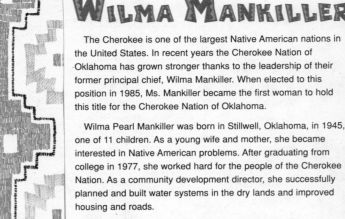

WILMA MANKILLER

The Cherokee is one of the largest Native American nations in the United States. In recent years the Cherokee Nation of Oklahoma has grown stronger thanks to the leadership of their former principal chief, Wilma Mankiller. When elected to this position in 1985, Ms. Mankiller became the first woman to hold this title for the Cherokee Nation of Oklahoma.

Wilma Pearl Mankiller was born in Stillwell, Oklahoma, in 1945, one of 11 children. As a young wife and mother, she became interested in Native American problems. After graduating from college in 1977, she worked hard for the people of the Cherokee Nation. As a community development director, she successfully planned and built water systems in the dry lands and improved housing and roads.

When she was first elected principal chief, many Cherokee doubted that Ms. Mankiller was the right choice to lead them. However, her hard work and dedication to making life better proved the doubters wrong. In fact, she served two more terms as principal chief. Although a medical problem prevented her from serving a fourth term, Ms. Mankiller remains an active spokesperson for Native American issues.

What impresses you most about Wilma Mankiller? _____

FOCUS ON ALL LEARNERS

ENGLISH LANGUAGE LEARNERS/ESL

Before they begin page 157, encourage students to discuss how plurals are formed in these languages.

VISUAL LEARNERS

LARGE GROUP Write the words *life, loaf, cliff, wolf, belief, radio, solo, potato, hero,* and *rodeo* on the board. Then ask one student to begin a story with a sentence that contains the plural of one of the words. Have another student add a sentence with a different plural, and so on, until all the words have been used.

KINESTHETIC LEARNERS

LARGE GROUP Write *knife, chief, bluff, piano, echo, tomato, trout, bacon, child, ox,* and *tooth* on the board. Have teams line up. The first student in each line writes the plural for one of the words, then the next teammate writes a plural for another word, and so on. The team that finishes first with the most correctly spelled words wins.

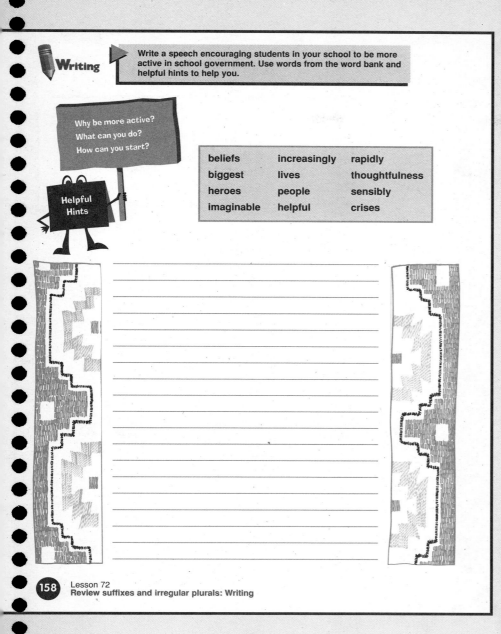

Writing

Write a speech encouraging students in your school to be more active in school government. Use words from the word bank and helpful hints to help you.

Why be more active?
What can you do?
How can you start?

Helpful Hints

beliefs	increasingly	rapidly
biggest	lives	thoughtfulness
heroes	people	sensibly
imaginable	helpful	crises

PARTNER

AUDITORY/KINESTHETIC LEARNERS

Have partners work independently to write a paragraph using words with suffixes that double the final consonant, drop the final *e*, and end in -*y* before adding the suffix. Then ask them to exchange papers and circle each other's words with suffixes.

GIFTED LEARNERS

Challenge students to find out more about the Cherokee tribe and its long history. Students can present what they have learned to the class.

LEARNERS WHO NEED EXTRA SUPPORT

Ask students to use what they have learned about suffixes and plurals to define *inventions, inventors, inventive,* and *inventiveness*.
See Daily Word Study Practice, pages 190-191.

CURRICULUM CONNECTIONS

SPELLING

The following sentences can be used as a spelling posttest.

1. **wolves**   The **wolves** looked like dogs.
2. **chiefs**   The two **chiefs** met to discuss the tribe's land.
3. **cliffs**   The **cliffs** are above the river.
4. **radios**   We played music on all the **radios.**
5. **potatoes**   I add **potatoes** to all of my soup.
6. **crises**   The patient has several **crises** before he recovered.
7. **oases**   The **oases** were the only places where we found water.
8. **olden**   In **olden** days there were no planes.
9. **mice**   **Mice** can be white and black.
10. **fungi**   Mushrooms are one kind of **fungi.**

SOCIAL STUDIES

Have students research the type of government their town uses. Help them contact the local seat of government for information. Students can then make a chart showing the names and offices of elected officials.

SCIENCE

Water is one of the most important needs for the Cherokee people and others living in Oklahoma. Students can research the climate of the area to find out the average rainfall and compare it to the rainfall in their own region. They can also learn more about how water is managed in arid areas like the desert southwest.

Lesson 73

Pages 159–160

Unit Checkup

Reviewing Suffixes, Plurals, and Syllables

Lesson Focus

PREPARING FOR THE CHECKUP

- On the board, write the heading *Adding Suffixes*. Write the following subheads at the top of four columns: *Words that double the final consonant*, *Words that end in e*, *Words that end in y or le*, and *Words with more than one suffix*. Have volunteers write these words under the correct heading as you read them aloud: *jogging, hotter, planning, hoped, imagining, changed, believed, powerlessness, successfully, joyfully, stories, sleepier, luckiest, probably, wiggly*. Then have students divide the words into syllables.

- Write the words *leaf, thief, cliff, scarf, radio, photo, potato, cello, wheat, shrimp, popcorn, moose, knife, wolf, cuff, banjo, kangaroo, milk, child, mouse,* and *tooth* on a word wall. Ask students to write the plural of each word next to the singular.

USING THE PAGES

Make sure students understand each set of directions on pages 159 and 160. Point out that the directions change after item 6 and item 14 on page 159.

159

Name _____

UNIT 6 CHECKUP

▶ Fill in the circle beside the word that is correctly divided into syllables.

1. ● won/der/ing   ○ wonder/ing   ○ wond/ering
2. ○ oa/tmeal   ○ oatm/eal   ● oat/meal
3. ○ cact/us/es   ● cac/tus/es   ○ cact/u/ses
4. ○ peop/le   ● peo/ple   ○ pe/ople
5. ○ butt/er/fly ○ butter/fly   ● but/ter/fly
6. ● pic/co/los   ○ picc/olos   ○ picco/los

▶ Fill in the circle beside the plural form for each word in dark print.

7. potato	○ potato	○ potatos	● potatoes
8. piano	● pianos	○ pianoes	○ pianist
9. life	● lives	○ lifes	○ lifves
10. hero	○ hero	● heroes	○ heroe
11. child	○ childes	● children	○ childrens
12. half	● halves	○ halfs	○ halfes
13. sheep	○ sheepes	● sheep	○ sheeps
14. leaf	○ leafs	○ leafes	● leaves

▶ Read each sentence and the two groups of suffixes that follow it. Notice the base word in dark print. Fill in the circle beside the suffix in each group that belongs in each blank. Then read the sentence again to make sure it makes sense.

15. Thomas Edison's **invent** ____ ____ is admired by all.
      a. ○ ful ○ ly ● ive ○ ness
      b. ○ ful ○ ly ○ ive ● ness

16. He chose to work on **seem** ____ ____ impossible tasks.
      a. ● ing ○ able ○ ly ○ ible
      b. ○ ing ○ able ● ly ○ ible

17. Edison **success** ____ ____ patented 1,033 inventions in all!
      a. ○ ion ● ful ○ ness ○ ly
      b. ○ ion ○ ful ○ ness ● ly

Lesson 73
Suffixes, plurals, syllables: Checkup **159**

FOCUS ON ALL LEARNERS

ENGLISH LANGUAGE LEARNERS/ESL

Before beginning page 160, generate a discussion about wolves and the fact that they are members of the dog family. Have students voice any knowledge or curiosity they have about wolves.

VISUAL LEARNERS

PARTNER Challenge students to work in pairs to design a word-search puzzle using words with more than one suffix. Suggest that students begin by brainstorming a list of words they can use. Encourage partners to exchange their puzzle with another pair of students.

KINESTHETIC LEARNERS

SMALL GROUP **Materials:** word cards

Choose a number of singular nouns and their plurals from each plural lesson in this unit, and make two sets of word cards. Then have students work in groups to place all the cards face down and then play concentration by attempting to match the singular and plural of the same noun.

Read the words in the word bank. Then read the story. Write the correct word from the word bank on the line to complete each unfinished sentence. Then answer the questions.

| beliefs | bounties | concentrated | debated | dedicated | defenseless |
| development | endangered | experiencing | observers | ranchers | wolves |

Wolves Ahead

In the 1800s, thousands of _____wolves_____ roamed North America. Today, biologists consider gray and red wolves _____endangered_____ in 48 states. Only about 9,000 wolves still live in the wild, _____concentrated_____ mostly in Alaska and Minnesota. However, biologists have been _____experiencing_____ success in reintroducing the gray wolf and the red wolf into their former ranges.

For a long time people believed that wolves were dangerous because they attacked _____defenseless_____ sheep and cattle. So local, state, and federal governments offered _____bounties_____ for wolves. These animals were killed by hunting, trapping, and poisoning. However, research from scientific _____observers_____ has found that these _____beliefs_____ about wolves are generally untrue.

In 1995, _____dedicated_____ scientists released several gray wolves into Yellowstone National Park as an experiment. These were the first wolves in the park since 1926. Farmers and _____ranchers_____ who live near the park are wary of this _____development_____ , so the experiment will continue to be _____debated_____ .

1. How do scientists know that the reintroduction of wolves in certain areas has been successful?

_____

_____

2. Are people interested in saving the wolf? How can you tell?

_____

_____

160 Lesson 73
Suffixes, plurals, syllables: Checkup

AUDITORY/KINESTHETIC LEARNERS

LARGE GROUP

Materials: index cards

Distribute to each student a set of four index cards numbered 1, 2, 3, and 4. Then read these following words one at a time: *awakened, operation, cheerfulness, joyful, painlessly, increasingly, quickened.* Ask students to show you how many suffixes are in each word.

GIFTED LEARNERS

Challenge students to write a short story about a group of people lost in Yellowstone National Park, using as many irregular plurals as possible—or using *only* irregular plurals.

LEARNERS WHO NEED EXTRA SUPPORT

Materials: word cards

Make and distribute word cards representing irregular plurals. Then ask students to write the singular of each word on the back of the word card. They can then use the cards for practice when working with a partner. **See Daily Word Study Practice, pages 190-193.**

ASSESSING UNDERSTANDING OF UNIT SKILLS

Student Progress Assessment Review the observational notes you made as students worked through the activities in the unit. Your notes will help you evaluate the progress students made with suffixes, irregular plurals, and syllables.

Portfolio Assessment Review the materials students have collected in their portfolios. You may wish to have interviews with students to discuss their written work and the progress they have made since the beginning of the unit. As you review students' work, evaluate how well they use these word study skills.

Daily Word Study Practice For students who need additional practice with any of the topics in this unit, quick reviews are provided on pages 190–193 in Daily Word Study Practice.

Word Study Posttest To assess students' mastery of skills covered in this unit, use the posttest on pages 135g–135h.

SPELLING CUMULATIVE POSTTEST

Use the following words and dictation sentences.

1. **cutting** We are **cutting** out newspaper stories about pollution.
2. **liking** I won't ever stop **liking** ice cream.
3. **activities** There are different **activities** every day after school.
4. **chimneys** Both **chimneys** need to be repaired.
5. **painlessly** We walked **painlessly** across the sharp rocks in our new boots.
6. **heavily** The street is **heavily** traveled.
7. **coyly** The children **coyly** peeked out from behind the curtain.
8. **wobbly** The **wobbly** chair had one short leg.
9. **wolves** **Wolves** are members of the dog family.
10. **chiefs** The police **chiefs** met to discuss crime prevention.
11. **radios** Before television, families listened to **radios** every night.
12. **potatoes** **Potatoes** are my favorite food.
13. **olden** We pretended to be on a wagon train in **olden** days.
14. **mice** Some people are afraid of **mice** and other rodents.
15. **fungi** There are pictures of poisonous **fungi** in my science book.

Teacher Notes

Assessment Strategy Overview

Throughout Unit 7, assess students' ability to use the dictionary to find information about words and their meanings. There are various ways to assess students' progress. You may also want to encourage students to evaluate their own work and participate in setting goals for their own learning.

FORMAL ASSESSMENT

The Unit 7 Pretest on pages 161e–161f helps

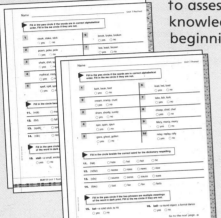

to assess a student's knowledge at the beginning of the unit and to plan instruction.

The Unit 7 Posttest on pages 161g–161h helps to assess mastery of unit objectives and to plan for reteaching, if necessary.

INFORMAL ASSESSMENT

The Reading & Writing Pages and Unit Checkup in the student book are an effective means of evaluating students' performance.

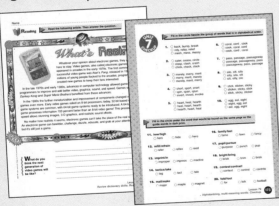

Skill	Reading & Writing Pages	Unit Checkup
Alphabetizing	171–172	173–174
Identifying Guide Words	171–172	173–174
Dictionary Pronunciation Key	171–172	173–174
Dictionary Respellings	171–172	173–174
Understanding Entry Words	171–172	173–174
Multimeaning Words	171–172	173–174
Homographs	171–172	173–174

PORTFOLIO ASSESSMENT

Portfolio This logo appears throughout the teaching plans. It signals opportunities for collecting students' work to place in individual portfolios. You may also want to collect the following pages.

❖ Unit 7 Pretest and Posttest, pages 161e–161h
❖ Unit 7 Reading & Writing, pages 171–172
❖ Unit 7 Checkup, pages 173–174

STUDENT PROGRESS CHECKLIST

Use the checklist on page 161i to record students' progress. You may want to cut the sections apart to place each student's checklist in his or her portfolio.

Administering and Evaluating the
Pretest and Posttest

DIRECTIONS

To help you assess students' progress in learning Unit 7 skills, tests are available on pages 161e–161h. Administer the Pretest before students begin the unit. The results of the Pretest will help you identify each student's strengths and needs in advance, allowing you to structure lesson plans to meet individual needs. Administer the Posttest to assess students' overall mastery of skills taught in the unit and to identify specific areas that will require reteaching.

PERFORMANCE ASSESSMENT PROFILE

The following chart will help you identify specific skills as they appear on the tests and enable you to identify and record specific information about an individual's or the class's performance on the tests.

Depending on the results of the tests, refer to the Reteaching column for lesson-plan pages where you can find activities that will be useful for meeting individual needs or for daily word study practice.

ANSWER KEYS

Unit 7 Pretest, page 161e (BLM 49)

1. yes	5. yes	9. sauce
2. no	6. no	10. fox
3. yes	7. hate	11. ball 2
4. yes	8. news	12. bat 1

Unit 7 Pretest, page 161f (BLM 50)

17. clam / clean	25. pronounce / prose
18. terse / tether	26. inch / include
19. foil / follow	27. knotted
20. stay / stream	28. erasing
21. cement / cereal	29. rangers
22. appear / arch	30. heroes
23. braid / branch	31. buildings
24. twine / ulcer	

Unit 7 Posttest, page 161g (BLM 51)

1. no	5. no	9. speak
2. yes	6. yes	10. rock
3. yes	7. mate	11. office 1
4. no	8. foil	12. stall 2

Unit 7 Posttest, page 161h (BLM 52)

17. consent / contest	25. crate / creep
18. malt / mangle	26. purge / quaint
19. depth / dessert	27. inspiring
20. rank / rate	28. capitals
21. burly / bushy	29. developed
22. prey / pride	30. locating
23. brick / brim	31. trophies
24. purple / quake	

PERFORMANCE ASSESSMENT PROFILE

Skill	Pretest Questions	Posttest Questions	Reteaching Focus on All Learners	Reteaching Daily Word Study Practice
Alphabetizing	1–10	1–10	163–164, 171–172	192
Guide Words	17–26	17–26	163–164, 171–172	192
Pronunciation Key	11–14	11–14	165–166, 171–172	192
Dictionary Respellings	11–14	11–14	167–168, 171–172	192
Entry Words	27–31	27–31	167–168, 171–172	192–193
Multimeaning Words	15	16	169–172	192–193
Homographs	16	15	169–172	192–193

▶ **Fill in the yes circle if the words are in correct alphabetical order. Fill in the no circle if they are not.**

1 bark, beak, bird
○ yes ○ no

2 cream, cramp, crust
○ yes ○ no

3 share, shortly, surely
○ yes ○ no

4 lead, led, load
○ yes ○ no

5 lake, lick, lock
○ yes ○ no

6 cheap, chief, chef
○ yes ○ no

▶ **Fill in the circle beside the correct word for the dictionary respelling.**

7. (hāt) ○ hate ○ hat ○ hot ○ hit

8. (no͞oz) ○ noose ○ nose ○ news ○ nice

9. (sôs) ○ source ○ sores ○ sauce ○ sues

10. (fäks) ○ fast ○ fax ○ fox ○ facts

▶ **Read the definitions below. Write the correct word and definition number to finish each sentence.**

bat—1. a solid stick. 2. to hit. **ball**—1. a round object. 2. a formal dance.

11. Janet got a new dress for the spring _____ .

12. She was disappointed because she really wanted a new aluminum _____ for the softball tournament.

Go to the next page. →

> ► Fill in the circle beside the guide words that could
> be found on the same page as the word in dark print.

17. clap	○ clam / clean	○ cleaner / clerk	○ civil / clamp
18. test	○ tent / terror	○ terse / tether	○ task / tasty
19. folder	○ focus / fog	○ foil / follow	○ forgive / fort
20. steak	○ stay / stream	○ stick / streak	○ steal / steer
21. cent	○ cave / cell	○ central / certain	○ cement / cereal
22. apple	○ anthem / any	○ appear / arch	○ arm / art
23. brake	○ brace / brag	○ brave / break	○ braid / branch
24. twitch	○ twine / ulcer	○ turkey / twain	○ turtle / twist
25. proper	○ profit / prone	○ pronounce / prose	○ protect / prove
26. incident	○ income / increase	○ in / incense	○ inch / include

> ► Fill in the circle beside the word for which the word
> in dark print would act as an entry word.

27. knot	○ knit	○ not	○ knotted
28. erase	○ traces	○ erasure	○ erasing
29. ranger	○ rangers	○ range	○ rang
30. hero	○ heron	○ herald	○ heroes
31. building	○ build	○ buildings	○ built

Possible score on Unit 7 Pretest is 31. Number correct _____

> **Fill in the yes circle if the words are in correct alphabetical order. Fill in the no circle if they are not.**

1 steak, stake, stick
○ yes ○ no

4 break, brake, broken
○ yes ○ no

2 poem, poke, pole
○ yes ○ no

5 lost, least, lessen
○ yes ○ no

3 shark, shirt, sparkle
○ yes ○ no

6 send, sonic, sound
○ yes ○ no

> **Fill in the circle beside the correct word for the dictionary respelling.**

7. (māt) ○ mate ○ mat ○ met ○ might

8. (fōil) ○ fall ○ full ○ foil ○ fowl

9. (spēk) ○ speak ○ speck ○ spoke ○ squeak

10. (räk) ○ rack ○ rake ○ wreck ○ rock

> **Read the definitions below. Write the correct word and definition number to finish each sentence.**

stall—1. a small, enclosed space. 2. to delay. **office**—1. a work place. 2. an important position.

11. The vice president called an emergency meeting in her _____ .

12. She instructed everyone to come immediately and not to _____ .

Go to the next page. →

> ▶ **Fill in the circle beside the guide words that could be found on the same page as the word in dark print.**

17. content ○ consent / contest ○ consider / construct ○ context / contract

18. manage ○ makeup / man ○ malt / mangle ○ mane / manner

19. desert ○ dessert / develop ○ depend / descend ○ depth / dessert

20. rarely ○ rank / rate ○ rain / rare ○ rash / ray

21. bus ○ burglar / burst ○ burly / bushy ○ bushy / butter

22. pride ○ pray / prey ○ pried / prime ○ prey / pried

23. brim ○ break / brick ○ brick / brim ○ bring / brisk

24. quack ○ quest / quiz ○ quail / quart ○ purple / quake

25. creaky ○ crab / creak ○ crate / creep ○ cream / crest

26. pursue ○ purge / quaint ○ puzzle / quaint ○ purchase / purpose

> ▶ **Fill in the circle beside the word for which the word in dark print would act as an entry word.**

27. inspire ○ spires ○ inspiring ○ spirit

28. capital ○ capitol ○ capitalist ○ capitals

29. develop ○ developed ○ envelope ○ development

30. locate ○ local ○ locale ○ locating

31. trophy ○ tropic ○ atrophy ○ trophies

Possible score on Unit 7 Posttest is 31. Number correct _____

Student Progress Checklist

Make as many copies as needed to use for a class list. For individual portfolio use, cut apart each student's section. As indicated by the code, color in boxes next to skills satisfactorily assessed and mark an X by those requiring reteaching. Marked boxes can later be colored in to indicate mastery.

STUDENT PROGRESS CHECKLIST

Code: ■ Satisfactory   ☒ Needs Reteaching

Student: _____ _____	Skills	Comments / Learning Goals
Pretest Score: _____ Posttest Score: _____	☐ Alphabetizing ☐ Dictionary Skills ☐ Multimeaning Words ☐ Homographs	

Student: _____ _____	Skills	Comments / Learning Goals
Pretest Score: _____ Posttest Score: _____	☐ Alphabetizing ☐ Dictionary Skills ☐ Multimeaning Words ☐ Homographs	

Student: _____ _____	Skills	Comments / Learning Goals
Pretest Score: _____ Posttest Score: _____	☐ Alphabetizing ☐ Dictionary Skills ☐ Multimeaning Words ☐ Homographs	

Student: _____ _____	Skills	Comments / Learning Goals
Pretest Score: _____ Posttest Score: _____	☐ Alphabetizing ☐ Dictionary Skills ☐ Multimeaning Words ☐ Homographs	

Spelling Connections

UNIT WORD LIST
Multimeaning Words, Homographs

stall
tire
office
desert
land
post

INTRODUCTION

The Unit Word List is a list of spelling words drawn from this unit. This list includes words with more than one meaning and homographs. To incorporate spelling into your word study program, use the activity in the Curriculum Connections section of each teaching plan.

The spelling lessons utilize the following approach for each set of words.

1. Administer a pretest of the words that have not yet been introduced. Dictation sentences are provided.

2. Provide practice.

3. Reassess. Dictation sentences are provided.

A final test is provided in Lesson 79 on page 174.

DIRECTIONS

Make a copy of Blackline Master 54 for each student. After administering the pretest, give each student a copy of the word list. Students can work with a partner to practice spelling the words orally and identifying the multiple meanings of a word or a homograph for appropriate words. They can also make and use letter cards to form the words on the list. You may want to challenge students to identify other words that have multiple meanings or that are homographs. Students can write words of their own on *My Own Word List* (see Blackline Master 54).

Have students store their list words in an envelope in the back of their books or notebooks. You may want to suggest that students keep a spelling notebook, listing words with similar patterns. You could also invite students to build word-wall displays in the classroom. Each section of the wall can focus on words with a single word study element. The walls will become a good spelling resource when students are writing.

Spelling

UNIT 7 WORD LIST

Multimeaning Words, Homographs

stall

tire

office

desert

land

post

My Own Word List

My Own Word List

My Own Word List

161k

Word Study Games, Activities, and Technology

The following collection of ideas offers a variety of opportunities to reinforce word study skills while actively engaging students. The games, activities, and technology suggestions can easily be adapted to meet the needs of your group of learners. They vary in approach so as to consider students' different learning styles.

● **ALPHABET SOUP**

Have groups of four students write each of the following letter combinations on small strips of paper: *ba, be, bi, bl, bo, br, bu, by, ca, ce, ch, ci, cl, co, cr, cu*. Tell them to place the strips in a bowl and mix them up. Students take turns closing their eyes and pulling one strip from the bowl. Each then writes a word beginning with that letter combination on an index card and places it on a table or desk. Succeeding word cards are added in the appropriate position to create an alphabetized deck. You might extend the activity by suggesting other letter combinations.

▲ **COLLECTIBLE WORDS**

Invite students to collect new words they learn. Using a notebook, students can create a personal dictionary by listing unfamiliar words as they are encountered. Encourage students to look up each word in another dictionary and create a complete entry including respelling, pronunciation, and primary definition(s). Suggest that students devote a double page to each starting letter and leave enough room between entries on a page to maintain alphabetical order. Encourage them to add illustrations as appropriate.

◆ **DICTIONARY PRACTICE**

Write these words on the board: *anxiety, bureaucrat, colonel, rancid, minotaur, decimate, frisky, hibernation, lieutenant, vagrancy*. Point out that the accent mark in a dictionary respelling shows the stressed syllable. Tell students to locate the words in the dictionary. As they do, ask volunteers to write the respelling for each word on the board beside the word and pronounce it correctly. You might challenge students to think of familiar words and write short messages in "respelling code" and exchange them with partners for decoding. An example is: thə foot´ bôl gām stärts at āt. (The football game starts at eight.)

■ WORD GUIDES

Groups of three or four can play "word guide." First, tell each member to consult a classroom dictionary and write three sets of guide words on a sheet of paper. Next, students can take turns playing "travelers" trying to find their way. The traveler asks each of the "guides," in turn, *Are you my guide?* The response is *I am. Walk between [followed by one set of guide words].* To move on, the traveler must say and spell a word that would be found on the same page as the guide words. If possible, allow groups to take up positions in different parts of the room and have travelers walk from one guide to the next.

✳ KNOCK, KNOCK!

Invite partners to play a variation of "Knock, knock!" The first partner says, *Knock, knock!* The second answers, *Who's there?* The first answers *An entry word* (such as *knot*) *and a companion* (*knots*). If the words are appropriate, and the companion word is listed with the entry word in a dictionary, the host replies, *Enter.* If not, the host says, *Come back later,* and the first partner tries again. After a correct exchange, partners switch roles.

● DICTIONARY WORK

Divide the class into groups of three or four. Then write these words on the chalkboard: *diagram, miniature, sergeant, cocoa, furrow, mileage, actual.* Tell group members to take turns looking up and pronouncing the words and reading the definitions. Suggest that they write sentences using these words.

▲ DEFINITION CHALLENGE

Have student partners work together. One partner says a familiar word. The other looks it up in a dictionary. The first partner then challenges the other to use one of the first two meanings for that word in a sentence by saying the number 1 or 2. After saying a sentence using the word in that specific context, the second partner hands the dictionary to the first and challenges him or her to form a sentence using the other meaning. Partners then switch roles.

◆ PEOPLE MAKE WORDS

Point out the etymology, or word origin, part of a dictionary entry. Tell students that there are interesting stories behind the origins of many words. Sometimes, words are named for people in history. Write the following words on the board: *sandwich, boycott, Ferris wheel, sideburns, macadam, maverick, cardigan, derby* (a race). Have students look up the words in a dictionary and volunteer the full names of the people behind the word origin. Invite individuals to use other reference works to research one of these people and then write a paragraph based on their information. Encourage them to share what they learn with the class.

■ PROOFREADING

You might consider having partners exchange paragraphs and proofread one another's work before it is collected. If classroom dictionaries contain a list of proofreaders' marks, suggest students find the symbols for a period, a comma, capitalization, lowercase letters, and indenting a paragraph and use them in their proofreading. If not, write the information as shown at left on the chalkboard and model the use of these symbols.

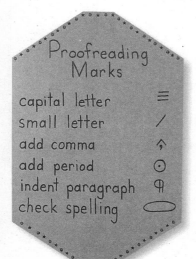

Proofreading Marks

capital letter	≡
small letter	/
add comma	⌃
add period	⊙
indent paragraph	¶
check spelling	⬭

When I play the drums with our **band**, I usually wear a purple **band** on my head.

✳ HUMOROUS HOMOGRAPHS

Write these homographs on the chalkboard: *bat* and *fly*. Discuss with students words spelled the same way that have a different meaning or origin. Then write the following sentences on the board.

The movie hero hit the vampire bat with a baseball bat.

The exhausted fly decided to fly home on a jet plane.

Have student work in small groups to brainstorm a list of homographs. Challenge them to create and illustrate humorous sentences using homographs. An example is shown at the right.

● DICTIONARY MALL

Make enough copies of Blackline Master 55 to distribute one to each student. Briefly discuss malls that the students might have visited. Remind students that malls sometimes have a theme (such as an outlet mall, or a furniture mall). Tell students to imagine that this is a floor plan for their "dictionary mall." Each store should specialize in a particular dictionary service. Explain that students should consider these services when naming each of the stores in the mall (for example, *Homograph Haven, Guide Words Gallery*). After they have named each store, they should create a "window display" by writing an example of the kinds of information customers can find there. You might wish to display the finished projects on your word wall or a bulletin board.

Technology

The following software products are designed to provide practice in dictionary skills.

Macmillan Dictionary for Children   This multimedia dictionary for students (ages 6–12) features more than 12,000 words, 1,000 pictures, and 400 sound effects. Some pages include hyperlinks that offer connections to semantically related words or word derivations. Several word games are included.
** Simon & Schuster Interactive
 P.O. Box 2002
 Aurora, CO 80040-2002
 (800) 910-0099

Reading Blaster   Hundreds of word-skill games offer students in grades 3–6 practice in alphabetizing, spelling, recognizing synonyms and antonyms, and following directions.

** Davidson & Associates, Inc.
 19840 Pioneer Avenue
 Torrance, CA 90503
 (800) 545-7677

Merriam-Webster's Dictionary for Kids   Students can use this online dictionary to find the meanings of 20,000 words and play a variety of word games.
** Mindscape
 80 Roland Way
 Novato, CA 94945
 (800) 234-3088

Name _____

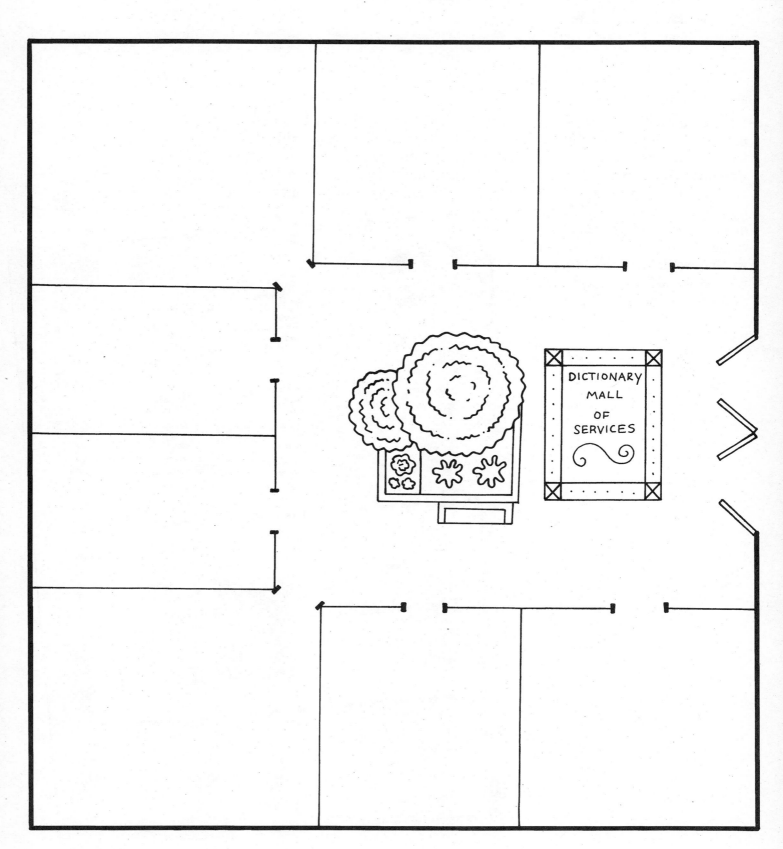

Home Connection

HOME LETTER

A letter is available to be sent home at the beginning of Unit 7. This letter informs family members that students will be learning dictionary skills, such as alphabetizing words, using guide words, and recognizing words with multiple meanings. The suggested home activity focuses on cartoon panels featuring multiple-meaning words and original puns. This activity promotes interaction between the student and family members while supporting the student's learning of reading and writing words with the targeted work study skills. A letter is also available in Spanish on page 161q.

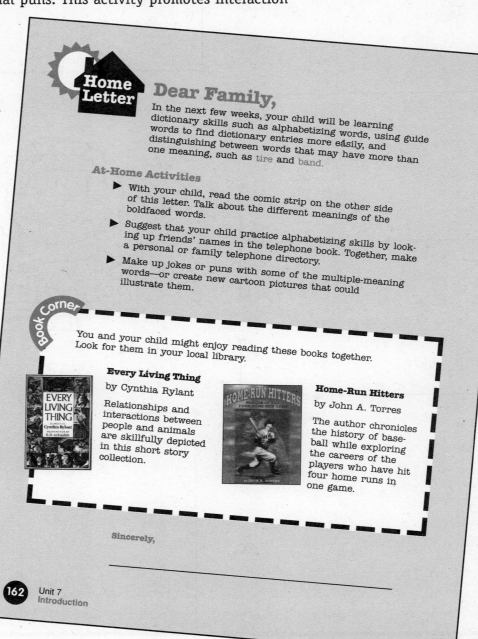

Carta para la casa

Estimada familia,

En las semanas próximas, su hijo/a va a aprender destrezas para el uso de diccionarios, tales como poner palabras en orden alfabético, el uso de palabras guías para hallar los asientos en el diccionario con mayor facilidad, y cómo distinguir entre palabras en inglés que tengan más de un significado, tales como **tire** (**llanta**, **cansar**) y **band** (**orquesta**, **liga**).

Actividades para hacer en casa

▶ Con su hijo/a, lean la tira cómica al dorso de esta carta. Hablen de los diferentes significados de las palabras en negrita.

▶ Sugiéranle a su hijo/a que practique su habilidad alfabética buscando los nombres de sus amigos en la guía telefónica. Juntos, confeccionen un directorio telefónico personal o familiar.

▶ Inventen chistes en inglés con palabras de sentidos múltiples, o creen una tira cómica que los pueda ilustrar.

Rincón del libro

Quizás a su hijo/a y a ustedes les guste leer estos libros juntos. Búsquenlos en la biblioteca de su localidad.

Every Living Thing
por Cynthia Rylant

Las relaciones y las interacciones entre gente y animales se relatan con destreza en esta colección de cuentos cortos.

Home-Run Hitters
por John A. Torres

El autor reseña la historia del béisbol al explorar las carreras de los jugadores que han bateado cuatro cuadrangulares en un juego.

Atentamente, _____

Unit 7

Dictionary Skills

ASSESSING PRIOR KNOWLEDGE

To assess students' prior knowledge of dictionary skills, use the pretest on pages 161e–161f.

Unit Focus

USING THE PAGE

- Invite students to read the comic strip on page 161. Point out that in each panel two people are talking. Have students look for something that is the same in each speech balloon.

- Invite students to discover why the same word is boldfaced in each panel. What does this have to do with the humor of the cartoon?

- Proceed through the page, helping students understand the dual meanings of each pair of words.

- Encourage students to express what they liked about the comic strip. Would they have been as confused as the characters on the baseball team?

- **Critical Thinking** Read aloud the question the character asks at the bottom of page 161. Have volunteers explain the misunderstanding in each panel.

BUILDING A CONTEXT

Write each of the sentence pairs from the speech balloons on the board, underlining the words that were boldfaced. Ask students to look up the boldfaced words in a dictionary. Help students find two meanings that fit for each word. Have them write the correct definitions on the board.

Read about a very confused baseball team. As you read, look for words with the same spellings but different meanings.

Unit 7 Introduction 161

UNIT OPENER ACTIVITIES

INSTANT REPLAY

Challenge students to act out the cartoon on page 161. Have some students pantomime the action while others narrate the speaking parts. Students with a knowledge of baseball might enjoy adding some scenes to the skit.

CLASS COMICS!

Students can design a class comic strip about an ongoing baseball game with themselves as team members. Encourage them to brainstorm confusing word pairs that would add humor. Point out that the words *bat, base, ball, catcher, slide, fly, steal, shortstop,* and *diamond* are all baseball words that have multiple meanings.

MANY MEANINGS

Write the words *back, band, deep,* and *might* on the board. Then ask volunteers to look up each word and count how many meanings are listed. Have students try to guess some of the meanings. Then have the volunteers share any definitions that the other students had not guessed.

Home Letter

Dear Family,

In the next few weeks, your child will be learning dictionary skills such as alphabetizing words, using guide words to find dictionary entries more easily, and distinguishing between words that may have more than one meaning, such as tire and band.

At-Home Activities

▶ With your child, read the comic strip on the other side of this letter. Talk about the different meanings of the boldfaced words.

▶ Suggest that your child practice alphabetizing skills by looking up friends' names in the telephone book. Together, make a personal or family telephone directory.

▶ Make up jokes or puns with some of the multiple-meaning words—or create new cartoon pictures that could illustrate them.

Book Corner

You and your child might enjoy reading these books together. Look for them in your local library.

Every Living Thing
by Cynthia Rylant

Relationships and interactions between people and animals are skillfully depicted in this short story collection.

Home-Run Hitters
by John A. Torres

The author chronicles the history of baseball while exploring the careers of the players who have hit four home runs in one game.

Sincerely,

_____

- The Home Letter on page 162 is intended to acquaint family members with the dictionary skills students will be studying in the unit. Students can tear out page 162 and take it home. Suggest that they complete the activities on the page with a family member and encourage them to look for some of the books pictured on page 162 in the library and to read them with family members.

- The Home Letter can also be found on page 161q in Spanish.

CURRICULUM CONNECTIONS ✳ • ◆ ■ ◆ •

WRITING

Have students write a character sketch of a character like Amelia Bedelia who is constantly confused by the multiple meanings of words.

LANGUAGE

Students can research another kind of word pairs—homonyms. Point out that homonyms are words that sound alike but have different meanings and different spellings. Give students the examples of *bored, board; hare, hair; nose, knows;* and *plain, plane.* Then ask them to discover their own homonyms.

PHYSICAL EDUCATION/MATH

Challenge students to work with partners to figure out the current standings of baseball teams in the National or American Leagues. If the season is over, students can look up the past season's standings. Ask students to show the wins and losses of each team on a chart that shows the teams ranked from best to worst.

BULLETIN BOARD

Students can create a bulletin-board display of multiple-meaning words. Have them look through joke and riddle books to find puns that they could picture in cartoon format. The title of the display can be "Double Trouble."

Lesson 74

Pages 163–164

Alphabetizing and Locating Words in the Dictionary

INFORMAL ASSESSMENT OBJECTIVES

Can students

✔ alphabetize words to the second and third letters?

✔ use guide words to locate dictionary entries?

Lesson Focus

INTRODUCING THE SKILL

Materials: dictionaries

- Have the following groups of words on the board and ask students to rewrite them in alphabetical order: *monument, category, traveler, recipe, quarter, battleship, blend, beaker, bubble, breaker; club, clip, clout, clam, cleaver.*

- Have students look up *monument* in their dictionary. Point out that guide words appear in dark print at the top of each dictionary page and that each pair of guide words indicates the first and last entry words on that page.

- Have students find the guide words for other words on the board.

USING THE PAGES

Be sure students understand how to complete the pages. When students have finished, suggest partners review their pages together.

163

Name _____

▶ Number the words in each column to show the alphabetical order.

RULE
When words begin with the same letter or letters, look at the second or third letter to put the words in alphabetical order.

1

microphone	1
middle	2
mistake	3
mystery	6
morning	5
modern	4

2

swaying	5
strawberry	4
seashore	1
skateboard	3
sickness	2

3

awkward	5
arrive	4
amount	2
application	3
aching	1

4

crayon	1
creek	2
crusty	5
cringe	3
crock	4

5

lotion	4
loneliness	3
locust	2
loaves	1
loyalty	5

6

southerly	5
sorrow	4
socialize	1
sometime	3
softening	2

7

blond	5
battery	2
blanket	4
bulge	6
beach	3
bath	1

8

thaw	2
trio	4
tunnel	6
tumble	5
talent	1
thief	3

9

payment	1
position	4
planter	3
pension	2
prance	5

Lesson 74
Alphabetizing **163**

FOCUS ON ALL LEARNERS

ENGLISH LANGUAGE LEARNERS/ESL

Although students can complete pages 163 and 164 without knowing what the words mean, encourage them to practice their dictionary skills by looking up words they are not familiar with in a dictionary.

VISUAL LEARNERS

PARTNER Pairs can play "guide-word challenge" by locating *trial, wring, flaunt, tribute, testify, cumbersome, dutiful,* and *cleverness* and taking turns writing an entry word and the guide words found at the top of the page on which the word appears.

KINESTHETIC LEARNERS

SMALL GROUP Write the following pairs of guide words on the board: *drapery, dust; shrimp, slam; wobble, zipper.* Ask students to come to the board and list—without using a dictionary—as many words as they can that would appear on the pages headed with these pairs of guide words.

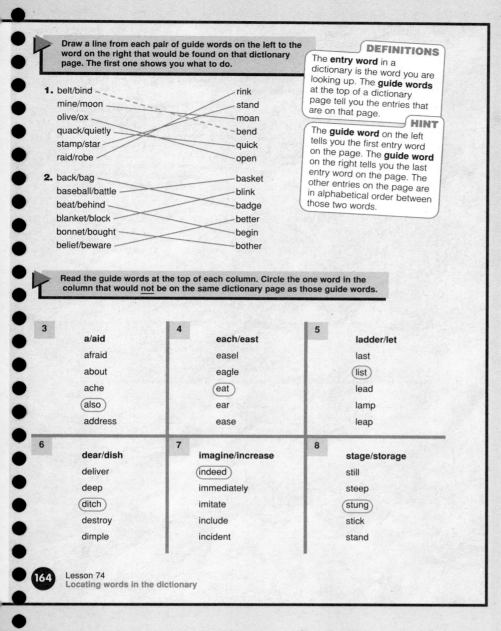

Draw a line from each pair of guide words on the left to the word on the right that would be found on that dictionary page. The first one shows you what to do.

1. belt/bind .... rink
   mine/moon .... stand
   olive/ox .... moan
   quack/quietly .... bend
   stamp/star .... quick
   raid/robe .... open

2. back/bag .... basket
   baseball/battle .... blink
   beat/behind .... badge
   blanket/block .... better
   bonnet/bought .... begin
   belief/beware .... bother

DEFINITIONS
The **entry word** in a dictionary is the word you are looking up. The **guide words** at the top of a dictionary page tell you the entries that are on that page.

HINT
The **guide word** on the left tells you the first entry word on the page. The **guide word** on the right tells you the last entry word on the page. The other entries on the page are in alphabetical order between those two words.

Read the guide words at the top of each column. Circle the one word in the column that would <u>not</u> be on the same dictionary page as those guide words.

3
a/aid
afraid
about
ache
(also)
address

4
each/east
easel
eagle
(eat)
ear
ease

5
ladder/let
last
(list)
lead
lamp
leap

6
dear/dish
deliver
deep
(ditch)
destroy
dimple

7
imagine/increase
(indeed)
immediately
imitate
include
incident

8
stage/storage
still
steep
(stung)
stick
stand

(164) Lesson 74
Locating words in the dictionary

AUDITORY LEARNERS

LARGE GROUP Say *before* or *after* and a word and call on a student who says a word that appears in the dictionary before (or after) the word you said. Then he or she says *before* or *after* and a word and calls on another student. Try to keep the words and cues moving quickly.

GIFTED LEARNERS

Challenge students to share interesting words they would like to use when they talk. Then have them create dictionary pages with guide words and an illustration or two.

LEARNERS WHO NEED EXTRA SUPPORT

Materials: tagboard strips

Before students begin the practices, suggest they write the alphabet on a tagboard strip to use as a cue card as they alphabetize words to complete the pages. **See Daily Word Study Practice, page 192.**

SPELLING

The following sentences can be used as a pretest for spelling words that are mulit-meaning words and homographs.

1. **stall** Will the car **stall** again?
2. **tire** I need to change the **tire.**
3. **office** Meet me at the **office.**
4. **desert** The **desert** is frequently hot and dry.
5. **land** I can see **land** over there.
6. **post** Help me set up the fence **post.**

WRITING

Portfolio Invite students to take a "sense walk," jotting down sensory words to describe things they see, smell, touch, and hear as they walk. After the walk, have them put their words in alphabetical order and use the words to write a description of the things they experienced during the walk.

SOCIAL STUDIES

Challenge students to devise their own language codes and use them to write secret messages or stories. For example, students could create a backwards alphabet code in which a=z, b=y, c=x, and so on.

LANGUAGE ARTS

Write *Wild Walter Winton wondered whether Wanda Whithers was watching Weather World.* Ask a volunteer to read the sentence, then cut the sentence into words and challenge students to put the words in alphabetical order. Invite pairs to compose sentences in which all the words begin with the same letter, cut the sentences apart, and alphabetize the words.

Lesson 75
Pages 165–166

Dictionary Pronunciation Key

Lesson Focus

INTRODUCING THE SKILL

Write these words on the board, one at a time: _April_, _boil_, _truly_, _thistle_, _western_, _trim_, _long_, _reach_, _this_, _treasure_, _border_.

- Have students use the pronunciation key on page 165. For each word on the board, challenge students to identify the symbol and key word in the key that matches the underlined letter(s).

- Write the following words on the board, omitting the numbers in parentheses that show which syllable is accented: _treasury_ (1), _medicine_ (1), _inspire_ (2), _society_ (2). Pronounce each word and ask a volunteer to identify the accented syllable.

- Instruct students to find the words in a dictionary to see if the stressed syllable was correctly identified.

USING THE PAGES

When students have completed the pages, correct the pages together.

Name _____

 Study the pronunciation key. Then follow the directions below.

HINT
The respelling that follows a dictionary entry shows how to pronounce the word. Use the pronunciation key in the dictionary to help you pronounce each respelling.

Vowels

Symbol	Key Words	Symbol	Key Words
a	cat	o͝o	look, pull
ā	ape	o͞o	tool, rule
ä	cot, car	ou	out, crowd
e	ten, berry	u	up
ē	me	ur	fur, shirt
i	fit, here	ə	a in ago
ī	ice, fire		e in agent
ō	go		i in pencil
ô	fall, for		o in atom
oi	oil		u in circus

Consonants

Symbol	Key Words	Symbol	Key Words
b	bed	s	see
d	dog	t	top
f	fall	v	vat
g	get	w	wish
h	help	y	yard
j	jump	z	zebra
k	kill, call	ch	chin, arch
l	leg	ŋ	ring, drink
m	meat	sh	she, push
n	nose	th	thin, truth
p	put	_th_	then, father
r	red	zh	measure

 Read the respellings below. Notice the symbols in color. Beside each respelling write the words from the pronunciation key that show how to pronounce that symbol. Then write the entry word for each respelling.

1. lēf	me		leaf
2. round	out, crowd		round
3. thōz	then, father		those
4. burn	fur, shirt		burn
5. koil	oil		coil
6. po͞ol	tool, rule		pool
7. sôrs	fall, for		source
8. no͞oz	zebra		news
9. äks	cot, car		ox
10. furst	fur, shirt		first

FOCUS ON ALL LEARNERS

ENGLISH LANGUAGE LEARNERS/ESL

Before they begin page 165, review the symbols that are used in respellings. Say each word for students and ask them to repeat them. Have students try to respell their own names using pronunciation symbols.

 VISUAL LEARNERS
INDIVIDUAL

Materials: dictionaries

Write _censorious, drought, historical, conventional, enchantment, habit, hydraulics, interfere, irritate, dispatch, energy,_ and _forlorn_ on the board. Have students copy the words, then use a dictionary to divide each word into syllables and mark the accented syllable.

 KINESTHETIC/VISUAL LEARNERS
LARGE GROUP

Materials: index cards

Have students use respellings to write their names on cards. Display five at a time. Have volunteers pick a card and hand it to the person it names.

Use the pronunciation key on page 165 and accent marks to pronounce each respelling below. Circle the syllable that is said with more stress, and then rewrite the word showing the correct spelling. You may use your dictionary if necessary.

HINT

When a word has two or more syllables, one syllable is stressed, or accented, more than any other. In the dictionary, an accent mark (´) shows the syllable that is said with more stress.

1. (rēd) iŋ — reading
2. (trub´) əl — trouble
3. (man´) ij ər — manager
4. (mem´) ər ē — memory
5. rē (välv´) — revolve
6. ther (with´) — therewith
7. di (sturb´) — disturb
8. (bil´) dər — builder
9. un (luk´) ē — unlucky
10. rē (fresh´) mənt — refreshment
11. (floun´) dər — flounder
12. kə (rir´) — career
13. ə (thôr´) ə tē — authority
14. (kan´) dəl — candle
15. (gär´) bij — garbage

Use the pronunciation key on page 165 and accent marks to pronounce each respelling below. Then circle the word at the right that goes with that respelling.

16. sim´ pəl — simmer, single, (simple)
17. də zurv´ — (deserve), desert, dessert
18. pas´ chər — (pasture), patch, pastel
19. ə slēp´ — assure, ashamed, (asleep)
20. baj — bug, (badge), bus
21. thur´ o — theron, thought, (thorough)
22. jin´ jər — jungle, (ginger), garage
23. ek splō´ zhən — explain, sxploring, (explosion)
24. soot´ ə bəl — suited, suite, (suitable)
25. gath´ ə riŋ — (gathering), gardenia, getaway

166

Lesson 75
Dictionary pronunciation key

AUDITORY/KINESTHETIC LEARNERS

SMALL GROUP

Materials: dictionaries

Write *anxiety, bureaucrat, colonel, rabid, manatee, decimate, frisky, vagrancy, truant,* and *hibernation* on the board one at a time. Challenge groups to find each word in the dictionary. The first group to find the word and pronounce it correctly earns one point.

GIFTED LEARNERS

Challenge students to choose a passage from a favorite book and rewrite it using respellings. Remind them to place accent marks to show the stressed syllables.

LEARNERS WHO NEED EXTRA SUPPORT

Suggest that students make a study sheet of the sounds they have difficulty with, copying the pronunciation key symbols they need to remember and choosing new key words that have special meaning for them. **See Daily Word Study Practice, page 192.**

CURRICULUM CONNECTIONS

SPELLING

Prepare slips of paper with one of the spelling words *stall, tire, office, desert, land, post* written on each. Put all of the slips of paper into a bag or box. Invite students to pick a word out of the bag to act out one meaning of the word for classmates to guess. Suggest that students use props if necessary. The student who guesses correctly, spells the word aloud, and writes it on the board.

WRITING

Portfolio Write the "coded" message on the board. Have students read the dictionary respellings and write the message as they decode it.

Kum too thə fôrt af´tər skool tə dā´. Bring ā mag´nəf i ing glas with ū. I kôt an in´tər ist ing in´sekt. I nēd yoor help too find out hwut it is kôld.

Allow time for students to write short messages using respellings.

LANGUAGE ARTS

Have students use dictionaries to find place names that begin with the same letter sound as their first names: Alexa from Alabama or Zach from Zimbabwe. Ask them to write the phrases on index cards with the place names written as respellings. Display a map of the world and have students exchange cards and locate their partner's place on the map.

166

Lesson 76
Pages 167–168

Dictionary Respellings and Looking Under the Correct Word Form

Lesson Focus

INTRODUCING THE SKILL

Write these respellings on the board.

(är´tər ē)   (hab ə́ tat)

(i mens´)   (mā jər)

(out grō)   (päk´ it)

(prez´i dənt)   (rub´ ish)

- Have students use the pronunciation key on page 165 to help them determine the word that each respelling stands for. *(artery, habitat, immense, major, outgrow, pocket, president, rubbish)*

- Write these words on the board and have them read: *colonists, colonist; briefest, brief; reducing, reduce; buries, bury; louder, loud; waited, wait.* Explain that the first word in each pair is a form of the second word. Explain that if students wanted to look up the first word in each pair in a dictionary, they would most likely find the second word as the entry word.

USING THE PAGES

- After they have completed the pages, encourage them to review their work together.

167

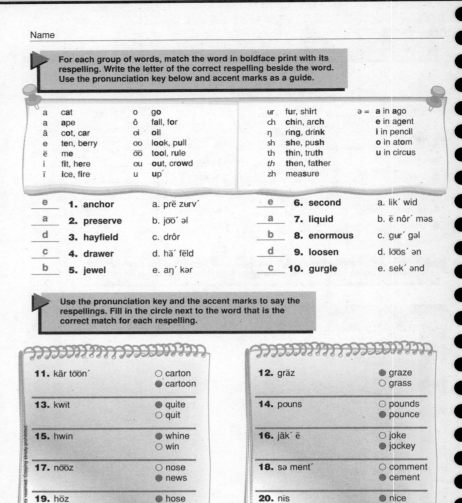

For each group of words, match the word in boldface print with its respelling. Write the letter of the correct respelling beside the word. Use the pronunciation key below and accent marks as a guide.

a	cat	o	go	ur	fur, shirt	ə = a in ago
a	ape	ô	fall, for	ch	chin, arch	e in agent
ä	cot, car	oi	oil	ŋ	ring, drink	i in pencil
e	ten, berry	oo	look, pull	sh	she, push	o in atom
ē	me	ōō	tool, rule	th	thin, truth	u in circus
i	fit, here	ou	out, crowd	*th*	then, father	
ī	ice, fire	u	up	zh	measure	

e **1.** anchor   a. prē zurv´
a **2.** preserve   b. jōō´ əl
d **3.** hayfield   c. drôr
c **4.** drawer   d. hā´ fēld
b **5.** jewel   e. aŋ´ kər

e **6.** second   a. lik´ wid
a **7.** liquid   b. ē nôr´ məs
b **8.** enormous   c. gur´ gəl
d **9.** loosen   d. lōōs´ ən
c **10.** gurgle   e. sek´ ənd

Use the pronunciation key and the accent marks to say the respellings. Fill in the circle next to the word that is the correct match for each respelling.

11. kär tōōn´   ○ carton ● cartoon
12. grāz   ● graze ○ grass
13. kwit   ● quite ○ quit
14. pouns   ○ pounds ● pounce
15. hwin   ● whine ○ win
16. jäk´ ē   ○ joke ● jockey
17. nōōz   ○ nose ● news
18. sə ment´   ○ comment ● cement
19. hōz   ● hose ○ house
20. nis   ● nice ○ niece

FOCUS ON ALL LEARNERS

ENGLISH LANGUAGE LEARNERS/ESL

Before students complete the puzzle on page 168, review the words hidden in the puzzle along with their meanings. Help students figure out what the entry word would be for each word found in the puzzle.

VISUAL LEARNERS

PARTNER Invite students to think of a "What is it?" or "What am I?" riddle and to write it on one side of a sheet of paper. Have them write the answer on the other side in the form of the dictionary respelling. Students may trade papers with a partner, try to answer each other's riddle, and decipher the respelling to see whether their answers are correct.

KINESTHETIC LEARNERS

PARTNER **Materials:** index cards

Have partners write the following words on index cards: *rosebushes, erasing, believed, loving, leaves, knives, loosened, loudest.* As each partner draws from the pile of cards, they say the word as it would appear as a dictionary entry word and then use the word correctly in a sentence.

Twelve words are hidden in the puzzle. The words may be written across, down, or diagonally. Circle each word and write it on the first line next to its definition. On the second line, write the word as a dictionary entry word.

HINT Entry words are often listed in the dictionary without suffixes such as **s**, **es**, **ed**, or **ing**. When you search for a word in the dictionary, look for the word without these suffixes.

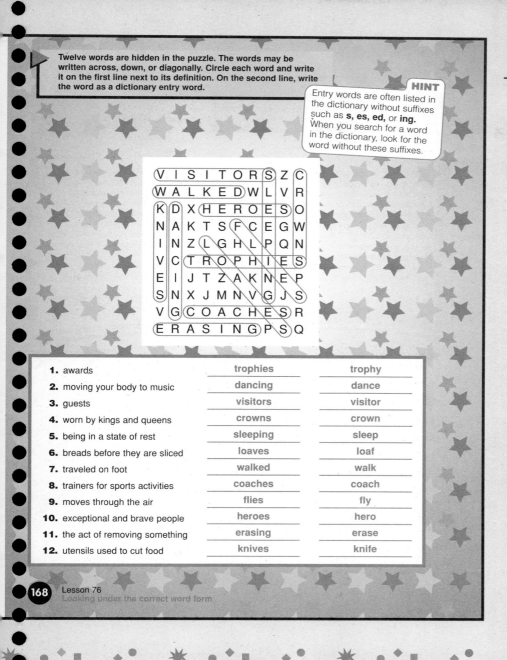

#	Definition	Word	Entry word
1.	awards	trophies	trophy
2.	moving your body to music	dancing	dance
3.	guests	visitors	visitor
4.	worn by kings and queens	crowns	crown
5.	being in a state of rest	sleeping	sleep
6.	breads before they are sliced	loaves	loaf
7.	traveled on foot	walked	walk
8.	trainers for sports activities	coaches	coach
9.	moves through the air	flies	fly
10.	exceptional and brave people	heroes	hero
11.	the act of removing something	erasing	erase
12.	utensils used to cut food	knives	knife

CURRICULUM CONNECTIONS

SPELLING

Ask these questions and have students answer each of them with one of the following spelling words: *stall, tire, office, desert, land, post.*

1. Where does a horse live? *(stall)*

2. What is round, rubber, and fits around a wheel? *(tire)*

3. In what room do people work? *(office)*

4. What is a region with little rainfall and a great deal of sand? *(desert)*

5. What part of the earth's surface is not under water? *(land)*

6. What helps a fence stand up straight? *(post)*

WRITING

Portfolio Challenge each student to create a dictionary of 20 unusual and interesting words. Have students include not only the meaning of each word, but also the respelling for each word. Have students write pronunciation keys at the front of their dictionaries.

SOCIAL STUDIES

Encourage students to research the history of dictionaries. Where was the first dictionary made? How do dictionaries for other languages compare to English dictionaries? Ask students to share their information with their classmates in an oral presentation.

ART

Invite students to make a beginning picture dictionary for the kindergarten class at school. Divide the alphabet into sections to give to groups of students and have each group decide on the appropriate picturable words to use. On a sheet of chart paper, students draw an illustration to accompany each letter and word. Then have students staple all the pages together and add an illustrated cover.

AUDITORY/VISUAL LEARNERS

LARGE GROUP Write these sentences on the board. Then have volunteers come to the board and write the dictionary entry word for each underlined word.

Greg <u>decided</u> to open a <u>recycling</u> center.

He <u>publicized</u> the center at <u>schools</u>, <u>stores</u>, and <u>libraries</u>.

Many people came and <u>deposited</u> glass and <u>crushed</u> cans.

The turnout was <u>larger</u> than Greg had <u>expected</u>.

GIFTED LEARNERS

Challenge students to make a crossword puzzle with different words from the lesson. Encourage students to complete each other's puzzles.

LEARNERS WHO NEED EXTRA SUPPORT

Review each symbol and key word in the pronunciation key together. For each sound, give students different examples of words. Then have students take turns working on an item aloud and suggesting an answer. **See Daily Word Study Practice, pages 192-193.**

Lesson 77

Pages 169–170

Multi-meaning Words and Homographs

INFORMAL ASSESSMENT OBJECTIVES

Can students

✔ identify and use multi-meaning words?

✔ identify and use homographs?

Lesson Focus

INTRODUCING THE SKILL

Write the following dictionary entry on the board.

> **hover 1.** to stay fluttering in the air over one place. **2.** to stay or wait very close by **3.** to waver (between)

- Explain that many words have more than one meaning and that each meaning is numbered in the entry. Point out that the most common meaning is usually first.

- Write these sentences on the board and read them aloud. *The racket kept me awake. I play tennis with a racket.*

- Ask what *racket* means in the first sentence (*a loud noise*) and in the second sentence (*a piece of sports equipment*). Help students conclude that the two words that are spelled the same and sound the same, but have different meanings are *homographs*.

USING THE PAGES

Give students help as necessary to complete pages 169 and 170.

Name _____

Read the dictionary entries. Decide which meaning of a word is used in each sentence below. Write the correct word and its definition number.

RULE

When there is more than one meaning for an entry word, the different meanings are numbered. The most commonly used meaning is usually listed first.

band (bānd) *n.* **1** a cord or wire, or a strip of some material, used to encircle something or to bind something together **2** a stripe of some different color or material **3** a group of persons united for a purpose **4** a group of musicians playing together *v.* **5** to unite in a band

fly (flī) *v.* **1** to move through the air by using wings **2** to travel through air in an aircraft or spacecraft **3** to cause to fly in the air **4** to move swiftly **5** to wave or flutter in the air, as a flag

interest (in´trist *or* in´ tə rəst) *n.* **1** a feeling of wanting to know, learn, see, or take part in something **2** a share in something **3** money paid for the use of someone else's money *v.* **4** to cause to care about or join in

serve (surv) *v.* **1** to work or work for as a servant **2** to promote the interest of; work for; aid; help **3** to perform a duty or function

train (trān) *n.* **1** a line of railway cars coupled together and operated as a unit **2** a line of vehicles, pack animals, or persons traveling together *v.* **3** to instruct or drill for a special purpose

1. During World War II (1941–1945), African American pilots wanted to ___serve 2___ their country.

2. They thought their ___interest 1___ in flying would be useful to the army.

3. The pilots wanted to ___fly 3___ planes in combat for the U.S. Army Air Corps.

4. At that time, African Americans could not ___serve 3___ as pilots.

5. African American leaders decided to ___band 5___ together.

6. Their aim was to ___interest 4___ the president in desegregating the armed forces.

7. In 1941 the army established a flight school at Tuskegee Institute, in Alabama, to ___train 3___ African American pilots.

8. This small ___band 3___ of pilots went on to make history.

9. While ___bands 4___ played, the Tuskegee airmen received medals for their heroism and bravery during the war.

10. They were proud to see the American flag ___fly 5___ in parades in their honor at the end of the war.

Lesson 77
Multi-meaning words (homographs)
169

FOCUS ON ALL LEARNERS

ENGLISH LANGUAGE LEARNERS/ESL

To build background for page 169, have students tell what they would think about learning to fly and why people who know how to fly might feel pride.

VISUAL LEARNERS

PARTNER   Challenge students to create word-search puzzles using words that are homographs. Before beginning, students may search through reading materials to find these words or make lists of their own. Invite students to exchange papers with a partner and solve each other's puzzle.

KINESTHETIC/VISUAL LEARNERS

LARGE GROUP   On the board, write the homographs *duck, jam, bat,* and *note.* Invite a volunteer to choose one word and then draw a sketch on the board or role-play a scene as a clue to the meaning of the word. Challenge classmates to guess the word and the meaning being described and then give the different meaning for the word.

Read these entries. Decide which word to use to complete each sentence below. Write the entry word and its number on the line.

HINT
Sometimes a word has a small raised number to the right of it. This indicates that there is another word pronounced and spelled the same way, but with a completely different meaning or origin.

hatch[1] (hach) *v.* to bring forth young birds, fish, turtles, etc. from eggs [Birds hatch their eggs by keeping them warm]

hatch[2] (hach) *n.* an opening in the deck of a ship, such as one through which cargo is moved into and out of the hold.

post[1] (pōst) *n.* a long, thick piece of wood, metal, or other material set upright for holding something up, such as a building, sign, fence, and so on

post[2] (pōst) *n.* the place where a soldier, guard, etc. is on duty [The sentry walks a *post* just over the hill.]

rank[1] (raŋk) *n.* a row of soldiers, vehicles, and so on, placed side by side

rank[2] (raŋk) *adj.* having a strong, unpleasant taste or smell [*rank* fish]

stall[1] (stôl) *n.* a section for one animal in a stable

stall[2] (stôl) *v.* to hold off by sly or clever means; delay by evading [He *stalled* for time.]

tire[1] (tir) *v.* to make or become unable to go on because of a need for rest; exhaust [The hike *tired* me.]

tire[2] (tir) *n.* a solid rubber hoop or tube filled with air, fixed around the rim of a wheel

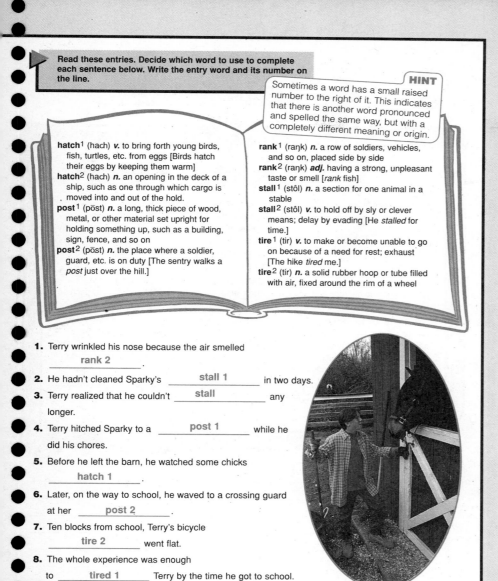

1. Terry wrinkled his nose because the air smelled ____rank 2____ .

2. He hadn't cleaned Sparky's ____stall 1____ in two days.

3. Terry realized that he couldn't ____stall____ any longer.

4. Terry hitched Sparky to a ____post 1____ while he did his chores.

5. Before he left the barn, he watched some chicks ____hatch 1____ .

6. Later, on the way to school, he waved to a crossing guard at her ____post 2____ .

7. Ten blocks from school, Terry's bicycle ____tire 2____ went flat.

8. The whole experience was enough to ____tired 1____ Terry by the time he got to school.

170 Lesson 77
Multi-meaning words (homographs)

SPELLING

Write the list words *tall, tire, office, desert, land, post* on the chalkboard and ask students to choose one to finish each sentence.

1. Don't kick the goal ____. *(post)*
2. Meet us at the principal's ____. *(office)*
3. You can see cactus in a ____. *(desert)*
4. Can you see ____ in the distance? *(land)*
5. One ____ on my bicycle is flat. *(tire)*
6. The horse must return to its ____. *(stall)*

WRITING

Portfolio Invite each student to write a humorous sentence using two words that are homographs, such as *the tiny fly will fly a giant kite*. Have students illustrate their sentences on chart paper and display them on a Homographs Wall.

SOCIAL STUDIES

Encourage students to find a relative, family friend, or neighbor who was alive during World War II and interview that person about the experience. What did the person do during the war years? If in the military, where was he or she stationed? If the person was in the United States, how was life different? Have students give oral presentations describing what they learned about life during World War II.

MATH

What chores are students responsible for in their homes? Have students take a class survey on chores such as cleaning, dishwashing, and baby-sitting. Tell students to brainstorm a list of chores and then survey their classmates and friends. Have students tally the results in a bar graph drawn on the chalkboard.

AUDITORY LEARNERS

PARTNER Have pairs of students conduct humorous conversations in which they use words that are homographs. Suggest that they brainstorm a list of suitable words before they begin their conversations.

GIFTED LEARNERS

Challenge each student to imagine he or she is a reporter during World War II, conducting an interview with one of the Tuskegee airmen. Students may write a newspaper article about the pilot or role-play and tape-record a dramatization of the interview.

LEARNERS WHO NEED EXTRA SUPPORT

Review with students the difference between a multimeaning word and a homograph by looking carefully at each entry word in both dictionary excerpts in this lesson. Have students give other examples of both multimeaning words and homographs. **See Daily Word Study Practice, pages 192-193.**

Lesson 78

Pages 171–172

Reading **Writing**

Reviewing Dictionary Skills

* ◆ • ◆ ■ • ● • ✴ • ◆ ● ◆

INFORMAL ASSESSMENT OBJECTIVES

Can students

✔ identify pronunciations and meanings of dictionary words within the context of reading an article?

✔ write a description using the correct meanings of words?

Lesson Focus

READING

Explain to students that they are going to read an article about electronic games. If they come to an unfamiliar word in the article, they can use the dictionary skills they learned in this unit to look up the word and learn its pronunciation as well as its meaning or meanings.

WRITING

Tell students that on page 172 they will time-travel to 2015 to interview a video-game inventor and write an article about the inventor's latest games. Encourage students to be creative as they make up details about the computer games of the future. Remind students to use the questions on page 172 to help them organize their articles.

171

Name _____

Reading ▶ Read the following article. Then answer the question.

What's Real?

Whatever your opinion about electronic games, they are here to stay. Video games, also called electronic games, appeared in arcades in the early 1970s. The first commercially successful video game was Atari's *Pong*, released in 1972. As millions of young people flocked to the arcades, programmers created new games to keep their fans interested.

In the late 1970s and early 1980s, advances in computer technology allowed game programmers to improve and add better video, graphics, sound, and speed. Games such as *Donkey Kong* and *Super Mario Brothers* benefited from these advances.

In the 1990s the further miniaturization and improvement of components changed video games even more. Early video games relied on 8-bit processors; today, 32-bit based video game systems are common, with 64-bit game systems ready to be introduced. A 64-bit video game processes information 700 percent faster than an 8-bit video game! This processing speed allows stunning images, 3-D graphics, and realistic sound effects.

No matter how realistic it seems, electronic games can't take the place of the real world. An electronic game can bewilder, challenge, dazzle, educate, and grab your attention—but it's still just a game.

What do you think the next generation of video games will be like?

_____
_____
_____
_____
_____
_____

Lesson 78
Review dictionary skills: Reading **171**

FOCUS ON ALL LEARNERS ✴ • ◆ ■ ◆

ENGLISH LANGUAGE LEARNERS/ESL

To build background for page 171, encourage students to talk about their favorite computer games.

VISUAL LEARNERS

SMALL GROUP

Materials: chart paper, strips of paper

Have students draw and cut out a computer screen with the heading *Homograph* in the middle of the screen. Then ask students to write homographs and illustrations of their different meanings on strips of paper and attach them to the computer screen beneath the heading.

KINESTHETIC LEARNERS

LARGE GROUP

Materials: strips of paper

Write pairs of guide words across the board. Then write dictionary entry words on separate strips of paper and distribute them to students. Have each student stand under the guide words where his or her word would be found. To continue playing, have students write new guide words on the board and different entry words on strips of paper.

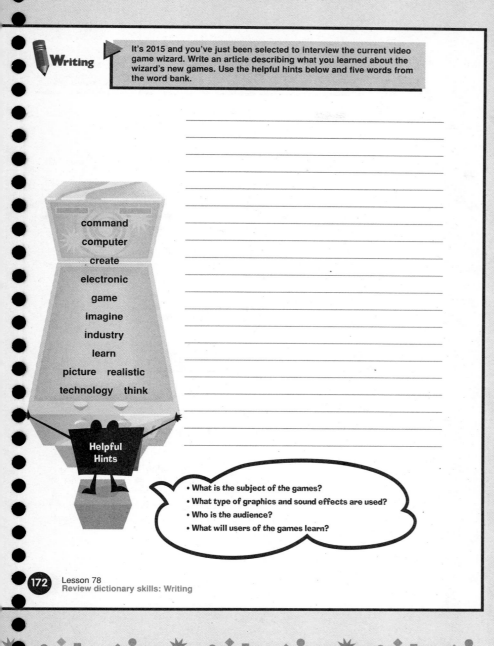

Writing ▶ It's 2015 and you've just been selected to interview the current video game wizard. Write an article describing what you learned about the wizard's new games. Use the helpful hints below and five words from the word bank.

Word Bank

command
computer
create
electronic
game
imagine
industry
learn
picture   realistic
technology   think

Helpful Hints

- What is the subject of the games?
- What type of graphics and sound effects are used?
- Who is the audience?
- What will users of the games learn?

SPELLING

Write the following sentences, one per card, on index cards or slips of paper. Write the list words *stall, tire, office, desert, land, post* in the same way. Distribute the twelve cards to students and let them quickly circulate. Those with a question will try to find the students whose word is contained in their sentence. When a match is made, the two students come to the front of the room and read their matching cards aloud.

1. Will you clean out the horse's stall?
2. I think the tire needs air.
3. The office of the president is very important.
4. Her voice did not desert her once during the entire production.
5. Will the ship reach land by tomorrow evening?
6. The soldier didn't leave her post until after midnight.

SOCIAL STUDIES

What did young people do for enjoyment before the advent of television and electronic games? Invite students to research the history of games and share with their classmates examples of different activities and games earlier generations of kids enjoyed. What are some games that are still popular today? (*chess, Monopoly*)

SCIENCE/FINE ARTS

How does a computer actually work? Challenge students to research the technology involved inside a computer. The school or public library will have many illustrated books on the subject. Have students make a giant cutout of a computer, labeling the inner workings of the machine.

AUDITORY LEARNERS

SMALL GROUP Invite students to read aloud the articles they wrote on page 172 while their classmates write down any homographs or multiplemeaning words they hear in the articles.

GIFTED LEARNERS

Challenge students to create their own "perfect" computer game. Would it be a mystery, an arcade game, an art or music product, or a sports simulation? Encourage students to have fun and be creative as they create this fantasy product.

LEARNERS WHO NEED EXTRA SUPPORT

Introduce some of the difficult and technical words in the article before students begin page 171: *commercially successful, programmers, advances, computer technology, 3-D graphics, miniaturization, components, eight-bit processors, processing speed, stunning images, bewilder, dazzle.* **See Daily Word Study Practice, pages 192-193.**

Lesson 79

Pages 173-174

Unit Checkup

Reviewing Dictionary Skills

INFORMAL ASSESSMENT OBJECTIVES

Can students

✔ use dictionary skills?

✔ identify pronunciations and meanings of dictionary words?

Lesson Focus

PREPARING FOR THE CHECKUP

- Write the following words on the board: *yourselves, denies, outskirts, demonstrated, overdo, bravery, overdue, broke, outweighing, densest, yours, braver.*

- Ask students to alphabetize the words and then write the dictionary entry word for each word.

- Write these words, one at a time, on the board: *amethyst, besiege, calamity, colleague, ether, futile, hostility, lichen, negotiate, ooze, precaution, reel, spiral, yucca.* Have a volunteer look up the word, tell the guide words it was found under, and pronounce it correctly.

- Have a second volunteer read aloud all the meanings, choose one, and use the word in a sentence according to the chosen meaning.

USING THE PAGES

Make sure students understand each set of directions on pages 173 and 174. Point out that the directions change after item 10 on page 173. After students have completed the pages, review the unit as you correct the pages together.

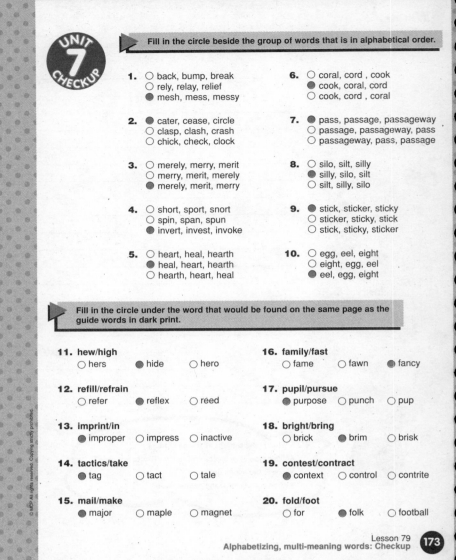

UNIT 7 CHECKUP

Fill in the circle beside the group of words that is in alphabetical order.

1. ○ back, bump, break
   ○ rely, relay, relief
   ● mesh, mess, messy

2. ● cater, cease, circle
   ○ clasp, clash, crash
   ○ chick, check, clock

3. ○ merely, merry, merit
   ○ merry, merit, merely
   ● merely, merit, merry

4. ○ short, sport, snort
   ○ spin, span, spun
   ● invert, invest, invoke

5. ○ heart, heal, hearth
   ● heal, heart, hearth
   ○ hearth, heart, heal

6. ○ coral, cord , cook
   ● cook, coral, cord
   ○ cook, cord , coral

7. ● pass, passage, passageway
   ○ passage, passageway, pass
   ○ passageway, pass, passage

8. ○ silo, silt, silly
   ● silly, silo, silt
   ○ silt, silly, silo

9. ● stick, sticker, sticky
   ○ sticker, sticky, stick
   ○ stick, sticky, sticker

10. ● egg, eel, eight
    ○ eight, egg, eel
    ● eel, egg, eight

Fill in the circle under the word that would be found on the same page as the guide words in dark print.

11. **hew/high**
    ○ hers ● hide ○ hero

12. **refill/refrain**
    ○ refer ● reflex ○ reed

13. **imprint/in**
    ● improper ○ impress ○ inactive

14. **tactics/take**
    ● tag ○ tact ○ tale

15. **mail/make**
    ● major ○ maple ○ magnet

16. **family/fast**
    ○ fame ○ fawn ● fancy

17. **pupil/pursue**
    ● purpose ○ punch ○ pup

18. **bright/bring**
    ○ brick ● brim ○ brisk

19. **contest/contract**
    ● context ○ control ○ contrite

20. **fold/foot**
    ○ for ● folk ○ football

Lesson 79
Alphabetizing, multi-meaning words: Checkup **173**

FOCUS ON ALL LEARNERS

ENGLISH LANGUAGE LEARNERS/ESL

Before beginning page 174, discuss jazz music and ask students to bring in any tapes of jazz they might have at home. If possible, play a song by Ella Fitzgerald.

VISUAL LEARNERS

SMALL GROUP

Have students page through the dictionary, looking for a difficult word. After they write the word on the board, others try to guess the meaning. Clues may be given if no one can guess the meaning of the word. The student who guesses correctly chooses the next word.

VISUAL/KINESTHETIC LEARNERS

PARTNER

Materials: index cards

Make word cards for the following words: *caretaker, bruise, bridge, carnivorous, breach, boundary, certainty, chessboard, bacteria, bystander, cacti.* Then have students working in pairs alphabetize the words. After the cards are in order, ask students to look up the dictionary guide words for each card.

UNIT 7 CHECKUP

Read the words in the word bank. Then read the story. Write the correct word from the word bank on the line to complete each unfinished sentence. Then answer the questions.

born	fifty	career	instrument
culture	interpretations	directed	popular
discovered	symphony	excelled	woman

The First Lady of Song

Ella Fitzgerald is the African American _____woman_____ known as the First Lady of Song. The popular jazz singer was _____born_____ in Virginia in 1918. She was first _____discovered_____ when she was 16 and won a talent show in Harlem, a center for African American life and _____culture_____ in New York City. She began her actual singing _____career_____ in 1935 as the singer in a jazz band. When the band leader died, she _____directed_____ the band.

This jazz great toured the world for over _____fifty_____ years. She performed with big bands, _____symphony_____ orchestras, and in solo appearances. She is best known for the clear tones of her voice and her personal _____interpretations_____ of jazz and popular songs. She _____excelled_____ at scat singing, using the voice as an _____instrument_____ by singing improvised syllables instead of words.

Although she died in 1996, Ella Fitzgerald's music is still _____popular_____ with people who love to listen to jazz. Her unique style continues to entertain her fans.

1. Why do you think Ella Fitzgerald is known as the First Lady of Song?

_____

_____

2. Why was Ella Fitzgerald a popular singer? Explain your answer.

_____

_____

(174) Lesson 79
Alphabetizing, multi-meaning words

Student Progress Assessment Review the observational notes you made as students worked through the activities in the unit. Your notes will help you evaluate the progress students made with dictionary skills.

Portfolio Assessment Review the materials students have collected in their portfolios. You may wish to have interviews with students to discuss their written work and the progress they have made since the beginning of the unit. As you review students' work, evaluate how well they use these word study skills.

Daily Word Study Practice For students who need additional practice with any of the topics in this unit, quick reviews are provided on pages 192–193 in Daily Word Study Practice.

Word Study Posttest To assess students' mastery of skills covered in this unit, use the posttest on pages 161g–161h.

SPELLING CUMULATIVE POSTTEST

Use the following words and dictation sentences.
1. **stall** Who is in charge of the cookie **stall** at the school fair?
2. **tire** Do you have a spare *tire* in the trunk of your car?
3. **office** Mom's **office** has the bright red door.
4. **desert** You can drive a jeep in the **desert.**
5. **land** The **land** around our house is muddy.
6. **post** That goal **post** is too tall to climb.

KINESTHETIC LEARNERS

LARGE GROUP

Divide students into two groups. Have students sit in a circle with a dictionary. One group member looks up a word, and whispers the meaning to his or her teammates. Then the team acts out the word for the other group. If the other group guesses correctly, they get to choose a word to pantomime.

GIFTED LEARNERS

Challenge students to find in the dictionary five words they have never seen or heard. Then have them write a short story that uses all the words. Ask them to read the story aloud, correctly pronouncing the new words.

LEARNERS WHO NEED EXTRA SUPPORT

Materials: index cards

Help students make their own alphabet card to help them with alphabetizing words. Have them write out all 26 letters on one side of an index card. Then have them practice alphabetizing the first and last names of the students in the class. **See Daily Word Study Practice, pages 192-193.**

Teacher Notes

Teacher Notes

Teacher Notes

UNIT 1　LESSONS 1–2, 7, 13–14

Words with the *k* Sound; *qu*, *kn* Words; Sounds of *ch*

◆ Write these words on the chalkboard and ask students to circle the letters that have the *k* sound: *check, hike, thicket, quick, practice, unique, kitten, knock, technique.*

◆ Make word cards for these words: *knight, knees, kept, kind, knock, knew, key, track, knew, tackle.* Have students sort them into two groups—words with silent *k* or words with the sound of *k.*

◆ Brainstorm a list of *qu* words. Then have students tell a group story, using at least one *qu* word in each sentence. Begin the story with *The quiet queen called a news conference. She yelled, "Quick! . . ."* Record the story on chart paper.

◆ Write the letters *k, ch, que, qu,* and *kn* as column heads on the chalkboard. Divide the class into two teams and have students take turns writing a word in each column. The first team to finish wins.

◆ Assign each student a word that contains *ch* and have students sort themselves into two groups: /k/ or /ch/. Use words such as *choose, peach, chore, chest, chance, inch, anchor, chorus, character, stomach, ache.*

◆ Write the following words on the chalkboard and invite students to circle any silent letters they see: *quick, knob, unique, knit, sign, koala, knave, foreign, kitchen, knell, kink, kick, knickers, cob, germ.*

◆ Write these words with *qu* on the chalkboard: *quiz, unique, question, oblique, quack, equal.* Have students circle the words that have /kw/ and underline the words with /k/.

◆ Write the following sentence on the chalkboard and have students supply the missing letters: *The gallant _ _ight rea_ _ed in his po_ _et, where he _ept his _eys to the uni_ _e old treasure _ _est in the _ astle.* If students need help, provide this list of letter combinations: *kn, ch, ck, k, c, qu.*

◆ Have partners write riddles to exchange with other pairs. The riddles should give a clue about a sound in a word; for example, *It covers a bed. The* qu *in this word has a* /kw/.

UNIT 1　LESSONS 2–4, 7, 13–14

Sounds of *c, g, f,* and *s*

◆ Write words with soft and hard *c* on cards, such as *ceiling, column,* and *cemetery.* Distribute the cards, have students read the words aloud, and tell whether the *c* is hard or soft.

◆ Give students cards for the letters *g* and *j.* As you read aloud a group of words, such as *gorilla, rage,* and *gym,* have students hold up the card that shows the hard or soft sound of *g* they hear.

◆ Have students scan their reading books and see how many words with soft *g* and *c* they can find in a given time, such as two minutes. List their responses on the chalkboard.

Daily Word Study Practice

◆ On the chalkboard, write a list of words that contain the sounds of *g*, such as *edge, George, eager, August, giant, agency, bagel,* and *garage.* Have students circle the hard *g*'s and underline the soft *g*'s.

◆ Make cards for words with /s/, /sh/, /zh/, and /z/. Then invite students to sort the cards into groups, according to the different sounds of *s*.

◆ Write words with the *f* sound on the chalkboard and have students circle the letters that make the sound. Use words such as *phony, affluent, photo, raft, frenzy, afraid, chief, graph,* and *effort.*

◆ Ask students to answer these riddles: *What hard* c *word is a desert animal? (camel) What hard* g *word names the head of a state? (governor) What soft* c *word names a breakfast food? (cereal) What soft* g *word names a precious stone? (gem)*

◆ Ask students to raise their arms if they hear a soft *g* or *c* word and clap if they hear a hard *g* or *c* word. Read words such as *coat, gentle, gymnast, circus, goal, giraffe, city, golf, stage, force,* and *cash.*

◆ Invite teams of students to unscramble these words and then sort them by hard or soft *c* or *g*: *galf (flag), acfe (face), vace (cave), ermg (germ), caft (fact), ehug (huge), dogl (gold), sesug (guess), nect (cent), stolce (closet), caned (dance).* The team that finishes first wins.

◆ Challenge students to supply words in which the letter *s* stands for /s/, /z/, /sh/, or /zh/. Have them write the words on the chalkboard, underlining the *s* in each.

UNIT 1 LESSONS 5–7, 13–14
Sounds of *wh, sh, th*

◆ Challenge students to write sentences on the chalkboard that contain words with both of the *th* sounds, such as *My brother traveled north.* Have them circle words with the *th* sound as in *then* and underline words with the *th* sound as in *thin.*

◆ Assign partners the sound of *sh, th,* or *wh.* Have them brainstorm a list of words, then write a tongue twister to share with other pairs.

◆ Write *ip, in, en, at,* and *ere* as headings on the board. Ask students to add *wh, sh,* or *th* to these endings to make as many words as they can.

◆ Ask students to hold up their hands when they hear a word that has /sh/. Say words such as these: *shell, magician, superstition, ceiling, finish, action, apples, harsh,* and *shine.*

◆ Write these words on the chalkboard: *special, commercial, appreciate, sufficient, harsh, magician, cashier.* Ask students to circle the letters that make /sh/.

◆ Write these words on cards: *where, when, who, why, while, whole, whose, whale, what.* Have students sort them into two groups—words that begin with /h/ and words that begin with /hw/.

◆ To help students focus on *sh, ti,* and *ci,* write these incomplete words on the chalkboard and ask students to supply the missing letters: *techni_ _an, fini_ _ed, pa_ _ent, spe_ _al, _ _ip, so_ _al, _ _ow, pu_ _, appre_ _ate.*

◆ Whisper to one student a sentence like this one: *The whales swim in the ocean in the harsh winter.* Have students whisper the sentence to each other, in turn. Then ask the last student to dictate the sentence. Write it on the chalkboard and compare it to the original sentence.

◆ Divide the class into three groups and assign them *sh, th,* or *wh*. Have group members create a list of words they find in their science books for their assigned sound, pointing out any differences in spellings and sounds.

UNIT 1 LESSONS 8–9, 13–14
Sounds of *sc, r, air*; Words with *gn*

◆ Write the letters *rh, wr, gn,* and *sc* on the chalkboard. Challenge students to write words with these letters that name household objects.

◆ Write these words on the chalkboard and have students circle the silent letters: *rhododendron, wrong, write, foreign, rhino, wrap, gnaw, rhythmical, wrist, sign, reign.*

◆ Have students practice *wr* and *gn* by filling in the missing letters to complete this sentence: *The President _ _ote in his campaig_ _ speech that it would be _ _ong to resi_ _.*

◆ Give each student a letter card for *gn, sc, wr,* or *rh*. Have students each hold up their card when they hear a word that contains their letters. Say words such as *sovereign, scar, wrong, wrestle, rhyme,* and *gnawing*.

◆ Write words with *sc* on the chalkboard and have students sort them into three columns by /s/, /sh/, or /sk/.

◆ Say the following groups of words: *gnaw, sign, foreign; scary, scurry, mascot; wriggle, wrong, rhythm*. Have students tell what sound they hear in all three words.

◆ Have students brainstorm a list of words that rhyme with *care*. Write the words on the chalkboard, noting which words are spelled with *air* and which are spelled with *are*.

◆ Have students complete the words in this sentence with *air* or *are*: *At the f_ _ _, Manuel did not d_ _ _ to st_ _ _ at his h_ _ _ in a mirror.*

UNIT 1 LESSONS 10–11, 13–14
Sounds of *ear*; Words with *ild, ind, ost, old*

◆ Ask students to touch their ears if they hear three words that have the same vowel sounds. Say these words: *heard, early, searched; bear, tear, clear; weary, nearby, gear.*

◆ Write *ear* on a card and consonants *h, d, n, g, s, ch, y, t, sm, p, b, cl,* and *f* on letter cards. Have students join a letter at the beginning and/or at the end of *ear* and say each word they make.

◆ Write the following words on the chalkboard and have students sort them into like vowel sounds: *fear, gear, smear, search, early, tear, bear, wear, yearn, heard, near,* and *weary.*

Daily Word Study Practice

- ◆ As you say these sentences, have students raise a hand when they hear a word with *ear: It is helpful to do research before you write a report. What did you wear to the party? The early bird catches the worm. Grandpa visits us each year.*

- ◆ Give each student a card that has a word with *ild, ind, ost,* or *old.* Then have them find other students who have words with the same vowel sound. Have pairs or groups say their words and use each one in a sentence.

- ◆ Have students make a list of words with *ost.* Then have them sort them into lists of words with the short or long *o* sound.

- ◆ Provide letter cards for *ld, nd, st, i, o,* and beginning consonants. Have students manipulate the cards to make as many words as they can with *ild, ind, ost,* and *old.*

- ◆ Invite students to unscramble these words: *stom (most), tosp (post), dolt (told), clod (cold), liwd (wild), dwin (wind), stohg (ghost), dol (old), lodcs (scold).*

- ◆ Write the word *wild* on the chalkboard. Have students substitute beginning letters to make new words, such as *mild* and *child.* At some point, substitute the *i* with *o* and begin again.

UNIT 2 LESSONS 15–17, 23, 28
Vowel Pairs *ai, ay, ee, ei, oa, oe, ow*

- ◆ Say a list of words and have students wave if they hear a long *a* word. Have them spell the word and identify the vowel pair. Use words like these: *time, stray, braid, true, tray, frail, shy, today, tree, grain.*

- ◆ Ask students to brainstorm and write on the chalkboard words that have the long *a* sound with *ai* and *ay* and long *e* words with *ee* and *ei.* Have them circle the vowel pair in each word.

- ◆ Write *ai, ay, ee, ei, oa,* and *oe* on slips of paper and put them in the bottom half of an egg carton. Have students toss a bean into one of the cups and say a word with that vowel pair.

- ◆ Have students use *oa, oe,* or *ow* to finish the words in this sentence: *Tomorr__, Farmer J__ will h__ the r__s in his garden and put up a scarecr__ with a red c__t to scare away the cr__s.*

- ◆ Invite students to make a list of words that rhyme with *low,* noting the different spellings with *ow* and *oe.* Then have them create two-line rhymes with their list.

- ◆ Students can create riddles by using words with vowel pairs; for example, *This fruit has the long a sound. This fruit was once a grape, but now it is dried up. (raisin)*

- ◆ Write a list of words with vowel pairs on the chalkboard. Then have students sort the words into the sounds of long *a, e, i,* and *o.*

- ◆ Write these words on the chalkboard and have students circle the vowel pairs that make the long *e* sound: *conceit, ceiling, protein, sleeping, succeed, receipt, neither.*

- ◆ As you say these words, have students hold up a letter card for *ee* or *ei* to indicate the spelling of the long *e* sound: *peel, receive, guarantee, leisure, agree, tree, green, receipt, deceit, cheese, either.*

UNIT 2   LESSONS 18–23, 28

Vowel Digraphs *ea, ei, ey, au, aw, ie, oo, ui*

◆ Write words with the *ea* digraph on cards. Then have students sort the cards into three groups, long *a* sounds, long *e* sounds, and short *e* sounds.

◆ Make a word ladder with the digraph *ea*, substituting beginning and ending sounds. As students make each word, say it and have students tell what vowel sound the digraph makes.

◆ Scramble words with vowel digraphs and invite students to unscramble them; for example, *rakeb (break), veela (leave), draye (ready), tena (neat), trage (great), clehab (bleach).*

◆ Write these words on the chalkboard and ask students to circle the letters that make the long *a* vowel sound: *survey, reindeer, neighbor, eight, they, hey, prey, weigh.*

◆ Give students letter cards for *au* and *aw*. As you say the following words, have students hold up the card that shows which letters are in each word: *saucer, gnaw, applaud, shawl, author, draw, faucet, awful.*

◆ Write *tie* on the chalkboard and have students make a word ladder by adding ending letters and substituting beginning letters. As students write each new word, have them pronounce it.

◆ Write the following words on the board and have students circle all the words that have the long *e* sound: *chief, believe, lied, pie, thief, brief, satisfied, niece, yield, field, dried, shield.*

◆ Write words with vowel digraphs and have students sort them into like vowel sounds. Use words like these: *they, spread, great, saw, belief, vein, author, fruit, recruit, guilty, good, build, juice, soon, foot, heavy, steak, threat.*

◆ Write *pool, wood,* and *blood* as column headings on three different sheets of paper. Tape each sheet in a different corner of the room. As you say each of the following words, have volunteers go to the corners and write the word under the heading with the same vowel sound: *snoop, raccoon, groom, took, gloom, crooked, shampoo.*

UNIT 2   LESSONS 24–28

Diphthongs *oi, oy, ou, ow, ew*

◆ Ask students to fill in the blanks with *oi* or *oy* to complete the sentence: *The b_ _ was ann_ _ed when his sister av_ _ded the t_ _l of digging in the s_ _l of their garden.*

◆ Write the headings *oi* and *oy* on the chalkboard. Challenge students to brainstorm words that contain each diphthong and write their words under the correct heading.

◆ Invite a volunteer to say a sentence that includes one or more words with the diphthong *ou* or *ow*. Have students write the *ou* or *ow* word they hear in the sentence and circle the diphthong.

◆ Have students change the *o* to *e* in these words and pronounce each *o-e* word pair: *know, now, crow, grow, throw, chow, blow, stow, flow, how, mow.*

Daily Word Study Practice

- Write these words on cards: *drew, jewelry, newspaper, scowl, proud, eyebrow, drowsy, join, destroy, annoy, avoid.* Have students choose a card to pantomime for the class to guess the word.

- Write these words on the chalkboard and have students circle the vowels that make the sound of the diphthong: *annoying, soil, mouths, prowling, shout, newspaper.*

- Distribute cards for *ou, ow, ew, oi,* and *oy.* Have students hold up their cards when they hear a word that has the same sound as their diphthong. Say words like these: *clown, enjoy, pound, renew, spoil.*

- Write the headings *ou, ow, ew, oi,* and *oy* on the chalkboard and one sample word for each diphthong. Have groups search for and list words with the same sound in a two- or three-minute time period, then read their lists aloud.

UNIT 3   LESSONS 29–34, 42
Units of Meaning; Prefixes *un-, dis-, ir-, in-, im-, en-, mis-, mal-, pre-, pro-*

- As you say each of these words, ask students to identify the prefix and the base word: *insightful, unintentional, unlawful, disappearing, insufferable, prolonging, uninhabited, untie.*

- Have students add a prefix to each of these words to make antonyms: *rational, happy, replaceable, possible, appear, advantage, credible, visible, continue, correct, manageable.*

- Ask students to add either the prefix *in-* or *en-* to each of these words: *scribe, habit, courage, rich, different, creased, circle, force.* Have them read aloud the new words.

- Write two columns with the following prefixes and words and have students match them to make new words: *en-, in-, un-, dis-, ir-, in-, im-; possible, rich, visible, available, credit, replaceable, creased.*

- Have students use each of these words in sentences: *behave, adjusted, trust, fortune, nourished, adventure.* Then have them add *mis-* or *mal-* to each word and use it in another sentence.

- Write these words on the chalkboard and ask students to circle the prefix in each: *disorder, disapprove, unlikely, disinterest, unorganized, disagree, unexpected, misled.*

- Make word cards for prefixes *pro-* and *pre-* and for the words *heated, motion, mature, tested, long, posed,* and *judge.* Have students pair the words with prefixes to make new words.

- Write the headings for prefixes *pro-, pre-, dis-, mis-, un-, mal-, in-, en-, im-,* and *ir-* on the chalkboard. Have students take turns writing a word using one of the prefixes until there are six words in each column.

UNIT 3 LESSONS 35–37, 41–42
Prefixes *re-, ex-, fore-, post-, over-*

◆ Write these words on the chalkboard and ask students to add the prefix *re-* or *ex-* to make a new word: *arrange, change, member, charge, place, plain, locate.*

◆ Have students write sentences that include words with the suffix *re-* or *ex-*, leaving a blank line for the prefix. Have each student read his or her sentence aloud and ask the class to supply the missing prefix.

◆ Write these words on cards and have students choose one to pantomime for the class: *recognize, recite, exchange, retrace, reconstruct, exclaim, relocate, replace, refuse.*

◆ Write these words and meanings in two columns: *to put off until later, message at end of letter, time before midday, nearest part of land, warn before; forenoon, foreground, postpone, forewarn, postscript.* Have students match words with meanings.

◆ Have students write the prefix *post-* or *fore-* before the following words to make words: _ _ _ _sight, _ _ _ _game, _ _ _cast, _ _ _ _mark, _ _ _ _war, _ _ _ _most. Have students use each word in a sentence.

◆ Write the prefixes *fore-, post-, re-, ex-,* and *over-* on word cards. Then write these words on the chalkboard and have students add a prefix to new words: *turn, change, season, react, claim, cooked, placed, priced, noon, hand.*

◆ Write the following words on the chalkboard and ask students to circle the prefixes: *reconstruct, excerpt, overcrowded, postscript, forehead, expect, reassure, postpaid.*

◆ Ask students to use the meanings of the prefix *over-* to tell what these words mean: *overpriced, overanxious, overtired, overgenerous, overheard, overworked, overheated, overflowed.*

◆ Divide the class into five groups and assign each group a prefix: *fore-, post-, re-, ex-,* or *over-*. Have group members brainstorm a list of words that contain their prefix, then read their lists aloud.

UNIT 3 LESSONS 38–42
Prefixes *co-, com-, con-, sub-, mid-, bi-, tri-*

◆ Write the prefixes *co-, com-, con-, sub-, mid-, bi-,* and *tri-* in one column and their meanings in the other. Have students draw lines to match meanings to prefixes.

◆ Write these prefixes and base words on the chalkboard: *sub-, mid-, bi-, tri-; marine, night, cycles, zero, winter, angle, life, cultural.* Have students match each base word with one or more of the prefixes to make new words. Then encourage them to use the words in sentences.

◆ Write these words on the chalkboard and have students circle the prefixes: *contestant, conquer, combination, comfortably, cooperate, costars, coexist, committee.*

◆ Write these scrambled words with prefixes *co-, com-,* and *con-* and have students unscramble them: *toscar (costar), pemecot (compete), tissnoc (consist), rocoteepa (cooperate).*

Daily Word Study Practice

◆ Challenge students to use one word with each prefix *co-, com-, con-, sub-, mid-, bi-,* and *tri-* to create a word-search puzzle that they can exchange with a partner to solve.

◆ Write the headings *co-, com-, con-, sub-, mid-, bi-,* and *tri-* on the chalkboard. Have students think of words that begin with each prefix and invite them to write the words on the chalkboard during the day.

◆ Write *sub-, mid-, bi-, tri-, angle, tract, side, point, mit, air, week,* and *weekly* on cards and distribute them randomly to students. Have each student match his or her card to a classmate's card to make a word.

◆ Write these meanings and words in two columns and have students match them: *take away, a train under the ground, noon, middle of the week; midweek, subway, subtract, midday.*

◆ Students can explain the meaning of or draw illustrations to show the following words: *submarine, subway, midnight, submerge, subtract, midpoint, midstream, midair.* Encourage students to use the meaning of the prefix to help them define or depict the word.

◆ Invite students to write riddles for the following words for classmates to answer: *triangle, bicycle, tricycle, tripod, bifocals, trillion, biplane, binoculars.*

UNIT 4   LESSONS 43–45, 50–51

Roots *pos, pel, pul, port, ject, aud, dict, duct, duce, duc, scribe, script, spec, spect, mit, miss, fac, fect, fic, feit*

◆ On the chalkboard, write *pos, pel* or *pul, port,* and *ject* in one column. Then write *put or place, carry, throw or force, push or drive* in a second column. Have students match the roots with their meanings.

◆ Write these words on the chalkboard: *transport, projector, adjective, posture, repelled, positive, reject.* Have students rewrite the root in each word in colored chalk.

◆ Give students word cards for these words: *subject, important, report, propose, projector, dispel.* Have them identify the root, tell what the word means, and use it in a sentence.

◆ Write *audio, counterfeit, dictate, deduct, reduce, description,* and *subscribe* on cards. Give each small group a card and have the group write a sentence using the word, substituting a blank for the word. Encourage groups to say their sentences aloud for the class to complete.

◆ On index cards, write words that contain roots and have students pantomime their meanings while their classmates guess the words. Use words such as *reporter, transport, deposit, introduce, educate, dictionary, dictate,* and *inspect.*

◆ Write these words on the chalkboard and have students circle the roots and draw a box around each of the prefixes: *dejected, permit, admit, facsimile, factory, speculate, special, defective, ejection, perfection, submissive, reporter.*

◆ Divide the class into groups, one group for each root studied. Challenge students to find and list words containing "their" root in reference books or textbooks during a given time period (such as two or three minutes). The group with the most words wins.

UNIT 4   LESSONS 46–48, 50–51

Compound Words, Possessives, and Contractions

◆ Invite partners to choose and discuss a topic, such as "My Favorite TV Program." Have partners take turns explaining their views and recording any contractions used in the process.

◆ Write *nurse's, mechanics',* and *mice's* on the chalkboard. Ask students to name other examples of singular or plural possessives they have learned and write sentences for each one.

◆ Write *foot + ball = football* on the chalkboard. Then invite students to take turns writing on the chalkboard other compound equations they know.

◆ On index cards, write *time, ache, work, stop, out, break, back, day, head,* and *light.* Have students use the cards to form as many compound words as they can.

◆ In two columns, write *tool, paint, jelly, blast, space; box, brush, fish, off, ship.* Have students match two words to make compound words.

◆ Write *you will, will not, do not, you are,* and *we have* on the chalkboard. Invite students to use a different colored chalk to make each phrase a contraction.

◆ During a two- or three-minute time period, have students look for and list as many contractions and possessives as they can. Let everyone read his or her list aloud.

UNIT 5   LESSONS 52–56, 60–61

Suffixes -er, -or, -ist, -ward, -en, -ize, -er, -est, -ee, -eer, -ent, -ant, -ful, -ness, -hood, -ship, -ment

◆ Say the words *helpful* and *happiness.* Challenge students to identify each suffix and its base word. Then ask students to suggest other words that have the suffixes *-ful* and *-ness.*

◆ Write *announcer, container, sculptor, actor, designer, digger, miner, spectator,* and *ranger* on the chalkboard and ask students to identify the suffix in each word. Have students give the meaning of each word.

◆ Students can use classroom objects to demonstrate the use of *-er* and *-est,* for example: *The yellow pencil is big. The blue pencil is bigger. The red pencil is the biggest.*

◆ Say each of these words, in turn, and have students identify the suffix and base word, then use the word in a sentence: *rescuer, scientist, dampen, darkest, engineer, criticize, statement.*

◆ Give each student a paper flag shape with *BW* (for *base word*) written on one side and *S* (for *suffix*) written on the other side. As you say each word, invite students to raise the appropriate side of their flags, depending on whether the word has a suffix: *different, dark, backward, appoint, absentee, idolize, coldest, container, bright.*

UNIT 5

Daily Word Study Practice

- ◆ Students can write a sentence and draw a picture to illustrate each of the following words: *peaceful, harmful, plentiful, useful, successful, armful, tenderness, beautiful, careful, darkness.*

- ◆ Write these words on the chalkboard: *beautiful, likelihood, civilized, resident, observant, creator, largest, plentiful, improvement.* Ask students to identify the base word and tell the rule for how the suffix was formed.

- ◆ Write *skater, loneliness, employee, cartoonist,* and *hitter* on the chalkboard. Have students write the base word and suffix for each word and describe the rule for each spelling change.

- ◆ Write these words on the chalkboard and have students add *-hood, -ship,* or *-ment* to make new words: *likely, improve, argue, friend, leader, amaze, author, child, equip, enjoy.*

- ◆ Invite students to pantomime these words with suffixes for their classmates to identify: *skater, artist, careful, argument, mountaineer, tailor, hypnotize, cheerfulness.*

UNIT 5   LESSONS 57–61
Suffixes *-able, -ible, -ion, -ation, -ition, -ance, -ence, -ive, -ity*

- ◆ Ask students to brainstorm a list of words that end in *-able* and *-ible,* such as *likable* and *responsible.* Then have them use the words to describe a person they admire. Have students fill in each blank with a noun to create a phrase: *likable* ____, *enjoyable* ____, *favorable* ____, *creative* ____, *dependable* ____, *active* ____, *accessible* ____, *responsible* ____. Examples are *likable child* and *favorable weather.*

- ◆ Give to students cards with these words and suffixes: *-able, -ible, reverse, move, perish, adjust, use, agree, like, sense.* Have students find partners to make new words. Encourage partners to write their words on the chalkboard and explain any spelling changes they make.

- ◆ Write these words on the chalkboard and have students circle the suffixes: *concentration, condition, addition, classification, celebration, inspection, graduation, imagination, nutrition, publication, pollution, ambition.*

- ◆ Distribute word cards with these base words: *correspond, appear, act, superior, observe, legal, confident, persevere.* Have students choose the suffix *-ance, -ence, -ive,* or *-ity* to add to each word. Call on volunteers to write sentences on the chalkboard that include their new words.

- ◆ Ask students to say the base word as you say words like these: *attractive, action, disturbance, inferiority, relaxation, tolerance, creative, sincerity, recognition, independence.*

- ◆ Write *-ation, -ition,* and *-ion* on the chalkboard in three columns and have students list appropriate words under each suffix.

- ◆ Write these incomplete words on the chalkboard and have students add *i* or *a: defens_ble, respons_ble, break_ble, reduc_ble, wash_ble, profit_ble, read_ble, knowledge_ble.* Suggest they confirm their spellings in a dictionary.

- ◆ Invite students to brainstorm a list of action words. Then see how many they can use as base words with the suffix *-able* or *-ible.* Have them write the new words on the board.

189

UNIT 6   LESSONS 62–63, 72–73

Words That Double the Final Consonant or Drop the Final *e* to Add a Suffix

◆ Give students letter cards for *b, i, g, g, e, r, s,* and *t.* Have them show how to spell *big,* then *bigger* and *biggest* by rearranging themselves and describing the spelling rule.

◆ Write these words and invite students to add the suffix *-es* or *-ed*: *graze, change, safe, hike, place, trade, approve.* Have students tell what letter they dropped from the base word to add to the suffix.

◆ Call on volunteers to come to the chalkboard and add the suffix *-ing, -ed, -er,* or *-est* to these words: *scrub, flat, get, dump, trim, rub, hard, wash, know, plug, clean, cut, fast, shop.*

◆ Have students write these headings at the top of a sheet of paper: *Final Consonant Doubled, No Spelling Change, Final e Dropped.* Then have them write four words in each column.

◆ Have students spell the base word in each of these words: *strangest, hoping, baker, dancer, nicest, raging, hopeful, increasing, defenseless, freezing, imaginable.*

◆ Write *like + ing = liking* on the chalkboard. Talk about the rule that creates the equation. Then have students write equations for *latest, hoping, scrambling, hiking,* and *placing.*

◆ Write these equations on the chalkboard and have students complete them: *cheap + ly = ____, grin + ed = ____, strut + ing = ____, jog + er = ____, lead + er + ____, wet + er = ____.*

◆ Invite students to circle the base words in *plodding, gutted, fanned, pronounced, approved, littler, nicer,* and *hiker.*

◆ Write these suffixes and words on word cards: *-ness, -ed, -able, -ful, -less, -ers, -ing, -ion, -ment, increase, teach, sneeze, disappoint, race, effort, pleasure.* Have students combine two cards at a time to make as many words as they can.

UNIT 6   LESSONS 64–66, 72–73

Words with More Than One Suffix, Adding Suffixes to Words Ending in -y or -*le*

◆ Give students word cards for suffixes *-ly, -ness, -s, -ing, -ful, -less,* and *-ed.* Invite them to add one suffix—or, if possible, more than one—to these words: *hope, increase, thought, amaze, mean, friend.* An example is *hopefully.*

◆ Say each of these words and have students hold up one finger if the word has one suffix, two fingers if it has two suffixes: *joyfully, painlessly, quickened, promised, widening, appointments.*

Daily Word Study Practice

◆ Write these words on the chalkboard and have students rewrite the first suffix in red and the second in green: *operations, peacefully, hesitatingly, enlightening, successfully, powerlessness, developments, lovingly.*

◆ Write these equations on the chalkboard: *ready + ly = _____, nimble + ly = _____, day + ly = _____, wiggle + ly = _____, dry + ly = _____.* Ask students to complete them and explain any spelling changes.

◆ Ask students to write a sentence for each of these words, leaving a blank for the word: *pebbly, dizzily, merrily, probably.* Encourage students to exchange their sentences with a partner, who will supply the missing word.

◆ Write these words on the chalkboard and have students add the ending *-s* or *-es* to each: *pony, baby, lady, valley, story, play, daisy, envy, beauty, monkey, birthday, delay.* Ask them to describe any spelling changes.

◆ Ask students to write the base word for each of these words: *occupied, easiest, busiest, worried, luckiest, rustiest.*

◆ Have students write these equations on the chalkboard and complete them, explaining the spelling change: *fancy + est = _____, pretty + er = _____, lucky + er = _____, worry + ed = _____, buoy + ed = _____.*

◆ Invite students to say the base words for these words: *sensibly, readily, healthily, bodily, sloppily, nobly.*

UNIT 6   LESSONS 67–69, 73
Plural Forms

◆ Write these words on the chalkboard and have students write their plural forms underneath: *wolf, chief, thief, loaf, cliff, reef, leaf, belief, safe, bluff.* Ask students to explain any spelling changes.

◆ Say these words and ask students to give you the singular form of each word: *beliefs, loaves, themselves, knives, chiefs, shelves, whiffs, wives, lives, halves, cuffs.*

◆ Write the following two sentences, one above the other, on the chalkboard: *Oh, no, I need a _____, right away!* and *Oh, no, I need two _____, right away!* Call out the following words one at a time and invite a student to come up and write the word in the sentence where it belongs. Invite a second student to write the word's other form in the other sentence. Use these words: *muff, scarf, loaves, leaf, wolf, shelves, chiefs, cuff.*

◆ Write the following phrases on the chalkboard and ask students to rewrite each phrase with the plural form of the underlined word when needed: *eight tiny <u>reindeer</u>, three bleating <u>sheep</u>, two tired <u>foot</u>, five swimming <u>bass</u>, six baby <u>mouse</u>.*

◆ Say these words and have students raise their hands if the singular and plural forms are the same: *wheat, man, bread, tooth, broccoli, ox, sheep, goat, shrimp, crisis, child.*

◆ Write the following words and ask students to tell if the word is plural, singular, or both: *fungi, alumnus, oatmeal, moose, goose, bacon, fish, feet, women, mice, sauerkraut, rye, cod.*

◆ Write the word *potato* on the chalkboard and have students write a sentence that contains both the singular and the plural form. Repeat with the words *woman, quiz, spy, shampoo,* and *stadium.*

UNIT 7   LESSONS 74–75, 78–79

Alphabetizing, Locating Words in a Dictionary, Dictionary Pronunciation Key, Respellings

◆ List a series of five words such as *become, bed, beanbag, beaming,* and *beaker* and ask students to alphabetize them.

◆ Call on volunteers to write their last names on the chalkboard. Then ask another volunteer to rewrite the names in alphabetical order.

◆ Have small groups of students write the names of their favorite breakfast foods on separate cards, then combine their cards and arrange them alphabetically. They can use a dictionary to confirm the correct alphabetical order.

◆ Write these words on the chalkboard: *metronome, microphone, mezzanine, mandible, meddle, miscellaneous.* Have students write the words in alphabetical order, then use a dictionary to copy each word's respelling.

◆ Locate guide words on a dictionary page and write them on the board. Then call out six words. Ask students if each word you name can be found on that page. Include words on the page as well as words from the previous and following pages as distracters.

◆ Have students use a dictionary key to write a secret message to a friend. They can check their respellings for each word in its dictionary entry.

◆ Have students copy a dictionary entry and label the parts *entry word, guide word, meaning, respelling,* and so on.

◆ Write these entry words on the chalkboard and ask students to use a dictionary to find the guide words for each: *disdain, fidget, joust, royalist, spelunker.*

◆ Write these respellings on the chalkboard and have students write the entry word each represents: *spyo̅o̅ (spew), fro̅o̅t′ lis, (fruitless), kâr′ frē (carefree), dub′əl (double).*

UNIT 7   LESSONS 76–79

Looking Under the Correct Word Form, Multimeaning Words

◆ Write these words on the chalkboard and ask students what other words in different forms they could expect to find in the entry: *early, relief, pronounce, graze, hundred, oasis.*

Daily Word Study Practice

◆ As you say these words with suffixes, ask students to identify the entry word they would use to find each word's meaning: *recycling, produced, originating, halos, jogged.*

◆ Invite students to use a dictionary to find and list ten words that have more than one meaning.

◆ Have students write two sentences for each of these words, using two different meanings: *door, nose, notice, rough, clear.*

◆ Brainstorm with the class a list of words that end with the suffixes *-er, -est, -s, -es, -ed,* and *-ing.* Write their responses on the chalkboard and have volunteers write the dictionary entry words for each suggestion.

◆ Ask students to look in a dictionary and make a list of five pairs of homographs. Challenge them to choose one set and write a sentence containing both of the homographs. Students' sentences may be serious or humorous.

◆ Ask students to find a word in a dictionary that has more than one meaning. Then have them use the word in a sentence for each different meaning.

◆ Invite students to explain (or illustrate) the different meanings of these words: *band, light, block, stand, file.*

UNITS 1–2, 4, 6   LESSONS 12, 14, 26, 28, 49, 51, 70–71, 73
Syllables

◆ Ask students to hold up their fingers to show how many syllables they hear in each word: *zucchini, oases, geese, broccoli, piccolos, patios, cliffs, beliefs, themselves.*

◆ Draw four columns on the chalkboard, each with a different heading: *qu, que, ck,* and *ch.* As a class, compile a list of one-syllable words containing each sound and write the words in the appropriate column. Repeat with two- and three-syllable words.

◆ Divide the class into small groups and allow five minutes for them to list as many two- or three-syllable words as they can that contain *ew, oy,* or *ou.* Then have each group switch lists with a neighboring group and divide the other group's words into syllables.

◆ Write the following words on the board: *extraneous, extravagant, extraterrestrial, extraordinary, extracurricular, superimpose, supersonic, superficial, superfluous, superior,* and *supersede.* Have students copy the words and divide each word into syllables. Encourage students to define the words by examining the word parts, and then have them each write a paragraph using as many of the words as possible. Invite students to share their paragraphs with the class.

Teacher Notes

Teacher Notes

Teacher Notes

Teacher Notes

Teacher Notes

Teacher Notes